Intimate Conversations:

Face to Face with Matchless Musicians

Also by Larry Ruttman

Voices of Brookline:
The Oral History of an American Hometown

American Jews and America's Game:
Voices of a Growing Legacy in Baseball

My Eighty-Two Year Love Affair with Fenway Park:
From Teddy Ballgame to Mookie Betts

Larry Ruttman: A Life Lived Backwards -
An Existential Triad of Friendship, Maturation, and Inquisitiveness

Intimate Conversations

Face to Face with Matchless Musicians

Larry Ruttman

Torchflame Books
VISTA, CA

Copyright © 2024 by Lawrence A. Ruttman

All rights reserved. No part of this publication may be reproduced, stored in or introduced into a retrieval system, or transmitted in any form or by any means (electronic, mechanical, photocopied, recorded of otherwise), except as permitted under Section 107 or 108 of the 1976 International Copyright Act, without the prior written permission of both the copyright owner and the publisher of this book, except by a reviewer who wishes to quote brief passages in connection with a review written for insertion in a magazine, newspaper, broadcast, website, blog or other outlet. For information, address Top Reads Publishing Subsidiary Rights Department, 1035 E. Vista Way, Suite 205, Vista, CA 92084, USA.

ISBN: 978-1-61153-505-1 (hardcover)
ISBN: 978-1-61153-477-1 (paperback)
ISBN: 978-1-61153-493-1 (ebook)

Library of Congress Control Number: 2024905506

Intimate Conversations: Face to Face with Matchless Musicians is published by: Torchflame Books, an imprint of Top Reads Publishing, LLC, USA

For information about special discounts for bulk purchases, please direct emails to: publisher@torchflamebooks.com

Cover design: Jori Hanna
Book interior layout: Susan Worst

Every effort has been made to give credit for photographs and art shown in this book. We apologize for any errors or omissions and will gladly make corrections in subsequent editions.

Printed in the United States of America

This book is dedicated to Susan Worst, with thanks for her assistance in the preparation of the manuscript.

About the Author

Larry Ruttman
Author, Historian, Attorney

Larry Ruttman, a longtime attorney and author, has won awards for biographical cultural histories about his famous hometown of Brookline, Massachusetts, *Voices of Brookline* (2005), and Jews on and off the field in Major League Baseball, *American Jews and America's Game: Voices of a Growing Legacy in Baseball* (2013), which was chosen the best baseball book in America for 2013 by *Sports Collectors Digest.* It also serves as a cultural history of American Jews since the Great Depression. He has recently written on his lifelong passion for classical music and its musicians in a book entitled *Intimate Conversations: Face to Face with Matchless Musicians.* Educated at the University of Massachusetts at Amherst, and Boston College Law School, Larry served as an intelligence officer in the United States Air Force in the Korean War. He was elected a Fellow of the Massachusetts Historical Society. His papers on his first two books have been collected by the Wyner Family Jewish Heritage Center (JHC), formerly of the American Jewish Historical Society (AJHS), and now in collaboration with and at the New England Historical and Genealogical Society (NEHGS) in Boston, Massachusetts, and collated, digitized, formatted, indexed, and published worldwide online. Larry has lived in Brookline since the age of two and has been married to Lois Raverby Ruttman for sixty years. He is going strong at ninety-three. He recently began a weekly podcast focused on what life has taught him about friendship, inquisitiveness, and maturation, entitled, *Larry Ruttman, One Man's Life, A Life Lived Backwards*, found on all platforms. Larry is amazed that Providence has granted him the privilege to "live his life backwards" in this late-coming and deeply satisfying labor of love.

Photo © Greg Spiers

"Life. Music is life. Music is a reflection of who we are as humans. Music tells us things that words can't, it ignites feelings in us that we didn't know we had, and it can reach a depth that nothing else can."

— SUSAN GRAHAM

Posthumous portrait of Wolfgang Amadeus Mozart by Barbara Krafft

Credit: from Deutsch, Otto Erich (1965) Mozart: A Documentary Biography. *Stanford: Stanford University Press., Public Domain, https://commons.wikimedia.org/w/index.php?curid=141841*

Contents

Foreword

The book you are about to read contains an array of interviews of musicians — composers, conductors, vocal and instrumental artists (both classical and pop) and a music manager. It is an unusual publication because very few books are devoted solely to interviews. Rather, interviews usually appear in such periodicals as *Opera News*, online in sites such as SongwriterUniverse.com, and increasingly in daily newspapers, such as the *New York Times*, where, for example, singers, directors, etc., discuss the new production of a pop album, an opera, or a new symphonic work.

The interviews in this book are not "puff" pieces; they touch on important musical and career choices, as well as personal issues that musicians face. Indeed. they could just as well be called conversations. They touch upon some of the musicians' musical mentors, their colleagues, musical meaning, and many other issues of interest for a general audience as well as those who specialize in musical narrative. In response to Larry Ruttman's open-ended questions, the interviewees provide insight into how artists think about music, how they have prepared for and sustained their careers, and which composers and performers influenced them.

Published interviews serve a number of purposes: they provide readers with an intimate connection to a public figure — personal details that augment one's familiarity with a known personality. Thus, when Susan Graham discusses her performances of Mahler's Third Symphony with Andris Nelsons, readers begin to understand her connection to the music. And when Ran Blake relates the kinds of dreams he experiences when he is performing, we are privileged to learn how he is inspired during his concerts. Interviews also provide biographical details that might otherwise be lost to posterity. They place an artist in a certain place at a certain time, which helps to populate a chronology of musical performances. Finally, interviews are extremely important to historians. Forty or fifty years from now, when a historian is researching the early decades of the twenty-first century, these interviews may provide him or her with factual information that is no longer readily available. In my research on music in New York City during the 1860s and 70s, for example, my knowledge of one of the important figures of the period, the conductor/composer Thomas Baker, was greatly enhanced by an interview he gave in the *Clipper*, a New York-based national weekly newspaper devoted to theater happenings and theatrical people.

Larry's choice of interviewees with whom to join in conversation provides readers with a wide perspective of musical substance that contributes to our understanding of the complexities that contribute to the art of music. I hope you enjoy reading these interviews as much as I did.

John Graziano
Director, *Music in Gotham*
February 2022

John Graziano is director of *Music in Gotham*, a database project, generously funded by the National Endowment for the Humanities and private individuals, which is documenting musical events in New York City from September 1862 through August 1875. His recent publications include the book *European Music and Musicians in New York City, 1840-1900*, and articles on John Philip Sousa, Harry Burleigh, the "Black Patti" theater orchestras in nineteenth-century New York City, Edward MacDowell's symphonic poems, *Lamia* and *Hamlet and Ophelia*, "Race and Racism" in the *Oxford Handbook of Opera*, and "The Many Faces of Rio Rita" in *The Oxford Handbook of Musical Theatre Screen Adaptations*. His recent lectures include studies of the concept of charisma, African American musicals, music and musicians in New York City in the latter half of the nineteenth century, and a study of Frank Loesser's *The Most Happy Fella*. He is Professor Emeritus of Music at the City College and Graduate Center, City University of New York.

Preview of the Famous Musicians You Will Meet in This Book and Their Thoughts; and Acknowledgments

---

As I have said before, any book has more than one author. Without the collaboration of others, there would be no book. For this one, my collaborators include all twenty-one of those musical artists who conversed so openly with me about their art, several of whom have become good friends. Their names, many of them familiar to you, appear below, with a short preview of what the story on each in the book is about.

At the start of each of these stories, you will find a photograph or illustration of the musician who is the subject of the story. At some point within the story, you will also find a photograph or illustration of the muse of that musician, some living, some gone. In the stories, the muse is discussed by the musician to a greater or lesser extent, along with many other musicians who have had a profound or meaningful influence on the musician. Thus, we come to know a plethora of artists who have inhabited this most mysterious and perhaps greatest of the arts.

Included also is the close group of people with the technical expertise, which I lack, to assemble and produce a book giving life to my ideas. I propose to speak of each with a short word about the contribution of each. They could collectively be called technicians, although that pedestrian word does not convey the art which these highly skilled and talented people provided.

To the MATCHLESS MUSICIANS portrayed in the book, as follows:

Composer John Harbison, whose honesty and forthrightness starts this book off with valuable insights into the creative process. A word of thanks also to his accomplished wife, violinist Rose Mary Harbison, for her hospitality and words, and to Sarah Schaffer, his longtime and faithful assistant, for her help, friendship, and enthusiasm for this endeavor.

Composer Joan Tower, whose bright, humorous, and open persona became the tower of strength I needed to write about her art and life.

Composer Robert Levin, whose articulateness told me more than I ever knew about my own musical muse, Wolfgang Amadeus Mozart, and who informed me how the gifted youngster Robert Levin became a teacher, composer, world-class pianist, and Mozart amanuensis.

Composer Unsuk Chin, who thoughtfully and generously told me of her inner compositional life in our long meeting and following ocean-spanning correspondence, to focus on her aspiration to become the original composer she already is.

Composer Osvaldo Golijov, whose Latin warmth, flair, and love of family taught me a lot about Argentinian music at the root of Osvaldo's original music now heard around the world. We share the belief that our two conversations, separated by fifteen years, have expressed his deep thoughts on music accurately.

A deep feeling of friendship was quickly created when I first met and conversed at length with composer Matthew Aucoin, whose honest and revelatory answers give us insights into the creative power that has resulted in his prominence lately as the composer of the opera, *Eurydice*, presented by the Met and LA opera companies, and as the author of his landmark book, *The Impossible Art.*

The archaic English idiom, "Hail fellow, well met," certainly applies to English conductor Harry Christophers, who referred to us as "Harry and Larry" within seconds of our introduction. Harry later told me how a kid from less-than-ordinary circumstances became a world-class conductor of early music without losing his early instincts and interests which make him such a fine fellow.

Conductor Charles Dutoit, maybe the greatest conductor living, who has visited every country in the world, is another rags-to-riches story. Charles vividly tells of his musical and world travels, which inform us about what it takes to lead the greatest orchestras and choruses in the world.

Conductor Gil Rose, the conductor who brings to our ears the best music not often heard by audiences today, gave me a tutorial on what the conductor does to lead an orchestra successfully to convey to us the intent of the composer. Thanks to Gil for this tour de force.

Conductor Martin Pearlman's pleasant demeanor belies the creative, knowledgeable, ambitious, and generous conductor, composer, teacher, and player within, who has created "Boston Baroque," known across the world for its beautiful and accurate presentations of music going back three or more centuries. Martin shares all of it with us.

Conductor Ben Zander is a unique man and musician whose service to his art, his listeners, and to his musicians of all ages in his two orchestras is legendary. His fame as an author and writer gives him the power to tell us his original and fascinating story with clarity and humor.

Violinist Anne-Sophie Mutter, one of the greatest violinists in the world, grew up as a small-town girl in Germany, and retains her plain-spoken personality to this day, along with her arresting appearance. She shares with us her art, growing up, charitable work, and philosophy in this conversation.

Mezzo-soprano Susan Graham has to be one of the most intelligent musical artists in the world. This charming diva, whose spontaneous words on music grace the first pages of this book, gives us insights to music as seen from the stages of the Met and other great opera houses of the world. A look from the inside!

The long-neglected viola is magical in the hands of violist Kim Kashkashian. True to her Armenian roots, she favors the music from that region of the world, as well as that of the European masters, and plays and teaches it all to her audiences and students. Kim tells us all about that, and her charitable work in the aptly named, "Music for Food."

I call cellist Larry Lesser a cellist and a president. Why? Because he is a world-class cellist and teacher, and served many productive years as the president of the New England Conservatory of Music. That is a story this articulate man tells colorfully. He caused to be printed my story on him in this book to be distributed to the big crowd at his eightieth birthday celebration at the conservatory. What a guy!

"A musician is what I am," proclaims the challenging and outspoken violinist Cecylia Arzewski, former concertmaster of the Atlanta Symphony Orchestra and now a successful author of a children's book. Outspoken Cecylia tells it like it is in no uncertain terms about musicians, the music business, people, and animals, especially her dog "Gustav." You'll meet him and her face to face in her story.

Pianist Aiko Onishi survived the historic firebombing of Tokyo in March 1945 to become a famous pianist, teacher, and writer, mostly in America, where she has long resided in California. Charming and gracious Aiko tells us of the art of teaching the piano and her continuing love affair with many of her former students.

Jazz pianist Ran Blake is a great pianist, composer, leader, and teacher. Everyone knows that. He is also a person like no other who has ever existed. A genius for sure, he has a unique style of speech which far exceeds mere digression! I have tried in his story to present that style in an understandable manner to show his brilliance and agility of mind. You will meet an incredible person in Ran. Play a game. Count the names of artists he mentions in this relatively short story. He can tell you lots about each one, an encyclopedic vision unmatched by any book!

Musician Eden MacAdam-Somer calls herself "Musician Extraordinaire." She is all of that and much more. Eden, despite those two words, is all about you, not her. That has been demonstrated by her work in Afghanistan and at the New England Conservatory. She is a rare multi-talented artist who combines that with an instinctive and fearless generosity. She tells you and me about her life in this memorable conversation.

Singer and songwriter Monica Rizzio describes herself as an "Americana Folk Singer." Indeed she is, and a good one, as well as music teacher in her own school, transplanted from the small town of Quitman, Texas, to Cape Cod, as a "Washashore Cowboy." She is also a woman of strong character who resists the sacrifices a pop artist is called upon to make to reach the top rung. She is her own person. You will want to meet her here and listen to her anytime.

Mark Volpe, recently retired as the president of the Boston Symphony Orchestra, started out as a clarinetist, became a lawyer, then advanced by leaps and bounds as an arts manager to the pinnacle of the Boston Symphony Orchestra. There he oversaw its rise to new heights in America and Europe, joining forces with the iconic Leipzig Gewandhaus Orchestra. Mark tells his story to conclude this book.

To the MATCHLESS TECHNICIANS who collaborated with the author in the preparation of this book:

Susan Worst, the dedicatee of this book, who formatted this book so true to the plan I suggested and did a thousand other tasks to make this the book it is. Susan, as she always does in our long association, lent her fine moral sense to the endeavor.

Holly Sullo, gifted artist, illustrator, who drew my logo, and became my good friend along the way.

That is only half the story. It is hard to find a trade publisher for a book on classical music. I was having a hard time. Holly said, "Why not self-publish the book? Once you do, you'll have an actual book with which to interest a publisher. I can help you with that." Holly's encouragement released me on an astounding creative adventure beyond the actual writing of this book, which called upon the honing of resources and talents I knew I had, and the discovery of others I never knew I had. The result is the book you now hold in your hand. I will write more about that adventure in my upcoming memoir, *Larry Ruttman: A Life Lived Backwards - An Existential Triad of Friendship, Maturation, and Inquisitiveness.* Maybe Holly Sullo should write a book on how to care for, feed, and inspire the nonagenarians amongst us!

Professor and respected musicologist John Graziano, of CUNY and Yale University, whose name and foreword give credibility to the serious intent of the book.

I found a friend and computer expert in Brookline High School senior, Elliot Stolyarov, whose ready smile on his handsome face signals his pleasant ways and generous spirit.

How lucky I was that fate directed me to Teri Rider, the CEO of my publisher, Torchflame Books, who combines her vast knowledge in that key field with a warm, giving, and agreeable persona that comforts me every moment I interact with her.

Likewise, I am lucky that Teri is assisted by and seamlessly combines with the talented, spirited, and youthful marketing master, Jori Hanna. Doubling as an illustrator, Jori stylishly, colorfully, and imaginatively created the magnetic front and back covers of the book.

Thanks too, to Chelsea Robinson for her expert copy editing, and knowledgeable literary sense in seeing this book's merits.

Janice Tsai, with whom I shared twelve of the most intensely productive days of my life when she lent her brilliant Harvard-trained mind to the final days of my composition of the last three chapters of the book. Janice organized and copyedited the long manuscript, critiqued my writing, especially of those last fifty pages, and exchanged countless emails with me, often until the wee hours of the morning.

As always, thanks go to old friend and publisher, Gene Bailey, for his advice and counsel all along the way.

Thanks too to Bridget Carr, the indefatigable and lovely longtime archivist of the Boston Symphony Orchestra, whose generous help in locating photos you see in this book is so very much appreciated.

Special thanks go to good friend Douglas Wolf, Esquire, intellectual property attorney at the foremost firm, Wolf, Greenfield, and Sacks, for his excellent advice from time to time on copyright law and other legal issues arising in the course of writing this book.

Deep appreciation goes to longtime and valued photographer Kathy Chapman, to whom I was led by drummer George Schuller, for extending herself mightily to locate the original print of two decades ago of her remarkable shot of two music immortals and close friends, Gunther Schuller and Ran Blake, which appears in Ran's story in this book.

I am happy to acknowledge an old and dear friend, Dr. John Caulfield, my next-door neighbor in Brookline when he ran his own research lab at the Harvard Medical School. He later served at Roche Pharmaceuticals in Silicon Valley, California, where his notoriety as a scientist expanded. He became friendly there with pianist, teacher, and author Aiko Onishi, befitting John's interest in the arts as well as science. Knowing Aiko was soon to visit Boston, and that I was writing this book, John introduced me to Aiko virtually. Virtually became reality, hence the story on the lovely Aiko. Later John apprised me of the well-known American Matthay Association, named after the legendary twentieth-century piano teacher, Tobias Matthay (1858-1945), through whose kindness, and the kindness of the Sowerby Foundation, I was able to obtain the telling photograph of pianist Frank Mannheimer and famous American church composer Leo Sowerby, which appears in Aiko's story. THANK YOU, JAWN, as I affectionately call him to this day.

Neil Rutman, my sort-of namesake, holds a distinction not duplicated anywhere! He is an award-winning national pianist and the boxing coach at the University of Central Arkansas. I asked if he ever hurt his fingers boxing. He never had! Neil was also a student of pianist Aiko Onishi. Aiko's special teacher was well-known pianist Frank Mannheimer. Neil sent me a hard-to-obtain photo of Mannheimer for Aiko's story in this book, which led to an even better one, alluded to above, which you see there. Thank you, Neil Rutman.

Let me tell you about Friedrich Kunzmann. Obtaining a photograph is often not easy. First you want the right photo, then you must locate the photographer to get his or her permission to use it, often for a fee. Dealing across the water compounds the problem. You do it because sometimes a picture is absolutely worth a thousand words. Famed violist Kim Kashkashian, who is featured in a chapter in this book, sent me to her contact at world company ECM Records of Berlin, Germany, to obtain a photo of her mentor, composer György Kurtág. Enter Friedrich! A gentleman par excellence, Friedrich turned up György and several others of note I bothered him for, never with a complaint, always with a smile across the sea. THANK YOU, FRIEDRICH!

In a similar vein, deep thanks go to Revna Karacabeyli, junior project coordination manager at Deutsche Grammophon in Berlin, for her hard, committed, and generous work in gaining for me the rights to use the amazing photograph of violin virtuoso Anne-Sophie Mutter you see in her story in this book. THANK YOU, REVNA!

I also wish to acknowledge all those photographers and illustrators who contributed to this book. I consider those pictures indispensable to its quality, whatever it may be. All are named in the credit accompanying each picture in the text, but it seems to me appropriate to recognize them here.

I want to thank model citizen and man, nonagenarian Justin "Jerry" Wyner, who has been a mentor to me for many years. Now in his ninety-seventh year, Jerry continues his lifelong work of preserving the rich history of Boston's Jewish community. Surprisingly, Jerry inscribed in his recent memoir that he was inspired to write it by my story on him in my book *Voices of Brookline*. His longtime interest in me encouraged me in writing this book and in my other endeavors. Jerry's incredible grip on life inspires me and others to persist day in and day out.

Last but very far from least is Cathy Jenness, my legal assistant for over twenty-five years until 2000. Why? Because, without accurate transcriptions of the conversations from which this book is made, there would be no book. It is that simple. Practically all of the transcriptions were done by Cathy. I have written before about this extraordinary woman and talented collaborator who made my life as a lawyer so much easier. We remained good friends after that. Cathy continued to help me from time to time. I asked her to help with these transcriptions, which consumed a lot of her time over and above her full-time employment. Was I surprised at how well she accomplished the task? Not at all, because that is who Cathy is. My debt to her is her gift to you as you read these pages. Thank you once again, Cathy, as our association nears the half-century mark, and your daughter, Samantha, too, who aided you from time to time. I also thank Sophia Willinger, now happily residing in Mexico City, who lent her talents to a few of these stories with ability and youthful enthusiasm.

List of Illustrations

The following are five handwritten letters to the author, Larry Ruttman, from famed composers John Harbison, Joan Tower, Robert Levin, Matthew Aucoin, and Osvaldo Golijov.

Dear Larry:

Thanks for the marvelously comprehensive essay. I learned a lot, and enjoyed the interview session thanks to your wide ranging interests and reassuring presence. Sarah joins me in admiration and thanks for your "reading" of the various subjects covered.

Best

JH

— John Harbison

Jan. 2, 2021

Dear Larry,

I reread your wonderful interview/article on me and was impressed with your choice of questions which often prompted me to talk about things in a more personal and subjective manner. You had clearly done your research on me which often resulted in "deeper" searches for answers from me.

It was absorbing reading.

Thank you for all that work and many thanks for the supportive title

Best wishes,

Joan

— Joan Tower

6 December 2020

Dear Larry,
What a pleasure it was to engage in lively conversation with you. I very much enjoyed your perceptive queries and thank you for involving me in your stimulating project.
With all best wishes,
Robert Levin

— Robert Levin

*

Dear Larry,

I still think back fondly on the interview we did back in 2017. It's rare indeed to meet an interviewer with your curiosity, perspicacity and patience. I do hope the whole book will see the light of day soon!

Yours,

— Matthew Aucoin

December 18, 2020

Dear Larry. It is an honor for me to be part of your enlightening and, as with your other publications, inspiring book. I hope you know how much I admire your work, your mind-opening interviews, and your restless spirit. With gratitude and best wishes

Osvaldo

— Osvaldo Golijov

Preface

Was it foreordained by some power in the ether almost sixty years ago, when I took my first serious step towards the appreciation of classical music by buying one of those then-popular, inexpensive ten-record music sets of the so-called best in the field, that the fork then taken would lead me to the publication of this book?

Listening to Russian pianist Sviatoslav Richter's rendition of Wolfgang Amadeus Mozart's sublime twenty-first piano concerto, I was literally stunned by the beauty of the sound I heard. Soon, listening to the rest of Mozart's twenty-seven piano concertos opened my eyes wider and wider. Each concerto was different, each was gorgeous. Many provoked sublime feelings, propelling me on an odyssey that continues to this day and forever.

Immersed as I was in building my legal practice, for many years I was a fan of classical music as time allowed. I soon came to know that my home city of Boston contained great musical institutions far beyond the number its size would suggest. There was and is, of course, the Boston Symphony Orchestra, Boston Baroque, the Handel and Haydn Society, the Boston Philharmonic Orchestra, Emmanuel Music, the Boston Modern Opera Project (BMOC), numberless choral groups, and many more. The New England Conservatory of Music (NEC), the Boston Conservatory, Berklee School of Music, Boston University, MIT, Harvard University, and Longy School of Music comprise an array of music schools hard to match anywhere else. Consistent with that, many musical figures of note inhabited Boston, and concertized for our pleasure, sometimes for pay, often for free.

Naturally, I took advantage of that atmosphere to breathe in as much as I could, particularly at three historic venues. Symphony Hall and NEC's Jordan Hall, both built around the same time at the turn of the last century, are considered to be among the best acoustic halls in the world and, incredibly, lie within a few feet of each other in Boston's historic Back Bay, a few miles from my home in Brookline. Not much further away is Memorial Hall at Harvard University, built not long after the Civil War to honor Harvard sons lost in that horrific fray, a place where the past is still redolent in its imposing statuary, and where the music of past and present sounds well in our ears.

Always interested in history, I read the programs of the concerts I attended, especially those distributed at the BSO, where the preparation of them has become an art form. Usually running close to one hundred pages, the BSO programs, written by expert musicologists on the music to be heard, give the concertgoer the historical background required to enhance the experience. Little did I know that my religious attendance to these small books was transforming me into a sort of amateur musicologist and equipping me much later in life to dream of writing a book like the one you are about to read.

And so it went until around age seventy, when I unexpectedly began to turn in my attorney credentials for those of a writer. First, I wrote a book about my hometown of Brookline called *Voices of Brookline*, which achieved a tad of national recognition. Then I took on another passion, producing *American Jews and America's Game: Voices of a Growing Legacy in Baseball*, which was chosen the best baseball book in America in 2013 by *Sports Collectors Digest*. Wow! This was more than I ever expected. The august and respected Massachusetts Historical Society, founded in 1791, elected me to be a fellow. Another august Boston institution, the New England Historical and Genealogical Society, reached out and collected my papers to be collated, digitized, and published on the internet! Then I published a memoir called *My Eighty-Two-Year Love Affair with Fenway Park: From Teddy Ballgame to Mookie Betts*, which enjoyed a wide distribution by the Boston Red Sox to their millions of followers.

Success breeds confidence, but did I dare tackle my other major passion of music? Only a layman, never a musician, hardly knowing an arpeggio from a diminuendo, I was on the cusp of eighty-five. Who would take me seriously that I could undertake such a big task at that advanced age? This was not a formula for confidence. I needed a trick to play on myself to get off the starting block. It came to me. Most books on music are written by musicians, talking to each other using technical terms, often about musical technique. I wouldn't do that. I couldn't do that. My mantra was how refreshing it would be for a music-loving layman to try to get into the psyches of noted musicians by interviewing them closely and horizontally as person to person, and not as a lay interviewer to a musician.

Did I really believe that? Maybe not entirely at the beginning, but it gave me enough to start. My first interview was with MacArthur genius grant winner and jazz pianist Ran Blake, already a good friend, who treated my inquiries with respect. When I asked him with questionable propriety whether he had self-confidence, he really buoyed my spirits when he said several times, "I've never heard that question before," as he struggled to answer. I discovered that my long-standing idiosyncratic habit of asking what might be thought to be inappropriate questions to draw out a subject could be applied with good results to celebrated musicians as well as ordinary folk.

Little did I know that I had just set out on the voyage of my life. The mantra I had adopted turned out to be true. Indeed, much could be uncovered from the minds of great musicians by asking questions person to person without any underpinning of technical musical knowledge. In this way, forearmed with facts about the musician's life, a personal connection could be quickly established which encouraged the interviewee to speak freely about their innermost thoughts.

An example of this is my interview of celebrated American classical and sometimes jazz composer John Harbison. Always gentlemanly and somewhat reserved, John answered my questions dutifully and well for about an hour and a half, at which point something sprang up between us which impelled John to answer deeply a series of questions probing into his psyche, attempting to get at the nucleus of his compositional power. What a mother lode of insights into the mysteries of musical creation from a master of music and words!

After I sent him a draft of his chapter, John Harbison wrote this brief warm note to me, convincing me I was on the voyage of my life.

Dear Larry:

Thanks for the marvelously comprehensive essay, I learned a lot, and enjoyed the interview session thanks to your wide-ranging interests and reassuring presence. Sarah joins me in admiration and thanks for your "reading" of the various subjects covered!

Best JH

And so it went with practically every interview. The conversations were revealing, the friendships warming; my feeling for music (whether classical or pop) was enhanced. I learned something new from each musician. The persona of each was fascinating. I suppose I could interject here what it was in the case of each that captured my imagination, but instead I invite you to the stories themselves. In each, I attempt to capture the essential quality and purpose of that musician's life, as becomes evident in the opening paragraphs.

I will, however, speak here generally of what I discovered about top drawer musicians on this more than three-year odyssey. Although highly anecdotal in nature, and not to be treated as fact, it is one man's impression gleaned from this array of twenty-one close encounters with virtuosos of music.

Musicians are articulate. Once their confidence is won, they talk revealingly about themselves and their art. Pauses, as well as laughs, came frequently, but only to allow time for a thoughtful answer to be precisely spoken. I surmise this articulateness is related not only to musicians' high level of education but also to the study and practice required to acquire the expressiveness needed to communicate true music.

There are a certain few composers whose names come up very often, the prime ones among them, not unexpectedly, being Bach, Mozart, and Beethoven. What is striking is that Mozart gets into practically every conversation. I've come to believe that musicians generally think of that master at the same level of love and respect as the level of jealousy and amazement with which Antonio Salieri was depicted as viewing him in the hit film *Amadeus*.

Even musicians who primarily perform love to be teachers (privately or in conservatories) of the next generation of musicians, enjoy collaborating and concertizing with their peers and students, appreciate and know the history of music, work hard at their art, and are proud that what they do brings pleasure to their audiences. In general, they seem to me to be humanistic, civilized, peaceful, gentle, humorous, charitable, and anxious to give back to others. To a person, they all believe they could not live without music.

That question on living without music was part of a set which included the seemingly simple, if not simplistic, question, "What is music?" The question was often met with silence and a pause to collect one's thoughts. The answers were wide-ranging, sometimes incredibly exact and meaningful as in the answer of Susan Graham, sometimes requiring a further question to flush out meaning from a mysterious answer, as in the case of Larry Lesser. Taken collectively, the answers suggest music is well-nigh impossible to precisely define but as pervasive and necessary to existence as are food, sleep, work, and procreation.

Have I been too extravagant in my evaluation of musicians? I think not. They are people after all, some better than others. There must be a few bad apples among them. Maybe Richard Wagner qualifies for that, a man who combined a surpassing mastery of composition and storytelling with a propensity to steal a wife, disrespect others, and foster hatred. But all things considered, it does seem that musicians are a special breed having the qualities enumerated above, perhaps made so by the music which sounds in their ears and souls every day.

What I do know to a certainty is that my few years with these musicians have given me two great gifts I never expected to receive in my lifetime. The first is their friendship and entrée into a world which has always fascinated me but into which I thought I'd never enter. The second is the revelations about themselves and their music which provided to me the wherewithal to pen this volume, which I hope will allow others to glimpse that inspiring realm.

No one knows where their journey through life will take them. To be an author was never planned. To write about my hometown, my favorite sport and its luminaries, my heritage, the history of my country, my ethnicity, the greatest and most mysterious of the arts, and, above all, the people in each of those, has been life-changing and extending. That continues. How fortunate I am!

LARRY RUTTMAN

Brookline, Massachusetts
April 8, 2024

George Gershwin, America's most original composer, who created masterworks of classical and popular music alive to this day, despite a life tragically cut short.

Credit: Photo taken in 1936 by Emmett Schoenbaum at RKO Studios during the making of "Shall We Dance." Used by permission of the Ira and Leonore Gershwin Trusts.

Part One

COMPOSERS

American composer John Harbison. Photo by Larry Ruttman.

CHAPTER
1

John Harbison: Composer, Instrumentalist, Pedagogue, and Man for All Seasons

"A Man for All Seasons" is defined in the Free Dictionary as a man who is successful and talented in many areas, and a man whose behavior is appropriate to every occasion. Such a man is John Harbison, who today very likely wears the mantle of America's most esteemed composer, and whose always appropriate and modest behavior has won him a place as a gifted pedagogue, now in his fiftieth year in that capacity at the Massachusetts Institute of Technology (MIT), where he holds the post of institute professor of music. In that time John has witnessed and contributed to its musical program, which has grown into one of the most respected in the country, drawing gifted students from everywhere under its umbrella. Recognition of his teaching talent resulted in a decade long tenure as the head of the composition department at Tanglewood, the summer home of the renowned Boston Symphony Orchestra. Interviewing John Harbison at his home in Cambridge for over two hours some months ago demonstrated the humility which makes him an unlikely candidate to sing a song about his own multiplicity of accomplishments.

The plethora of events honoring him in the 2018-2019 season must be cited to do that. The summer of 2019 will mark the thirtieth anniversary of the founding of the Token Creek Chamber Music Festival in their other home in the village of DeForest, Wisconsin, by John and his inspirational wife, master violinist Rose Mary Harbison. His love of Johann Sebastian Bach comes to further fruition in score and print in his composition and book, both carrying the title of *What Do We Make of Bach?* His opera *The Great Gatsby*, originally written for the Met, was reprised in December 2015, and again in May 2017, at the Semperoper in Dresden. New recordings demonstrating his prolificity are being issued under the

Naxos, Sony, and Albany labels. Although a theatrical approach combined with his bent for poetry and prose, not to mention his own writing ability, is evident throughout his career, that tells only part of the story of a prolific composer whose oeuvre has touched many musical forms from the very small to the very large, including solo instrumental, chamber music, song, liturgical music, vocal, choral, ballet, concerto, symphony, opera, and last but not least, jazz, which may be accounted as his starting point. Indeed, John Harbison is a man for all seasons. As I write this, only two nights ago at a concert honoring John Harbison's eightieth birthday at Jordan Hall at the New England Conservatory of Music, and only two days after the Boston Red Sox won the 2018 World Series, I unexpectedly experienced for myself a delicious rendition of Harbison's mastery of any and all forms. His *Diamond Watch* (2010), for two pianos with baseball lyrics to match, is fun and nostalgic, dedicated to renowned economist Peter Diamond, also an institute professor at MIT, whose interests include baseball, like so many brilliant people who read the box scores before breakfast. In sharp contrast was *Mirabai Songs* (1983), whose evocative score for soprano, flute, clarinet, percussion, harp, violin, viola, cello, and double bass, based on the words of ecstatic religious poetry written in sixteenth-century India, expresses love through the metaphor of sexual union with Krishna, the Dark Lord, bringing release to Mirabai from the burden of losing her husband to war while still in her passionate twenties. Hearing only those two pieces is enough for the listener to recognize the omnivorous talent of John Harbison.

Reading here about the other facets of John Harbison's life will be enough for the reader to gain perspective on why, in accord with the dictionary definition, this softly spoken, laid back, and yet powerful musician behaves appropriately to every occasion.

"John, what I'm trying to do is get into the psyche of composers, especially as to how they derive inspirations and what they can they tell us about composing. One never really can find out how a person becomes a great composer, but you can ask some questions. I know you grew up in a musical family, that your dad, Almore, studied composition, and your mom, Janet, wrote songs, and both of your sisters, Helen and Margaret, are musicians. Do you think that growing up in a musical family was a big help to you in becoming the composer you are? Were any of them mentors to you?"

"Yes, sure, I heard a lot of music. My dad studied musical art. At one point he wanted to be a composer, so he taught me a lot of basic things when I was really young. He played a lot of music that I was interested in. Then later on, my sister was a professional cellist, and I worked with her as a colleague."

"What are you composing right now?"

"I'm writing a piece for a large orchestra and organ that sort of has something to do with Bach."

"Was that a commission? Will it be orchestral?"

"It started out as just an idea from a conductor friend of mine, Ludovic Morlot, the music director of the Seattle Symphony, and he thought that I would be interested in writing for organ and orchestra. I wrote three pieces for the organ when I was a graduate student, so I guess that was in 1963. It's not a symphony. It's kind of a dialogue, an antiphon; it's really about a kind of dramatic encounter between Bach and a modern orchestra."

"You studied with Walter Piston and Roger Sessions, both American composers. Have either one or both of them influenced your music a great deal?"

"I think it's really important when you study with somebody to find out about their music. I'm a little surprised sometimes to run into young composers who are studying with a composer, and I ask what piece of that composer they know, or what is it about his music that interests you? They sometimes aren't that curious about their teacher. I certainly paid a lot of attention to what Piston and Sessions were writing. So as a student, and as a performer too, I wanted to know the music from that standpoint. Also, my teacher in Berlin was composer Boris Blacher. I had a chance to hear a couple of his operas when I was his student. I think it is an important part of studying with someone to hear their music just to know what they're saying to you."

"Speaking of Bach, I understand you think of him as the composer most influential to you?"

"I would say sure, I keep thinking about Bach all the time. This year as a performer I will conduct five weeks at Emmanuel Music in Boston, so that is five Bach cantatas there and an entire program of Bach at Tanglewood this summer, so I'm still really involved in learning Bach."

"So, what is it about Bach that inspires you?"

"Well, it's the best music you can find. Bach is always writing at a high level. A lot of composers are less committed in the area in which they work. I think Bach was fully committed."

"How would you compare the works of Mozart and Beethoven to those of Bach?"

"They're all at a very high level. To me, Bach has an edge on any other composer because his ambition for what music can achieve is somehow more comprehensive. That is not to say that those composers are not ambitious. Any time that you are with them they seem to be absolutely sufficient. But for me Bach just remains. The more I study him, the more I find both the consistent level of excellence and also his exploration of every aspect of what music does seems to me the most thorough."

"Yet he almost fell out of sight after his death."

"Actually, he didn't. I think he fell out of sight to the large public of that era, which wasn't interested in older music. Among the core of musicians, he remained very strong even though he didn't have much of a public career. They knew about him for certain. Throughout, Mozart, Haydn, and Beethoven, all of them,

German composer Johann Sebastian Bach, muse of John Harbison

Credit: portrait of Johann Sebastian Bach by Elias Gottlob Haussmann, public domain, via Wikimedia Commons.

were very fully cognizant of what Bach meant despite the fact that they weren't hearing his music publicly performed. They had his scores, and they played his music for themselves."

"I was talking with Rose Mary about Mozart's understanding of life as shown in *The Marriage of Figaro* and his other operas. I said to her that he held up a mirror and said, 'Hey folks, this is the way you are,' as opposed to Beethoven saying, 'This is how I'd like you to live.'"

"I totally agree that is what Mozart's operas do."

"Did Bach try to instruct us on how to live?"

"In different terms than Beethoven, he did. It's very realistic in a way because what you basically go through are the basic interpretations of the Lutheran literature in that people get themselves into terrible trouble and have to ask for forgiveness. That's the plot line to almost every Bach cantata. It's implied that the problems that they get into are the problems that we're into now. The difference, of course, is the mechanism of how we now try to deal with those tragic consequences is much more psychiatric than of the higher power, very similar to what Mozart does in his operas. Mozart's view is a much more tolerant and Italian view, that these forces are just running like fire through the whole society. Everyone gets tangled up, and we hope we all live through it. To me it's much more Mediterranean. I think some of that comes through in *Idomeneo* and then later in his three Italian operas with librettist Lorenzo da Ponte, *Figaro*, *Così fan tutte*, and, even more, in *Don Giovanni*. They're all on the same subject, that the world can't handle these desires and urges and struggles except by trying to pick yourselves up and figuring out how to go ahead, and maybe punish the worst offenders. But, of course, in *Figaro* that's not what happens at all. In *Figaro* we try to reabsorb everybody back into society. *Così fan tutte* is the scariest one because of its harsh view that if you put the original couples back together, they're now with the wrong one. So, in a way, that's a cynical piece. That is their last statement of the problem."

"Were Mozart and da Ponte the best collaborators ever?"

"You can make an argument for Wagner collaborating with himself. He had a very large embrace of humanity. *Die Meistersinger* is very womanly and humanly inclusive. There's a lot of wonderful human engagement in that piece."

"Mozart led a seemingly pedestrian life. So where did all that understanding come from? Was it from traveling?"

"Smart, incredibly smart guys are extraordinarily perceptive. Mozart's father provided to him a very cultured upbringing, sort of like Mendelssohn's family did. He was presented with the highest artistic models that existed by his father, just like Mendelssohn as a kid read Shakespeare plays. I think a lot of it starts right at the beginning. Wagner had to get it himself, but he found it. He read the classics he educated himself incredibly rigorously. I think that's what it takes to give you a chance to grow something. It's easy to look at Mozart's playful side, his wise guy side, his egomaniacal side, but clearly he also must have been incredibly sharp. It takes a lot more than mere instinct to make operas as comprehensive as those of Mozart with such subtlety of thought. That takes a lot of intelligence and a lot of culture. None of that is just happening simply by genius. It's happening because somebody is there who puts many, many things together that are there needing to be assembled."

"His letters show some of that."

"Yes, you can see how smart a guy he was there. Nobody was ever more aware of music needing to be apprehendable by the whole audience made up by different classes of people. That was the listener's side. Mozart says that straight out in his letters a couple times. He's one of the few who actually lays that out there."

"You're talking more about Mozart than Bach?"

"We know so much more about Mozart. Bach is harder to track. You look at the Bach reader, and it's a bunch of documents, although his quarrels give you some picture of his life. Bach was very angry about authority. In most of his correspondence he's complaining about people mistreating him. It's instructive. Bach is mainly in very subservient positions working for people whom he doesn't really respect."

"Maybe the piece that you're most noted for is *Gatsby,* which you wrote for the Metropolitan Opera. It had mixed reviews but it's being revived and it's played. Are you satisfied with the work you did on *Gatsby,* for which you wrote both the libretto and the music?"

"I certainly wanted to write more operas than I've written, but that's a question of opportunity. At a certain point it is foolish to write operas for which there are no performance plans. That was the position I was in after *Gatsby*, so that is why I haven't written more operas. When I started writing as a composer, I always thought writing opera was what I had mapped out. The first two I wrote were with no performance prospect. That is a difficult start for an opera, that is just to have it on the page. Then I did get a chance with the third opera, *Gatsby*, but as you say, the reviews were mixed enough and the piece was heard enough that I think it sort of closed off my opera opportunities. So I moved in other directions. But I would have to say that wasn't voluntary on my part. I just had to write what I had real chances to hear."

"James Levine was the musical director of the Boston Symphony Orchestra when he commissioned you to compose *Gatsby* for his twenty-fifth anniversary at the Met. You also were awarded the Oberlin prize by the BSO. You've done a lot of work with the BSO, so might you speak a little bit about the combination of those forces in your life, Levine, the Met, and the BSO? When did you first meet Levine?"

"I was in Salzburg writing a paper about opera. Levine was there and liked the paper I wrote defining the difference between the feeling of the passage of time in the real world and its passage in the presentation of opera, and the amazing idea of Wagner where he wanted some things to pass in real time on stage, an idea which he obviously had studied and used. That is one of the reasons Wagner's operas are so unusually provocative. They are spellbinding! Remarkable! I took the scene where Isolde finally shows up in the third act in *Tristan*, and she is sighted near the shore. She takes forever — you can't believe how long it's taking her to get there — but what is happening is that she's crossing that terrain in real time, as Wagner often did, and its stunning effect is very excruciating. I compared that to the scene at the beginning of Verdi's *Otello* where Otello is in the shipwreck, then he's on shore, then he's right here, and it's all done in a few seconds. It's like movie time. It's like in a flash. It's the way Verdi moves the action forward. There is no realism. It's just a brilliant scene. In Wagner a lot of the so-called action in his operas is just as it happens in the real world. It's like what you're living, so, of course, it feels really long, I mean really, really long sometimes. It's like, get on with it! Whatever he's trying to do, he succeeds. Wagner is such an amazing artist!"

"I guess after that James Levine became a pivotal figure in your life?"

"Any composer who writes orchestrally at all has to have the conductor link. If you don't have that, you probably won't wind up spending much time around the orchestra because you have to have a chance to hear a piece move from place to place to gain an evaluation of the piece. Levine, among other things, kept giving me varied sorts of orchestral opportunities, which I accepted, bringing me to my orchestral phase. Thanks to him, I had a period of about fifteen years where I composed a large series of orchestral pieces. The way I moved from my opera renditions into a very different area came as a surprise to me because I never thought orchestral music as such was what I was naturally fitted for. But as I kept on doing it, it certainly turned out to be where I really put in the biggest phase of my career."

"Were the pieces mostly symphonic?"

"Yes. There are six symphonies, I think eight concertos, and two big sets of orchestral songs with a singer, and some shorter pieces. So, as said, it was a complete surprise to me because I never felt the idea of the orchestra was what drew me into composition. What did was much more about operatic singing with small groups of instruments, which is not really where I spent as much time as I expected. But I'm glad to have written orchestral music. A composer needs a conductor as an interpreter. That has been true all the way through history. You need someone who will put it out there."

"I've always thought James Levine is a great and inspiring musician."

"He is a phenomenal musician. I've been lucky to have sat with great conductors like Blomstedt, Haitink, really amazing people! But Levine was something unusual. He internalized. He was a slow learner, actually not a quick study, but he absorbed the piece and always came back to it. There was a sense of going way past just the outline of the piece and reaching some sort of very internal sense of what the piece was supposed to achieve. So I got that in a lot of instances with Levine. That was a big opportunity. I don't think I saw it coming, nor as I look back on it now, do I see it as anything but a positive development."

"It certainly was a great opportunity. It gives much greater scope to your career?"

"When I finished the sixth symphony, I thought that's it, I don't need to do more. I'm done with symphony. So this chance to do this very unusual idea of Ludovic's for organ and orchestra is just another way to stay around the orchestra a little longer. It's funny because I've never had any interest in orchestration. I never taught it. I did badly in it; it's where I got one of my lowest grades in school. My sense of orchestration has always been that the notes will describe the instrument, and that orchestration is not like a set of techniques. I was always amused because a couple of kids from Harvard came to study orchestration with me in the early days, and I always had to tell them, 'I don't have a thought about orchestration, or even a sense of the technique.' To me every phrase is just to listen for the sound, which you probably already have in your ear when you write the note down. And that's been really the way I've navigated all through, so I'm much more sympathetic to what I would call the idiosyncratic orchestrator, the ones who really may not be who we think of as good. Schumann would be a great case — he's one of my favorite orchestrators — or Haydn whose orchestra sounds extremely distinctive. It's almost entirely just a set of choices rather than a preconception. So my life with the orchestra has proven much more attractive to me than I thought it was going to be starting out."

"Wasn't it tough for American composers to get their stuff played then?"

"That's right. When I started learning composition, no one thought about writing for orchestra because no one was getting played at that stage. We had a big change in this country about 'Let's hear orchestral music from American composers,' which occurred in the 80s. I was one of the beneficiaries of this seeding by various orchestras with composers. I was sent out to Pittsburgh and to LA, in the role of resident composer writing for those orchestras. Collectively, I think we all changed the relationship with the orchestra very emphatically. It was a whole new way of thinking. Really, twenty years before that you wouldn't write an orchestral piece because you didn't think anybody would play it."

"When you were playing mostly jazz did you think then you would become a classical composer?"

"For a brief time in college I was really enjoying being a jazz player. I began to imagine a career in jazz. I think people get enthusiastic about jazz and you sort of blind yourself to the fact that the career possibilities are extremely slim. I made the choice in a clear moment that I was going to be a concert musician in a primary way. I had a lot of good friends that I was playing jazz with. I really liked them. I enjoyed that world, so I never really left jazz as a player. But I'm really very realistic about it as a professional world. It's even more fragile as a niche than the concert music world. It wasn't when I started out in jazz. Jazz then was in the position of rock now. Then there was a huge sea change in the 50s, and the same clubs that were jazz clubs turned into rock clubs, and jazz has never come back to be the central popular music in the country again. Now jazz is really a small slice of the action. Even symphony orchestras have way more influence in the larger cultural life than jazz."

"Is Rose Mary a jazz enthusiast?"

"Yes, she's also a jazzer."

"I see she comes from Wisconsin, where you founded the Token Creek Chamber Music Festival with her way back in 1989."

"We've done a lot of music out there. For about thirteen years we included a jazz element in the festival. We tried to do a festival that was both a jazz and concert music. I started really playing a lot and working myself back into shape. We hoped for some of the audience to take an interest in both sides. Not as many did as we hoped for, but we did certainly have some who came to do everything. We did big jazz concerts. All of them were sort of thematic. We were exploring pop composers of the past and trying to do an inventory of the tunes we like, which was similar to what I was doing with the vocal jazz group back here at MIT. It interests me a lot to understand, say Jerome Kern, in a synoptic way, to really immerse myself in those tunes to get a sense of what he's doing as a composer. I have done the same thing with concert composers."

"Rose Mary told me how you met musically, so to speak, and that you've been married around fifty years. Is she a big influence on you?"

"She played a lot of Bach, like me. Of course, Rose Mary is a big influence. She's much more than influential. I would say she's more thorough and exacting than I am in many ways. Rose Mary has very high standards. We met playing Bach in the Princeton University orchestra. She has turned into a very excellent jazz player too."

"Did you teach her jazz?"

"No. She just started playing. It was quite a while ago, back probably in the early 70s. We played quite a lot of the jazz thing. It sort of took over quite a bit for a while. I never tried to do it without staying in decent shape. It's different when you're improvising. You have to be able to fire off very well under a certain kind of moment. Certainly when I am playing a lot of jazz, I usually try to make sure I've gotten myself in shape for that."

"Do you and Rose Mary ever play together at home?"

"Oh, sure. Very often just the two of us. It's easy because we live alone. We've played a lot of things here that we don't ever perform. Rose Mary plays the violin, and I play the piano. I used to play viola a lot but keeping up both instruments got too I hard, I guess, although I love playing viola. I did a lot of that at our festival. We sometimes just read Mozart sonatas for an evening. Not that I'm a good reader, but if nobody is listening, it's OK."

"I asked you about Mozart's understanding of life. Where would you say yours comes from? Your own life experiences, reading, other sources? I ask that now, John, having read about you and spoken to you enough to realize that you think about many things."

"All composers have a lot of time where you just think about stuff. I mean it's a profession where you won't probably join a meditation group because you do enough of that. The social side of it is present, but a lot of it isn't that way. I think that aloneness is where composers figure out what they think and where their minds are kind of lodged. It's built into the profession. It's something that you can't do if you don't have any appetite for it."

"Do you ever just sit there and think about things when you're not composing?"

"Yes, that is what we call composing. But unless you're trained in meditation when you sit down to compose, everything that is running through your head is going to come through there. I'm just always waiting for the useful stuff to show up, but you can't will it to come."

"What might you be thinking about? Current events?"

"Yes, you could be thinking about anything, but what you're hoping is that at some point your mind will come up with something that is useful for what you're doing. You just have to be ready. I've learned not to reject the very unpromising things which I used to not bother with. I won't reject them now. You don't know what is going to be helpful. Of course, since I've composed a lot, I will not want things that I would have been happy with some years ago because I now have a much more precise idea of what I want to do. Unfortunately, that can be a hazard or a handicap, but it's just a byproduct of having been around quite a while. But you never know which little chord or little line fragment is going to take you in a good direction, and that's what you're sitting around waiting for."

"How would you describe your compositional process? Is it from the outside, the inside, from dreams, impressions, experiences, literature, nature, light, color, life itself?"

"It could be anything. The main thing is that you're always looking for some musical idea to push its way out to sort of take the lead. It's just like someone, some musical material, volunteers to take you forward. It could be any element. I just hang on to whatever wants to go forward. Just thinking about the kind of thing I want to hear next, kind of hoping it will show up. Of course, there are little pragmatic things that are very different, which are based on skills that I know I always have, like arranging a known tune or something like that. There you are just working with stuff you know how to do. But that is the problem with composing. Much of composing isn't stuff you know how to do."

"So you just personalize a musical idea which volunteers itself, so to speak?"

"Yes, and it's probably going to be something not arbitrary. It's going to be something like what you've been looking for. You have a certain area of eligible sounds or chords. It can be almost any material that is in some way translated into music. It is in a general place where your mind is available to hear it, and you wait for it. I compose a lot more slowly now because I just schedule myself to be more open. I don't want to have that kind of pressure anymore. I really think that it's almost like you recognize something that you had been planning to do, that you weren't ready to do before. And you can only do it at any given time. I look at my early pieces. I've listened to them. I think, boy, there's so much there. I really would love to do that. I can't do that anymore. At any time your skill set is completely different, even from two years before. So I'm very envious of myself. One of my very good friends says, 'God, you're about the only person I know who is envious of yourself!' I agreed, because I was always saying things back in the 70s that I could really do this or that. Yeah, let it go. But you can't carry that stuff along. You just have to pick up other skills. I do get envious of my earlier self. I'd say there are things I just would love to do now I could do then, but I can't do them now."

"When you compose, is the notation just an afterthought, or do you sit at the piano and compose from note to note, idea to idea, or put differently, what is your compositional process?"

"I don't use specific notation in the early stages. I do notate, but not in the usual way. Occasionally it has a pretty clear shape, but sometimes it really has to be heard later. I do put something down so it won't get away, so I won't forget it."

"Do you hear music in your head? If so, please tell me about that?"

"I do hear music in my head. Mostly it's useless for my purposes. Just not stuff I would want to compose. It's just static, reiterated things that go through your head that are not useful. Every once in a while I find something in my head, and I say, 'Oh wait a minute, that's not just a momentary glitch, that's something I might want.'"

"Do you ever hear a known composition of yours or anybody else? Do you hear the actual instruments?"

"Oh, sure. There are whole pieces of mine or of other people that I can still remember all the way through. If it's like a classic piece that I've heard lots of times, you hear the whole damn thing. It's like you have the recording."

"When it comes, does it become a bother or can you wipe it away whenever you want?"

"That's the difficulty with being a performer. To be a performer of say a Bach cantata, you have to study the piece, you have to really know how it goes, and to have a really good concept of it to put it before others. Sometimes that's very much in conflict with being a composer because the piece sticks around and is not useful to you. It's just occupying a piece of your consciousness. I've known musicians who do a lot of conducting who say, 'I can wipe it off, it just disappears.' Unfortunately for me it's never like that. I carry the piece I'm performing around, and that's just interference in a way."

"So when you're in a conducting period, can you compose?"

"Well, I have to make a big effort to just get to what I'm trying to think about, and to get the piece to go away for a while. I'm always amazed by composer conductors who move back and forth easily. I just can't do it."

"When you're hearing music, is it mostly classical or mostly jazz, or whatever?"

"All kinds of stuff, just everything."

"Does hearing music in your head ever interfere with normal life? Not musical life, just life?"

"Yes, particularly if I'm having memory trouble or I'm just trying to recall something and I get stuck somewhere. Then it's very distracting."

"When you conduct, are there some things you conduct without the score?"

"I used to do that, but I don't do that anymore. I did it before I got my cataract surgery. It was not by choice. I had very bad sight troubles, so I had to conduct virtually from memory. But I wouldn't take the score away even if I could just see its outline. It was pretty difficult. My sight is pretty good now after the surgery. Cataract surgery is pretty amazing."

"Here is a simple question, not so simple maybe. What is music?"

"Well (long pause), I would have one opinionated view of what a real musical idea is as opposed to a kind of reflex, or the difference between a concerted action and a twitch. A musical idea is one which has some sort of consequences which moves and has an urge through time. For me the difference between music and everything else is that eventually music blocks out a number of seconds, and you can't choose when to pay attention to it. You can run it back in your memory, but unlike a book where you pick it up and put it down, or a painting which you can look at and then walk away from it, the composer of a piece of music ideally has legislated that you have to stay through the whole piece. To me that is the most important and singular characteristic of music, that it has a duration and requires a specific period of attention. No other art does that."

"I believe that. But is that an answer to the question of what is music?"

"No, it isn't. But it's an important part for me."

"It certainly answers the question of what characteristics music has for you, but what about a question that doesn't involve you, the abstract question of what is music? Is it a vibration in the air? What is it?"

"I have no idea; I have no answer for that."

"How would life be without music?"

"I just don't cross that bridge because from the age of three I could pull the records out of the shelf that I wanted to hear even before I could read the names of the composers because I knew by the length of the type who the composer might be. What is music? I'm just passing on that. I really don't have any idea. I have no idea what the answer is to that question. I have to read a philosopher like Susanne Langer for that. Bach had the theological answer, which is great, but I don't think you can make that stick any more. He said that music was the model of the structure of the universe."

"Absolutely it is. John, what level of satisfaction do you derive from all you do musically?"

"I just think I'm one of the fortunate people who is in a profession in which I get to do quite a bit of any day doing something I want to do. Still, life is full of an awful lot of time doing something you don't want to do. In this profession in which I always wanted to be, there are certainly some long stretches when I get to do what I want to do. I know quite a few people, even some of the graduates of MIT, who haven't had that experience. I get reports from the field that a lot of their day is spent doing what they don't want to do. I feel the difference between those times of the day when I'm doing something I want and when I'm not. So a lot of people out there wind up being dissatisfied."

"I would think that music is certainly well able, if not uniquely, to give a person that level of satisfaction."

"Of course. Bizet said on behalf of all musicians that at times in their lives music is a beautiful art but a pretty miserable profession. I think he said it because that mirrored a huge part of his life where he was buried in tasks and not getting recognition."

"Maybe he would have lived longer if things had gone better?"

"Bizet had it tough. I know what he meant because we've all felt that way about it. Nevertheless, the first part is important. It is a beautiful art. Despite the fact that artists have a lot of wonderful material that they work with, a lot of them always, as a class, are very dissatisfied. It is not what I've felt, and it's one of the reasons I have a dog."

"Should musicians be running the world?"

"Not from what I've seen, I don't think so. I've often thought that the arts should be really run by somebody like Red Auerbach."

"(Laughs) He loved Chinese food. He was a great coach, a fantastic leader."

"He was. He ran a merit-based system, and the arts are very seldom purely a merit-based system."

"Are you going to tell me it's based on connections and stuff?"

"Yes, I'm going to tell you it's based on that, and perhaps happenstance, luck, connections, politics."

"So we've had a lot of musicians who were as talented as the ones we know, but because of their lack of political connections or whatever never really made it?"

"I believe that, I believe that for sure. I think that's definite. The more one gets around the more you believe that."

"Do you believe that your music will live on for a long time after you're gone?"

"I don't think so. I used to be really worried about that question, and I took some steps about four or five years ago. I made this decision that since there are a lot of my pieces that really just sat in my own files since I've written them and had performances of them, but that I didn't think anybody would listen to now,

I started about five years ago to listen to everything I've written. I've almost gotten through it and it's been a mostly terrific experience. It's one of the best decisions I ever made, and it's released me from that question because now someone has heard it."

"Oh, you mean you have heard it?"

"Yes, I heard it. I realized that given the way that culture seems to be going, and looking at the music that I valued when I was a student coming up, I was very enthusiastic about it and I was performing it. None of that music is with us anymore, with the exception maybe of Messiaen."

"But wasn't that mostly popular music?"

"No, I'm talking about concert music. Popular music will stay with its generation. In a few unusual occasions it will be prolonged somewhat artificially, but mostly it stays with its generation and will be guaranteed to do that. Concert music has not done well sticking around during my lifetime. It's no longer that kind of art. The only music from the sixties that is widely played is music that, in my aesthetic judgment, I don't believe to be of first quality."

"Is classical music dying out, or do you think first-quality music today will survive?"

"I don't think so. Classical music is going to be more and more niche oriented. To me the real surprise is that I don't think Boulez was entirely right when he said that. In fact it turns out he was actually wrong when he said that Shostakovich was the Meyerbeer of his generation. We know that Meyerbeer was very popular in his lifetime, but now he has almost completely disappeared. However, the reverse has happened with Shostakovich, who is the only composer from the sixties and seventies who has fully survived in the public mind. To me his music is not first-class, and so that indicated to me a bleak survival for concert music, including the loss of a great many valuable things. Messiaen is still hanging around in some form. Some things have survived but it's taken tremendous energy for them to survive."

"Let's talk about Emmanuel Music, John, which I know is close to your heart. Just to introduce this line of questioning I know that you were very close to the late esteemed conductor, Craig Smith, when he was the director there. You were one of the founders. I believe your Pulitzer Prize-winning composition, *Flight into Egypt*, had its genesis at Emmanuel. I read that the piece derived from the book of Matthew in the King James Bible, and also involved not only Craig Smith but your wife, Rose Mary. Please talk a little about your long connection to Emmanuel Music."

"Emmanuel Music from the very beginning became a kind of small community. You would call it a collaborative community because the original cantata performances were really structured around Craig and his friends, and conservatory classmates that he could convince to sing and play voluntarily. Gradually funds were found and raised through the church and outside to make it more stable and to ensure that the cantatas went on every week. But the spirit of Emmanuel pretty much retained that sense of people really choosing to ground their weekend in this music, people who are really enthusiastic about the repertoire. I think Craig was the biggest force. His spirit was very inclusive and very purely derived from the musical purpose. Given how long it went on under Craig, almost four years, I would say there was much less of a political sense and much more of a collegial sense about it."

"What was it about Emmanuel Music that appealed so much to you, John?"

"Well, I remained close to Emmanuel pretty much through the whole thing. Probably a high-water mark was [when I was able to conduct for] about fifteen weeks a couple of times when Craig went to other jobs. He was conductor at the La Monnaie Symphony Orchestra in Belgium for a while. I stayed close to the idea of the weekly Bach cantatas which is the heart of Emmanuel. There always have been a lot of other activities there, but the cantata on Sunday is really why the performers find their way there, and it's also the place that they learn more about Bach cantatas and what they are about. That leads into an area of my music that has been pretty consistent of working in church music, which is really not a very highly developed area in the United States, compared to Europe where it is probably a little more developed. Emmanuel and oratorio groups like the Cantata Singers are quite distinctive to Boston. I've written a lot of music because of that, enjoying the sense that when I write something for the Emmanuel choir that their audience has heard a lot of other music that I have heard and are grounded in the same sorts of musical issues. So for me it was the most meaningful audience with which to hear the music because we had been hearing Schütz motets, Bach cantatas, and quite a few contemporary pieces that Craig would play. So it stayed solidly in my catalogue all the time to be doing that kind of work. We did it at eleven o'clock on Sunday mornings! If you can sing that music then you can really sing anything (chuckles)."

"You were commissioned by the Pontifical Council in Rome to do a piece called *Abraham* which was officiated by Pope John Paul; Rav Elio Toaff, the Chief Rabbi of Rome; and Abdulawahab Hussein Gomaa, the Chief Imam of the Mosque of Rome. What did that commission mean to you, and how significant was that in your musical and personal life?"

"It was something that I was very ready to do (long pause). I was impressed by what John Paul was trying to accomplish. It was a fascinating experience. I knew a lot of music history dating back to when the Vatican was the musical center for the world, and the Vatican choir was commissioning and likely performing the most important music in the world in the 1500s into the 1600s. I was very startled and impressed when in the run up to that concert the Pope issued a statement that the Catholic Church needed to reclaim its musical legacy all the way back to Josquin. Somewhat of a reversal of trend was implied by that statement. The interaction with the committee which was involved in that performance was fascinating because it sent a lot of what I call hints about what kind of music they were hoping to hear. I did not find that intrusive because that's been a part of the commissioning process since the beginning of music, but I took that in and focused the composition in an interesting way for me. I've never had a piece of mine premiered before that large an indoor audience. That was amazing! It was a very long and complicated project in terms of all the ancillary events, and the dealings with the Pope and the Vatican, but it was extremely interesting for me to see what about that institution is ancient still, like arcane requirements of what kind of paper I was to use, and what is extremely highly computerized now, and aware of everything that is happening in the world."

"Are you religiously oriented?"

"Yes, I think I am religiously oriented. I go to Emmanuel. I can't define it too specifically. My parents both were religious. That was their profession. My father was a historian of the Reformation, and my mother was an editor for a magazine of the Presbyterian Church, so they were both thinking about that all the time. It was their life."

"One quite interesting piece I read about you was on your seventy-fifth birthday party at Kresge Auditorium at MIT. That article spoke of your love of jazz and songwriting. No question you have a broad range in your various interests. Tell us about your songwriting."

"Songwriting has always been a big thing for me. Some of my first songs are from when I was in high school. I've always kept that up because I'm fascinated by what a rare and difficult skill songwriting is. I don't think I have the ability of the great songwriters who really were able to spend a whole career writing in that very tight and small genre, but I still like doing it. I grew up as a jazz player knowing a huge number of songs. I didn't even know who wrote them for a while, but eventually I kind of put that into an order in my head. It became important for me to know. To me songwriting is a highly developed and strenuous form of music to which our country has made a contribution. It requires tremendous good luck to be successful."

"This plays into something else that happened at that birthday party. You had labeled eight of your songs which lacked lyrics as rejects, so you set your students to work in writing the lyrics. How did they do in your estimation?"

"The only way that anyone seems to be able to write lyrics is to write them out of what they're worrying about, so what they wrote was kind of what I expected them to do, which is their telling of some story that is on their mind. I think that never changes in that medium. The only ones that people really can grab onto either as writers or even as listeners are coming from some sort of direct experience. They didn't worry about stylistic issues about how they connected to the music."

"I know the teaching has been a big thing in your life. That shows in the method of your teaching. Please reflect on your experience in teaching and how valuable that is in your lifestyle."

"It really is important. I think one of the things I've gotten out of working with students is I've learned more about how people listen and about what it is that is retained from the experience of hearing music. That has been very helpful because I think the composer spends a lot of time as his own receptor, but the students are different. First of all they are of a different generation, and if you stick around as a teacher the students change in terms of what they receive and what is important to them, and you find that certain kinds of artistic things appeal to them at different moments in time. I think that that keeps you aware of what the constants are because you're always looking for what can carry forward. That is not to say that you're trying to find the constants just to refurbish old things. You're trying to see how the art of music stays alive for these people who make it too. I've always felt that I needed to keep some connection because I need to know what they're hearing."

"Do you always like what they are hearing?"

"Occasionally I put myself in the situation where I don't understand what they are hearing, and I've had to withdraw and go teach something else, particularly when I was trying to do a course for non-concert music writers. It was at the height of the heavy metal period. At the beginning of every semester I tell the students to bring in the thing you're listening to most. I had a couple years where I came in and I just couldn't hear it, that is I could hear it but I didn't want to hear it, and at that point I thought this is a moment for me to step away. I thought the culture will probably evolve and change, but this is not a group to which I can usefully contribute any aesthetic guidance right now. That was in itself constructive. But I think the main thing about teaching is it really never repeats itself. Every group is different and everyone has their own issues about how they prepare to perform. I find tremendously inspiring the fact that the main thing I do as a teacher and as a coach of my own pieces is that I just try to teach people to read a score. That can mean literally the signs on the score, or it can mean listening with a sense of what was intended, or what we're trying to produce. And over and over I go in to coach one of my own pieces and the students say, 'Oh, thanks you really just opened up the whole piece.' But I never say if it says forte, here play loud. I think everyone needs encouragement to read the score vigorously. We who teach, we carry around the score. That's about all we ever do, teach the importance of the score."

"Do you think you've taught them things about life, not necessarily musical, but just how to live?"

"Well, you try to (long pause) create an environment in which they can do well and find the balance between living and setting some standard which will keep them working. I've often had trouble with the kind of student who doesn't want to work because I don't feel very comfortable with injunctions and stern threats. I'm sure there are situations where that's useful. I think it's a lesson in how to get along with people. In every generation of students some are coming from a different place, that's for sure. But I think one of the things that is interesting about music, and it may be true for people who teach literature too, is that you come in with the score encouraging the students to take it on very vigorously. The score isn't something initially to interpret. The presentation of a piece of music is not just there to find your own way with it. The first thing you have to find is what the composer intends. I think that is one of the things that we teach. Because talented people will always move to the next level and find out why they're there, but that's not what we have to tell them. We have to tell them there's somewhere to start from this point. Where is the starting point? Take a peek and go back to the starting point."

"Will you continue teaching indefinitely?"

"I hope so. I want to figure out how to do it. I like particularly teaching where I can play in an ensemble. To me that is where I can do the most efficient job. With my Vocal Jazz Ensemble at MIT, my being in that group is crucial to me. Likewise with concert music. I'm playing in one of my groups right now, and to me that is a helpful way not to have to talk about everything. I think playing in an ensemble is a really good way to summarize some of the things you don't always have to talk about, a real quick way to get into a piece without having to say anything elaborate."

"MIT is famously directed to engineering and all those type disciplines. How big is music at MIT?"

"It's very large although we have very few music majors each year. Surprisingly, there are enough though to make a dent in the profession. One of the reasons it's such a nice place to work is because we're not expected to be scholarly. We're supposed to be artistic. I think at MIT we haven't had to act like a university department because we're not a technical school."

"Do you ever think of it in terms of teaching your students humanistic values that they can carry into the technical work they will do?"

"I think you have that role wherever you teach at MIT. I think one of the things we think about trying to impress upon them is the fact that if you wish to study an art seriously, it requires as many stages of knowledge as the stages of exploration in the scientific disciplines that they study. Because one of the things that the founder of music at MIT, Klaus Liepmann, insisted on was battling to get his courses in music ranked on the same scale as the science courses. It took some years, but now it's basically established. Now, if you're doing advanced work in music as an undergraduate, it is a discipline like the others. We have some fantastic students. I've always felt my Vocal Jazz Ensemble was as good an ensemble skill wise as the Lincoln Center Chamber players and many other groups I've worked with."

"The reviewer summarized the evening as you sitting unobtrusively at the piano through it all and providing accompaniment and support to your students. Is it a fair statement to describe you as unobtrusive?"

"Depending on the situation I think backing up singers is a really particular issue. I worked with one of our really marvelous jazz pianist students about that whole thing. I used him in vocal jazz occasionally to work with the singer, and to learn to get the singers out in the best light that can be. It's like being a Schubert player for a Schubert song cycle. You have to really be able to play, but you have to know how to be unobtrusive. I wouldn't be so unobtrusive if I were conducting a symphonic concert. You know that a concert has to be led, but I think there are certain collaborative things where you really get the best result if you get into the right role. I know some collaborative pianists who are really great at it. To me it's really specific skill."

"How about your speaking style in front of a group? Do you like that role of talking to a group?"

"I used to like it more. I used to depend on just working from notes. Now if I have something fairly substantial to say I usually have to write it out. I did a Haydn lecture at Lincoln Center about a month ago, and I wrote it out. I don't depend on making it up on the spot anymore. I'm not satisfied with that. What I say extemporaneously is not as good."

"John, how existentially threatened do you think mankind is?"

"I think it's very, very fragile. Rosie was asking me, because I read the Bible more than she does, what does the Bible say about irresponsible, catastrophic behavior. I said we've got *Armageddon*, and we've got *Revelation*. In terms of the nuclear age that's not fantasy! So it always depends on a combination of leadership and broadly based social moral responsibility which has really slipped to an unpredictable level. I think what we're learning is how many big societal problems remained below the surface waiting to come up to the surface again."

"Has this threat been reflected in your own experiences?"

"Yes. Rosie and I were in Mississippi in 1964 in very risky situations for that whole Freedom Summer, and, incredibly, felt a sense of amazing change evolving, a sense of movement and some progress towards greater tolerance. However, you don't need much change in the government to realize that that change was much less definitive than it seemed. So we look around now and we find out that the intolerance is still there."

"The United States as we know it could just disintegrate!"

"Yes, and of course the Obama presidency was very confusing as it turns out because what it did was to stoke up a lot of racial animosity and resentment that just burned away and waited for the moment someone would lift the lid."

One can hope that the lid will soon be lowered before it is lifted any higher. If the reverse should happen, we'll need all the folks with clear heads who are short on animosity for their fellow humans to act appropriately in that circumstance. We'll need those folks who are "men and women for all seasons." Among those would surely be John Harbison, sitting to play, standing to resist.

American composer Joan Tower. Photo courtesy Joan Tower.

CHAPTER
2

Joan Tower: A Tower of Strength and Love

What can you say about a woman who is elegant in every way; who is liked and admired by everyone; who is a feminist to the core and says so to the world; whose music is so muscular and powerful that it belies her gentle and loving demeanor; whose lusty laugh makes one feel good and ignites your own laughter; who rebelled against authority as a teenager growing up in South America; whose adventurous father was her model and muse forever; whose innate curiosity about composers, players, conductors, and teachers of music inspired her to excel at all four callings; who thinks of music as her "food" without which she might die; who comes to all of us as a gift from God? You can say that woman is Joan Tower, one of a kind, and America's foremost woman composer ever!

"Joan, I'd like to start off with something that was played here in Boston, which is a very famous composition of yours called, *Made In America*. I noticed that in your liner notes written a while ago you said that perhaps composing it was your unconscious reaction to the challenge of how do we keep America beautiful. We're really challenged these days. What do you think the future holds for the survival of American democracy?"

"It's a very scary time right now because everything is so unpredictable with a leader who has so much power and doesn't know what he's doing. It's a lot worse for sure than when I was writing that piece. It is anxiety provoking on every level, especially the healthcare level with which I'm involved with my brother who had a major stroke ten years ago leaving him half paralyzed up and down his body. I'm his advocate here. He's in a nursing home, so I've been in the middle between my brother and the medical establishment."

"Do you think we'll remain a democracy?"

"I think we have enough inner and infrastructure strength to hopefully maintain the democratic ideal, but I can't predict."

"You have written that in your growing up years you were in Bolivia mostly, sometimes in Chile and Peru, because your father was a mineralogist working in South America?"

"Yes, he was a geologist and a mining engineer."

"Was he an influential person in your life?"

"Yes, definitely, because of two reasons; he had a real passion for what he did. He loved the earth and the study of minerals and the formation of natural things. He loved it so much that I wanted to go to the Colorado School of Mining! It affected me that much. I couldn't get in because I couldn't get past the math test, which was actually a blessing in disguise, because that was not where I was really headed. My father also had a genuine love of music. His mother was a pianist, so he was around music all of his life and loved that part of me. A third thing was that he was a feminist used to strong women. He had some quite strong sisters who were very successful in their fields. Those were the three reasons I adored him (laughs)!"

"Do you think your life as a musician would have been different if you hadn't spent those years in South America?"

"Absolutely, absolutely! I was very much affected by the Latin dance culture, as well as the Inca culture, in both of which I participated. In the Latino culture dancing is enjoyed on a regular basis. They celebrate everything they can in order to dance (laughs), so dancing and percussion became a part of my early life there. I don't think that would have happened if I had stayed in the United States because the United States doesn't have that level of dance built into the culture the way Latins do. So yes, in that sense it affected me dramatically! But I was also studying classical piano and being introduced to Chopin and Beethoven and all those other great composers at a young age. It was a nice balance. Both of those things affected my music deeply."

"I get the impression that you're an outspoken, sort of rebellious, person who goes her own way. Do you think that being in South America played a part in that?"

"No, I think that was just part of who I was. South Americans might have acted differently towards me because of the difference in background. I was an American in a Latin culture. I was known as '*la gringita*,' meaning 'Little American,' so I was treated differently by the Latinos, as were other Americans there, as well as Germans and other foreign nationals. But the rebelliousness? No, that came from us."

"Did you date any of the South American guys?"

"Yes. I was after them like a torpedo ship (laughs). I had Latin boyfriends, and I partied a lot because it is a dancing, partying culture, and I loved it! I also had an American boyfriend in Peru, a Marine. I remember all those people."

"I read some of your quotes, and it seems that you were certainly a very normal young woman interested in those guys out there."

"Oh, sure. I was a rebellious thing. I was put into a private school in Santiago which was supposed to discipline me. It was an international school for upper-middle-class international people where their parents could drop their kids off for a while. It was a boarding school. I hated the place. You had to wear green uniforms with white gloves and brown pumps. It was horrible! So what I did was (laughs) — I remember this distinctly — to climb the walls to get out. There were walls all around this school. It wasn't a prison, but it was sort of like a gated community for young women who needed an education. So I climbed the wall and went to the nearest hotel, the Hotel Carrera. I remember this distinctly. I would go up to the swimming pool up at the top, and pretend I was one of the guests, and order Coca-Cola and stuff. They never bothered me, they never asked who I was. I would swim and have fun. Then I'd go back and climb the wall back into the school. No one ever noticed it (laughs)."

"Joan, you've been a star not only as a composer, but as a pianist, a conductor, and as a teacher. Which do you like the best of all of these?"

"I've always been curious about things connected with music, so when I worked with conductors, I was curious about what conducting was about, how conductors relate to the people in front of them, how do they learn scores? So I took up conducting. The piano has always been my life. I've always been interested in performers who are on the other side of the page from what you create. Composing was a curious thing too because that was getting into music in a very different way than performing or conducting. Teaching is also like that, but teaching is more like trying to help a young person get what I call a 'fuel line' into music so that it will be a lifelong lasting thing for them which they can do all their lives. Creating that connection has been very exciting for me. It works on most of them — I'd say ninety percent — to get that 'fuel line' going. It's not necessarily a question of talent or chops. It's a question of commitment, so that has been a very interesting and different way into music."

"I know you describe yourself as a feminist. Have you found many barriers set up against you because you're a woman composer? How did you become a feminist?"

"It's funny how you come into an historical and political social context, and you sort of adapt to whatever that context is in order to do what you want. When I came into the music scene in the 70s in New York, I didn't know that women were completely ignored in the past. I was just doing my thing, doing the best I could, surrounded by a lot of talented men who were getting lots of prizes, and I wasn't. I was like, 'Oh, that's the way it goes, fine, fine, I'm not a good enough composer to get any prizes' kind of thinking. I was OK with that until I started reading feminist consciousness raising books. In the 60s and 70s, there was a big wave of feminism coming along at that time. I started reading a lot of books by all the feminist writers, and I was like, 'Oh my God! I didn't know (laughs)!' It was literally consciousness raising for me. Then Nancy Reich, a feminist musicologist, came to Bard to teach for one semester. She had written a biography of Clara Schumann. Nancy taught a course called, 'Women in Music.' Music history courses had always been extraordinarily boring for me. But when Nancy Reich started talking about the history of women in music I was like all eyes, all ears, my hand was up the air all the time (laughs). I was at every class and started reading the books that she recommended. We did a couple of festivals of women in music together. She gave me all kinds of music by women that was hard to find which we would pass on to the players. Nancy had an extraordinary influence on me and opened my eyes and ears to the whole history of women in music. That experience became my basic reason for becoming more of a feminist because here it was all tied in with music. Suddenly I discovered I had no idea that the history was so bad. Women were just not being represented at all for a lot of reasons. The historians uncovered these earlier women who basically had relations to men who were in power, like Fanny Mendelssohn had her brother Felix, Francesca Caccini of the Baroque era had her father. There were all these connections. Hildegard of Bingen wrote music in the twelfth century which survived because she was the director of a convent and had a lot of power at a time when most women didn't, so her power was sort of unusual. So to make a long story short that is how I became a feminist."

"I've always been fascinated by some of the women composers, Fanny Mendelssohn especially. I don't know if Felix died because he was in mourning for her, but he died not too long after she did?"

"They were very close and that could have been a reason, but I don't think anybody will ever know exactly. Felix was not supportive of her going public with her music, and that is interesting. He admired her and loved her, but he thought it was politically incorrect because they were upper class German, and I think he just would have been embarrassed by Fanny going public. I think it was hard for her because she was very musical and talented and had the chops that he had because they were trained exactly the same way. But at eighteen she was told to go get married and he was told to go make a career in music."

"You must be happy to see feminists are coming to the fore because of the 'Me Too' movement?"

"'Me Too,' yeah! It's very encouraging. I have to say so because I see it affecting older people like me. It has been like a groundswell to support women who are older, and people who have been kind of ignored. I see it happening all over the place."

"Tell me, Joan, do you think it will continue or die down? I mean not only the 'Me Too' movement, but the whole thing about those kids from the high school down in Florida where there were those mass killings. We're seeing horrific things in our society that we've seen before, but now the opposition to them seems to be sticking, and may change the way things are?"

"Exactly! And those kids! They are empowering themselves. They suddenly have a voice in society on a real issue which impacts their own lives. I was crying throughout that whole thing on TV with these teenagers coming out and speaking about their friends dying in front of them, and with that young woman who just stood there and faced the camera for six and a half minutes. It was a very strong, very powerful, very pure, and not politically based but personally based."

"How would you describe your compositional process, Joan? Is it from the outside in or from the inside out? Do you get inspirations from dreams, impressions, experiences, literature, light, and color?"

"It's from the music itself. Basically, it's from the inside out because I think for me knowing what drives the music is in the music itself. In other words, if it doesn't drive forward, I'm not doing something right. It's an organic process for me always. It's like writing a novel. I start with a character and I watch the character closely and see what that character could be. Are they feisty, are they lyrical, what are they? Then they interact with other characters, and the other characters start to have an identity too, so it's like watching something emerge which has to emerge within a context that is a strong narrative. Do you want to know where I get that from? Basically it's from Beethoven because I played a lot of Beethoven sonatas when I was growing up, some of his trios, and some of the concertos too. I loved Beethoven because he had such a strong sense of organic structure, an ability to take risks now and then. He would throw the piece in a different direction intuitively. It was just fascinating to play him, and then I started noticing that that kind of architecture actually had an effect on me compositionally."

"Would you say Beethoven is your muse?"

"Yes. I would say that when I wrote my piano concerto, which is an homage to him, he walked into the room. I said to him, 'I really would appreciate it if you would leave (laughs), I don't want you around here.' He said, 'Nah, I'm just hanging out. I'm not going to bother you. Just hanging out here.' He hung out so much that three of his sonatas came into the piece, three sonatas that I had played which I loved. They are in that piece, not as literal quotes, but you can hear them."

"Which sonatas were those?"

"The first one is not easy to hear, but it's the from the 'Le Adieux' sonata. What is so interesting about that first movement is the alternation of pretty slow and very fast music. Then the second part has that last theme from the Opus 111, the oldest of his sonatas (sings it). So the Beethoven relationship between those two parts is pretty clear. The last one is from the last movement of the 'Waldstein' sonata, which I never could play well because it has too much power. I would get too intense. I just couldn't do it. But it's in there."

"Joan, explain what you meant when you said Beethoven was in the room."

"Not literally, of course. This happened while I was composing the piece. What I mean by that is that his music kept coming into my room because I was writing a piano concerto and playing a lot of his piano music and concertos. He just kept coming up in my piece, so finally I accepted him and brought him into the piece rather than turning him away."

German composer Ludwig van Beethoven, muse of Joan Tower

Credit: Ludwig van Beethoven par F. von Stuck (Musée de la musique, Paris). Photograph by Jean-Pierre Dalbéra, https://creativecommons.org/licenses/by/2.0/ CC BY 2.0

"I'm interested in that particular occurrence because I want to ask you some questions about music you might hear in your mind as part of the compositional process. How real was that experience? Did you actually talk to him? Was it surreal? Of course he's long gone, but that intensity could result in a sort of bizarre experience. Was it anything like that?"

"No, nothing like that. It's just that his music lives on very clearly, so his presence is very clear. It's more like his music walked into the room, not his person."

"I know that you have a feeling for strong composers who rouse our feelings a lot, like Tchaikovsky, so the question is, do you feel a kinship to any other composers, whether living or dead?"

"Stravinsky had a big influence too, again another viscerally powerful composer, in his early works particularly, like *The Rite of Spring* and *Petrushka*. I wrote a piece called 'Petroushskates' which is actually dedicated to him. All of his early work had a huge influence on me."

"Yes, he became different as he grew older."

"Yeah, he got very mental. I think as he grew older and the twelve-tone movement was coming in, he felt his early music was too visceral. He kind of disowned it. Anyway, Stravinsky's early music was influential, and then music of particular pieces influenced me, like Messiaen's 'Quartet for the End of Time.' We played that piece for seven years with my group, the Da Capo Chamber Players. We never got tired of it. It had a profound effect on me in a way that I felt that I could have the courage to write slow music. I wrote a piece called 'Tres Lent,' which is for cello and piano, based on the last movement of that quartet, which is an homage to Messiaen and that piece."

"Do you hear music in your head? Do you hear the actual sounds or do you only imagine what the music sounds like?"

"That's a tough question. We were talking about Beethoven. You know he went deaf, but before that he had become an amazing improviser. Bach and Mozart did too. They all had this relationship to music where they would improvise for an audience, whatever audience that was. In Beethoven's case that was a salon audience, in Bach's case it was a church audience, but they each developed a very powerful inner ear. This is just a theory of mine, that the stuff they improvised had become a part of their inner ear, so that when Beethoven went deaf, he had all of that stuff in his ear. It was a reality inside his ear. I think that is what happens to a lot of composers. The experience becomes part of their persona. It's like brushing your teeth. After a while you don't think about it, you just know what to do, right? It becomes a part of the mechanics of who you are. I think most composers get to that point where they can do that. Now some composers have perfect pitch, so they can hear things without even having any experience. They can always count on it because they can hear it. For the rest of us it's not so easy. You have to develop that over years. I compose everything at the piano, so I'm hearing it right away at the piano. I'm pretty good. I can get around the piano and I can count. I'm very good with rhythm, so I have some talents. I still play the piano because I want it to be a real time event. Time becomes an important factor in how you're conceptualizing it. You're actually living the time, so I'm sort of a composer who is a performer who composes."

"Yes, because you are considered a terrific pianist, so that's the way you would do it."

"I'm mediocre, I only got to the second level etudes of Chopin (laughs), but I can play. I played a lot of contemporary music, so I learned how to count with other people in an ensemble. I'm at the piano, so it's not in my head so much, which I don't always trust."

"As far as composition goes, as you said, you sit at the piano and compose from note to note, idea to idea, to put it together. Is that a fair statement?"

"Yes, but it's always retracing back to the beginning. I don't just add things in kind of intuitively. It's being generated by the stuff before it. Everybody thinks that when you compose intuitively you just kind of easily find things out. Actually, it takes a lot of work to pull it from the beginning and make it work if you're really listening to what happened before. It's not that easy to write like that."

"Joan, do you listen to a lot of other people's music?"

"I do a concert here at Bard every semester with Blair McMillan who is a wonderful contemporary pianist. We present a program called 'Music Alive' which is living composers, every year twice a year. So we have to do research and to listen to get that to work. I heard a lot of music on panels. I kept up with the younger composers that way, and once in a while I take those panels just to catch up on the younger composers, like at the American Academy of Arts and Letters. I don't sit down intentionally and listen to music because I don't have the time. I know a lot of music already. It's not like I have to. I have to catch up a little bit on the younger composers, but I pretty much know the older composers."

"Do you have a lot of thoughts on pop music? I guess on the Bard campus there must be lots of pop played?"

"I don't have a lot of thoughts about pop music, except that it looks like a healthier culture from the outside than the classical music world because they keep up with new stuff all the time. It just seems to be healthier in the sense that it's more engaging on a critical level from an early age on up. Once in a while my students will play something for me, and sometimes it's fascinating in terms of the technology that they use. There is this one English kid named Jacob Collier who creates his whole orchestra by himself, plays all the instruments, and sings at the same time. It's all him. He's got the technology to do it and the visuals to do it. It's absolutely fascinating what he's doing, although his music is a little bit repetitive and low-key. But I shouldn't comment because I really don't know enough about that music."

"It seems like classical music is going downwards and pop music is going upwards, so I don't know where it will all end up. Joan, you once made a very interesting comment which I'll quote back to you, 'I think there will have to be more of a tie in between classical and pop to bring classical into a more contemporary framework and to bring pop into a more sophisticated framework.' Do you still stand by that one? I think you might have said that to Bruce Duffy a long time ago."

"That was a long time ago! I was acting like I knew something about the pop world. Now I'm a little more humble (laughs), but basically, yes, I still agree with that."

"Maybe the main purpose of this book is to get composers to reveal their musical minds so we'll know what went on in Mozart's or Beethoven's head that allowed them to create such wonderful music?"

"I see it as impossible to talk about, basically. There are some composers who are very articulate who will try to answer that question, and will probably answer very nicely, very rationally, and very cogently, but maybe the music they write is not so interesting. I think it would be very, very hard for Beethoven to articulate what he did and how he did it. He might talk about the form, but talking about form is like talking about making love. How do you describe that? Like, I did this and I did that and I did this and I did that. We've got too many books talking about form as the ultimate, but it's not the ultimate. Actually, composing is an intuitive thing. Beethoven had great instincts and so did Bach and so did Mozart, but they each came at it in a different way and through different practices too. I think it's impossible to talk about that deep inner thing that makes those few people so great."

"I guess music itself is sort of beyond dissecting."

"That's right. We have all these books about it which can be totally misleading. Like theorists will do an analysis of my music, and I get these five-hundred-page dissertations on a solo clarinet piece. I have no idea what they're talking about. I don't have a clue. When they call me and ask me questions I'm dreading, I can't answer their questions. I just can't, but they think by talking to me, the authority on the subject, they're going to get rational answers which will really further their dissertation. It's not. I can't do it. People like theorists scare the holy bejesus out of me. You know what it's like? It's like somebody describing your intestines to you, your inner organs. Like, do you know your intestines are about three inches longer than seventy-five percent of intestines of women in your age group? Do I need to know this (laughing)? It's that kind of feeling, actually."

"Joan, you said, 'My whole life is music. If you put me on an island without music, I would die pretty soon.' Let's say you were on a desert island with another person, that all your needs were taken care of, but for some reason there was no such thing as music on that desert island. Would you really die, do you think? Do human beings need music to stay alive? Is music so central to our existence that we can't live without it?"

"Music is my food. It's not everybody's food, but it's mine. I think once my hearing starts to go, or my ability to play the piano goes, I think I'll start to cash it in. That will be it. I don't know, who knows? Maybe I'll be very happy not to have to do it (laughs). I don't know I can't predict that."

"This is interesting. I interviewed Cecylia Arzewski just recently, a very fine violinist who was the was concertmaster of the Atlanta Symphony Orchestra for twenty years. She always had an ambition to record Bach's *Sonatas and Partitas for Solo Violin*, which she finally did. After the last note was recorded, although only in her late sixties, she put down her violin and has never picked it up again, even though she's still fascinated with music. She said I'm not a violinist, I'm a musician, so that was never my life."

"Did she do something else in music?"

"She describes herself as a great listener now. She has written a book on music which is going to be published at some fairly early date."

"That's great! She had other ways of getting into music, and being around music."

"Right. I bet you would find ways to enjoy music even if you lost your ability to hear and play."

"I probably would. I'm very resourceful, I would find other ways."

"Tell me something about your piece, *Island Prelude* for oboe and strings, which you wrote with love for your husband Jeff Litfin?"

"There is a kind of a backstory to that. We've been together 45 years now, and he's a very feisty guy too. I think that's why we've lasted so long. I pictured the oboe part as this long, big bird flying around a tropical island, and Jeff is the bird. That is the backstory to the piece. I was trying to write a slow piece. I did fine up until about the fourth and a half minute, and then I gave in. That's where the piece kind of falls apart, actually. That is between you and me. Don't tell any oboist that."

"Is Jeff a musician?"

"He studied the piano. He didn't have the opportunities that I had growing up, so he had to learn the piano by himself without a teacher, but he was amazingly determined. The first piece he learned was 'Claire de Lune.' He knew it because he had a recording of it. He slowly imitated the recording because he wasn't too good at notation. He could play it after a year. I think it was then that he became a cellist. Jeff later developed carpal tunnel syndrome, so he had to give up both the piano and the cello. He has a terrific ear, and he's one of my best critics. Jeff has really good instincts about music."

"Joan, what do you hope the listener or the audience takes away from listening to your music?"

"Engagement."

"Do you hope to change their lives in any way?"

"Oh no, no, no! I just hope they're engaged with the piece on some level."

"Let's talk about your teaching. I know you've been over there at Bard a long time, something like 45 years."

"Yes, I love teaching, always have. I have all different kinds of students. I have beginners, I have advanced, I have players who compose, I have composers who play, I have people who like minimalist music, people who like Ligeti, people who write in very different styles, some very conservative, and some who are very cutting edge. My success in teaching is allowing each to develop a voice in any of those styles."

"I bet some of them have gone on to great careers."

"One just got played by the Detroit Symphony with Leonard Slatkin conducting. Leonard gave me the ultimate compliment. He said to the composer, Connor Brown, that, 'You don't sound at all like Joan.' That was a huge compliment because he's done a lot of my music and knows it pretty well."

"I attended a class by Larry Lesser over at NEC. That is exactly what he wants his students to do. He doesn't want them to sound like him; he wants them to develop their own voice and to play with passion."

"Do they actually sound different? I mean he can say that, but do they actually sound different?"

"They do sound different. An advanced cello student of his at that class played a sonata for cello and piano by Frank Bridge which didn't sound all that great the first time around. Then Lesser spoke to them, told a few stories, told a few jokes, played a little on the cello, and when they played it again, they were terrific!"

"OK (laughs)."

"An interesting thing one of your students said is, 'Joan is no BS, you can get inside her head and have a full relationship with her.' It sounds like you become real friends with your students?"

"That is true, actually."

"Joan, I will say to you there may be some other question I haven't asked that you yourself can ask and answer which would really shed light on this discussion?"

"I have one thing which I always talk about that is really important to me. It is the composer as opposed to the performer thing. You know there was a split in the beginning of the twentieth century when the composers and the performers sort of parted. The composers went to the university and became theorists in the mid part of the century, and the performers went into the conservatory and became performers. Before that it was much more mixed. All the people we've been talking about were performers. Beethoven, Mozart, and Bach were hugely fantastic performers. We lost that somewhere, and that loss became a crucial problem for classical music because it meant that the composer was no longer out in front of the audience. Now the composer was in the background somewhere. Something I have been trying to do in my own little way is to get performers to compose and composers to do more performing, so they are both on both sides of the fence more, like choreographers and playwrights, which are the nearest art forms we have where the principals are on both sides. In the music world, as said, it's become much more separated. It's partly because of notation. Notation has enabled people to take a score and go to Europe without the composer. That is not true in the dance world. It's a different notation in the dance world, and in the theatre world, very different, not quite so specific. So you need a director there, you need a playwright there, you need the choreographer or the ballet master there, to show you the steps or the speaking parts. It's a very different kind of creative process in those fields from the classical music world. So I think we need to get back to composers and performers doing more on each side. Like in the pop world."

"Thomas Adès is one guy on both sides. He conducts, plays, and composes."

"He's an exception actually. How many can be named other than him? There are people like Esa Pekka Salonen who composes on the side of his conducting. Leonard Bernstein was the last big name who did both, but his composing suffered. He wasn't so active later as a composer. Anyways, there aren't many, very few."

"You're in that category, Joan."

"No, not anymore because I don't perform that much now. I did enough of it to help me along to be a better composer."

"I think one of your favorite people is Leonard Slatkin?"

"Leonard Slatkin changed my life, basically, because he recorded my first orchestra piece, *Sequoia*, and played it with something like six major orchestras. He then commissioned me to write other pieces and made me the composer-in-residence with the Saint Louis Symphony Orchestra. He just completely changed my life. I owe a lot to him. He introduced me to the orchestra world and helped me grow."

"Another artist you're associated with is singer Dawn Upshaw?"

"Yes, Dawn has become a friend and colleague at Bard. I just met her a few years ago and wrote my first and only song for her. I'd never written for the voice before. I did it because she loves composers, and I just felt I had to try to do it even if I'm not a vocal composer. She is going to do my 80th birthday celebration here at Bard with her entire vocal group in September."

That interaction between Joan Tower and Dawn Upshaw stands as a metaphor for Joan's whole life, a life defined in a few words from Luke, "Give and you will receive." Joan has, without stint, given to her parents, brother, and husband, to her fellow musicians, to her collaborators, to her students, to her fellow women, to her beloved music, to all people from everywhere, and has received back from all of them gifts in accord with the Biblical maxim. Would that more Joan Towers inhabited our planet!

CHAPTER
3

Robert Levin: Pianist, Professor, Mozart Amanuensis

Is Robert Levin Wolfgang Amadeus Mozart reborn? Not quite, but close! His ability to inhabit the mind of that master almost two centuries after his demise eerily marks him as Mozart's amanuensis. In 1967, during his college years at Harvard, Levin completed a sketch that was discovered in 1962 to a fugue Mozart intended to conclude the Lacrimosa of his *Requiem*, and the completed fugue was premiered within a performance of the work in that year. His completion of the entire Mozart *Requiem* was undertaken between 1989 and 1991 and premiered by noted choral conductor Helmuth Rilling in Stuttgart in August 1991. Later it was recorded by Boston Baroque under the direction of Martin Pearlman, convincing many auditors, including this one, that Levin's completion was prime among several going back to that of the master's pupil, Franz Xaver Süssmayr. In fact, there are now about ten recordings of Levin's completion of the *Requiem*. Not only that, Robert Levin made an even larger completion of Mozart's Great Mass in C minor, commissioned by Carnegie Hall and premiered there in 2005 by Rilling. Levin began a career as a world-famous concert pianist and harpsichordist in his middle years, again following in Mozart's footsteps, bespeaking the extraordinary musical mind which has brought him world recognition as a composer, conductor, instrumentalist, writer, musicologist, and professor of the humanities at his alma mater. A musical prodigy, Levin fortuitously studied in France with iconic pedagogue Nadia Boulanger as a teenager, honed his understanding of many masters over his lifetime, never losing his fascination with Mozart, and completing other of his works to the point where it might be said Mozart revealed his musical mind to Levin, who has passed on that revelation to us. At the same time, in these pages, Levin reveals his own musical mind, and his deeply analytical, musicological, and philosophical ideas about music. A three for one trifecta bound to fascinate and enrich any lover of

American composer Robert Levin. Photo by Larry Ruttman.

music. I met with the articulate and engaging Robert Levin at his lovely home in Cambridge, Massachusetts.

"Robert, it was a long time ago that I became aware of you at a concert over at Memorial Hall at Harvard while you were still a student."

"The concert you're referring to was on May 18, 1968, to be precise. It was a bit later at a concert conducted by F. John Adams with the Harvard Glee Club, in which my work finishing a Mozart fugue for the *Requiem* was played. The fugue had been discovered only about five years earlier in a sketch leaf. But there were two other Mozart concert pieces I completed and played at that May concert which were part of my Harvard undergraduate thesis, one a movement of a double concerto for piano, violin and orchestra, and the other a clarinet quartet, not the famous one but a different one in a different key. The orchestra that we put together was conducted by John Harbison, and his wife, the wonderful violinist, Rose Mary Harbison, played the double concerto premiere, and the Mozart violin sonata K. 454. Then I played the K. 503 piano concerto which you remembered when you contacted me."

"In high school you studied with Nadia Boulanger, the very famous French music teacher, so you were a bit of a child protégé yourself. What did she equip you with that enabled you to learn how to compose like Mozart, and complete fragments by him, which is almost like being him?"

"She said that first and foremost the responsibility was to cultivate the fantasy and the imagination of a young musician, and allow searching, risk-taking, the development of a personal language, and beyond that to be utterly ruthless in matters of discipline. So she taught technique, she taught an extraordinary awareness of and sensitivity to the subtlest details in a piece of music. By pointing out those things she developed in her students a fascination with the rhetoric, with the technique, with the architecture, and with the details of scoring. Anything, in fact, that was worth talking about received her attention, and by demanding of her students a vision that was equal to that of her own she pushed people to surpass their own expectations and to set standards that at times seemed frightening. I got bony fists in the ribs if I failed to sight read perfectly the orchestral score of a work of Stravinsky, for instance. I was thirteen at the time and burst into tears because it was the only thing that I could do, at which point she turned into a tender grandmother and said, 'Oh, no, I shouldn't get upset.' Of course, she loved me. A few minutes later I was sight reading and she was hitting me with her fists again. But all of those things were more of the jumping through hoops of immediacy, especially when one was as young and impressionable, as I was. But as the years went by I became more and more aware of the enormity of what I could do which, at the time, did not strike me. I was so enthralled by the fervor and eloquence of what she had to say, the power of her observations and understandings, and because I was at an age at which I did not feel intimidated, simply because I was basically a child at age twelve when I first went over there, and worked with her until I was sixteen, that I just assimilated what she propagated."

"Sounds like you visited and studied with Nadia Boulanger on several occasions?"

"I studied with her during the summers of 1960-1964, from age twelve to sixteen, and during the academic year 1962-63, which would have been my junior year in high school, which I skipped by providing proficiency in French and doubling up on English and History. I was twelve when I first arrived at Fontainebleau and sixteen when I left. I then attended Harvard from age sixteen to twenty."

"That is a quite young age to get to Harvard."

"I arrived at Harvard at sixteen as a freshman, and it suddenly hit me like a proverbial ton of bricks that there were all sorts of things that I took for granted that I could do that these people at Harvard could not do. There were only two reactions that I could have to something like that. One of them was to become arrogant and the other was to become humble. I chose humility because I realized that without the extraordinary happenstance of my ear training teacher telling my parents when I was twelve that I could continue to be musically educated in New York, but that if I wished to make giant steps, the only way forward, the ideal way forward, would be to go to France and work with Nadia Boulanger."

"How did that happenstance happen, so to speak?"

"My uncle was the musician of the family, He stayed in Paris for four years, then came back and discovered that I had perfect pitch. So when this idea came up of my going back to France to continue work with Nadia Boulanger my parents couldn't afford that. My uncle said, 'I'll take the brat, I'll pay for it and I'll go with him.' Then when the fall of 1962 came along, Nadia Boulanger said he's learning very well but it's really not very valuable to have only these two months of the year to work. If he were here the whole year imagine what we could get done. My parents said why not, realizing that it is very hard to make your way as a musician, very, very difficult. Here I was doing music as a part time activity as a high school kid. How could I possibly have the wherewithal to decide whether I really cared so passionately about this that I would be willing to risk everything, including solvency, in order to pursue this path? That year in France was a very dramatic one. I got homesick, I decided to go home, Boulanger found out about it and screamed at me. At the end of that year my parents' bet paid off because I came back to my senior year in high school, and for me a life outside of music was unthinkable. So at that point, when seniors in high school are very vague about the direction their lives are going to take, for me everything was absolutely decided. So that was really the bellwether moment in my life."

"Well I would think it was the decisive moment in your life because to discover exactly where you would be going in your life at such a youthful age is something that a lot of people would like to have happen to them. I enjoyed being a lawyer but I didn't discover that I could write until I was your age. You never know what is going to unfold so that I'm happy I lived long enough so I could get to this. I guess Nadia Boulanger was the main mentor in your life?"

"She was, though I had others that were of significance. I was fortunate that when I was only 9 years old, from 9 to 13 I studied composition with Stefan Wolpe, one of the darlings of the avant-garde in America. Originally from Germany, he was an extraordinary figure, irascible but full of humor and life. It was extraordinary to be so young working with a master like that. Later at Harvard I took Leon Kirshner's composition seminar. He said that whatever meager gifts I had were completely destroyed by Nadia Boulanger, which did not endear him to me. But nonetheless Leon and I had a close relationship during those undergraduate times. People who have a proclivity to music tend to display it rather early. You hear music and you sing it back, which was my case."

"What did you sing?"

"What I sang gives one a very good view of the eclectic nature of what I would call a typical Roosevelt era Jewish middle-class upbringing in America. I sang 'la ci darem la mano' from *Don Giovanni*, 'I'm as Corny as Kansas in August' from *South Pacific*, and some American folk tunes in a very staccato delivery, which shows what was being played in my home. I was five when my uncle came back from Europe and heard from my parents that I was singing all the time. He tested me and figured out that I had absolute pitch, then started giving me ear training and solfege to teach me pitch and sight singing. That gave me pretty much a twelve-year head start on anybody who would go through a normal musical education. Then my uncle went out and found piano teachers. He got me into the Chatham Square Music School in lower Manhattan where there were the flotsam and jetsam of World War II musicians who had come to America to escape the Nazi, and were starving and needed money. These were people who got subsistence from teaching music. Every Saturday I would go to lower Manhattan and for fifteen dollars got a private lesson in piano, an ear training class, and a theory class, which turned out to be private composition lessons with Stefan Wolpe. It seems unimaginable by today's standards, but that was the trajectory of it, and, of course, as soon as I could learn to read music, I started to write it."

"Would you credit Boulanger with giving you this idea I've read about that compositions could be completed or go differently than as we know them?"

"She was not afraid to offer compositional advice. At one point she decided that my writing was far too harmonically oriented. I was writing for piano and there were chords and chords and chords. She said that I had to get away from that. She told me I needed to compose a sonata for flute and clarinet without piano. So I just had two lines to compose. It was a very wise kind of move. However, she would listen to a piece and say maybe you ought to hold that note just another second or two seconds longer. And often when she did that either the discourse would be immeasurably enhanced by that exquisite little detail, or at other times that was like pulling out the bottom card in the house of cards and you realized that when you saw that, that the whole thing was just no good at all. She would never say anything like that, never. She was always giving positive advice."

"Robert, you are a world-class pianist. Did Boulanger's wisdom help you there too?"

"In my own work as a performer I've learned from how she taught me composition, which is to say that I feel that an interpreter is an actor, and that our job, like that of an actor, is to slip inside the skin of not just the composer, but inside the piece. Doing that one internalizes the values and the characteristics of the piece of music in such a way that there is no possibility of separating the identity of the performer from what the performer is saying from the lines that have been given by the composer."

"Can you tell us of an example of that?"

"A couple of years ago when I gave my farewell recital at Harvard none of the pieces on the program were by Mozart, Bach, Beethoven, or Schubert, which people expected from me. All of the pieces were pieces that were dedicated to me, including one world premiere. And I couldn't have been happier when Jeremy Eichler's review in the *Boston Globe* said that the most impressive thing about the concert was my ability to slip inside the skin of each of these composers and give an idealized presentation that was completely idiomatic to the language of these composers. In other words he opined that I succeeded in doing what I was trying to do. I couldn't have been happier."

"How did you become so attuned to Mozart?"

"Like almost everybody else the music that I wrote as a kid sounded more or less like Mozart. It is a strange thing that most people who start to write music when they're kids tend to write in the style of Mozart. There is something about the seeming simplicity of his music that I think strikes a young person as rather clear. But that leaves open, of course, the question of what sort of music perspicacious young musicians would have composed before there was a Mozart. Perspicacity exists throughout the centuries, so I suppose when Bach was alive people probably wrote in the style of the Baroque, but that, of course, with its rigorous intellectual content would have been something a little bit harder to assimilate at the age of five or six. Anyway it is what people do. In my own teaching career I can bear witness to the fact that young women and young men who have a certain inclination to classical music tend to write music that sounds like Mozart."

"I'm not a musician but I know I was attracted to Mozart. That's what brought me to classical music at the late age of a bit over thirty. I remember the first piece of his I heard was the twenty-first piano concerto in C major, the so-called 'Elvira Madigan.' I said to myself, 'God that is beautiful.' And then I started listening to the other twenty-six Mozart piano concertos and I said, 'Is there any one of them that he wrote that isn't beautiful?' This is kind of a lay question if

Austrian composer Wolfgang Amadeus Mozart, muse of Robert Levin

Credit: Portrait of Wolfgang Amadeus Mozart by Joseph Lange - http://www.mozartforum.com/images/Mozart_(unfinished)_by_Lange_1782.jpg, Public Domain, https://commons.wikimedia.org/w/index.php?curid=1068061

ever there was one. Do you think Mozart was the greatest composer who ever lived?"

"Look at Bach, look at Beethoven, look at Schubert, look at Mendelssohn or Brahms or Schumann, look at Stravinsky, I'd say look at my friend who lives a quarter of a mile from here, John Harbison, my friend who lives six miles from here, Yehudi Wyner. Every age generates people of wisdom, of power, of drama, of tenderness. I do think that what separates Mozart from virtually everybody is that he has a knack for characterization and for the understanding of the human condition, which is equaled, as far as I am concerned, only to Shakespeare. That's something quite different. That's not about whether you think the music is beautiful. When you go to the opera and you experience *The Marriage of Figaro*, or *Così fan tutte*, or *The Magic Flute*, or *Don Giovanni*, and six people are standing on the stage and singing simultaneously and you can figure out who everybody is and what each is singing about, that is miraculous."

"I've experienced that miracle in Mozart. Please go on."

"In an Italian opera, whether it's by Donizetti or Bellini or Rossini and you've got six people on the stage, the top soprano is singing the top note of the chord and the bottom bass is singing the bottom note, and they are all singing in exactly the same rhythm because that's a lot easier to write, and it creates more or less the same dramatic situation."

"But that's not how Mozart works. Just to listen to the music when Don Giovanni slays the Commendatore at the beginning of the opera. You have this frightening moment when Leporello is filled with horror contemplating the grisliness and awfulness of this scene in which the Commendatore is expiring, whose weakening pulse and flagging energy as he prays for help which will not come, is expressed in his music, and there is Don Giovanni commenting on the enormity of this situation. These are three completely different perspectives, and every single one of them can be picked out from listening. It is really something uncanny, and, of course, great theatre which is something that we absolutely expect from Mozart."

"Does Mozart do that in all his operas?"

"Yes. That is what life is all about. In *Così fan tutte* these two stupid little men are prompted into this wager that they can create infidelity by the two sisters who are their respective fiancées. Who are the dolts in that situation? The title is *Così fan tutte*, freely translated as 'women are like that,' but in fact the idiots are the men not the women. The women are the victims of deceit and their feelings are real, and when Fiordiligi finally yields, her anguish is overwhelming. Of course, the idea that in these seductions they are going to try to seduce the fiancée of the other is really quite scary. At the end of the opera there is no indication either from the libretto of Lorenzo da Ponte on the one hand, or in Mozart's music on the other, whether at the end the sisters go back to the original pairing at the beginning of the piece, or whether they remain reversed, which is pretty terrifying and absolutely modern, if you want to look at it that way. Beethoven of course loathed that opera because he found it to be immoral."

"It seems Beethoven was much more straitlaced than most?"

"The difference is that Beethoven was an idealist and Mozart was a realist. The thing about Mozart is he never claims to show people otherwise than how they are. He places no judgment on those things. We know that Don Giovanni is a monster. We know that he seduced a thousand and three women in Spain alone, and yet when he raises his champagne glass and sings the champagne aria everybody in the audience wants to go to his party because Mozart makes it possible for every character to elicit the empathy and sympathy of the audience. That's not what most opera composers and dramatists do. When you have the grand inquisitor showing up in Verdi's *Don Carlo*, you know that this is a bad guy. Nobody likes Alberich in Wagner's *Ring Cycle*. It is not for want of affection or involvement in his characters that Mozart is like this. It is because he has this uncanny ability to understand what makes human beings tick."

"Which opera of Mozart's do you think was the earliest that exhibited his understanding of human nature?"

"That comes around twelve years old in the earliest things that he is writing, in *Apollo and Hyacinth* and in *La Finta Semplice*. Yes, they are the works of a child, but a very precocious child."

"Was Mozart's depth of understanding helped by his many travels?"

"Mozart was a very shrewd observer. One of his biographers suggested that he was a kind of magic mirror. That he refracted everything that he heard. He went all over Europe. He was in what we now call Germany and Austria. He was in the low countries, he was in France, he was in England, in Italy, of course, and he heard music everywhere. Everything he heard he assimilated and managed in his treatment of it to go it one better. He had this sympathetic, kind of tactful, and maybe partially conscious. partially subconscious understanding of things. When he got the first real challenge in his life provided by the earlier music of Handel, and especially, Bach, when he was twenty-five years old, it precipitated an intellectual and compositional crisis in which he is finally confronted with music that he couldn't instantly make better. So he wrote fugue after fugue, one after the other, because he realized that this was not just something that was easily learned but was intellectually challenging. It was something that was enormously powerful and he needed to master that. At the end we got the G major string quartet, the fugue in C minor for two pianos, and finally we got the 41st symphony, the *Jupiter*, where he proved that he could do all of those things. But it was a huge battle, as it was for Beethoven who followed him. Composers when they get older turn to Bach, and Bach becomes the final mountain to climb. Mozart was able to unite basic elements of national style from country to country and absorb into his language elements of all of them. As a result he could supersede the individual languages of these national styles. Rossini, who came after Mozart, himself said in earlier times that the Germans were the masters of learning and rigor, and we in Italy were the masters of feeling and melody. But then along came Mozart and we were beaten on our own ground because he could do everything that we could do and then some. I think that does say something about it."

"Give us an example of that from one of Mozart's Italian operas."

"I never get tired of hearing *The Marriage of Figaro* for that reason. It is a hit show. It's what Rodgers and Hammerstein tried to do, what Lerner and Lowe tried to do. Everybody tried to do it whether it was *Fiddler on the Roof* or *Hello, Dolly!* or *South Pacific* or *Oklahoma*. The hits just keep on coming in *Figaro*. You don't know which one to whistle when you walk out after each one of the acts. The situations, of course, are slapstick comedy except when they are heartbreaking. There is something so sublime about the moment when Figaro realizes that the woman disguised as the countess in the dimly lit garden in the fourth act is actually Susanna, his betrothed. At that point he starts to make violent love to her, making her so furious she starts to beat him. She can't believe that he could be so unfaithful to her. Figaro says, 'Oh these blows are the sweetest things. I recognized your voice.' She says, 'My voice, you recognized my voice,' and immediately she melts. And that's the way we are (laughing)."

"Robert, I would ask you this question about Mozart. The facts of his life are pretty pedestrian, at least as we understand them. And despite some of the things that he liked to pursue, whether it was billiards, parties, other women, or great sopranos, he would tell his wife, Constanza, to behave herself at Baden-Baden, and don't do anything I wouldn't do, which is sort of a joke. How did he get that way? How could he understand human nature so well?"

"His father, Leopold, who was essentially his only formal teacher, was extraordinarily educated. He was an enlightenment figure. He always seems to know what is going on. Mozart arrives in Paris in 1778, and in the postscript of one of his letters to him Leopold writes that the American minister, Benjamin Franklin, is in Paris, perhaps you have met him; that the thirteen English colonies have declared their independence from Great Britain, and France is helping them, so it will be interesting to see what happens. Leopold is writing from this tiny little provincial town of Salzburg, yet he knows this kind of thing. He knows that Franklin is in Paris. So he gave Mozart a complete musical education, but also Mozart was able to write in German, French and Italian. So this was an education that was not at all superficial. We also know Mozart was fascinated by numbers for his whole life, sort of a numerologist before the word was coined. His sister, Nannerl, reminisces that when he was a child he would take chalk and write numbers all over the walls and the floor of the house."

"We hear a lot about the Mozart effect. Do you believe in it?"

"Some think it is ridiculous. But I'm not so sure it is so ridiculous. Mozart was able to write music which is enormously complex and sophisticated, a fact which was actually recognized by the people of his own time and for which he was reproached. It was said his music was too complicated, it had too many notes, so people complained about this. If you can write music like that and clothe it in such a guise that it seems to us simple and direct, isn't that actually helping you to think more clearly? You're processing information of complexity which seems to you simple. If you can make something complicated seem or sound simple, I think it says something about a particular art which goes beyond the sensuous delights of moment to moment that you experience listening which are, of course, overwhelming because Mozart is a very sensuous composer."

"Was Beethoven a sensuous composer?"

"Beethoven is only occasionally a sensuous composer. There is nothing good or bad about it, but Mozart was fascinated with the erotic and Beethoven was aiming at an idealized sense of human dignity and human liberty. So one admires both equally. That Beethoven was able to survive the tragedy of his deafness and the final years of his life when various diseases were all competing to see which one would kill him first, and in the indescribable physical agony which accompanied his every single day, to be able to write those late piano sonatas and those late quartets, is unimaginable. Mozart had scarlet fever when he was a kid and probably that weakened his heart in such a way that it may have precipitated his final collapse, but it is hard to imagine any artist in history who overcame the obstacles that faced Beethoven, and overcame them in a more glorious, more sublime, and kind of other worldly way. To listen to those late quartets it is still one of the most modern things you can do."

"Robert, I have another memory of the time twenty or more years ago when you substituted at the Boston Symphony on very short notice for the ailing Alfred Brendel to play the Beethoven second piano concerto?"

"As a result of that the Boston Symphony said you really saved us big time, we owe you something, we are going to engage you on your own, what would you like to play? I said why don't you ask Yehudi Wyner to write me a piano concerto? They said, 'That's what you want?' I said, 'Yes that's what I want.' The result of that was Wyner's piano concerto called, *Chiavi in Mano*, *Keys in the Hand*, and it won the Pulitzer Prize in 2006. So that has a happy ending!"

"I guess there are some people who don't like Mozart?"

"My feeling is anybody who thinks either Mozart is simple or doesn't like him just doesn't get it. There are musicians, and well-known musicians, who didn't like Mozart. Florent Schmitt, a French composer, refused to let a composition prize go to the young Jean Francaix because he said he wrote music which was just as bad as that by Mozart. So there have been people like that, but more often than not you have those who idealized Mozart, including in no particular order Haydn, Beethoven, Mendelssohn, Schubert, and Grieg. Tchaikovsky adored Mozart, even writing a piece called *Mozartiana*. Grieg wrote second piano parts to four of the Mozart piano sonatas. Mahler and Stravinsky closer to our own time were Mozart fans."

"I've read that *New York Times* publisher Arthur Hays Sulzberger, back in the forties, had a strong aversion to Mozart. You have said that in order to complete

Mozart fragments you had to learn how to compose in the style of Mozart. How did you do that?"

"I had to subject the music to the kind of examination that Nadia Boulanger had taught me to do. That is to see the forest for the trees, the individual choices of pitch, to understand the counterpoint, to understand the character that accrues to having a doubling of a note, and a chord like so or like so, higher or lower. She showed me that all of those things are subjective but carry with them an expressive context."

"Thank God for Nadia! Please go on."

"To finish a piece by Mozart, the first thing you have to understand is what the unfinished part of the piece which survives is, how much of the piece is that, what architecturally is implied by what's there, and how much can be extrapolated. His working methods tell us a great deal about this. For instance when he is writing a concerto, what he normally does is he scores out the entire opening tutti. There is one exception to this rule, but the others are all like that. The whole tutti is done, then when a solo instrument comes in, then only the solo instrument is written, and if and when the solo instrument pauses, he goes to the violin, the bass, and the orchestra, and as soon as the solo instrument resumes, he goes back to that. If you look at Mozart's manuscripts, as I have in the flesh, not in facsimiles, you will see different tints of ink on every page which shows that he has written down the music in layers."

"Why did he do that? It sort of runs counter to the idea it was all in his head and he just copied it off his brain, so to speak."

"Why? Because Mozart is a short order cook. He may be in the middle of writing a piano concerto and suddenly a knock on the door comes and someone wants a wind serenade. That will bring in money and he has to feed his wife and kids, so he has to put the piano concerto aside and then go and write this wind serenade, or maybe write an opera, or write whatever it is that will bring in the money. If he has written the whole orchestral texture out bar by bar for the concerto, maybe he'll get ten or fifteen bars on the page and then he will be interrupted, and when he comes back to it after six days or six months, he won't remember what it is that he had in mind."

"I guess even Mozart had to eat and keep tabs on where he was in the score?"

"Yes, that is very frustrating and inefficient. Instead what he does is to write out the principle voices all the way through, and when suddenly the oboe comments on what the violin does, he goes from the violin to the oboe and then back to the violin. You can see that by looking at the color of the ink. Sometimes you see as many as four different colors on every page. I'm not talking about red and blue and green, I'm just talking about what the chemist mixed, dark, jet black, gray, brown, brown with a yellow tint, brown with a green tint, brown with a gray tint. You can see this. It shows the efficiency of Mozart's working method. When I started to work on such things, I did what he did."

"Can you give us an example from one of your completions?"

"When I completed an oboe concerto from 1778, I wrote out the whole solo oboe line. When the solo got to the middle of the piece, I wrote the first violin line and solo, thinking if I adopt his working methods that is going to get me closer to his way of thinking. So I did that."

"Where in Mozart's completed compositions is this particularly apparent?"

"Look at the three piano concertos that he wrote in the 1782-83 season, K.413, K.414 and K.415. Each piano concerto has three movements, nine in all. All of those movements have the same four tints of ink. You've got to realize that what that means is this man is composing nine separate movements simultaneously in his head, and at every stage from the first principal voice to the last one he is checking things through to be sure he's got all of what is in his head onto the paper. This is not the same thing as a painter painting seven pictures at once because you can see the entirety of the canvas, but you can't see and hear the entirety of a piece of music."

"Sounds confusing for anyone, even Wolfgang Amadeus Mozart?"

"It's bewildering! I don't think we have an example parallel to that from any other composer in history. That doesn't mean that he did it with facility. Mozart said later in his life that no one realized how hard he worked, and I believe that. I don't think his late music is any less hard and worked and thought through than, say, Beethoven's. It is just with Beethoven we have all of those sketch books, whereas 90% of the sketches that Mozart made were thrown out by his wife. She was protecting his legacy, but we are sort of sorry about that."

"Robert, you have said that if we want to save classical music it better be dangerous and adventuresome. Could Mozart, or any composer, have reached that standard better by finishing some of their compositions differently, or extemporized them differently, so that they would have been just as good or even better?"

"Sure. You have Bartók providing alternate endings to some of his pieces, and we also have from other composers alternate versions of pieces. There is a great deal of that. Bach takes a movement of a Brandenburg concerto and throws out the violin and replaces it with a four-part chorus. It becomes a movement from one of his secular cantatas. Of course, there is the idea of the sublime as opposed to the journeyman's approach to the daily necessities of composition. We tend to assume that everything is according to a sublime aiming for the stars and for all time. But then there was just what might happen on a particular day. Say Mozart wrote a piano concerto with no trumpets and drums played before the emperor. Then a couple of weeks later he decided to play the concerto again and found out the emperor was again coming. So at the last minute he quickly added trumpet and drum parts because he thought the emperor would be bored hearing the same piece. Does that mean the version with trumpets and drums is definitive? No it's not. You like trumpets and drums, it sounds fine to have the trumpets and drums, but it doesn't mean anything. Maybe three weeks later or ten years later he might have revived it, and suddenly decided he needed a flute or some other instrument. He added clarinets to the *Haffner Symphony*, which weren't there before. Those were practical decisions, not necessarily aesthetic ones. You've got two versions of the great G minor 40th symphony. One has clarinets and one doesn't. So you see what Mozart is trying to do. It is purely a commercial kind of thing. If you can play them without winds you don't have to hire wind players, so it costs less. It is not an aesthetic judgment."

"Robert, do you think that classical music will survive?"

"I think that the survival is going to depend upon people's understanding of how important it is to their existence. The only thing that is going to save the world of classical music is that if musicians realize that when you give a performance of this piece its effect is so transformative, so shattering, that those people who attend stagger out of the concert hall not good for much of anything for hours. And that they will wake up at three in the morning realizing that there is something about this music that they have never realized before, and that it has changed them forever. You have to keep people up at night. If Beethoven doesn't seem to be as overwhelming an experience as *Mission Impossible III*, that's not Beethoven's fault, that's our fault, because after all what classical music does, what all great art does, is to hold up a mirror and tell the audience, 'You look, if you have the courage you look. Do you not recognize who you are?'"

"I'm hoping for that every time I go to a concert. How do you as a teacher try to get your students to play in a way to elicit such feelings?"

"These things are huge matters of our consciousness, and they need to be overwhelmingly powerful. They can only be powerful if we have the kind of understanding of musical language and the dramatic curve that comes from having the kind of musical training that I got from Nadia Boulanger, and that virtually nobody is getting any more. That's the problem. The problem is that people are being trained technically in as whiz bang a way as has ever been the case in music history. The basic technical competence of every violinist in every conservatory in the world surpasses all but a half dozen people fifty or seventy years ago. But I'm sorry, just playing loud and fast ain't it, you see. Great playing can only come if we educate people to understand the exquisite details that give this art its murderous power. That's what I got when I worked with Boulanger, and that's what I taught at Curtis when I ran the Theory Department there. People who loathed those classes came back to me twenty or thirty years later when I was soloing with the orchestra, and said, 'I want you to know how much I hated every single moment in your class, and I also want to tell you that now with hindsight I could not be more grateful because you gave me the tools that I needed to understand music in a way that enabled me to get the job that I've got, and to keep it.' It seems to me every teacher should have as their fondest wish that her or his pupil will surpass what they have been able to achieve. I don't see any way that I, in this system that we have now, can communicate as much as ten percent of what I know. How can I be optimistic about the future?"

"What do you concentrate on with your students?"

"When I go down to Julliard as a guest professor and work with these people, they come in with an expectation that they are going to get something that they don't get somewhere else. What I work on with them most of all is a dramatic rhetorical understanding of what it is about a particular passage in relation to a hundred other passages that gives them the knowhow, the savoir-faire, to be able to negotiate the shoals of any number of pieces of music because they understand the principle behind the aesthetic promulgation, and don't get simply trapped by essentially getting fixes, their shot of heroin. The aim is that they walk out of there and feel great."

"Is that enough to teach them?"

"There is another problem. You don't want to teach piecemeal solutions. You want to give people the wherewithal to understand themselves and what they must do, which is what Nadia Boulanger did when she taught me composition. As I said, she got inside the language and evaluated it and made it better. And that's what I try to do when I teach the piano, what I've tried to do when I've taught theory, when I've taught all of the various things that I teach. This is the essential thing. To give people an insight and an ability to allow their imagination to flourish through a sensitivity to, an excitement of, and a knowledge of processes and rhetorical and expressive features. And that can be done. Doing it creates a thirst in the student for more."

"How did you come upon your methodology of teaching?"

"I stopped studying the piano when I was sixteen years old to concentrate on my studies at Harvard. Much later, I had to figure out stuff about playing the piano for myself that was not a gift. I became clinical and diagnostic about my own playing. Then when I started to teach the piano in Freiburg, Germany years later it made my own playing so much better because I had already developed this clinical approach to things. You as a lawyer understand these things perfectly well. You have to figure out what your solution is going to be, a piece of unfinished business that is seeking an end. From that point of view the difference between that and taking an unfinished piece by Bach, or Mozart, or Beethoven, and trying to figure out how it could go is not so far apart."

"When did Mozart first know that he could compose better than others?"

"I think Mozart became aware of his superior abilities at a very early age. I'm reminded of what pianist Malcolm Bilson told me once when he came back from his first recording of Mozart concertos with Sir John Elliot Gardner in London. I asked him what it was like. He said, 'You know it was like making love for the first time in your life, you are so excited to be doing it you have no idea whether you are doing it well or badly.' I think there are moments in Mozart's life as a child where he realizes he can do stuff, and he is very excited by it. But that kind of excitement comes in waves, and it gets more and more prodigious. By the time he is fourteen, fifteen, sixteen, he is already writing pieces that are well worth hearing. Mozart is making a progression of these things. It is an incremental thing, and it gets better and better and better. I think by the time he is 17 or 18, he realizes that he is writing music which is as good as anybody, that's for sure. When at 24 he writes the opera, *Idomeneo*, it is an explosion! This opera apparently remained his favorite opera until the day he died because it was a coming of age for him. You can find things in *Idomeneo* that turn up later in *Don Giovanni*, in *Figaro*, in *The Magic Flute*. There is a sense he is writing for the greatest orchestra in the world. He's using the Gluck aesthetic of the chorus. His later operas don't have these great choruses in them like *Idomeneo* does."

"I just heard it in Met Live HD. I was thrilled by it over fifty years ago hearing it live at the Kresge Auditorium at MIT when it was not in the repertory."

"One can sense the degree of excitement. In fact you can read the letters Mozart writes to his father throughout the composition of *Idomeneo*, just as you can with *The Abduction from the Seraglio*, and what Mozart says about what he is composing, and why he is doing certain things, and how people are going to react to them, and so on. You don't need to put words in his mouth. Fortunately he is writing for his father, but in a way he is writing for the ages. The same can be said of when Mozart later wrote to Leopold of the piano concertos K.413, K.414, and K.415, that they are a happy medium between that which is brilliant without falling into the pitfall of being too vapid, and that there are some passages that only connoisseurs will understand but that the rest of the audience will not help but be pleased by, albeit without knowing why."

"Sort of like when Mozart wrote for six characters and one knows what each is saying when all are singing at once. Here he writes a piece and it reaches everyone one way or another."

"It's fantastic. That I think is what you should tell any performer today. You play in such a way that some people in the audience will figure out what it is you are doing and realize that you've got the goods. The other people will say, 'I don't know what's going on here. I've heard a lot of people play this piece. This person here has got something, but I can't fathom it, I can't figure it out, but it is sensational.' That's what you do. You never aim just for the gallery because the people who are the smartest people in the audience are the people that you must not disappoint if you really want to aim high. And that's what Mozart figures out. He is constantly talking about what the audience will like. And he knows how to do it. He says that in his *Paris Symphony*. He says there is a passage that I knew that the audience would like, and sure enough, when the passage came the audience all started to applaud in the middle of the movement. Nowadays we discourage people from clapping between movements, like they do in a jazz club. He also said that because he knew they were going to like that, he took care to bring it back towards the end of the movement. You know what, they started applauding all over again. This is not a guy who wanted people to sit in rapt and pious attention. He wanted to get a rise out of them. He knew perfectly well what it took to do that. The thing is that this music was written at a time when there was not a culture gap between art music and vernacular music. And there was not a gap between writing music and performing music, both of which exist today."

"I guess *The Magic Flute* is an example of that?"

"Who came to *The Magic Flute*? Well, the emperor came and the aristocracy came and people like Salieri came. But the blacksmiths and the green grocers came. And they listened to Emanuel Schikaneder, the librettist and first Papageno, singing his little opening song which basically sounds like a pop tune. Mozart knew that he could bridge the gaps, and that at certain moments the aristocracy or connoisseurs would weep from the profundity of the action and music, and that the other people would be borne along by the catchiness of the tunes."

"I've always been amazed by *The Magic Flute*. It's a seemingly simple opera which appeals to everyone, whether children or adults, on a multiplicity of levels, some profound. How did Mozart accomplish that?"

"He knew what he was doing. Beethoven was astonished by *The Magic Flute*. It is the progenitor of the great German operas. You wouldn't have *Der Freischutz* or *Oberon* by Carl Maria von Weber without it, you wouldn't have *Fidelio*, you certainly wouldn't have the Wagner operas. This idea of being able to bring everybody together to get rid of those barriers is something that could very well save music for the future. Since everybody who composed in those days performed, and virtually everybody who performed composed, even singers composed. It would be nice if we had more people like that today. For example, my wife is going to be soon playing some pieces by Earl Wild, a fantastic virtuoso and a very clever composer of not so simple paraphrases of his own and other people's music."

"Robert, how important is composing to you, considering your skill as a player, conductor, teacher, and in other areas of music?"

"When I got to know John Harbison, I was a senior at Harvard. He said he was a composer. I asked him to show me his music. I saw the music and I thought this guy's got it, why should I continue to struggle to write my music that no one is going to play. It is more important for me to play this man's music."

"John wrote me a letter a couple of weeks ago in which his handwriting looks like musical notes. You've probably seen it."

"I have, it is like beautiful calligraphy."

"I put that letter away because it is so beautifully written, both the form and the words he wrote. Do you think Mozart thought his music would live on after his passing?"

"I don't think he had any doubt about that. After all, he lived in an age when most music was being played for the first and only time. If anyone wanted to hear a piece that they liked again, they had to insist that it be repeated immediately because they had no reasonable expectation of actually ever hearing it again. Music was all based on premiers. premiers, premiers, and premiers! Playing pieces from previous generations was not something that was done. Therefore when Mozart got to know Bach and Handel it was an acquaintance with earlier music that was not really part of what most people received as an education. Haydn and Beethoven got to know Handel and Bach too, and revered them, but it wasn't until further into the nineteenth century that the concept of repertoire emerges."

"In studying Mozart especially, it seems he valued his own music on a higher level than the music of other contemporary composers, save perhaps Haydn, and worked very hard to get it right. I read a recent book by your associate at Harvard, Christoph Wolff, *Mozart at the Gateway to His Fortune*, where he quite convincingly expounded on that in Mozart's writing of the *Requiem*."

"I still feel that some of these composers in the back of their minds had at least a hope and perhaps an expectation that their music would live in the ages to come. It is hard to know because they were so bound to the strictures and pressures of daily existence, to earthly cares, that they didn't have very much time to think about things like that. They had to work at breakneck speed to get done what they were doing. On the other hand, I also say that if a composer like Beethoven or Mozart or Bach or Brahms had as their goal to merely write better music than anybody else, they could have written music that was a tenth as good as what they wrote. They weren't simply trying to write better music. They were trying to write music to a standard that was so unaccountably, breathtakingly high that actually anybody else who proposed to write a piece of music could have just put a bullet through their brain because there was no point. I wouldn't say that comparing only Mozart and Haydn, for instance. When you listen to so much of the music written at that time, there is nothing wrong with it. It is perfectly fine. But if you just flip the record over and then play a piece by Mozart or Haydn for the same combination of instruments, you figure, 'Oh, forget about it. It is just not going to work.' You can listen to a Humboldt string quartet and it sounds really good. Then you put on a Beethoven quartet, and you say, forget it."

"Beethoven, Haydn, Mozart, and many others wrote divertimentos and serenades that were meant to be background music. Did they give those their best shot?"

"Yes, they had an inability to create shoddy work. it's just the way it is. I think it is that extraordinary capacity that music has. Even if we don't think we're listening to it and it's in the background and we are talking, it sneaks in and it starts to affect our heart rate and, of course, like a great Hitchcock suspense film, we start playing games and trying to guess what's going to happen. Once you start to guess what's going to happen you are roped in. It's the pea under one of the three walnut shells. The audience has to be right a certain number of times. Otherwise it will stop listening."

"Do you play and record Mozart concertos on the piano or on the harpsichord?"

"The recordings have been done mostly on period piano, but I've done some on Steinway, and I alternate performances both on Steinway and on period pianos. I do both."

"So do you use the harpsichord very much?"

"I usually do Baroque pieces on harpsichord."

"Not Mozart concertos?"

"No. That was not as ideal, although the word Mozart used to describe the keyboard solo was 'clavicembalo,' which is the Italian word for harpsichord. He did that straight through the K.503. That was a generic thing. Beethoven also uses the word 'clavicembalo.' "

"Can the harpsichord be as expressive as the piano?"

"Yes, but using different parameters. The most important thing about the harpsichord is articulation. It is the speed where the slowness of attack gives an extraordinary amount of flexibility to the discourse. It is how you pronounce the consonants, so to speak. So I learned a great deal playing the harpsichord that I then brought back to my piano playing. And when I teach piano, I'm constantly impelled to point out to these students that they are not thinking enough about touch. They play everything loud or soft, but the speed of their touch is mostly undifferentiated, so it deprives them of a very important expressive means."

"When you are home and you are playing for your own pleasure what do you play?"

"Both, or all three. But a couple of years ago I was doing C. P. E. Bach with Nick McGeehan, and also with my wife, Ya-Fei Chuang. There is a double concerto for harpsichord and piano, so my wife played the forte piano part, and I played the harpsichord part. Then we did another concerto, a fantastic B minor concerto by C. P. E. Bach. He wrote about thirty or forty of these harpsichord concertos. Wonderful pieces. And I did that on the harpsichord. So I have a good time."

"For a while I've heard someone playing very beautifully in another part of the house. Would that be your wife? What is the music?"

"Indeed it is. She's a very fine player. That is Chopin. She's practicing for her next public appearance. She teaches at the New England Conservatory."

"Do you have a favorite among all the instruments?"

"No, each one teaches me something about the other. It is very useful."

"Do you consider your primary calling in your musical life to be a teacher?"

"Well, that's what Nadia Boulanger evidently thought. She never said anything to me about it because she was much too wise to do that. But when Rudolph Serkin wrote her and asked her whom she could suggest to lead the Theory Department at the Curtis Institute of Music, she told him to get me. I was twenty at the time. In 1979, the year of her death, she summoned me to Fontainebleau to teach at the American Conservatory there where she had served since the first year in 1921. She asked me to do all of the teaching that she had done. It was only a month later after she passed away that I began to put the pieces of the puzzle together and realized that there was a pattern to this, and that what she had decided was of all of the things that I could do that teaching would be the thing that I could perhaps do the best. It has now been almost fifty years, so I can't say she was wrong, but my own identity is really very much connected to performance."

"Well sure, you've made your greatest fame there, but in your mind what do you think?"

"I feel that the teaching is a matter of idealism and also a matter of responsibility to try to pass on the things that I've been privileged to learn. I not only got to absorb the aesthetic of the whole French tradition through Nadia Boulanger and through some of her colleagues, but I played for ten years with violinist, Felix Galimir, and I coached with violinist, Rudolf Kolisch, and thereby got a connection to the whole Viennese aesthetic of music-making. To have had the privilege to work firsthand with people on both sides of that divide is something that immeasurably deepened my life and profoundly affected it. If I had just been working with students of those people in this country, I still would have gained a great deal, but doing it firsthand is another matter. And those lights have all gone out. The only person who is left from that generation is Menahem Pressler. Claude Frank left us a couple years ago."

"Robert, while we still have some time, I would like to ask you some questions about what goes on in your psyche about music and musical composition, what it is, and what it means to the human race. Let me start with this one."

"Do you hear music in your head, and, if so, do you hear the actual sound or only imagine what the music sounds like?"

"Yes, of course I do. There is nothing remarkable about this. We read silently and can either pass directly to the meaning of the words or hear them phonetically. Musicians can do this with sounds. And I have a choice of hearing actual sounds or a synthesis of the content of the score without the individual timbres of the specific instruments."

"Whose music do you hear?"

"Whatever I choose. And of course I hear music that no one before me has composed, at least as far as I can ascertain."

"Does music you hear sometimes come unbidden?"

"Yes, music comes of its own accord as well. What can be maddening is a little snippet of music that I must examine and turn over and over and over until I can guess what it is. Sometimes this process lasts only a few seconds, but it can also last days or even longer."

"Can you turn it on and off at will?"

"If I start to think about non-musical things, it will sometimes dissipate, but there is what the Germans call an earworm, *Ohrwurm* — a tune or a phrase that repeats over and over and won't let go. This can drive one a bit crazy."

"Does it ever interfere with normal life?"

"No."

"Is it classical music or some other genre?"

"Mostly, but other genres like jazz and rock sometimes join the party."

"Is the phenomenon a pleasure or a pain?"

"I am thankful for it, as it keeps me connected with music in a creative interchange."

"Have your greatest aural experiences in music, excluding concerts you have led, occurred inside or outside your head?"

"The greatest aural experiences in music that I have had are concerts given by great artists. Of course I feel tremendous excitement and motivation in my own performances, but the kinesthesia of performing oneself can sometimes distract from the powerful reaction to music made by others as one listens. Listening inside the head is stimulating and creative, but rarely surpasses the excitement of live performance."

"How do you compose, the notation being merely an afterthought, or do you sit at the piano and compose from note to note, idea to idea. Or put differently, please describe your compositional process?"

"I compose in my head, not on paper. I used to go directly from the inner ear to notation with pencil or pen on paper, but in the present age of notational software I often compose directly into the notation software called *Sibelius*. This holds me up a bit, because I could write faster than I can do computer inputting, but it spares me having to input it afterwards. I do it the same way in completing Mozart fragments."

"Where does music come from and to where does it go?"

"This is ultimately a mystery. When does an idea come into my head? What prompts it? I do not know. I have experienced writer's block just as writers of prose and poetry do. When ideas come naturally, it is a blessing. And it can come in the middle of the night, even within a dream. Sometimes notating it can be elusive."

"What would life be like without music?"

"There is a wonderful *New Yorker* cartoon that shows a desert, with a discarded auto tire and other detritus, captioned 'Life without Mozart.' Life without music would be bleak, lacking an elevation and thrill of the spirit that music inspires more than any other art form."

"Could humans live without music?"

"Fortunately we need not try. It is everywhere, in every culture, and in each of those cultures it both reflects life and acts as a design for living."

"What is it that speaks to you within music that you don't get from any other artistic form?"

"It is not the uniqueness of music, but the power of its expression that I find extraordinary. Music would seem to be the most abstract of the arts, but Mendelssohn said that of all forms of art he preferred music, because with it one could be so much more precise. Given that he drew invidious watercolors and sketches and wrote poetry, he knew of what he spoke. So the paradox is that it seems to soar untrammeled by literal contexts and yet can evoke the most piercing and precise emotions."

"Is the particular way a composer solves a technical musical problem, among many solutions, amount to the audible style of that composer so that he can be thereby distinguished from others, Mozart from Schubert or Mendelssohn for example?"

"Music can be about problem solving, writing a fugue, say. But it is primarily about expression, depiction, representation, and ideals. One distinguishes composers through their style, which is a synthesis of melodic, harmonic, rhythmic, textural, rhetorical, and architectural factors. These elements can overlap without making it impossible for us to tell one composer from another."

"What is music?"

"The late Robert Sarnoff of RCA sent a letter out to a lot of people asking what music was, and one of the people he wrote was composer Arnold Schoenberg. Schoenberg's answer is devastating. Schoenberg wrote that music is the art of sounds which can create the greatest euphoria or the greatest despair."

"That makes music sound extremely powerful? Just how powerful is it?"

"I think almost anyone would agree that music has a more powerful effect on people's sensibilities than anything. If you were to ask a teenager what most defines them, they would say my music, meaning of course the music that they love to listen to. But Mendelssohn's idea that music is much more precise indicates the fact that music does what people do. Music shows how people gesticulate, what their facial expressions are, how they move, how they express themselves, what kind of clothes they wear. Mozart starts with courtly music of the eighteenth century from the baroque, and he creates sounds and gestures that evoke a certain way of living. Just as we can recognize in a movie that it is shot to depict Elizabethan England, we can hear Mozart's music and understand that music is both of its own time and transcends all time. So from that point of view music gives us insight into our fellow human beings in a way that reaches directly into our visceral emotions without requiring the translation of words, and without depending upon a visual component, although you get both in opera. You don't get that in a piano sonata or a violin concerto or a symphony or a toccata for harpsichord. The drama that unfolds from music is self-defining so it opens a window to anyone who cares to look out of it. It grabs us and transforms us. It is very hard to build up a resistance to music."

"Robert, one can't think of all the questions, but as our conversation has gone on and considering the several subjects we have discussed, is there anything that you think that you should say to complete what you've said?"

"There is no human emotion that does not have a counterpart in a particular piece of music and what it is capable of inducing that mutates and develops from age to age. So ecstasy in a piece by a modern composer is going to be different from ecstasy in a piece by Bach, but we feel it all the same, just as Supreme Court Justice William O Douglas once said he couldn't define pornography, but he knew it when he saw it or read it. We can hear these emotional states in the music because, of course, art exists always, and, in the end, I think exclusively to communicate. It does not have an independent existence because a score of music, like a book on a shelf, is not heard, is not read, is not appreciated. It is the capacity of the music to be sounded in front of people who have never heard it before and who immediately find themselves in a situation of astonishment, of terror, of intrigue, of bewitchment, of all sorts of human states that emerge purely from sound, that gives it life. I think we need to understand that, but the ability of the music to convey those things is dependent upon the ability of the performer to perceive them and to communicate them. Music will not be sensuous if the performer does not understand it to be. So everything in the end depends upon the medium that stands between the creator and the audience, and the ability to refract the light and to create a sense of existence that requires no words, no description, but comes imminently from the succession of sounds from second to second which in itself is utterly mysterious and miraculous. How would you explain it to somebody from some other planet? How would you explain why you would hear a certain moment in a song by Schubert and you would start to weep uncontrollably? Perhaps you don't even understand the German which is being sung to the song, but you hear something and all of a sudden you just start to sob."

"I know. It's happened to me."

"Thank God it happens. And one of the frightening things is imagining those Nazis listening to a string quartet by Schubert, wiping away their tears, and going to a telephone and ordering fifty people to be shot. It makes you wonder, what are the humanities? What is the morality of this? And that's something I didn't say. So good. I'm glad you asked me this."

"Plainly you see music far more inclusively than merely performing it for an audience."

"I stress to all of the musicians with whom I come in contact that the act of performance is profoundly moral, that to walk out on stage and perform is a moral act. It is not what you do merely but it is why you do it, how you do it, and to what end you do it. Because if you do it to communicate to an audience the essence of the dilemmas that confront them of their own nature, then you are performing something which has an almost sacred spiritual dimension and power. You are like the imam or the rabbi or the priest or the reverend in front of whom the audience suspends all defenses and allows themselves to be shattered by the message because there is a faith in the morality of what is being said. If instead you use such a sacred communication — and it is no less sacred being by Schubert than it is being from the New or the Old Testaments or the Koran or whatever it is you are reading — if you use that situation that you have and that power only for your own aggrandizement, you are a monster. One cannot do enough to protect oneself from the mountebanks, from those hypocrites who use the great truths of our civilization for such petty and prosaic and indefensible purposes. I think that ultimately surpasses all of the other considerations I've been speaking about."

"In these times where there are a lot of existential threats to mankind, can music reduce or allay those threats, or can music be helpful to find a way for mankind to continue to exist?"

"Music has always had a more than symbolic importance. Bernstein conducting the Beethoven Ninth after the fall of the Berlin Wall, for example. Think of the number of Koreans and Chinese who come and study music in the West. There is something very liberating about all of that. A lot of them stay in the West, a lot of them go back. It is hard to say what are the consequences for society of that. I believe that ignoring the power, and the moral and spiritual dimensions of music relative to those existential dangers, is so extreme that those of us who firmly believe in what we have, have no alternative but to pursue them until the last breath we draw."

That Robert Levin in the twentieth and twenty-first centuries should be the amanuensis of Wolfgang Amadeus Mozart from the eighteenth century seems fitting and proper, perhaps even eerily predictable, given that both of these musical prodigies have joined hands across the abyss of over two hundred years to communicate music in man's never-ending search for himself and his salvation.

CHAPTER
4

Unsuk Chin: Composer and Great Lady

This story began problematically in the noisy lobby of the Colonnade Hotel in Boston's Back Bay, where I first met composer Unsuk Chin in November 2015 to interview her for this book. In these adverse conditions we bonded within minutes and undertook a conversation which finished transoceanically almost two years later. What came out of our conversations is to both of us a minor miracle because Unsuk Chin is a rare combination of great compositional talent, incisive intellectual power, clear and revealing articulateness, innate honesty, and the willingness to share the innermost recesses of her psyche. Her remarks here offer us a rare, perhaps unique, glimpse into the mind of a great artist to bring us, almost microscopically, as close as we'll ever get to the nucleus of compositional power.

One would not think that suffering to write her own music and taking many years to accept herself is a good recipe for success. In the case of the now internationally admired and tradition shattering composer, Unsuk Chin, it proved to be the right mix when combined with her continuously strengthening, always persisting, and powerfully persevering persona. In 1985, at twenty-four, she boldly embarked from Korea to Hamburg to study with the renowned and iconoclastic Hungarian modern composer, György Ligeti. Their fraught relationship foundered when Ligeti criticized the sensitive young woman's music, which lowered her mood and not long after impelled her to break free of Ligeti to seek her future in Berlin. Slowly coming to believe in herself, Unsuk rose from her disappointments to begin composing works in her uniquely personal style which were individual and drew on various sources. Painstakingly composing music she hoped would be original, Unsuk persevered for the next decade, believing that her traditional classical training, combined with her willingness to

Korean-German composer Unsuk Chin. Photo by Priska Ketterer

burst out of its boundaries, allowed her to compose using that training while also using and fusing any other musical styles, from anyplace and everyplace, including her dreams and inner life. Unsuk Chin also mastered English during these years so that now in these pages she is clearly and completely able to convey to us in her revealingly honest answers how the inner dynamics of her psyche contribute to her genius as a composer. It may be that her explication of how she creates her music is one of a kind in the literature. Unsuk Chin's modest remark to me that she is still unsatisfied with her music seems to be the key to her perseverance, and augurs well for more of her original music to reach our ears.

By the time I met Unsuk Chin in late 2015 when her original and well-crafted composition, *Mannequin*, was to be given its American premiere by the Boston Symphony Orchestra, which had co-commissioned it, Germany and the world had proclaimed fortissimo that Unsuk Chin was in a prime position among world composers, mainly because of the originality of her music. In interviewing her I sought to plumb the depths of her mind and the details of her life experiences to reveal the sources of her compositional power.

"Unsuk, you are here in Boston for the premiere of your composition *Mannequin* by the Boston Symphony Orchestra. So let's start with that. You've said *Mannequin* is imaginary choreography. I know that you live in a world of imagination listening to your opera, *Alice in Wonderland*, and your other music, so what is your definition of imaginary choreography?"

"For me as a composer imaginary choreography is to make music with an abstract imagination of choreography, which I think can be a fantastical and deceptive art which tries to defy physical laws to make the impossible appear possible. So in this work I tried to create the feeling of weightlessness by means of breakneck virtuosity, timbral 'smoke and mirrors,' and other musical mirages. For me that is one of its essences. I aimed at something comparable when I wrote *Gougalon (Scenes from Street Theatre)*, which was performed by Alan Gilbert and the New York Philharmonic. In that piece I attempted to compose an imaginary piece of folk music from beyond a classically cultivated sphere; that is, folk music that has never existed apart from in my mind. As for *Mannequin*, If one day I will see this piece choreographed for ballet or dance on the stage, I imagine the feeling could be very strange or very unusual for me because I've never seen any of my pieces choreographed. When I composed *Mannequin* I had some very strong and vivid imaginings. I tried to put those trance-like visual pictures into the music as directly as possible. So it's like in a trance, like in an abstract language."

"Has anyone tried to choreograph this yet?"

"Not yet, because this piece is very new, and after the premiere in April in London, I revised it, so it's extended now, it's longer, and the first premiere will be here in Boston. I expect someday, somebody would choreograph this piece."

"I'm guessing that if that happens, you'll have to give up some control to the choreographer and others involved in the production. Have you had that experience in writing opera?"

"I have. When writing an opera, during the composition, one controls and sets up every parameter, including the stage directions. But then comes the moment when you give it to the stage director and he makes something completely different out of it. As a composer, you can feel very helpless and powerless at that moment, but, ultimately, it's a good thing since the director needs to have his own vision so that the opera works on stage as theatre. In opera, it is very rare that everyone involved — composer, stage director, conductor, singers — are content with the result because it's such a complex machinery. My opera, *Alice in Wonderland,* was premiered in a staging by the German stage director, Achim Freyer. He is an iconoclastic stage director. He changed all my stage directions. It was not easy, but on the other hand, he is a great artist and had such powerful and unforgettably unique ideas. One always needs to stay open-minded."

"It seems to me that the way you wrote *Mannequin* was from the inside out because it sort of came from the imaginings in your mind, and then you wrote the music. Is that how you composed *Alice in Wonderland*?"

"Yes, but here it's very different because *Alice* draws on a very realistic E.T.A. Hoffmann story named, *The Sandman.* Therefore, my imagination was more narrative and realistic, and my pictorial imaginings were more real than for some other pieces. It is more like musical storytelling. I tried something here which was very new for me. Of course, I used materials which I have used in my other pieces, but the character of the piece is very different because in this piece there is a lot of surreal, even psychedelic feelings. This atmosphere is more stark and strange, so you never can be quite sure what is going on or know whether it is dark or bright. So you can't judge whether the child who is the protagonist in the story is mad or the society around him is mad. The title of my piece can be understood as an allegory, since the main character of Hoffmann's strange tale is torn between hallucinations and reality, as is the whole story, which could be seen as an early example of magical realism since he feels himself controlled by a number of macabre 'puppet masters.' Hence the title of the piece."

"It seems like you filtered E.T.A. Hoffmann's literal story through your own vivid imagination so that there is a lot of Hoffmann in it but more of you?"

"It's not a mere retelling of Hoffmann's work. I was interested, however, in a couple of images in Hoffmann's tale, in its overall atmosphere, as well as in his experimental film like and elliptical style, which shows what a subjective affair perception can be, and how it constantly blurs the border between dreams and reality. I just took aspects of the story which especially interested me and used them very freely for my own means. Oh, of course, this story has existed for a long time, and I read it. But I have my own imagination, and I wrote my own music (laughs)." *[E. T. A. Hoffman (1776-1822) was a leading influential Prussian Romantic writer of many talents, being also a composer and a jurist, whose stories were inspirational to Offenbach's opera, "The Tales of Hoffman," and Tchaikovsky's, "The Nutcracker ballet", and other nineteenth-century works of art.]*

"Well, let's go again to *Alice in Wonderland*, for which you composed the music, and co-wrote the libretto with playwright David Henry Hwang. You said about that opera that you wanted to compose a piece that would be intellectual, simple, and communicative. Can it be intellectual, simple, and communicative all at the same time?"

"Yes. Definitely. I don't want to compare my music to Mozart but his music may appear to be very simple, but in fact it has lots of layers and complexities. His music means something to everybody, even to people who have never heard much music. Everyone gets something from Mozart, even musicologists who know everything about music on the conceptual level. For me, that kind of music is the best kind of music, very simple on the surface, but you can go deeper and you can find something more, and there is no limit to that. So it's intellectual too."

"I keep saying, how many times can you hear *The Marriage of Figaro*? But every time I listen to it, I'm carried away."

"It's huge, yeah, yeah, it's completely crazy music. Crazy. Great !"

"He seems to understand everything about human life. How was he able to do that?"

"I don't know (laughs)."

"Unsuk, don't tell me Mozart is your favorite composer?"

"(Laughs) Yes. Yes."

"He is? Unsuk, we've found each other! Did the music for *Alice* come to you from knowing the story, knowing what it was you were writing about? Or is it something you made up on your own?"

"I think my opera *Alice in Wonderland* is closely related to the story by Lewis Carroll. Of course, I used a lot of different materials. I used other pieces. But this *Alice in Wonderland* is quite different from all my other pieces because it is a kind of simple music with lots of different, complex layers. So on the surface it has a certain simplicity, but if you go deeper, there are lots of things to discover, and ultimately nothing is quite as it seems. I decided to write in this style of music after I read *Alice in Wonderland*, because on the surface there is no meaning, but if you dig deeper, there is a lot of complexity. It is considered a story for children, but it has inspired philosophers, psychologists, mathematicians, physicists, filmmakers, and avant-garde writers. This is hardly a surprise because in all of the layers of these visionary dream stories, in which everyday reality and physical laws are being transcended by means of absurdities, paradoxes, and wild leaps of logic, the subject is really people, their psychology, and all of life. If you can find those layers, it is fascinating. So I decided to write this simple music to mirror *Alice in Wonderland*. I tried to find a musical equivalent to Lewis Carroll's style. On one hand, I played a lot with musical semantics and hidden meanings in order to try to correspond to Carroll's intertextual games. So, the musical language of the piece might be likened to a musical hall of mirrors with a certain dose of irony. Some listeners were irritated because of this surreal approach which includes sweet, simple songs but also screeching noise, rap parodies of coloratura arias, and so on. The other aspect is that Carroll's book takes place in a dream world having different physical laws which clash violently with the physical laws of our everyday reality, and that is something I tried to capture musically." *[Lewis Carroll, (1832-1898), English jack-of-all-trades who was primarily famous as an author for his perennial masterpiece, "Alice's Adventures in Wonderland," and its sequel, "Through the Looking-Glass" but also shone in such diverse fields as photography, mathematics, and logic, not to mention his long service as an Anglican deacon. Carroll was also noted for his talents at word play and fantasy. He is still popular today. "Alice" has inspired many works in diverse artistic fields, including Unsuk Chin's opera of the same name first presented at the Bavarian State Opera in 2007, to be followed by her new opera, "Through the Looking Glass," commissioned by the Royal Opera, Covent Garden, to be presented in their 2018-19 season].*

"Did the music exist in your mind before you wrote it?"

"Up to a certain degree, yes. When I read the story, I immediately had the inspiration for some kind of wordplay and play of numbers which links directly with the music. As so often, I was late and there was not so much time. Then it went really smoothly right up until the end. The adrenaline rush usually helps me. I wrote and wrote and wrote (laughs)."

"Did it take you long to write the whole opera?"

"Two and a half years. There were a lot of note papers because there is a lot of text and the music is very fast. I wrote and wrote and still it was not ended (laughs)."

"What is your favorite form of musical expression? I'm talking opera, of course, concerto, and symphonic music, since you've been successful in all of those, and more?"

"I really have no preference. I write for different genres and different types of musicians. I cherish different challenges, including electroacoustic music which I have not done for a while but which was formative for my musical thinking. I am quite picky before I accept a commission because I want to make sure that might have something original to say for that particular genre. It would not be inspiring for me to limit myself to one mode of expression."

"You said, 'I'm attracted by virtuosity.' You also said you like to make difficult pieces. What do you mean by those statements?"

"Yes, because for me, the act of composing is very virtuosic. Every time I try to go beyond my perspective, I'm really suffering and trying to do something new, something I've never done. Therefore, I also ask the musicians performing the piece to do the same thing. I really like seeing these people on the stage trying to go beyond their possibilities, beyond their abilities. So, for me it's very important that it be hard for me and for them. Maybe I am a bit of a sadist, but I like to see musicians sweating. I think it creates a very special kind of energy! Anyway, I've been lucky because of a number of excellent musicians I've written for flourish in these challenges, musicians such as Alban Gerhardt for whom I wrote my cello concerto, Viviane Hagner who premiered my violin concerto,

Barbara Hannigan who premiered *Le Silence des Sirène,'* the sheng virtuoso, Wu Wei, for whom my sheng concerto was composed, the Korean pianist, Sunwook Kim, and many others. I will shortly start to write a work for German violinist, Anne-Sophie Mutter. I am hugely looking forward to working together with her."

"Well it's a good thing, because if the players stretch their abilities, they're going to be able to do more stuff. Do the performers pick up on that?"

"They do. When I was younger this process of composing and making music was relatively limited by my own personal possibilities. If I have an idea, I write a note, I hear it, and then I judge whether it is good or not. Nowadays, I think making music is a very wide concept, so lots of other people should also be involved — the conductor and the whole is orchestra. It is very important. The great performers are those who discover aspects in a piece you couldn't imagine hearing before. Now I'm aware that a composition exists only partly before it is interpreted. Before I was a bit arrogant and approached the musicians with the notion that they should simply do their work and play what I've come up with. But eventually, when I became more experienced, I realized it is not that simple. We owe the fact that we can continue to exist as composers, and to survive as artists, to the musicians who through their skill first bring our scores to life. Also, I didn't realize how very important the different theories of music were. I just saw it all too simply. So I made it hard on myself. Also, without the audience, you don't need the music. Why do I compose music? For myself? No. I compose for the people who want to hear this music. So if the audience is there and they are involved in this process, concentrating on the music as it is being played, that is a very important part of the music, even though if the audience is very small. One should never try to give the audience something they already know. One should challenge them, take them seriously, offer them something they didn't knew was existing. For me, there lies the *raison d'être* of art. Sometimes there are people who are booing, but that is also part of the process. When my opera, *Alice in Wonderland,* was premiered in Munich, it was the opening of the Munich Opera Festival, so, it was a very different audience from the other performances. Many of the people simply attended in order to be seen, not in order to learn to encounter a new work. In the other performances you had a critically informed and curious audience, but in the premiere most of the attendees probably rather would have preferred to go to a performance of a musical or a light operetta than to a premiere of a new work. They didn't know Carroll's story and intensely disliked the surrealism of the production. So, from some parts of the audience you could hear ferocious booing, which actually is not that uncommon in Germany. In a weird way that gave me energy, I had the feeling that, 'Wow, I may have touched a nerve. It was fun!'"

"When you write music, do you sit at a writing table and try to think up the music? Or are you sitting at the writing table, maybe like Mozart did, and it's already all in his mind, and he just writes it down? Or is it somewhere in between?"

"(Laughs) When I compose, I need a very long time for preparation. This ripening of ideas needs over five years in my mind to become mature. Even before I start to write the first note, I need lots of time. It is a most difficult process. To translate my idea into the various notes and dynamics, I need total control of the parameters. Normally, I sit at the table and I think and think and at some point I write the note. I never use the piano or a computer."

"So really, you're writing off your mind?"

"Yes, it's from my head directly to the paper."

"Most composers use the piano or a computer in composing. Why don't you, Unsuk?"

"Although I love playing piano, I never compose at the piano, even when I write for the piano, since that would only be distracting for the compositional process. As to the process itself, the ideas are already there before I start drafting out a new work. The entire process, from the first ideas appearing in my head to their gradual ripening and then writing them down in individual sketches, can extend over a very long time frame. In my case, I actually reject up to, let's say 98% of my initial ideas and inspirations. And then comes the moment when I must begin to flesh out the piece. Occasionally, that turns out not to be working, and that's the most critical phase of the composition process. But if I have really gotten off on the right start, then it usually goes relatively swiftly right up to the end. It's not a straightforward process. You suddenly move away from a certain idea and look for an alternative possibility. Perhaps you come back to it in a roundabout way. And sometimes what remains at the end is actually only a little bit away from the original thoughts. All the same, there can be substantial differences in the process from piece to piece."

"How many minutes of music can you compose in one day, and how long does it take you to do that?"

"One day? It depends, maybe nothing, sometimes nothing, and sometimes a couple of seconds. But no more than ten seconds a day. So it's a very difficult process. I need even more time for an orchestral piece. Usually large-scale works need the most time, but sometimes writing a short piano piece can really take time, since writing idiomatic music for piano is fiendishly difficult. If I have very strong feelings towards the piece, and the work in process is going very well, then I can write a piece within two months. *Mannequin* took more than four or five months. And then I needed two months for the revision."

"John Cage said that the audience completes the music, that the listener travels only the distance the music allows him to travel, and then the listener is on his own to complete the distance to interpret the work on his own and make it his own, perhaps even hearing something in it the composer didn't even think about. Does that make sense to you?"

"It does. Good music has so many facets, so it allows for very different kinds of ways it can be performed or how it can be perceived. One should never say this is the way the piece should sound and this is what it means. No. Even great composers, especially the great ones, often cannot explain what they are doing. The work they create is more clever than they could ever imagine. At times, they are like somnambulists. It's better that way since it is good that art can address and touch the nervous system so directly. Susan Sontag has rightly stated that, 'Real art has the capacity to make us nervous,' but that interpretation of it makes it conformable and impoverishes it by setting up a shadow world of meanings. That's exactly what I feel, too."

"You also said words to the effect that you don't take yourself seriously at all. I don't see how you could be who you are without taking yourself pretty seriously. Did you mean that, or were you being ironic?"

"(Laughs) No, no, I conveniently keep a distance from myself so I can speak about my music in the third person. Music is not self-expression. One has to alienate, to keep a distance from themselves. I think I'm a little different from other composers like that. I know a lot of my colleagues who are composers who really love themselves and their own music. Of course, I love my own music too. I'm the creator, but at the same time I can keep a distance and then look at my music as a third person, I can't describe how, but I can do that."

"So maybe you can just stand back and say, well okay, I'm famous and I'm well known, but I'm just a human being?"

"I never think I'm famous. I have no idea about that. Also, it is not so important. Growing up I was never respected, not even in Europe for a long time. So I got used to that. I needed lots of time, more than thirty or forty years, to come to myself, recognize myself, and respect myself."

"Unsuk, we've talked a lot about music. We'll come back to that. First, please tell us about your youth in Korea, and coming to Germany?"

"It was a difficult time back then. It was less than a decade after the Korean war, the country was devastated and the people were traumatized. I was lucky to discover music at a very early age. I began to play piano when I was four, and from the first moment I felt a really strong connection between the instrument and my body and soul. I played some simple stuff at first, but by the age of six or seven, I knew music is something for my whole life. I just knew it. My father, who was a Presbyterian priest, taught me some rudiments of music and a bit of score reading so that I could accompany his services on a small organ. Thanks to that I learned the basics of harmony, and also acquired practice in sight reading transposition. As the churchgoers' singing grew louder and they become excited, the pitch rose, so that I constantly needed to transpose. It was hard work at that age, but good practice. We were poor, so I also earned money for the family by playing at weddings. I was sometimes given a free meal on such occasions."

"You've said that, in your mind, to be a composer is a greater thing than to be a pianist? How so?"

"That was from my music teacher in school who recommended to me to become a composer. He was a composer himself. I just wanted to become a concert pianist, but there was no money to receive lessons. One day he called me in and told me that being a composer is much better because as a composer, you can still play piano, but as a pianist, you can't compose (laughs). I was twelve, maybe thirteen, then. Of course, I knew about all the great composers by then, like Beethoven, Mozart, and Bach from listening to any recordings I could get my hands on. I admired them, but I never thought to become a composer myself. It was a new horizon. At first, I didn't understand my music teacher's friendly advice. I thought he simply meant that I was not talented, so I felt completely devastated. However, in 1974, there was another occasion which presented me with reality. The young Korean pianist, Myung-Whun Chung, now one of the world's great conductors, won the second prize at the Tchaikovsky Competition. I realized that since he was only eight years older than me, the time was running out for my ambition to be a concert pianist. Indeed, without a solid technique and constant tuition, one cannot really embark on such a career. However, I later studied piano, and even though I don't perform in public, playing piano remains one of the greatest sources of happiness and inspiration in my life. I practice as often as I can."

"It sounds like this teacher was pivotal in your life?"

"Yes, I was lucky to have this music teacher who believed in my talent and encouraged me by saying that I will be able to make something of myself. Thanks to his intervention, I could stay in the afternoon in the school's music room that contained hundreds of records and listen for hours. This was a great opportunity since records were scarce in those times. So, that was where I encountered the gamut of Western classical music. The most modern music I heard was by Stravinsky. I especially remember *Petrushka* and his violin concerto. I was overwhelmed by the colorfulness and novelty of Stravinsky's music. My teenage love was Tchaikovsky."

"When you listened to all those records, Tchaikovsky, Stravinsky, Mozart, Schubert, Brahms, what were you saying to yourself? Wow, this is a whole new world! I've never heard anything like this, this is great, or that it's just another kind of music?"

"No, it was really great. The first time I heard Western classical music, I was very young. I played piano, very simple stuff. Then I heard Beethoven piano sonatas and things like that. I had never heard this music before. I had no education in this type of music, but it was, 'Oh, this is amazing, Bach, Beethoven and the others are amazing!' So it's sparked me very directly. But it's no surprise. I think many of the strongest and most immediate emotional musical experiences take place when one is a child, even though one cannot yet grasp it on an intellectual level. In fact, I think continuing to perceive things in a childlike way is a sine qua non for artists. That is the only way to stay creative. Making new art is not about applying recipes or concepts or theories, but it is trying to keep oneself open to new impulses and perceptions, while constantly and self-critically working on one's skills and techniques. It's a constant fight between intuition and rational self-control."

"And amazingly you are now writing music for that tradition, the likes of which we've never heard before?"

"I hope so! (laughs)."

"How did it go when you reached college in Korea?"

"The way to get there was thorny. Since I had had no private tuition, I had to manage myself. I had no idea about the strict rules and regulations for the entrance tests. One had to use certain harmonies, and one was not allowed to use a ballpoint pen. In the entrance test, I composed something in a post-Debussy style, but I was expected to do something more traditional, so I didn't pass the exam. I failed twice. So, there were two years during which I felt to be a complete failure, and, in the eyes of the society, I certainly was a failure. I drowned my frustration by drinking and taking pills. In the third year, I finally passed. I was lucky because I got to study with Sukhi Kang. He had studied in Europe with the famous émigré Korean composer Isang Yun. He had this pioneering spirit and was really instrumental in bringing all the avant-garde trends from Europe to Korea. I and his other students were very lucky to have this first-hand experience of modern music. He showed us recordings and scores of the important European modernist composers and organized concerts of unheard new music. Sukhi Kang encouraged me to send my works to international competitions. I won some. I had some success with my music at Seoul National University. So I wrote to Gyorgy Ligeti applying to be his student. He accepted me, and I went off at twenty-four to be his student in Hamburg. I had encountered Ligeti's music in Korea in Sukhi Kang's class, and of the European modernists, Ligeti was the composer I admired most." *[György Ligeti, (1923-2006), highly respected prolific Hungarian avant-garde composer of contemporary classical music, whose wide-ranging interests included literature (Hoffman and Carroll among many others), painting, architecture, mathematics, and science].*

"What would you say, what was the main thing you learned from Ligeti?"

"To be more tough and hard and critical on myself. It is the most important thing. Before I came to Ligeti, I was already like that to some extent, but not enough. He also taught me how to judge music. His thinking about music was on the highest level. At the beginning it was very difficult for me to understand him, but now I understand what he meant at that time. I was very young and naive. I didn't realize how very important different theories of music were. I just saw it too simply. So it was a difficult time for me."

"I understand that after a period with Ligeti, he told you that your compositions were OK, but they all were just copying others, and that was not the way to go. That couldn't have made you feel very good?"

"In the long run, it was the right advice. Ligeti had noticed that my early works, which I have now withdrawn, were skilled imitations of mainstream avant-

Hungarian-Austrian composer György Ligeti, muse of Unsuk Chin

Credit: Photo of György Ligeti by Marcel Antonisse / Anefo, CC BY-SA 3.0 NL, via Wikimedia Commons

garde music, but nothing more. Deep inside myself, I knew it was true. Still, during my time with Ligeti, I composed *Troerinnen*, a work for female singers, choir, and orchestra based on a play by Euripides. It's my official opus 1, since I still allow it to be performed. It's the first work where I tried a stylistic turn. It is rather different from how I write now. It's a rather emotional work, and there is even a lot of pathos in it. After that, I felt empty, and clueless as to what to do. I couldn't compose for three years. I made the very good decision to leave Ligeti."

"Where did you go?"

"I moved from Hamburg to Berlin and tried to restart and find myself. I started to compose in a studio for electroacoustic music. In the beginning, I didn't know anything about computers and had to come to grips with this immense complex apparatus. I said to myself that I will, after all, become a composer if I learn to deal with this apparatus! And so it was. It was one of the formative experiences for my music and for the way I now write for instruments. In the electronic music studio one can research, as with a microscope, the inner life of sound, its molecular level, and make many interesting discoveries. After a few years I wrote an instrumental piece, *Akrostichon-Wortspiel, Seven scenes from fairy tales for soprano and ensemble*. It is still one of my most performed compositions. I started slowly to compose again."

"Did being a woman and from Korea present obstacles to you?"

"I'm very often asked how it is to be a female composer. That is hard to say because I've never been a man (laughs). I do belong to a minority in my profession. Some people actually still seem to believe that classical music has been exclusively written by dead European males. I have not pondered much about prejudices during the thirty years I've been in the business since that would have been stifling for my compositional work. I've just tried to do my own job as well as I can and not think about what other people might believe since that's something I couldn't change anyway.

"Frankly speaking, it's not so easy to work in Europe as a woman composer from Asia because people have certain expectations from a woman. My work didn't meet their expectations, and nobody accepted me. So it was tough at the beginning in Germany. I had almost fifteen years without any performances in Germany. No concerts at all. I had most of my concerts abroad. Now I am older than fifty, and things are easier. In Germany the thinking of some people was, 'Why doesn't she compose what we believe to be her tradition, Korean traditional music? But I wanted just to try to compose music that was individual and drew on various sources. Such identity discussions can be really troublesome. As Amartya Sen, the Indian philosopher, has put it, the identity of an individual is essentially a function of their choices. If people are seen in terms of one dominant 'identity,' they are being denied a very important liberty to choose their identity themselves. I wanted to compose music that was individual and drew on various sources."

"Sounds like there were considerable roadblocks in Germany?"

"Yes. When I came to Germany in the eighties there were not so many women composers. But in Germany, it's not just being a woman or a man, it's also being a foreigner and from the East because in Germany they have a very strong tradition, and it's hard to accept people from outside as a composer."

"Tell us about that tradition."

"German composers have a very strong German tradition. It is good because they can stand on this base and then go afield, but there are not many possibilities to escape the tradition. Actually, they don't want to escape. I don't have that kind of strong tradition in composing music. Therefore, I am influenced by classical music, but I can use any other materials I wish to and do infuse my music with other musical styles in a selective manner. So I feel really free. I find the example of American maverick composers very inspiring, wonderful inventors such as Harry Partch, Conlon Nancarrow, or Charles Ives. This is something that would not otherwise have come to me living in Germany. Of course, I have great colleagues in Germany, and the music life there as a whole is amazing, but I feel a bit frustrated about the overall sphere of German new music, its dogmatism and sectarianism."

"Does your music draw at all on Korean tradition, or just upon influences from all over."

"Some from Korean traditional music, but hidden, and not as a main influence. I always make my own music with many materials. You never can see a direct influence from certain music in my music. So this is always like a sauce. You put garlic in, you don't see the garlic, but you can taste it (laughs)."

"Would you say, Unsuk, that your music is original? Like nobody else?"

"I don't dare say that, because my vision is to become an original composer, and my music should be much more original. I'm on the way, but I can't say that yet."

"Does your music sound like you?"

"I can't say. Maybe other people can judge whether my music is like that or not. I hope it's not like that on the surface because I feel that music should not be self-expression. For me it's just my music. I'm always trying to compose my own music. That means I have to find myself and my own music, and right now I can't say whether I can ever find my own music, but it is worth it to try, and worth my voyage to see if I can find it. Paradoxically, this means that I always have to look out for something new which I didn't know was existing. Every new work should attempt to be different from the previous one. At least that's my ideal."

"What is your music based on?"

"In contemporary classical music there is music that may appear to be just noise containing microstructures of sounds, but some is also quite interesting. You can learn something from this music. My music is based on Western European classical music, European contemporary music, and lots of other things, influences from very many different times and regions. I can take this material, this tradition, and develop it in my own way. After all, we live in a globalized culture, and I prefer to keep on that track rather than to stick to a so-called 'truth.' On the other hand, it is necessary to remain self-critical, since different styles can't just be combined haphazardly. You have to accept that imitation and combining styles in an unfiltered manner is not an option. I envy the giants of Viennese classicism like Mozart and Haydn. At that time there was a valid universal musical grammar, so, you didn't have to start from scratch with every new work. In fact, some of my colleagues perfect a certain individual style so, as it were, they are writing variations of a certain piece time and time again. That is a possible way, but it's not my solution, I try to reinvent myself. The only way to progress is to attempt something I haven't attempted before. The philosopher Isaiah Berlin once categorized writers into two categories: the foxes and the hedgehogs. He was referring to a Greek parable. The 'foxes,' he said, draw on a variety of experiences and don't believe that the world can be reduced to one single idea, while the 'hedgehogs' view the world as a central, all-embracing idea. I think I belong to the former category."

"So it's an ongoing trek. Will it ever end before you leave us? Let's say you live to a hundred, will you still be going on that voyage?"

"I have no idea (laughs)."

"Are you attracted to music other than Western classical music?"

"Oh, yes, absolutely. We have lots of different music. For example, gamelan music in Java, or in Bali, is amazing! For them it's like a Beethoven symphony. They have an unbroken tradition. It's a collective experience, a utopia come true because many of the performers are laymen and there is no estrangement between the individual and the collective. The parts in itself may be simple, but the whole is very complex, and the degree of perfection and refinement is stunning. We can't do this kind of music here because the specialization required by notated Western classical music is a completely different approach to art. But it's wonderful. I have myself been influenced by gamelan music. I stayed in Bali in the 1990s for a while. I also studied it a little bit and notated some of it. It was surely an influence on my double concerto for prepared piano, percussion and ensemble, or for my piano etude Number 1. But one may not notice this influence on the surface."

"Do you think there is something better about Western symphonic music?"

"Traditional Western classical music is really very strong, and a very significant cultural phenomenon in the history of mankind. I think that, yes. Nevertheless, there is much fascinating music other than European music."

"Do you have any mentors now?"

"Not really. Earlier in my life, I met some very important musicians at the right moment. The first one was my teacher in Korea I spoke about. Then I came to Germany to Ligeti. I thought he didn't help me at that time, but his lessons and everything he taught me did help me as my career went along. Maestro Kent Nagano commissioned a couple of pieces, including a violin concerto which was very important on my work list *(for which Unsuk won the Grawemeyer Award, probably the most esteemed prize in the world awarded to composers).* I have met and worked together with wonderful conductors, like Sir Simon Rattle, the conductor of the Berlin Philharmonic Orchestra, Myung-Whun Chung, the great Korean conductor who invited me to be the Composer-in-Residence of the Seoul Philharmonic Orchestra, where I founded a new music series, Alan Gilbert who introduced my clarinet concerto with the New York Philharmonic, Esa-Pekka Salonen, who invited me to run the Philharmonia Orchestra's new music series in London, Venezuelan conductor, Gustavo Dudamel, Finnish conductor of contemporary music, Susanna Mälkki, and many other wonderful musicians.

"But mentors? No, not really. Sometimes you have colleagues with whom you can talk about your work, but it's rare. As a composer, I guess one is ultimately alone. I'm quite alone. (laughs)."

"Who would you say are the composers who have influenced you the most?"

"All the great composers. I have no preference, I studied Ciconia, Bach, Scarlatti, Mozart, Beethoven, Romantics like Schumann and Chopin, also Debussy and Stravinsky, all the way up to avant-garde composers and modern composers like Ravel, Webern, Xenakis, Grisey, and many others. All the good music influenced me. They're all wonderful!"

"We seem to gravitate back to music, Unsuk. (laughing) Where do your inspirations come from?"

"I think inspirations come from everything I do and I see and I experience, my everyday life. Often they come from music I listen to, and also from books, films. From physical phenomena. From everything, everything."

"From things that are inside you, like dreams?"

"Yes, dreams too. But I don't see any musical notes in my dreams, so it is not an immediate effect. My dreams have nothing to do with the music directly, but all the colors and images I see in my dreams give me positive energy and vision to continue this very difficult process of composing."

Unsuk Chin descriptively expanded on the inspirations she receives from her dreams in an interview some years ago with her famed music publisher, Boosey and Hawkes, as follows: "My music is a reflection of my dreams. I try to render into music the visions of immense light and of an incredible magnificence of colours that I see in all my dreams, a play of light and colours floating through the room and at the same time forming a fluid sound sculpture. Its beauty is very abstract and remote, but it is for these very qualities that it addresses the emotions and can communicate joy and warmth."

Fascinated now by my probe into the innermost recesses of Unsuk's psyche, I sought to go even deeper, and more broadly.

"Do you hear music in your head, and, if so, do you hear the actual sound or only imagine what the music sounds like?"

"I hear the actual sounds quite precisely in my head."

"Can you turn it on and off at will, or does it come unbidden? Does it ever interfere with normal life? Is the phenomenon a pleasure or a pain?"

"Usually I can turn the music on and off at will, but when I'm especially impressed by a work of music, it can become an earworm, yes."

"Have your greatest aural experiences in music occurred inside or outside your head?"

"It's difficult to compare since these experiences take place at different levels. What I heard in my mind's ear when I read a score can be a powerful experience, but it's still essentially an abstract one. I never cease to marvel at the skills of great musicians."

"Have your most beautiful and/or most profound hearings of your or any composer's music occurred inside your head? If so, please tell us about that."

"Well, it's always difficult to describe musical experiences in words, but the experiences I have when I read a score or when I think about music are different from the experiences of listening to music since they are still more abstract than the latter. The sheer sensuality of sound of a great performance is always a cause of amazement and delight."

"What is music?"

"That is a very good question. Music is a wave we hear, a certain wave from the air, physically speaking, that you can possess and touch. You can do that, but you can't explain it or describe it. While it can cause immense delight, both emotional and intellectual, it is physics at its core. And, yet, it exists on an altogether different qualitative level than sound waves. Music may have analogies with language, with mathematics, with games, or with rituals, but it is still different and it exists in its own realm. So, I eschew any further attempt at definition, and quote Igor Stravinsky, 'Music is given to us with the purpose of establishing an order in things, including, and particularly, the coordination between man and time.'"

"What would life be like without music?"

"As Friedrich Nietzsche said, 'Without music life would be a mistake.' In order to live we need air, and in air there is always a wave, even a noise, so mankind will discover this noise and some sounds and organize them into musical structures. Mankind would automatically find the music, discover the music. I'm very interested in astronomy. I always read and find out about the history of the cosmos from the Big Bang onward, and how our own sun system was created. It's an amazing story. Our universe is so huge and our sun system is so tiny, a little thing, and the earth is really tiny. And then we have this air in our atmosphere, which is so fragile, but therefore we can survive here, this tiny little atmosphere where mankind discovered the music. But space is empty. there is no air in space. Space is silent. If you play music there, you can't hear anything. Making music and listening to music is really our privilege on this earth. I think it is a logical product of human intelligence, of the human mind."

Unsuk Chin's interest in astronomy and the cosmos inspired her appropriate large-scale composition chosen to inaugurate the new Lotte Concert Hall in Seoul in the summer of 2016, described by Boosey and Hawkes, as follows: "Scored for choir, children's choir and orchestra (including an orchestral organ part), *Le Chant des Enfants des Étoiles* offers poetic reflections on our physical relationship with the cosmos."

In that same year Unsuk was chosen to be the Artistic Advisor of the highly regarded Seoul Philharmonic, for which she had already served as Composer-in-Residence for a decade, and as the Artistic Director of their new music series. Across the world in London, Unsuk continues her affiliation with the Philharmonia Orchestra, overseeing its "Music of Today" series.

"Unsuk, are you worried about the future of classical music?"

"I really worry about the future of classical music because everything is becoming more and more commercial, and more and more like an event, even in Europe where there have been rather strong and unbroken state structures in order to protect non-profitable art. The concert business is becoming more and more about mere glitz, good looks, and other superficialities. Some classical concerts are organized to have only certain pieces on the program and exclude other worthy pieces.

"For example, the Beethoven Eighth Symphony may not be included, but maybe the Beethoven Seventh Symphony will be because the house is always trying to please the people and draw a big audience. This is a big misconception. Such a thing as 'the audience' does not exist, since it consists of many different people. We can't offer people something we think they want to experience since they don't know what they want unless we present it to them. They want to be surprised and challenged, even if they don't know it themselves. At least many of them do. It is always the supply that creates the demand and not the other way around. But in the present situation the repertory is becoming more and more narrow. There is no space for lots of very sophisticated and exciting music. Even a great composer like Haydn is not being sufficiently performed. When I started to do programming at the Seoul Philharmonic, I tried to do something about this, with themed programs and lesser known but good music. But it is always difficult. Sometimes it feels like you are fighting against gravity!"

"Has the computer revolution had much to do with the problem?"

"Yes. The problem, of course, is about much more than just repertoire choices. The standing of classical music in today's world is becoming more and more difficult, and I believe this has, at least partly, to do with the last few decades' revolution in the information sector. I believe its challenges cannot even yet be foreseen. The problem already starts in schools where music education is dwindling. The aesthetic tastes of children are said to form before the age of nine. So, if people are not being offered access to classical music by that age, it can be hard for them to ever get fully acquainted. Not even being offered the chance to form their own taste and knowledge of art is a tremendous loss, a huge problem. So I do worry."

Unsuk Chin is beaming her intellectuality on this worry following her appointment as a member of NYU's Institute for Advanced Study working group of "scholars, musicians, and arts administration professionals," gathered to seek answers on the troubling issue of the future of classical music in a world where attention spans are fast diminishing.

"How is classical music different than pop?"

"Well, sometimes when I saw the spellbinding artist, Michael Jackson, perform, and the performance was perfect and thousands of people attended, I would say, 'Whoa, we in contemporary music composition will never, never reach this.' But our music is different, our music can survive longer than that kind of pop music. I don't know if this is a difference. Maybe we can't and we shouldn't compare."

"As long as people are around, do you think Mozart, Brahms, and Bach and those people will ever go out of style altogether?"

"No. I think their music will survive. If we were alive at that time, we would have known their Michael Jacksons, but now we don't know who they were. Although the people who understand classical music may not be many at any one time, if you count its audience over a two-hundred-year span, it is huge, so we have continuity. Maybe there should be more educational projects to try to make a fusion between classical and popular music to try to reach young people and more people through some special educational project."

"Unsuk, you have been quoted as saying your life has changed a lot since you came to Europe, that your life is different now, and that you're a different person. Do people really change, or might you be pretty much the same person?"

"I think there is a part of me which has changed, but there is a very great part of myself which is the same. There are a lot of amazing things that have happened to me. I'm now more of a person, I guess more mature, and I see now the worth in my life with wider eyes perhaps (laughs)?"

"After thirty years in Europe, Unsuk, do you consider you are an Eastern person, a Western person, a world person, a musical person? Who are you?"

"I think I'm me? I think I'm a cosmopolite. I'm kind of a mixture of all, I think. I can't say to what degree I'm still Korean or to what degree I am German. Maybe if you say typical Korean, then I'm not a typical Korean. And even when I lived in Korea, I was not a typical Korean, whatever that entails. I was quite different from what was expected by the society back then, and therefore I had lots of difficulties there. Now I'm just me. (laughs)."

"Do you find it easy to get along with people?"

"Oh, I think at this point easier and easier. Maybe up until ten years ago I stressed out a lot, but now things go easier and I'm more relaxed. Composers can be tormented souls, you know? (laughs)."

"Unsuk, you've taken a longer trip than most people. What are the personal qualities in your character that you've always had that have made it possible for you to make this long trip, and to keep traveling on it?"

"I think it's that somehow I've always believed in myself. Otherwise, I couldn't have survived those difficult times when I was young. If I really want something, I have to succeed at it. I don't know what the English word for this is?"

"Perseverance, persistence?"

"Yes, yes. I still have not attained things I want. It is to become a really original composer. It is my target of my life. I can't say I am there yet, so I'm still unhappy and unsatisfied with my music (laughs)."

"I would say that's a good thing. If you were satisfied, you'd never write anything good."

"Yes, when I came to Germany thirty years ago, I had some small successes at the beginning. At that time, I had a couple of composer colleagues, almost the same age, almost the same career. Some of them were getting very easily satisfied with themselves. They got married. I got married too. They became professors, and things became more easy. I don't know where they are now. At the beginning they were very active, but within five years there came new rising stars. Move forward three or four years and my colleagues were gone, and others are rising, and so on. That's life. It's a crazy profession. I saw these people thirty years ago. The important thing is that I'm still here (laughs)."

"Tell me about your family life, Unsuk?"

"My first marriage was to a German guy. He was a sound engineer. So we worked together in the electronic studio I spoke about. I composed and he assisted me, so that was a very good collaboration. We were together for ten years. Later I met my second husband, Maris Gothoni. We married and had a son. He is Finnish. At the time, he was a well-known concert pianist. He gave up his original career. Now we are making programs together for a contemporary music series, so he is a concert dramaturge and kind of my manager, helping me a lot. He is hugely curious about literature, music, and film, so this knowledge has also influenced me. For instance, when I composed my cantata, *Le Chant des Enfants des Étoiles,* about physical phenomena or cosmological themes, and was looking for suitable texts, Maris suggested hundreds of different poems from different countries. In the end, I could use only eight, but it was helpful to have all the options!"

"Sounds to me like this marriage has had a positive effect on your life and career?"

"Yes. I really became more relaxed than I was before. Before I was physically more tired, but I could manage even though I was always under stress and tension. Now I have less time, but I can manage the time better. After my son was born, my career went really well. I composed a couple of very important compositions that are central for me. So this type of new life is really positive. When I was pregnant I had to work. It was a secret that I was pregnant because I had a deadline. So I had to work until the end of my pregnancy. Then after the birth of my son, I had to work again on my violin concerto, So I started that when he was three months old and that was a strain. But it all went fine (laughs)."

Indeed, it has all gone along fine. The coalescence of Unsuk Chin's natural talent and her determined persona have already brought to the world a plethora of original compositions from the deep recesses of her mind, and her essential humility combined with her strong sense of self promises that she will never rest satisfied until she believes, if ever, that she has reached her goal of composing original music.

Argentinian-American composer Osvaldo Golijov. Photo by Yoni Golijov, Osvaldo's son.

CHAPTER
5

Osvaldo Golijov: Composer, Professor, Innovator

All of us, to a greater or lesser extent, are the product of our genes and experiences as we navigate the adventure of life. So too are the expressions of artists affected by their experiences in life. Some artists, like some people, seem to absorb practically every memorable experience and person they encounter from childhood on, somehow filtering those through their creative processes, to produce works of unique depth and meaning. In music, it is said that Wolfgang Amadeus Mozart was such an artist. How else can we account for the astonishing depth of his understanding of human nature expressed so beautifully, for example, in his opera, *The Marriage of Figaro*, synthesizing seamlessly all previous musical and life influences on him, when measured against the relatively pedestrian facts of his own short life?

Similarly, Osvaldo Golijov, growing up in Argentina in a close transplanted Jewish Yiddish speaking musical family from Romania, studying there and in Israel and America with musicians of note, absorbed a kaleidoscopic array of musical influences from his family and his musical mentors and colleagues. As Osvaldo's utterances make movingly clear, at the same time, and to this day, his sensitive, warm, and inquisitive persona reached out eagerly and passionately to people of all walks, every place, and to diverse ideas, some, like Catholicism, far afield from his roots and Jewish identity, all of which entered his mind to ignite his imagination to compose music striking in its originality and expressive power.

Perhaps it is impossible to completely articulate the mysteries of musical composition, even for an articulate composer like Osvaldo Golijov? Is it not true that music is the most mysterious and elusive of the arts? Here and gone, as it were, leaving its indescribable imprint on the psyche of the listener! But we are bound to try to unravel that mystery. Where better to start than by investigating the manifold arc of a composer's life?

One advantage I had approaching that conundrum was having known Osvaldo for over a decade, since I interviewed him for my book, *Voices of Brookline* (2005), my lifetime hometown and his adopted one. When Osvaldo warmly greeted me at his artistically and amazingly furnished apartment, respectfully preserved in a condo building converted from St. Mark's Methodist Church, a classic nineteenth century Richardsonian Romanesque structure in the style of Boston's famed Trinity Church, and listed on the National Register of Historic Places, neither of us expected our conversation would last so long or reach such depths. At we parted and hugged in the Latin manner of his homeland, we expressed to each other that no previous interview in our respective experiences had been so all-encompassing.

Whether the future great composer sits at the piano like Mozart did at age five with his esteemed father, Leopold, or under the piano like Osvaldo Golijov did at age five at where his beloved and gifted mother was playing the classics, the results of this synergy among parent, child, and dynamic instrument appears to be a formula which worked wonders with Wolfgang, and to this point has worked wonders with Osvaldo too.

Osvaldo tells about that response to my very first question, "What is your very earliest memory of playing music as a child?"

"Well my earliest musical memory is being under my mother's piano and playing. She was playing and I was playing with my toys. But she would practice, so that the piano was almost like a second womb for me. And then I think that my earliest memory of myself playing was playing the introduction of the slow movement of the *Tempest* sonata of Beethoven. I forget how old I was, maybe five, and I realized that it had two lines, and when one stayed in line, so to speak, the other went up. So it was the first realization that two different things could go on at the same time in music and be more beautiful that way. I was trying to figure that out. Like perhaps other children would disassemble a clock and try to reassemble it. So for me it was that question mark. 'How did Beethoven make that work?' It was really something that obsessed me."

"I know there were a lot of musical influences that you were exposed to when you were a child. There was your mother, of course, Jewish liturgical music, klezmer, Argentinian composers like Alberto Ginastera, Gerardo Gandini, and Astor Piazzolla, new tango, classical, other stuff too," I remarked. "But of all those many influences, which one do you think now, as you look back upon it, has had the most influence on your music?"

"Childhood. In my childhood the greatest influence was Bach, Beethoven, all the music that my mother played. Right now, as I said, I feel that I'm going back to that world. Yes, after exploring so much of, as you said, Jewish traditions and the tango and other Latin American music, I feel that I'm going back to the questions of Bach and Beethoven. Who knows? Maybe I'm getting old (laughs)."

"Bach and Beethoven — that's great. Was your mother a performer? I know she was a teacher."

"Yes, she was initially a performer, but then there were four children and it was very hard for her to keep up a performance schedule and raise four kids, so she became a teacher. Absolutely my mother was a very, very important influence. She was the first one to not only teach me the piano, but to tell me the difference as to what made each one of these composers unique. You know, Beethoven different from Mendelssohn or Schubert or Bartók. Everything. It was great! It was great!"

"Musically, what was the main thing you learned from your mother?"

"I don't know how to put it in words. I remember her always being very excited about new stuff. She was always catching up to the fashionable element of the new stuff, and saying to me, 'OK, but how does this compare to what someone like Bartók or Beethoven did?' That is the ideal. Those people were really serious. Music was music to them, of course, but also a way of living, a philosophy of life, an ethos. And I think that's the main influence my mother had on me."

"Is this going back to the master's liable to change your style of writing music as you go forward?"

"Yes, yes, I think so. I think I'm becoming different. I think that it's natural. Absolutely! For any composer to keep growing. Who knows? I think it's wonderful! Even if you remain very youthful, like yourself, you probably look at life differently than when you were younger."

Knowing how true that is, I asked Osvaldo, "When you listen to different composers now, and maybe to a piece you've never heard before, and you don't know who the composer is, can you pick out the composer?"

"I can, most of the time, pick out the composers I know. I think as you get older you know more and more music. I am more and more curious to learn. So I play a lot on the piano, all kinds of scores, all periods. But I wish I knew lines of Shakespeare like I know themes or sections of pieces by the great composers."

There was the Bard out of nowhere, showing Osvaldo's inquisitive, humanistic, and creative mind. I asked him to expand a bit.

"I was hanging out over the weekend with an actor and his wife. And they know so many lines of Shakespeare and it's so beautiful to hear them speak them."

"Have you read much Shakespeare?"

"I read it mostly in Spanish, but now I'm reading him in English, and it's not so easy for me."

"Not so easy for me either. But there are so many composers who have followed Shakespeare. And you may find something you want to write about."

"The thing is you have to think that Verdi already did that. He did *Macbeth, Otello* and *Falstaff.*"

As Osvaldo grew to manhood in Argentina he came under the influence of other great musical masters, most notably the celebrated pianist and composer, Gerardo Gandini, and the revered master of the *nuevo tango,* the new tango of Astor Piazzolla. For Osvaldo, Gandini was the link back to the most famous of all

Argentinian classical composers, Alberto Ginastera, and the bridge forward to the influential Piazzolla. Osvaldo spoke of all three, reminding us of his deep roots in the Latin music of his homeland which he has shaped into a new classical sound of our time.

"Gandini was my main teacher in Argentina. He was a student of Ginastera, who was the most famous Argentinian classical composer. He was a contemporary, later than Bartók and Ravel. He wrote in the 50s and 60s and was a wonderful figure! Gandini was his student and was an astonishing pianist. In one of those great twists of fate he ended up being the last pianist for Astor Piazzolla. What Gandini taught me was how to bridge the so-called high with the so-called low. How everything is a continuum and not to have musical prejudices, and to be free. Gandini knew so much. He was music, he was really music, all music embodied. I loved Piazzolla's new tango and now I love old tango as well."

It must be remembered that Osvaldo's youth was spent in the authoritarian atmosphere of Argentina at that time, and in the shadow of the Catholic church, which both hung over the country's small Jewish population made up in part of immigrant East European Jews like the Golijovs escaping the Holocaust. Fortunately, he was able to build on his musical base of family and that trio of Argentinian masters when he left his homeland at twenty-two to study first in Israel with composer, musicologist, and pedagogue, Mark Kopytman, and then in America with avant-garde American composer, George Crumb, at the University of Pennsylvania, where Osvaldo earned his doctorate.

"Mark Kopytman was another wonderful teacher. Very strict, very rigorous. He gave me I think a very wonderful training in counterpoint, harmony, and theory. He also taught me composition and orchestration."

What was it about American original, George Crumb, that rubbed off so well on the relatively *tabula rasa* mind of the youthful Osvaldo Golijov?

"I think George Crumb is one of the great composers that America has produced. One of the few composers with an absolutely unique, true, and original voice. And a courageous man because when he was writing the music that today remains as one of the wonders of American music, he was totally swimming against the current. He remained pure and a real poet of sound. When the zeitgeist in the seventies was very cerebral, and the music sounded very gray and anonymous, his music remains with us — evocative, sonorous. colorful, and poetic. It's a great accomplishment. You can't quantify it. He created magic with intangibles. The other composers were more into the tangibles."

Bostonians and Philadelphians may argue over which city is the cradle of independence and liberty. Osvaldo Golijov will not take either side. He has lived in both, and both figure significantly in the American experience that has provided the free atmosphere required for his creative work. Once in America, Osvaldo has never left, although his peripatetic journey as a citizen of the world

Argentinian composer Astor Piazzolla, muse of Osvaldo Golijov

Credit: Photo by Carlos Ebert. CC BY 2.0

continues every day through family and his own travels through time, space, and his imagination. Does he consider America to be his home?

"I don't want to say a cliche, but I came with nothing and I was accepted. I was given a voice and room for my musical voice. I was allowed to grow. And to be free, which I was not in Argentina. I recognize that some people are oppressed in America. Not me, but there is a lot of work to be done. I'm sort of restricting myself to Massachusetts, which I love. I love Brookline too. Brookline is a beautiful place. Despite tremendous problems which are really monumental, there is a spirit of freedom in America. I cannot imagine I would have grown as a human being and as a musician this much if I had stayed in Israel or Argentina. I am very grateful that I raised my children here. Very grateful indeed. The human quality here is incredible. Even if you travel on the MBTA, you see the books that people are reading. It's impressive. You say, 'Whoa, I love that.'"

Perhaps reflecting the divisions now plaguing America, Osvaldo added:

"I think I would feel the same in New York or California. I don't feel so connected to other places in the country where I've been. I don't feel that I belong so much. I think that's natural."

So how does an Argentinian Jew emerging from that Catholic bastion come to write an astounding musical composition on a Catholic passion which vaulted Osvaldo Golijov into the attention of the world amid huzzahs, bravos, foot-stomping, shouts, weeping, and tumultuous applause from the public, musicians and public alike. One European newspaper said, "Forget new music. Forget old music. Forget Europe's music tradition, Osvaldo Golijov's '*Pasion*' is incomparably unique." That is the history of *La Pasion segun San Marcos*, the *Passion According to Saint Mark* (2000), premiered in Stuttgart in 2000, and in America the following year by the Boston Symphony Orchestra, written combining Latin and African musical styles including flamenco, bossa nova, rumba, mambo, tango with dance and theatrical elements, into a never before heard kind of classical composition.

Perhaps ironically, the work was commissioned by Stuttgart choral conductor and teacher, Helmuth Rilling, to commemorate the 250th anniversary of the death of seminal composer, Johann Sebastian Bach, who represents the European style of classical composition as much as, if not more, than any other composer. The answer tells us a lot about the composer and his adopted country.

"I believe that I wouldn't have written the *St. Mark Passion* had I not been teaching at Holy Cross (highly rated undergraduate Catholic Jesuit administered liberally oriented liberal arts college, located in Worcester, Massachusetts). Holy Cross allowed me to study Catholicism, and, first of all, to lose my fear of Catholicism and Christianity. Secondly, I was able to study and immerse myself in Catholicism. Actually, I studied with a student of mine. I took one year to do that. I came with a lot of questions, she came with books, and we sat once a week for an entire year. I tried to understand it all, and I read a lot of a liberation theology as well, because that is so important in Latin America (liberation theology is an interpretation of Christian theology favored at Holy Cross and developed in Latin America, but not fully accepted in the Catholic hierarchy, which emphasizes a concern for the liberation of the oppressed). I think Holy Cross was essential. I would have totally rejected Rilling's invitation to write the passion had I not been teaching at Holy Cross."

"What is the main joy you get from teaching at Holy Cross where you were appointed the Loyola Professor of Music in 2007?"

"I would say to me the main joy is the continual discovery of 'the other.' You know it's a challenge to grow up Jewish in a Catholic country with a certain fear of Catholicism because unfortunately the church hierarchy there was aligned with the anti-Semitic hierarchy of the army. So I was kind of scared of Catholicism. That was despite having so many wonderful Catholic friends. So to come here and teach at a Catholic college, and to discover the wonders of that culture and the Jesuit mind is a beautiful thing. It's a challenge. It's to get out of your comfort zone. That is always a good thing. I think everybody should do that. I don't like to give advice, but that's my only piece of advice to everybody. To not be so much in your comfort zone all the time."

Like Mozart, Osvaldo's life and music have been powerfully influenced by family, especially by births and deaths within it. A crucial event was the death of his beloved mother in the very same week in which his first child was born. Asked what single event of his life was the most life-altering, Osvaldo said:

"My first child was born and my mother died in the same week. I was faced with a new life I was responsible for, and to lose my mother at the same time was traumatic. Life and death so close! Six days apart. My daughter was born. Then my mom died. It was expected but it still hurts. She was only fifty-seven. I couldn't be with her because my daughter was born here and my mother was in Argentina. My daughter was born with a little bit of jaundice, so we were not allowed to fly there. It was hard."

Life and death! Asked what has inspired him the most apart from music itself, Osvaldo spoke again of family:

"My children. Being a father. Discovering them. Following them in life. How they have become people. Thalia is twenty-seven. She's in Israel doing a master's in international conflict mediation. Jonathan — we call him Jonny — is right now at the Cannes Film Festival working with Laura Poitras, the director of the Snowden documentary, *Citizen Four*. Anna, whose paintings you see on the wall, is a junior at the University of Miami."

The more Osvaldo talked of how his family influenced his personal life forwards and backwards, the more its profound influence on him became apparent.

"I cannot name one. At the beginning my mother, and my great-grandfather and great-grandmother. Now my youngest sister. She is a child psychologist. She works with mothers who have attachment problems with their children. You wouldn't think that is possible but it's possible. I go to visit her once or twice a year. My great grandfather and grandmother because they came to Argentina from Romania, a different world. He was religious and a carpenter by trade. He spoke almost no Spanish, only Yiddish, so he was a mysterious but great figure. Both of them died in their nineties. I adored them because they had been through so much. They even had lost some of their children as grown-ups, but they kept the faith, they kept living, they kept choosing life. And that is a major accomplishment (laughs). My father was also influential. He was a great guy, and actually my father is becoming more influential now, even though he died almost twenty years ago. I don't know why. Maybe it's because his wisdom was more subtle. He talked a lot and was very humorous. The more I remember things that he said the more I believe he was a wise man."

Oddly enough, one of the most profound influences on Osvaldo's creative life has been his now-sundered marriage and alliance with Neri Oxman, the noted Israeli-American MIT architect, designer, and professor.

"I learned a lot from Neri. She is a little bit like Bach in that she believes everything comes from one thing. Organically from one cell, so to speak. And that is like Bach, who was different than Beethoven, and Stravinsky in our time, who were masters of oppositions. So to Neri, who could be higher than Bach? It's a challenge when you speak with Neri because she's a great artist and a great mind. Her influence made me a more rigorous composer, perhaps less colorful on the surface but more solid inside. I think what I learned from her is the unity of all things, seeing the world as one system and not a collection of different things. That is what drives her life. It's like that great essay by (Russian-English philosopher) Isaiah Berlin, *The Hedgehog and the Fox*. Neri is the hedgehog. She knows one thing but that thing is very, very big, like the hedgehog. Whereas the fox knows a lot of things but none of them is so big. That incredible essay essentially divides artists into those two schools. Stravinsky's a fox, Schoenberg is a hedgehog, Bach is obviously a hedgehog. Berlin said that Leo Tolstoy, whose ideas in *War and Peace* were central in the essay, was a fox who thought that he was a hedgehog."

It might be said that the musical influences on Osvaldo Golijov are not only Catholic, but also catholic, following upon his mentor Gandini's advice to bridge the so-called high and low. Thus, Osvaldo has a place in his pantheon ranging from Bach, Beethoven, and Ma to Dylan, Cohen, and Kendrick Lamar. An alliance still thriving is the one between Osvaldo and famed master cellist and world citizen, Yo-Yo Ma, the founder of the Silk Road Project uniting musicians and musicianship all along that ancient highway of commerce, to which Ma conscripted Osvaldo Golijov as one of its composers.

"A person whom I admire and I'm lucky to consider as a friend is Yo-Yo Ma who lives nearby. When we meet it's always a substantial conversation we enjoy. Helmuth Rilling because he saw potential in me and just said, 'do it.' I want to single out Geoff Nuttall, the leader of the famous St. Lawrence Quartet, who has affected me very much. Geoff is like a brother, a brother who challenges me and makes me grow. He released a collection of my works on an album called *Yiddishbbuk* which got two Grammy nominations.

"But I'm talking about all music. Oh yes, doesn't matter, everybody needs a different kind of music. I don't know Bob Dylan or (the late) Leonard Cohen personally, but I love both of them. Kendrick Lamar I think is a monumental genius. He's a rapper. But he's to rap what Beethoven was to music. I mean he truly has expanded the vocabulary in a cataclysmic way, and, like Beethoven, he has these high ideals. It's like he's the channel of the *Black Lives Matter* movement. He's the voice of a whole social justice movement. Because of him, other artists have grown enormously. Like Beyonce with her new record. Kendrick's influence on her was overall, and she leapt like ten leagues because of that. So it's like when Beethoven came onto the scene and completely molded Schubert and Schumann and Mendelssohn and all of those people. So it's a miracle to watch. I guess the genre of hip-hop rap was ready for someone of that caliber. And he has emerged."

Having come this far in investigating the sources of Osvaldo Golijov's musical power, have we penetrated to the core of that conundrum? Certainly not, but Osvaldo's answers to questions directed at his ideas about music and his own musicianship do shed some light on that everlasting mystery.

"As I compose, I feel that there is one song going on all the time in the universe and all that we can do is to catch little pieces of it. Of course, the great composers catch much more. I think that the true composers or songwriters, whether classical or popular — it doesn't matter, you know — either tap into that song that is running through the universe or don't tap into it. And if you tap into it, you tap into part of that river. The great ones swam or sailed longer stretches of that river than the small ones. But everyone that is true taps into that music which already exists.

"To my mind, George Crumb had the most beautiful and true definition of music. But now I have to remember exactly how he articulated it because it was so good. I think he said that 'music is a system of proportions in the service of a spiritual impulse,' the impulse of the soul, you might say. And to me what is beautiful about that definition is that he doesn't even talk about sound. He says music is a system of proportions. I feel that that is the truest definition because your soul has an impulse, but if you just go literally 'oh,' that's not music. But if you go 'OHHHH, it's already music. So then you notice that it's waves, it's relationships. Maybe relationships is a good word too. Relationship between pitch and time. And it's perfect. It's perfect because music is like that. It's vibrations in the air that have ratios, proportions, and relationships. I like that definition. It comes from the soul. If it doesn't come from the soul, it's not music. And if it doesn't articulate it in those relationships, it's not music either. I love his answer because everyone else talks about the sound."

"Sounds like you might think music is mysterious and elusive, Osvaldo?"

"Always. Even the music that seems to be most transparent, when you try to understand it in full, it's mysterious again. Sometimes music is elusive, sometimes it's right there with you. I think there is music that is almost like breath. Like Verdi. I love him. Puccini is amazing, but I like Verdi much more. Verdi has truth, and like Shakespeare, he has tapped into the core of what it means to be human. Mozart too."

"How about Wagner?"

"Wagner is also a giant. When I get into a Wagner mood it's like a period of intoxication, and you think this is the greatest thing ever. He is incredible. But then when I get out, I might then listen to a simple Verdi aria and say, 'I'd rather stay with Verdi.'"

"Where does music come from and where does it go?"

"Music comes from many places. Sometimes it comes from what nature brings into you, sometimes from the great questions of life and death, sometimes from emotions like love. But basically anything that affects the human spirit can become music. Anything that comes either from inside or from outside through you can become music. You are just a vessel. Some people do everything. Once again I come to Beethoven. Beethoven had everything: tragedy, humor, nobility. He tackled so many of the aspects of what it means to be a human being on this planet. Some composers, Chopin for example, specialize in a small area of the soul, but that is important too, and he found more and more nuances in that. Music then goes back to humans, back to their ears and to the souls of the people that listen, I believe. And then to the universe (laughs)."

"We've talked a little about what music can do that the other art forms can't do?"

"I think that what music can do is to stop time, which is a huge thing! Stop time! Like when you said earlier, Larry, that you went to hear *Götterdämmerung* at noon and you exited at six, it all went by so fast. Those six hours could have been six seconds, six years, six thousand years! Time ceases to exist. Music can also bring you back to mythical time, like for Jews at the Passover dinner. You don't compare it to the day before and the day after, you compare it to a Passover dinner forty or fifty or sixty years ago, right? So music exists in that other realm of time that is not day to day."

"Maybe that's why Einstein played the violin."

"Einstein said that the greatest human being ever was Mozart (laughs)."

"Yes, he said that. Well, Mozart is my favorite, but I think yours is Beethoven."

"I guess. For a while it was Mozart too. I changed, but I think I'm going to die with Beethoven."

"So is music the greatest art?"

"Music is everything. Music is emotion, but it's also philosophy, science, transcendence. It's everything, everything. Music is what we choose in the most important moments of our lives. I don't think human beings can live without music. When you take the T, you see everybody with headphones. Everybody needs music. It's a vital need."

"Do you consider yourself to be a melodic composer?"

"I would consider myself mostly a harmonic and melodic composer as opposed to a rhythmic one, even though I have done a lot with rhythm. I think the center of my being is harmony and melody, predominantly harmony."

"Do you hear music in your head?"

"If not you cannot (laughs), you cannot write it."

"Would you say it comes from the outside in or from the inside out? Dreams? Impressions?"

"I think it's both. The good pieces are where there is an inside out idea but also an outside in idea. And sometimes one is the first and sometimes the other is the first. But there has to be a meeting point. So the inside out idea has to find the best way to be articulated by the outside in. And the outside in without an inside out is nothing. It's just a shell. If it's only from the outside in, you have just a great conceptual idea but you don't have the material, the musical substance that makes it memorable, so in that case it is nothing. Both alone are the problem. I think that the best is when there is a confluence of both impulses."

"What do you think the future of classical music is, Osvaldo?"

"It's interesting because I think the definition of classical music is changing, right?"

"Well, you're doing it."

"In my way, I guess. Many things not meant to be classical become classic, right? The Beatles will be classical. They are already classical I think. But to take classical as we understand classical, I don't think that the great composers will die. No, I think that they did something that is forever. Picasso said that all great art is in the present. And it's true. When you look at a Picasso it is present today, and also Egyptian art is present today. There is no past and no future. All great music lives in an eternal present. That's true. So anything that gives you that impression of being alive, like the piano sonatas of Beethoven, will live. Who cares if he wrote them two hundred and some years ago?"

"Well, how about the pop music of Kendrick Lamar?"

"I think he will live. It's like Miles Davis, Louis Armstrong, and the Beatles. Like Frank Sinatra, who was incredible! They'll all be around in a hundred or two hundred years. Anything that speaks to your soul in a deep way will stay."

As said, Osvaldo's music is the end product of all he has experienced. That includes the many books on philosophy he reads. Asking him whether "humans have ever been without music," elicited this questioning response.

"I don't think so. I'm reading a lot of evolution books. I'm reading Richard Dawkins's, *The Selfish Gene*, which is an old book but great [Richard Dawkins, English ethologist, evolutionary biologist, and author]. I think music must have some evolutionary function. I think it's been there from the beginning. And it's there everywhere. I think there is no culture without music. Cavemen had it.

Even whales and animals have music. Whales have incredible songs. Of course the birds do. That's all true."

"So Osvaldo, what single idea or realization in the course of your life was the most life-altering?"

"I'm obsessed with the relationship between free will and no free will (laughs). That's why I'm reading all these biology books because I can see that a lot of things that you think you do out of free will are preconditioned by your genes and by evolution. The idea is that an astonishing chain of events led to a symphony to be composed and performed — a succession of miracles. And that everything is really, really connected, from the big bang to this very hour. I wonder whether all philosophy, psychology, music, and all of those other disciplines are only the first veil of something that is pure biology? So I don't know if there is any free will. That's what I'm trying to find out. But I guess I will die without knowing, like all the philosophers. You ask me whether everything is predetermined. That could be. Not every little detail, but the general course of things. I feel that we are like leaves being blown about. I don't have an answer, but the more I read the more fascinated I become with this. With the implications that evolution is responsible for most everything. That it's not so much people who are responsible."

"From your reading, and the building of these ideas in your mind, is your musical composition affected?"

"Oh, yes! Yes, because you realize that once you start reading all of these things you see the relationship between melody and harmony in a whole different way. And rhythm and orchestra. You realize that this is just one more expression of genetics, perhaps. The genome is also a musical concept."

It may be that a true artist can be discerned by his measurement of his own talent against his view of his place in the cosmos. Osvaldo's words, drawn from three different parts of our conversation, speak to that.

"Do you view your own music as unique, as many observers do? Is there any other composer who is like you?"

"I don't know. Maybe there is (laughs). In the end, I think that I'm pretty unique. I think so."

"You once said to me, 'If I had to die tomorrow I would like to have left music that speaks to people.' You said, 'I don't want to die as a distinguished composer. I want to be a composer who is loved or hated, admired or dismissed, as cheesy. Rather than being stuffy, I'd rather be cheesy, like popular musicians are, but at least they touch people's hearts.' Do you still have that feeling?"

"I do, because I am of the kind of composer that errs on that side. I feel pretty much the same. To me classical music is music that transforms the listener, that takes the listener on a journey of change."

"What are your greatest ambitions for the rest of your life?"

"I think the greatest ambition is to end each day knowing that I was a good man, that I did the best I could do in my work, that I was good to the people I love and love me. Something good, a good action. Of course I want to write a lot still. To keep exploring different aspects of the human soul, and how to express that musically."

I stated at the outset that Osvaldo Golijov was the product of his open acceptance of influences from all sources. Although he considers himself a classical composer without the resources to compose popular music, his remarks have already shown the profound eclecticism which informs his music. Osvaldo expands our own understanding of the pop music phenomenon.

"What is it that pop music has that gets all those people excited, rhythm, melody, what?"

"It's relevant to its time. It catches the spirit of the time (snaps) like this. It's hard to pin down. We spoke about Frank Sinatra. What is it about Frank Sinatra? It's the quality of his voice, the storytelling in his voice, the mythical quality — the myth of the time. At that time he was, or what he created, was the paradigm of what people wanted to be. Smooth, in command, romantic, but restrained, vulnerable. So it's hard to define. Can you produce stats which define Frank Sinatra like people try to do with sports stars? No. But I do believe that you are right that there are some rhythms that speak to an era better than others. I don't think there is a universal answer to that question."

"Which has a deeper effect on people, pop music or classical music?"

"(Laughs) Depends on the person. And depends on the music. I think pop music can have humongous effect, a very deep effect. I can see that the music of Bob Dylan in the early 60s had an immense effect. The music of Aretha Franklin had an immense effect. Bob Marley, Miles Davis, Jimi Hendrix, the Beatles, they affected the collective spirit of the world."

"I recently read your friend Philip Glass's memoir, *Words Without Music.* As you know, he writes a lot for the cinema, as well as opera, just as you do, and he said that music has such power that it lifts up any work and carries the spectator through a piece whether it's opera, theater, dance, or film. So he's giving music the paramount place in the piece. Is that true?"

"It's absolutely true. You can prove it yourself. Get a stretch of any movie that you like with and without the music. You'll see how the music really has an absolutely disproportionate impact on the movie and to how it appears. A great musical theme for a movie by someone like John Williams, Ennio Morricone, or Nino Rota, can, in a minute or less, encapsulate the whole two hours of the movie. The music can really put everything together."

"Glass also says all music, without exception is ethnic music?"

"True, true... Do you remember Isaac Bashevis Singer? He won the Nobel Prize for literature. He kept writing in Yiddish. A journalist asked him, 'You know, you speak great English. Why do you choose to write in a dialect instead of a language?' Singer replied that, 'A language is a dialect with an army and a navy,' (repeating an adage popularized by Yiddish scholar Max Weinreich, who had heard it from an attendee at one of his lectures). With an army and navy! And it's the same with music. All German music is ethnic music. All Latin American music is ethnic music. All music is ethnic music. I completely agree with Philip."

"Would you say that musicians are tolerant of other musicians, and more tolerant of other people generally, both personally and with respect to differences in outlook, political positions, religion, national origin?"

"I think so, especially chamber musicians and jazz musicians because you have to play with so many different people. I wouldn't say that would apply for orchestral musicians because they play always with the same people so they can develop their own little tribes and cliques. But if you're a jazz musician you have to play with different people almost every night. Then you have to be tolerant by force, and you have to listen to each other. You have to listen! And that's what the world needs. People who listen to the other. You cannot make music if you don't listen. That already makes you more tolerant."

Not that Osvaldo Golijov is perfect. Who among us is? He told us about his troubles meeting deadlines on musical commissions, a failing that plagued him so much that he stopped accepting them, although it must be added that many great composers, including Beethoven, Verdi, Mahler, Stravinsky, and a chorus of others, have had the same problem, usually for the same reasons, lack of readiness or lack of quality to satisfy the master.

Osvaldo told me of some of his other traits he might do without. Or maybe not. Let the reader decide. Often flaws are the obverse of good things that lend humanity to a person.

"I'm not a good pianist. I'm OK. I like to read music on the piano, to improvise, and to write. But I never had the patience to really study, to practice seriously, and that shows. If I had it to do over again, I would practice more piano (laughs). I would practice all those scales that I didn't. I wish I could play better. I have no idea to write a piano concerto because my problem with the piano is that I play good enough to play, but in a way that limits me. I don't play strings but I have a great imagination and feel for the strings. I have no limits with the strings. I have limits of what I can do on the piano, which is not much."

"What personal qualities do you wish you had in greater measure? Or maybe some that you don't have at all?"

"(Sighs): Some more discipline. At times I'm not disciplined. It is important to be disciplined. At times I seem to be floating, but sometimes I float too much (laughs)."

"Well, Osvaldo, I could be a lot more disciplined. Would you say that you're a free spirit and do what you want to do, and let the Devil take the hindmost, as I guess I do."

"Yes, I'm that way. I mean I'm not a wild person. But sometimes, like when I am drawn to biology, I will spend hours and hours and hours and not do anything else. And if something interests me, I will go for it."

Unsupported claims of plagiarism rising to a crescendo in the *New Yorker* concerning Osvaldo's *Siderus* honoring Galileo, were distractingly made against him, although those were lowered to a diminuendo or silence by Michael Ward-Bergeman, the very composer he supposedly plagiarized when both worked together, asserting there was no plagiarism. So let the academicians and journalists argue, while the musicians collaborate. Osvaldo can take comfort from musical history there too. Many composers, again including the great Ludwig van, have been similarly accused, Beethoven from Mozart's wondrous piano concertos, and Johannes Brahms in his belated but powerful first symphony from Beethoven's ninth. As Osvaldo stated, "Music comes from music." So it is across all art. How many of Shakespeare's plots were borrowed? Would we have *The Marriage of Figaro* had not Mozart and da Ponte looked to Beaumarchais?

In fact, Osvaldo has given a good deal of thought worth attending to a variety of subjects, musical and otherwise. And he has been through a variety of experiences. I asked about some of them to flesh out further the portrait of the artist and his persona.

"Is there a difference in the way instrumentalists play if they're from Europe or the Far East or America? Does their performance reflect their background?"

"I would say so. Although there is a country called music and everybody belongs to it, each of us has an accent, just like I have an accent in English. As an artist emerging from Argentinian and Jewish culture I play or compose differently than one emerging from European or American culture because you are shaped differently. You absorb different sounds from your birth through your childhood, and I think that affects you. You cannot escape it. It has affected me."

"Do you think we would be better off with women running the world? Women are thought to be more tolerant."

"I think so. That is something I hope for. I think that women will probably think again one more time before sending people off to war (laughs). I want to think that. For instance, Angela Merkel is a very good leader. A very impressive leader. Absolutely (laughs). I think it is motherhood. Motherhood! Carrying a being inside gives a woman the capacity to think one more time than a man before sending people to war. Yes, that is what I think."

"How about musicians governing the world because of what you were talking about, their traditions of collaboration, cooperation, and community?"

"Astor Piazzolla used to say that if the world were run by musicians it would be a better world. Probably it's true but it will never happen (laughs), because musicians want to play music. And because there are people that crave power. That is their music. Power."

"Should musical artists be socially conscious?"

"It's an interesting question because we just spoke about the most recalcitrant great composer, Richard Wagner. You cannot get much worse than he was as a human being. And yet his music is great. I think that part of the greatness of Beethoven was that he cared. I'm disappointed in Wagner that he didn't care. He was an egomaniac. I don't think that Beethoven was an egomaniac. I don't think that this guy Kendrick Lamar is an egomaniac. I think they are socially conscious.

I think that is good. Mozart who didn't seem to be socially conscious, was socially conscious. He was in *Le nozze di Figaro* and did it with humor. It's the best way."

"Osvaldo, what are your thoughts about humanism, existentialism, and the hope that humanity will survive?"

"I hope I'm a humanist. I don't want to be presumptuous. You can always do much more than what you do. As to existentialism we will probably at some point either destroy ourselves or evolve into another species. We are not the end of the road. We're still metamorphosing. In Dawkins's book it's the theory of evolution from the point of view of the genes. In other words, we are just carriers of the genes which are playing with us. We are vehicles for our genes. We are the vehicle of a genome that will reconstitute itself in a different way."

"What about life after death?"

"No, I think we just disintegrate. But everybody leaves something behind that affects the world. I think one of the motivations for creating music is to leave something behind. But I think it's the same motivation that makes you want to raise children. You want to leave something of your own, you want to leave love. Music is a form of love. It doesn't matter. Nobody remembers what happened before you were born. The world didn't exist then, and the world won't exist after you die, and that's OK."

Even that short remark exhibits the nuance and complexity of Osvaldo's musical and philosophical mind. Surely there is truth in however those words are interpreted. One truth is that Osvaldo Golijov's music and spirit will be with us long after he leaves.

CHAPTER
6

Matthew Aucoin: Composer, Conductor, Pianist, and Maverick

One might wonder what significance there is in the fact that Matthew Aucoin's tense and dark opera, *Crossing*, about Walt Whitman's care of wounded Civil War soldiers, had its acclaimed premiere in 2015 in Boston's century-old Shubert Theatre only a few weeks after the composer's twenty-fifth birthday, just as Wolfgang Amadeus Mozart's dramatic and accomplished opera, *Idomeneo*, about human relationships on the isle of Crete in the wake of the Trojan Wars, had its premiere in 1781 in Munich's storied Cuvillies Theatre a scant two days after that composer's twenty-fifth birthday. Is that uncanny similarity why Matthew Aucoin has been compared to Mozart? That is a striking coincidence but a doubtful notion. Could it be because this still youthful prodigy, who is unsure where destiny will take him despite his recognition of his own talents, appears to be walking in Mozart's footprints step by step in matching time, and thereby being seriously thought of as the Mozart of the twenty-first century? That makes more sense, although none of us, including Matthew himself, would put money on it. It is a fact though that like the master, Matthew Aucoin wears hats as a composer, conductor, and pianist, as well as a poet, lyricist, and writer, whose maverick critiques on music reach our eyes and ears as have Mozart's in his famous letters to his pedagogic father, Leopold. Matthew Aucoin incredibly wears other hats too, one as a genuine and revealing conversationalist, the hat he wore to his astounding meeting with me.

These talents combined with his deeply held feelings for connecting with others, a spirit of generosity, the courage of his convictions about his music and himself, and the imagination to project his thoughts into the future, make him an interviewer's delight who can impart to us the secrets of composition and music-making lying in his psyche waiting to be uncovered. Who better than Matthew? Indeed, when better, before the demands of his work and his public, along with

American composer Matthew Aucoin

Credit: Photo copyright © John D. and Catherine T. MacArthur Foundation. Used with permission.

the natural contraction over the years of his willingness to sit and talk for some hours amid the breezes and passersby in a public park in Boston's Fenway minutes after a taxing rehearsal of *Crossing,* as he did with me in our very first meeting, will limit the freedom of youthful expression Matthew now radiates, as he strives to give full meaning to each answer?

I reminded Matthew when our conversation began that almost sixty years separates us in age, and that if his career continued even close to that far along the comet like trajectory it so far has traveled, that many people then will be fascinated by his open explications today of his life to this time, and his thoughts as to what his future might hold. It is in that spirit that the following affecting conversation unfolded.

"Matthew, how are you today?"

"Great now. Very full day. I sort of feel that afterglow. I was exhausted during the lunch break, but I feel better now. I think it was a good day."

"It's often the case you get energized by the things you do. A little while ago, because your name is the same as some guy down in Philadelphia who jumped up on the stage with Bruce Springsteen, you said to me that you wish you were *that* Matthew Aucoin."

"Right, you asked if it was me and I said no. I wish it was me. I guess I'm a second-generation Bruce Springsteen fan. My dad was playing Bruce for me before practically anything else, certainly before any classical music. I was two or three. It's not something I listen to much now, but certainly I have happy childhood associations with *Born to Run* and even the earlier albums. So, nostalgically, if Bruce Springsteen invited me to jump up on stage I'd be there in a heartbeat."

"Was your choice of going to Harvard based on an idea of music being a pariah in education, and it being secretly treated badly while it is pretended outwardly it is special. I believe you said let's give music its place at the table with literature, art, and painting. I grasp the idea, so the question is did you go to Harvard because you wanted to get a broader education?"

"Yes. I didn't have much experience with conservatories because I didn't go to an arts high school, I took piano lessons privately. I didn't do any kind of pre-college program at New England Conservatory, or anything like that. The homework I did about their curricula made me think that it was not the kind of environment in which I could develop my potential in multiple fields. Actually, the real reason I went to Harvard is that I had a couple of life-changing encounters with really great poetry."

"By what poets?"

"Wallace Stevens, Hart Crane, Emily Dickinson, Elizabeth Bishop, mostly Americans actually, in the year before I would have been applying to college. Poetry was the only thing that had ever really challenged music for me. Throughout college I wrote a heck of a lot more poetry and essays than I did music. I didn't actually write much music in college, believe it or not. For most of those four years I was trying to decide whether I was going to be an English professor or a poet who made a living as a teacher of literature, or a musician. It was really a neck-and-neck struggle. I wasn't expecting to jump into the deep end of the music world the way that I did. My senior year of college a bunch of things happened at the same time that made it feel fateful. Also, my mentor on the literary side, Jorie Graham, told me she thought I really needed to give music a go. I'm not sure if that was because she thought I didn't have the chops poetically."

"I doubt that."

"I think she sensed that if I didn't do it then, the chance might not come again."

"I have a feeling that that was good advice. In that program I looked on YouTube at that lecture you gave over at Harvard about your Civil War opera, *Crossing*, I forget the name of the professor who ran it?"

"I think it was Professor of Humanities, Homi Bhabha."

"Right. He said you need to be able to read music to criticize and understand it, and you said reading and listening deeply to music is just as good. As a layperson, I was happy you said that. Is that true? Can I, as a non-musician, appreciate music which makes me feel deeply as well as a musician who can read the music?"

"I really don't think that musical literacy is the make or break. I think there are plenty of people who have a certain fluency for whom reading music comes easily but who don't necessarily feel or grasp pieces as deeply as certain other people who can't read music. I don't think that's the same."

"What is?"

"(Long pause) There I'm at a loss. I don't know what. I guess 'openness' is the first word that comes to mind."

"That might be, that's good. It's like if you are open to other people, you can accept any person."

"Yes. Openness to what a piece of music wants to do to you. This kind of gets into one of my least favorite words that's in vogue right now, which is 'accessibility.' The idea that a piece of music needs to be made accessible, the way that a building needs to conform to a fire code to be accessible. I have always thought that actually has it backwards because I don't think that we access pieces of music. I think pieces of music access us. And I think that often what people mean when they say a piece of music isn't accessible is that it is too intense or too demanding. It's not like the piece of music is a structure that you're entering. It's entering you. If what it has to say is too intense, then that can make certain people very uncomfortable, musicians as well as non-musicians. So this is why I think openness is the key thing. It is sort of a willingness to hold yourself open even when what rushes in might be quite intense."

"So I think the prof's idea of breakfast is different than your idea of breakfast. His idea is sort of elitist and technical, and yours is take is as it comes."

"If you wanted to write a thirty-page paper on late Berg it might be useful to be able to read music, but I don't think there is really any good music that requires literacy in order for its impact to be felt."

"Another subject that came up in that lecture was whether your multiplicity of interests, or anybody's interests, help or hinder composition. You said then you had to rewrite *Crossing* from the beginning, and now you are rewriting the rewrite to some extent."

"Yes."

"And you also said you're not yet a master of subsuming all those interests into a musical composition you can live with on the first try, but that it can be done. Do you think you are approaching that point as a musician where you can do that?"

"Yes, to an extent. I hope I'm still growing. I think the reason that I've revised *Crossing* so much is that I started talking about it and working on it in 2012 which is the year that I graduated from college. So I was twenty-one. At the time I was an English major. I didn't have anyone holding my feet to the fire when it came to my compositional technique. Man, have I held my own feet to the fire over the past few years to make sure that there is not an instrument in the orchestra that I don't feel comfortable with testing its limits, but not going beyond those limits! And understanding harmony, notation of challenging rhythmic ideas, singers' breathing capabilities, a million things. I think the first go of *Crossing,* written in 2012 and 2013 was just a not fully mature version of myself. I'm glad that a lot of people were moved by the piece, but I said to myself, if it's going to keep being performed, I need to get it up to my current standard. I think also that I have focused my interests in the past couple of years. I think of myself as a composer full stop. I do conduct, I do sometimes play the piano, I do sometimes write essays, but I get up every day and work on composing. I think on a technical level it's beginning to pay off."

"You can't do all that full stop. I think being a composer is a great thing, and I think that it is the right choice now, but you're not going to give up the other things, you're going to do them."

"In due time. It feels like now that I'm getting to a place where I don't feel that there is any aspect of my technique that I need to go away and work on for six months. There might be time soon for some of the other things."

"We know what you said in those two essays on Verdi and Walt Whitman's poem, *The Sleepers.* Would you stand by those now or would you amend them or write them differently?"

"I don't think so. That's the ironic thing. Maybe my prose writing chops were in better shape than my musical chops back then."

"So tell me, Matthew, speaking of *Crossing,* do you think opera is one of the greatest forms of music?"

"I think it's the form with the greatest possibilities. It is the most ambitious in the sense that the ideal of opera is to pay attention to every human sense, to visual art, to dance, to music's vocal and instrumental sides, to poetry and drama. That is stupidly ambitious, psychotically ambitious! So I think that the essence of opera is kind of the dream of the union of those things. It is the most ambitious thing imaginable for human artists. But I also think that for that reason opera is usually very bad. It doesn't take very much logistically for a great violinist to give a great violin recital. You just stand up and play, and that can be a life-changing and intimate experience that doesn't require eight weeks of technical rehearsals and millions of dollars. I would never claim that an opera is higher or greater than a solo violinist playing the Bach chaconne. Plenty of solo recitals have been among my favorite musical experiences. But I do think that what opera can do when everything comes together, and that's probably one time out of a thousand, is to give you the uncanny sense that our emotional lives have been made physical, and it's been sort of manifested that our internal worlds are somehow externally present. I think opera is better at that than any other art form."

"I know you think Mozart and Verdi did that. Do you think that anybody since them has done it pretty well?"

"Yes. My vote for the greatest achievement in the art form in the twentieth century would be a tie between Berg's *Lulu* and Stravinsky's *The Rake's Progress.* I think that they achieved a comparable transparency of emotion and transcendently beautiful music through almost opposite means. I think Stravinsky was really shameless and fearless in his belief in some of the cleanest-cut classical forms. *The Rake's Progress* is basically a numbers opera made up of very clear-cut arias and duets and ensembles that actually form that classical clarity of form which he believed, when fused with his own volatile approach to rhythm, would yield something that felt true to him. Whereas Berg went all the way out into the left field of Schoenberg's brand-new twelve-tone method, and then somehow managed to liquify it and fuse it with his own sort of romantic sensibility. So I think for me *Rake's Progress* and *Lulu* are in a league of their own in the past hundred years."

"Let's talk of your own operas, *Sandover, Hart Crane, Crossing, and Second Nature.* Which is your favorite?"

"At this point I think of *Sandover* and *Hart Crane* as student pieces. There are things in them I'm affectionate about, but I don't really think of them as my operas in the sense that they are not published. I'm not sure I would authorize a performance of them in their current form. I think that the most recent version of *Crossing* will be my favorite. I've made some cosmetic revisions in the last two years. Not revisions that affect the dramaturgy too deeply, but a slight expansion of the orchestra, little surgical nips and tucks. So nothing on too large a scale, but kind of pervasive cosmetic revisions. I think that this new version will be something that I'm fond of. I should speak of the piece I am working on now, which is an adaptation of Sarah Ruhl's play, *Eurydice.* Sarah is doing the libretto herself after her own play. That one is only about sixty percent written, but I think it is a step forward."

"Would you say that *Crossing* is a combination of a personal story about Walt Whitman with something larger about the Civil War?"

"Definitely. It's a personal story that can't be separated from the macro story of what was happening in the country at the time. It didn't feel especially topical when we did it two years ago, but it feels uncomfortably more so in 2017 than in 2015 for the obvious reason that I think a lot of us are being woken up out of our daydream about various overarching political issues. Obviously race relations is the most salient one. Sort of realizing that maybe things aren't as rosy as some of us thought, or as some of us younger folks were taught that these relations had gotten rosier. So all of a sudden I think the figure of Whitman as a hopeless optimist — his optimism is all consuming, he just can't help himself, he is sure that the forces of progress and goodness are going to win — makes him look even more naïve now. That is intentional. I wanted to show the flaw of that side of his thinking. For me it strikes a little bit closer to home this year."

"You said Whitman was an omnivore. Were you an omnivore? Were you reading everything in sight? Do you still? Is that good for composing?"

"I think I was. That's a great phase of life. But I think if you stay an omnivore then what you should be is a critic, basically. I had a fantastic professor at Harvard, name of Steve Burt. Professor Burt, who now identifies as a woman, had consumed every piece of culture known to humanity. Somehow she managed to read every new book that was being published. Somehow, she also knew every obscure Australian heavy metal band from the eighties. It was just completely absurd. And she writes poetry as well as criticism, but I think in her case she's at her best in her criticism because so much of her life force clearly is spent on digesting everything that's out there. And I think if you are going to be a composer or a poet, at a certain point in your life you need to be an omnivore just to see what is going to shape you, to see which artists in various fields are going to be the decisive ones. You need to cast the net pretty wide to find those. In my case I found the poet, Paul Celan, and the composer, Thomas Adès. If I hadn't really done some digging, I don't know if I would have crossed their paths. But I think if you stay an omnivore you might not hone one skill."

"Speaking of Thomas Adès, you mention that you think his opera, *Powder Her Face,* is so much better than his opera, *The Tempest*? Let's talk briefly on your thoughts about Adès as a composer. I know you think he is different than you are. Do you know him?"

"(Pause) I do know him. Actually, I was an assistant conductor on *The Tempest* at the Met. I would be lying if I said anything other than Adès has been the decisive musical influence on me both because his music opened up certain possibilities that I've followed in different directions than he has, but also because I saw the cracks in the wall through Tom's music."

"That sounds like a lot! Please expand on those?"

English composer Thomas Adès, muse of Matthew Aucoin

Credit: Photo by Marco Borggreve. *All rights reserved.*

"Well, we still live in a musical world where there is this myth of tonality vs. atonality. Musicians and critics alike have a habit of saying this piece was tonal, that piece wasn't tonal, and I've always felt that it's a spectrum, that it's really a fluid and unstable spectrum, with levels of stability that range from pure chance — aleatoric music — to serialism, which claims to be totally organized. It is a sliding scale between tonality and atonality. I think what Adès's music does is not just simply that he recognizes that there is a spectrum, but he takes familiar tonal materials, chords that Mozart used, chords that have been around for a while, and he somehow makes them behave in a more volatile manner. Instead of tending towards resolution, they tend towards expansion, so that a major chord or a series of fifths tend to spiral on top of one another in a way that opens out into space. It's kind of exhilarating and it is also scary because the expansion implied might go on forever. Therefore it can be very difficult to end a piece when you are working with it in Adès language. But I think he basically has invented an alternate grammar for pre-existing musical material, and that's really exciting. So even though I think my music tends towards slightly more cyclical rhythmic structures, whereas Adès's rhythms are always kind of in quicksand rather than cycling, my pieces tend to come full circle whereas his open out into space. I learned a lot from him. The question you pose of *Powder Her Face* vs. *The Tempest* boils down to the libretto. It is hard to screw up *The Tempest,* but Meredith Oakes, his librettist, sure did. She really made a mess of it. She boiled Shakespeare's incomparably beautiful language down to these embarrassing rhyming couplets. It is all, 'you are my slave, go to your cave.' It's really embarrassing. And what surprises me is that Adès didn't stomp on it and say, this is not OK. I suppose the outlines of the drama were intact and he was able to weave his musical world, or maybe he doesn't mind as much as I do. Who knows? But I think the real difference is that *Powder Her Face* has a libretto by Philip Hensher, an English writer and critic, that is subtle and witty, and somehow simultaneously is written in modern British English and slips effortlessly into verse when it needs to, whereas *The Tempest* is desperately trying not to be Shakespearean. I'm not sure whether that is out of a fear of pretentiousness or whatever, but for me, as a result, the only thing I think of throughout the entire piece is the original Shakespearean language."

"Matthew, before going any further, I want to ask you about your compositional process and your thoughts and feelings as you compose. How would you describe your compositional process? Is it from the outside in or from the inside out. From dreams, impressions, experiences, light, color?"

"I've never been one to draw on dreams or mystical impressions, or to sit around under a tree waiting for the lightning of inspiration to strike. I have faith in the inherent dynamism of musical materials — the notes and rhythms that are the building blocks of musical matter — and I live in the hope that if I engage with the material on its own terms, music will emerge. In other words, I start small. I start from a tiny musical atom, or musical molecule, and start stringing things together to create chemical reactions."

"How about nature, stories, literature, music?"

"I'm most inspired, as I said before, by the inherent dynamism of musical materials, by the organic life that's contained within them, and the miraculous way that notes and rhythms can speak to us and make sense of their own accord."

"How do you notate what you compose? Is the notation merely an afterthought, or do you sit at the piano and compose from note to note, idea to idea."

"I do usually work at the piano, pounding away until I can *feel* the music I'm trying to write. Stravinsky said he had to feel the music in his fingers, and I sympathize with that attitude. If you have an intimate relationship with an instrument — I'm on pretty good terms with the piano, though maybe you'd have to ask the piano how it feels about me — then a physical connection to that instrument can be a vital lifeline. If something's wrong, if a chord is awkwardly voiced, or if a rhythm isn't notated right, your body will tell you."

"Do you hear music in your head?"

"Sure, all the time."

"Do you hear the actual sound, or only imagine what the music sounds like?"

"I'm not sure there's a distinction."

"Whose music do you hear?"

"If I'm working on a piece, then I often hear the part that's giving me trouble. Let's say I get stuck at a certain moment and decide it will be better to go take a nap and come back to that part tomorrow. Inevitably I will hear, like a broken record, the exact passage that I can't seem to solve, played over and over again in my head. It's a kind of torture. But productive torture."

"Can you choose the music you hear?"

"No. Can any of us choose our earworms?"

"Have your most beautiful and/or most profound hearings of your or any composer's music occurred inside or outside your head?"

"I've had many joyful experiences in the concert hall, both as a performer and as a listener, but some of my most intense musical experiences are internal ones. I feel fortunate that I can read a score like a book and hear what's on the page. As a result, there are some pieces that I would be wary of performing live. Some of Mozart's music, for example, can easily be ruined, or at least tainted, by live performance. My happiest experiences of some Mozart pieces have been through reading the score in silence. To me it feels like reading poetry. Not all poems need to be shouted out into a big auditorium."

"Wow, Matt! That is something I've never heard before. It suggests many questions to me immediately. Which pieces are those, which of them do you read in silence, have you heard live or conducted any of them? What do you think Mozart would think of your idea? Did he intend any of those pieces to be private not public? Was Mozart a poet?"

"I certainly don't think Mozart composed pieces abstractly. He composed them to be performed, often on very short notice. Obviously he was a consummate performer himself. But even so, there are moments in *Figaro* and *Zauberflöte*, as well as in certain of the piano concertos, the earlier movements of the *Requiem,* and the last few symphonies, that are so tender, so exquisitely balanced, that it's easy for even a great performer to distort them merely through the act of rendering them in sound. The miracle of Mozart's music is that you don't sense the effort it took to compose it. You certainly sense the effort with Beethoven, for example. Just compare the E-flat chords that open Beethoven's *Eroica* symphony with the E-flat chords that open Mozart's symphony number 39, K. 543, in that key. With Beethoven, I can feel the enormous pressure that must have built up in order for him to release those chords. The beginning of the piece is clearly the culmination of some unseen struggle, the boiling-over of some massive pressure. But the chords that open Mozart's symphony just seem to already be there, waiting for us."

"Is that why it might be tainted by live performance?"

"Look, live performance involves physical exertion. It takes a deep physical effort to shape sound into music. When the music itself gives us evidence of the effort of its creation — as in Beethoven, or Berg, or Janáček, or Thomas Adès, or almost any composer in history — then it feels right to mirror that effort through the physical act of bringing it into sound. But there is a mysterious *givenness* to Mozart's music. A more-than-human ease to its emergence. It feels aesthetically risky to take on the responsibility of bringing it into sound. That's not to say, of course, that it isn't worth trying!"

"Do you feel akin to any other composers, living or dead?"

"Let me be clear that I'm not comparing myself to this composer, since that would be hilariously immodest, but I admire and try to emulate Stravinsky's approach to music. He pulled off a seemingly impossible tightrope act in maintaining his musical integrity no matter what 'style' he was writing in. He was totally fearless. He wasn't afraid of seeming radical, as in his early days. He was equally unafraid of seeming stodgy, as in his so-called Neoclassical period. Such things just didn't matter to him. Musical curiosity and a hunt for beauty and truthfulness were all that mattered. His most amazing achievement may be that he successfully tuned out all the nonsense around him — the stupidity and narrow mindedness of the mid-twentieth-century musical cabals, constantly at war over the wrong things — even after he was mega-famous."

"Can your music be distinguished from other composers?"

"That's for others to decide, not me!"

"What were the most important public and private events in your career in the last few years?"

"Many people have had faith in me, often before I quite saw what there was to have faith in. The people at the Met, for example, who hired me as an assistant on Thomas Adès's *The Tempest.* When I auditioned, I was a twenty-one-year-old college student with no experience at that level. And then there was Diane Paulus, who had unwavering faith in *Crossing* throughout its three-year gestation. The same goes for Christopher Koelsch at LA Opera, who created this position called artist-in-residence for me, which has allowed me to really spread my wings."

"Same question as to your life?"

"Oh, that's easy. Meeting my boyfriend, Clay, three years ago was the most important thing that's happened to me as an adult."

"Is he a musician? Tell me about him?"

"Yes, Clay is a musician, and plays the baroque bassoon with various orchestras. The ones he plays with most regularly are Tafelmusik in Toronto, American Bach Soloists in San Francisco, and the Trinity Wall Street Baroque Orchestra in New York. He is starting to play with Boston Baroque, under Martin Pearlman."

"Tell us how conducting your composition, *The Orphic Moment,* went in Salzburg in February 2017. Was that a signal event for you musically?"

"Yes, *The Orphic Moment* has led a charmed existence so far; I'm not sure any of my other pieces have traveled so much. It's been done in Salzburg, Brooklyn, Boston, Rockport, Toronto, LA, Santa Barbara, and most recently at Lincoln Center with the Orchestra of St. Luke's. The reasons for this may be largely practical, since the piece is only seventeen minutes long and requires a fairly small orchestra. I do think my obsession with the Orpheus story pays off in this piece. My conception of Orpheus is that he's a total narcissistic monster, and his famous backwards glance is very much a calculated decision, since he knows that Eurydice's second death will be fruitful for his music. The whole piece takes place in the few seconds before he turns around. It's a kind of twisted erotic game for him. Usually my pieces have a long gestation period, with plenty of tortured revisions, but I wrote *The Orphic Moment* in one brief burst in March 2014. I think the whole thing was written in under a week. Sometimes — very rarely — you get a gift, and you have to accept it!"

"Same question as to *Crossing* being a signal event, for which you were rehearsing today, soon to be put on at the Brooklyn Academy of Music?"

"It was very special to do a piece about Walt Whitman at BAM, since Whitman himself was an opera nut who attended opera in Brooklyn. That was not in BAM's current building, but in its predecessor. That said, I think of *Crossing* as something of a student piece, since I came up with the idea for it when I was just a few months out of college. Much of the music is somewhat immature. So I have a complicated relationship with the piece. I have affection for it, but I'm also way, way beyond it by now."

"I know you've said *Figaro* and *Otello* are your favorite operas. Great choices. What about Wagner and Puccini?"

"Reminds me of that great Bernstein line. 'I hate Wagner on my knees.' It's like you might hate him but you've got to recognize the power there."

"When I heard *Götterdämmerung* live in HD I said to another guy leaving, 'I can't believe that I came in here at noon and it's now six o'clock. It seems like it all passed very fast.' Osvaldo Golijov said to me that music changes time."

"Actually, I do agree with you that the great Wagner operas put you into a trance. You enter this state where you're not sure how much time has passed but you just want to sink into it. I do love that experience. I've had it a few times. I really think Wagner is admired for the wrong reasons. The things that I love about Wagner are kind of the opposite of the things that are conventionally held to be great about him. My understanding of the conventional wisdom is that people admire Wagner's capacity to bring it all together into these massive forms, to create the architecture of all fifteen hours of *The Ring Cycle,* to write the libretto and this dazzling orchestration, all of that. I don't always find that Wagner's forms, the shapes of the operas, are especially satisfying on the macro scale. There are major issues of pacing. I think that's because he wrote the librettos first and then stuck to them very closely. So there are times when the music is kind of enslaved to the pacing of the epic poem so the opera goes on much longer than it needs to. But what I love about Wagner is the kind of moment-by-moment tenderness. I think that if you take any thirty seconds, or a minute in isolation of the mature operas, it's really exquisite. Strangely, to me, it feels quite human even when the characters are superhumans."

"Are you talking about *The Ring*?"

"Yes. So I love Wagner, I love every moment in isolation. I just think Wagner cheats in the way that he strings them all together. I suppose that's what you can do when everything is chromatic."

"Puccini?"

"I'm not just trying to be obnoxious, but I also think people sometimes get Puccini backwards. I think Puccini is like a technical master. I think he's one of the most skilled composers ever, ever, ever. The understanding of how to write for an orchestra, the subtlety of the harmony, the sort of quicksilver changes, the sophistication, are all really impressive. When I look at a Puccini score, I'm just stunned by how well it is all executed. Maybe it is because he is Italian and people have this stereotypical sense of Italians writing from the heart rather than from the brain. I actually think Puccini wrote from the brain, and I find the pieces on the emotional level manipulative rather than true. I feel kind of dirty after a Puccini act. I've never conducted a full Puccini opera, and I don't know if I ever will, because in the past when I have studied them I've found that they become less rewarding the more time that I spend with them, whereas Verdi always becomes more rewarding the more time you spend with him."

"Do you think Puccini is up to the level of Mozart and Verdi?"

"No, but nobody is. I think he's earned his popularity, but he is not in my personal pantheon."

"Are you as confident of your talent as Mozart seemed to be when he told the elector who thought he used too many notes, 'Only as many notes as are required.'?"

"I think we live in such a different artistic landscape that while I'm very confident in my capacity to execute my ideas, I don't feel the same kind of objective confidence about the worth of those ideas. I think if you grew up in the Austrian Hungarian scene in the eighteenth century you were probably only exposed to a certain kind of European music and to a series of criteria for what quality was in music. And by any standard, Mozart knew that he was the best working in that milieu. He was like, 'I know objectively I can play better, I can harmonize better. Of course, I am the best.' He wasn't a jerk about it, but he knew. Whereas today, my music is more adventurous than many, but also I'm writing for orchestras, I'm writing pieces for piano and violin, I'm working within a pretty ancient tradition, and I'm writing notes. I'm not exclusively having my players drag their bows across the backs of their violins. Basically what I am getting at is that there are many aesthetic world views right now. I think growing up in the age of Spotify and YouTube it is possible to be exposed to so many of those. I heard some pieces by this young composer, Ashley Fure, who works mostly with non-instrumental objects. She records and notates for them. She does write for instrumental ensembles sometimes, but it is all extended techniques. A couple of her pieces that I heard were so powerful and so viscerally satisfying. She clearly is following cosmic physical laws about the ways that these overtones from scraping this object work. It really gave me pause and made me think, gosh, should I just be working with noises rather than notes. This is a whole other world. I want to keep questioning the worth of what I do, but I do have confidence in my skills. I just don't want to be too bold about what the worth of that is."

"Well, building confidence is an ongoing experience. I would imagine such an event was the time as a Harvard student you famously conducted *The Marriage of Figaro* at Dunster House?"

"I would say it was because we had an orchestra that was much better than any undergraduate non-conservatory orchestra should be. It was just the most stellar group of players and an unusually sympathetic hard-working cast. It wasn't the first thing I ever conducted, but it was the biggest in scale. It certainly did make me think, 'OK, I can do this.'"

"Matthew, I'm impressed by some maverick ideas you have which are very different than some accepted ideas. That is really refreshing. You have already stated some. I'm reminded of a segment you did I saw on YouTube when you analyzed the Count's apology to the countess at the end of *The Marriage of Figaro.* You described what the pervasive mood was at that time, the countess as superior to the count, and the scene being kind of sad. I had never thought of it that way. Were you the first one to see it that way?"

"I don't know. I didn't knowingly take it from anybody. I bet the people who have understood it that way are singers who have sung those roles. I think I've been influenced in my understanding of it through the way that certain great singers have done it. And so I think it is their choices that have led me in a way to that insight."

"Did you talk to some of the sopranos who played the countess about this?"

"No. I have talked with the great, great baritone, Peter Mattei, about the count. Peter is wonderfully outspoken and can be very loquacious as an artist. The way that he identified with the count and made him so sympathetic was to get angry at the count in the way you get angry at yourself when you do something stupid."

"Do you think Mozart when he composed it saw it the way you analyzed it?"

"I do think Mozart saw this dynamic. I do think that it's there intentionally. Why else repeat it in that way? It's the lovers interval, he is projecting. I'm getting chills even just thinking about it. That gesture is the musical equivalent of lying prostrate before somebody."

"You can't take that music as just asking forgiveness in a perfunctory way. The count really means it."

"I think he really means it, and I also think kind of implicit in the whole musical texture is the tragedy that his good intentions are not going to last. I think he is saying I'm so sorry, I'm so sorry, but I think what he means is, I'm so sorry that I am this person. He is not saying he is going to change. The poignancy of it is that everybody has this moment of clarity about their own weaknesses, and there is this cathartic communal moment of getting through it together, but that doesn't mean it is all better. And that's the wisdom of the creators because it would have been so easy for the music to say, presto, it's all fixed. That's not what is being said."

"Matthew, Mozart had this uncanny understanding of human nature when he wrote *Idomeneo,* which we marvel at, in his early twenties, but you seem to have that understanding too. Where does that come from? How did you get that?"

"On one level I want to say that I learned that from Mozart. I think there are people out there with extreme emotional intelligence who aren't artists themselves, and there are artists out there who lack a certain kind of emotional or social intelligence, panache, comfort, call it what you will. I think even though I think of myself as fundamentally an introvert — you sort of have to be an introvert to be a composer — I do think I have always been able to connect one-on-one with others, to display a degree of compassion and a desire to listen closely to friends. I think this is a crucial ingredient in having been blessed with really great friends."

"It is funny you say that, Matthew, because I make friends even at this age with young people, older people, all people. Friendship is a great thing. A friend is somebody you can tell things to."

"It opens you up and you learn things when they open up to you. I totally agree. And I've had friends who have brought me out of my shell, and I've had friends that I've brought out of theirs. I think what I am getting at is that, especially for opera, it is not enough to be virtuosic with the orchestra or in any other technical sense, you also have to have compassion, and have to be interested in the inner lives of others. We always hear about Mozart as one of the greatest touring virtuosos as a kid, but there were plenty of kids who have been touring virtuosos. Somebody who lived an extraordinarily long life who saw both Mozart and Saint-Saens, said that Saint-Saens was better as a performer. Why don't we think of Camille Saint-Saens as being anywhere near Mozart's league? Because Mozart had this emotional understanding, and this emotional neediness, he just needed to be loved, which is why he went after all these women and really got close to whomever he met in his life. And I think it is that characteristic coupled with musical intelligence and a voracious musical appetite and a need to really master every form that distinguishes Mozart. When you bring all those things together you might have an opera composer. I'm realizing this just talking with you. I do think there is something there. I was never like the class clown or the most popular kid or anything like that, but I always had a one-on-one way of connecting with others, and maybe that plus my musicianship will make me an opera composer."

"Well, you may be an introvert, but you don't seem like an introvert to me."

"I guess I'll take that as a compliment."

"So at the Met you worked with James Levine. What are your thoughts about him?"

"It was a nice experience. I actually met Maestro Levine right before he left the BSO. I was a freshman at Harvard and somehow he caught wind that the Lowell House Opera Company was doing *Otello,* which is a piece that most professional opera companies can barely handle. So it was totally insane that LHO was mounting *Otello.* I think Levine must have thought to himself, this I have to see, a semi-professional *Otello* in some dining hall at Harvard. I'm not sure exactly how he heard about my activities as a coach pianist, but he took an interest, we actually met up, and he coached me a bit on Verdi, and conducting Verdi specifically. I was eighteen at the time and had never conducted anything. I was just dipping a toe in the waters of the opera world, so I completely had to pinch myself that I was sitting in a room with a piano with James Levine. Immediately after that he had to leave the BSO and was pretty much incommunicado for the next three years. Ironically, he didn't have anything to do with my being hired at the Met, but shortly after I arrived at the Met he was able to get back there. I ran into him in the hallway, and it's like, 'Hey weren't you that kid at Harvard a few years ago?' And then I did a system on the production of *Figaro. Figaro* seems kind of inescapable. To be frank, by that time he wasn't at his best, and it was a very hard moment at the Met because it was the summer and fall when it looked like there was going to be a strike any day, so tensions were high. The countess in the production was fired because she couldn't sing the role, Levine was in bad shape physically, it was just unpleasant all around. So I really do wish that I could have worked with Levine more closely at some point. I think it would have been really illuminating."

"Have you had any contact with him since then?"

"He said something that pissed me off recently where he opposed the idea that the Met should be doing more new operas. The gist of what he said was that 'some people say that they think the Met should do a new piece every year, but I say I wish there were an opera every year that was worthy of the Met.' To which I wanted to say, 'You know Maestro, if you look at the La Scala schedule from 1858 you're going to see a bunch of forgotten operas, and also you will see *La Traviata.*' The only reason *La Traviata* was written was because they were doing a lot of different new operas. If they only did one every five years, we wouldn't have *Traviata,* or any of those pieces, because you have to try and fail. You have to fail a lot to find the good stuff, and I think under Levine the Met didn't even try. So it is really disingenuous to complain about there not being enough good operas when you personally have prevented them from being programmed. And then you go to a Levine performance of *Der Meistersinger* and it's the greatest thing ever, and you sort of say to yourself, 'Well, of course, this is all he wants to do, he's the best in the world at it.' But it's not fair to composers to talk that way."

"Can opera houses succeed half producing traditional stuff and half doing new stuff?"

"I think that the ideal ratio for a big house is half repertory and half newer pieces. Why? Because half is still plenty for familiar pieces. If the Met did half and half, which seems inconceivable, that would still be fourteen productions of canonical operas every single year. And when I say new, I don't mean it has to be a world premiere. In a way it is every bit as important for an opera done two years ago to reach different audiences. That is because in an age when most operas don't get recorded, a premiere in a particular city is as good as a world premiere. It is the first time those people are hearing it, which is a big thing. So I think it will be essential for the survival of the art form for houses to begin to move towards that ratio. Opera Philadelphia is doing it really well right now, although, of course, it is a smaller company. Whether that is financially sustainable is another question. I kind of doubt it. On the practical side, I think that we are going to see a lot of smaller scale pieces. I don't think that is necessarily a bad thing. It is actually a whole other conversation. I am in the process of founding an ensemble with some friends for smaller scale projects."

"You are. That sounds terrific. Tell me more about that, Matthew?"

"Yes, it's a company of singers, dancers, instrumentalists, a director, and a composer. We call ourselves AMOC, American Modern Opera Company, but pronounced 'a-muck, as in 'to run amok.' And the reason that we are doing it is that I know by now who my favorite colleagues are. I've worked all over the world, I know who the really great artists are, who are of the younger generation, and I want to make stuff with them. I don't want to be beholden to this system that you see in opera houses of every single production has a different cast, so basically it is strangers working with each other anew every time. I think that is so stupid. Why not build deeper relationships with colleagues that you actually want to work with. And with AMOC we are going to do smaller scale things. Ultimately I hope that my smaller scale pieces will be written for them. It is an opera company on the model of a rock band. I hope it works."

"You have said that one won't change the world as an opera composer, one should do something else for that. Do you have any ideas about doing something else non-musical?"

"I should have said that as a composer through music you can't change the course of external public events. I definitely think you can change people's inner lives, and that that's just as important on some level. But on a fundamental level of what our priorities should be, of course it is more important to be feeding people who need food. It seems that human beings as a species do not prioritize certain life essentials as distinctly as one might expect. You might think that before turning to something as frivolous as making art we would have taken care of widespread hunger and poverty, but no. There was art in the caves. It's not something that emerges later, it is actually parallel. So I guess I have faith that it must be a basic human need for others because it feels that it is for me. I do believe I'm doing something that is one of the fundamental human needs. But as far as having an effect on the course of events and on others' fears, I think of myself much more humbly in that way than I do of myself as a musician. I just think of myself as a private citizen who doesn't know that much, who is lucky enough to have some friends who do know a lot more, and to whom I can turn. I have one friend who is a brilliant political reporter who absolutely knows the charities in the world that are the most effective, most lives saved per dollar and so forth, so I'm always consulting him about which ones I should support. I have other friends who are really active as protestors, especially in this age of Trump, and who will remind me to get out there and help or write letters. So these are all activities that for me feel quite separate from making art. I know for some people they are intertwined but I've never bought that."

"Do you see yourself at any age getting more heavily involved in politics or conservation or whatever as a social activist? Do you feel that strongly about it or do you think you have to stay pretty much with what you do?"

"No, I would like to. I would like to be more involved than I am in various issues, including environmental ones. I already feel that I should make more time. What do I do? I go to a protest, I write a letter, I give some money, but those are things that don't actually take huge amounts of time or energy on a daily or weekly basis. So yes, there is some guilt in the back of my brain about that. But I think there will also be a time for it in my life."

"Let's talk about the future, Matthew, and some things about your personality as you understand yourself. You can answer or not answer. I'll refer to your main positive and negative personal characteristics. Let's start with the negatives."

"OK. First thing I would say is that I'm a mess in the sense of messy. I've never been able to keep a room or house organized. The weird thing is that I'm relatively ascetic, so sometimes I can live without buying bare essentials, and yet the room is still a mess of papers and things like that, so it's really bad. My boyfriend, Clay, is much better at this than I am."

"Lots of artists are that way. Are we still on negative characteristics?"

"Extreme disorganization. I have a tendency to put things off, especially when my work is consuming, which it usually is. Then I put off everything else in life. Paying bills and things."

"So you're a little bit of a procrastinator?"

"I think those are the things that crop up the most."

"Is that the worst you can say about yourself? I'm glad I'm not being asked these questions."

"No, I'm trying to think, actually (laughs). I suppose you should ask other people how they feel about dealing with me."

"Do you have any trouble dealing with an orchestra you are rehearsing?"

"No, though sometimes I move too quickly. Sometimes I kind of jump to the next thing before an idea has sunk in. I think really great conductors have an ability to pace things such that the orchestra kind of relaxes into what is happening, and I don't always do that. I guess another negative quality that I've tried to be better about is that I'm not always good at keeping in touch with people, or remembering birthdays, or calling family members, things like that. But I think I'm getting better."

"So let's talk about positive characteristics. Don't be modest, Matthew. I don't know that I'd be so bold as to say we are doing this for posterity, but we may be."

"I think generosity."

"My wife, Lois, taught me that one over the course of a lifetime. She is naturally generous."

"I think definitely it took meeting Clay and being with him for the past couple of years that has made me a better person in a lot of ways."

"I take it that you are talking about generosity towards others as opposed to giving money."

"Yes, definitely. The only other positive characteristic that I can affirm having without question is my total commitment to what I do. I don't have ulterior motives when it comes to making music. I just want to write the best music I possibly can. I work like a dog to do it. I don't know if that is a morally good characteristic — that is an interesting question — but I think artistically it is very helpful."

"If we had had this conversation when I was sixty-five I wouldn't have known quite what you were talking about. But now I know exactly what you are talking about. I'll tell you something, Matthew. I liked the law, and I guess I was rated as a good lawyer, but I never gave it the total commitment I have to writing which I never even knew I had a talent for until I was seventy. And come to find out the best part among all the other good parts is just doing it. It is life enhancing, totally absorbing, and good for one's health."

"Yes, it is a big deal! It gives a shape to pretty much every day. I have not observed weekends since probably high school (laughing). In high school weekends really matter (laughing)."

"Are you open or closed to others? Do you think we covered that one?"

"I'm an interesting blend, I think. It is all about the situation. Certain situations really open people up. I've never been someone who owns the room at a party. That kind of social situation doesn't light me up. On balance though, I think I'm more social than misanthropic."

"Funny or sober?"

"More funny than sober."

"Egotistical or modest?"

"I think (laughs) I care about presenting modesty, but I have an understanding or maybe a mistaken opinion of my own capabilities that is not always what I present. So you can take that however you wish."

"No, I understand perfectly. When the *Kirkus* reviewer of my baseball book called me 'odd, eccentric, idiosyncratic, charming, and inquisitive,' (laughing) I said to myself, that's me."

"There you go. That's it."

"I think the next one is would you call yourself a humanist?"

"Yes. I guess there are multiple forms of humanism. I'm a humanist in the sense that I think human beings really matter because we can feel. Our extreme senses mean that it really, really matters not to cause suffering and to make the best of our powers of sensing things."

"What would you say that your philosophy of life is? Is it something that can be boiled down to 100 words or less (laughing). I'm just kidding."

"If it were one word it would be to give. I feel like what I'm doing when I'm writing music is just like pouring out something that is latent in me, that actually is unformed until I spend my hours and my days giving it a form. This is going to sound corny but I completely believe that everybody has something unformed in them."

"Yes, they do. I believe that. That's why you try to respect everybody. People surprise you."

"Right, you never know what it is until you look. I think the whole goal of education should be to assume that everyone has something that is latent which can be shared, and to help figure out what it is because it's complicated. I don't know what the larger purpose of existence is, obviously none of us do, but I do think that the purpose of living a particular human life is to figure out what you can give and unleashing it. Articulating it doesn't make it sound all that satisfying, but it feels satisfying. That can also mean giving to others, giving love, giving help. I think for some people the essential thing that they have to give is direct help to others. Someone is a born doctor or a born firefighter, whatever, but for some people it is something less direct like a piece of art. That is what it is for me."

"Are you religious?"

"I don't subscribe to any particular organized religion but I somehow consider myself a really religious person. I was raised Catholic."

"Do you go to church at all?"

"No, the way I tell it is that I'm in a family of lapsed Catholics now. I lapsed first and my parents followed suit. I think it was already in their minds. When I was eleven or twelve, the age when you start having to take classes for confirmation, I was being raised on some weak watered-down Catholicism. Maybe if I had had the fear of God struck into me it might have been different. But these ladies volunteering at Sunday School didn't know the first thing about the Bible, so it was easy as a precocious youngster to just see through it. You ask a question and no one knows the answer. So I basically believed that many forms of Christianity and American culture in the 1990s were basically incompatible with each other. It just doesn't work to say you are so special, you are the center of the universe, and also to fear this, to fear that. It didn't add up for me, and so by the time I was heading towards confirmation I said to my parents, 'Look, can I just not be confirmed?' They said 'Sure, just don't tell Grandma!' Then a year or two later they told me that they were leaving the church, but I think their reasons were different than mine. They left because they were so disgusted with how the Catholic Church in Boston handled the pedophilia scandal. My dad, who covers theater for the *Boston Globe,* covered that story. He is probably a minor character in the movie *Spotlight.* He was writing some of those stories and I think for them it was a loss of faith in the institution more than any of the attendants."

"Speaking of your parents, do you have siblings?"

"I have a younger sister, Christine. She is twenty-one and a senior in college."

"Is she a musician?"

"No, she is taking both women's and gender studies, and theatre. My dad became a theatre critic right about when she was entering high school. Unfortunately it was right after I went off to college so I didn't benefit from that quite as much. Christine probably saw two plays a week with him for four years. So she got this incredible theatrical education. She is doing great at Barnard College in New York City."

"Do you consider yourself religious, even though you are a fallen away Catholic?"

"I do, yes."

"Given what you've said, what does that mean? Does it mean you believe in God?"

"I consider myself religious. I think it's that I don't believe that the cosmos has unfolded randomly. I think in a way I align myself with the various kind of Gnostic forms of both Judaism and Christianity which believe that there was a God and that God maybe is the impetus for the universe in a weird kind of after effect. I have the feeling that there was a kind of consciousness at the root. The Big Bang is a flash of insight, the Big Bang is a moment of clarity for some unimaginable consciousness, but I don't think God predicted all the aftereffects of the Big Bang. I don't think God predicted us. I think we've grown out of this initial event. To relate it to the micro level makes sense as an artist. You start with an idea, and then you see this cosmos unfold that is nothing like what you expected it to be. It makes sense. It is also terrifying because there is no end in sight and there is no plan."

"Do you think there is an afterlife?"

"Not for us humans. I'm paraphrasing Kafka here. I don't think that I, Matthew Aucoin, the individual, will keep being conscious after my body dies, I really don't think that. But I do think that all of our consciousnesses are tapping into a very deep well, and so the very fact that an individual can emerge means that there is some kind of hidden template. So I guess I have faith that life will go on. I also think that my consciousness as an individual is a part of that. I'm becoming less articulate. No, I don't believe in individual afterlife though."

"I'm not going to ask you if you think you are a genius, although many have said that. Let me put it this way. Do you think you have what might be called a genius?"

"Not my favorite word (laughing). What interests me about the way people have thought about this is that in the European tradition people talked about artists having a genius rather than being a genius."

"So what do you really think about this?"

"I think I have ideas. I think I have technique. When you put those together a lot can happen. But look, the reason I'm being cagey with this one is that there was this flood of things written about me when I was twenty-three or so. There was an article in the *Wall Street Journal* and in the *New York Times*, Matthew is this and Matthew is that, and the reason the accolades made me so uncomfortable is that I didn't know how big the features were going to be. I knew there was going to be an item. It was in advance of the premiere of *Crossing*. I didn't know I was going to be on the cover of these publications. I didn't know I was going to get the kind of attention that I did. The reason that it made me uncomfortable was that they acted like I had already achieved the things that I hope I'm going to achieve. And it felt like bad karma to act like I've already done things. Of course, I do have a high estimation of my potential, but I don't have an especially high estimation of the things that I wrote two or three years ago."

"Anthony Tommasini in the *New York Times* thought *Crossing* was great!"

"He did, which is great. It is good that he thought so. My own review would have been totally different, though."

"Do you think you can attain the reputation of top people like Mozart, Verdi, Beethoven, Wagner, and Stravinsky?"

"I think that depends a lot on whether there keeps on being a canon the way there has been. Seems like it is in vogue at the moment to tear apart the centrality of these figures. Personally, I do think that all of the composers you just mentioned are as present as they are in our minds because they really were the greatest composers. Again, I would have to say I think the potential is there, but who knows? It is not impossible."

"What besides early demise or illness or accident could stall your advance. Are there any personal characteristics which could hold you back?"

"No, I don't think so. I think I am going to keep doing what I am doing as long as illness or untimely demise don't get in the way."

"Would you say that you want to do great things?"

"I want to write the best music I possibly can, yes."

"In your own mind, Matthew, do you think that you are destined, or have been chosen to do great things in music? Do you ever put your head down on the pillow at night and say, 'God, I've gone a long way so fast and I love what I'm doing, I love giving, and I just think that I can give so much more.'"

"Sure, I have said that. I think I can do so much more. I think it is kind of impossible in this lifetime to definitively distinguish between luck and destiny. I like making a distinction between being lucky and being fortunate. I think the word lucky implies total randomness, whereas in being fortunate there is an element of chance but also you are fortunate because of who you are. And I think I've been both lucky and fortunate in having a lot of people give me support that I thought I wouldn't have, that I really wouldn't have dreamed of. Why was I trying to become a conductor in college? Because I assumed that I would never be able to make a living as a composer. I just figured that if I was going to do music that I would have to make a go of it as a conductor which in itself is a difficult path for a musician. But as it turns out, I conduct for pocket money, but I could live as a composer. That's crazy and that's something that a lot of composers who totally deserved it did not get. The answer to your question about would anything else stall my progress, the thing that could stall it is a loss of time. At the moment I'm incredibly lucky to be able to control my time, to be able to say for this month I'm going to go to Vermont, not answer my cell phone, and just write this piece, because there I can live in it. In a country where the arts are not supported in any central way, I don't want to assume that that's going to be the case for the next fifty years. So there is nothing in my personality that I could imagine getting in the way of my desire to make music, but there are a million external circumstances that could."

"I think people make their own luck, as you have said."

"I would agree with that."

"How do you see your future unfolding given all the interests you have. I think the best thing to do here is to just read them and you'll tell me which of those you might give significant time to. Here we go. Opera composer, orchestral composer, chamber composer, song composer, librettist, poet, piano virtuoso, conductor, writer essayist, critic, author, pedagogue, conservationist, public citizen, politician, author."

"I'll go down the list with you. Actually, I don't see myself as an opera composer more than any other kind of composer. At this point I feel more and more like I'm just a composer and that instrumental works are pretty much as essential as the operas. So opera composer, yes, obviously. Orchestral composer, yes, just as central. Chamber composer, yes, just as central. Song composer, the same. All of that wrapped together under the composer banner. Librettist, much less. I probably will do my own libretto again in my lifetime, but I tell you I am loving working with Sarah Ruhl on the current project. It's so nice to not have to do everything myself. So that sharing of the load for operas is really a great relief. Poet, yes, I'll come back to that someday. I'll be writing some more poems, but I don't know when. Piano virtuoso, not at all. There was probably a time in high school when my right hand could match pretty much anybody's right hand. My left hand was always far behind."

"I noticed when you were conducting the orchestra at the rehearsal today that your fingers are much longer than mine."

"I do have long fingers. I've always had a very good reach; I can reach a tenth or an eleventh at the piano. But what is really curious is that even though I'm mostly left-handed, and I write with my left hand, at the piano my left hand is a lump compared to my right hand. So I was never really capable of mastering the most demanding Chopin or Rachmaninoff, the stuff that requires two hands to really be powerhouses. Conductor, sure, I feel like I conduct for pleasure because I love it, I love the adrenaline of it, I love performing, but I'm not a career conductor. I'm not looking to be music director anywhere. I don't want the responsibilities of having to hear every audition and conduct every goddamn Tchaikovsky symphony every time that there is a gala. I want to be a free agent and conduct when I want. In that sense the career of Thomas Adès is once again a model."

"There are similarities in our personalities, Matthew. I think that has something to do with why this conversation is going so easily."

"Yes, definitely. Writer essayist, yeah, that will come back into the mix. Critic, not so much. Author, I suppose yes in the sense of as a writer-essayist. Pedagogue, that's a good question. You know most of my composer colleagues who are around my age are in doctoral programs and they are already teaching or planning to teach. I love what little teaching I have done, the master classes and visits to various schools. But I actually think that I wouldn't want to teach composition. I don't know what form it would take. Maybe coaching chamber music or teaching literature, who knows in what capacity, but I don't see it as being central for a while."

"Why not teach composition?"

"Because it is so personal, because picking what note comes after the previous note is a really personal thing. I know that composition teachers are essential. You need to be able to impart certain skill, but there are plenty of people who can impart the basic skills. For the really special stuff it somehow feels intrusive. I don't know. Maybe I'll feel differently in ten years. Conservationist, totally amateur. I have an interest in those issues but no expertise. Public citizen, who knows what form that can take, but sure. Politician, no, no chance."

"What is music?"

"It's activated breath. Yes, that is what it is. It's breath, it's the breath of whether it's a voice or a wind instrument or it's the breath of matter. It's a very hard thing to articulate. A violin is a little machine but we, in playing it, treat it like an organism that can speak. So in a quite a literal sense it's the breath, it is what emanates from the organism, and we as human beings and all the other creatures activate their own breath. But they don't make instruments to make other kinds of sounds, but we do. It's the breath of matter."

"What would life be without music? Could you live without music?"

"It would be dry. I don't think music is a freestanding thing, it goes back to what I said about art being in the caves. Music is in so much of what we did. It's hard to even picture a world without music because there is music in speech and there is music in everything that happens, so it's actually not separable."

"What is it that speaks to you within music that you don't get from any other artistic form?"

"Catharsis. Transformation of violence. I think there is a certain kind of physical power or intensity that is required to make a beautiful sound. Playing a clarinet or an instrument is a physical thing which requires a kind of mastery of violence. It is violence transformed into beauty. I think music serves one of the great functions in our world in that it is a release in the way that sports are. It is a rechanneling of an impulse that could do great damage into something that is very beautiful."

"Sort of like Mozart's remark that no matter what is happening on stage the music should be beautiful. Like when the Commendatore was being slain by Don Giovanni. I love the way that his heart stops beating just as the music diminishes and stops."

"Yes. I don't think what I just said is incompatible with that. Even in Mozart the level of mastery requires a kind of controlled violence."

Would that humankind could control violence and transform it into beauty as music does. Certainly a conductor like Thomas Adès on the podium is doing that as he slashes the air with his baton to lead the orchestra to harmonious effect, just as a harpsichordist like Robert Levin in the pit does it as he strikes the keyboard before him with vigor and expels beautiful sound from the instrument, just as a mezzo soprano like Susan Graham does sharply taking in the breath needed to sing her beautiful aria on the operatic stage, or just as when a gifted athlete like Mookie Betts violently swings his bat at a crucial moment before tens of thousands and unleashes a beautiful parabola in the sky to release us from the stress and tension of everyday life. Petroglyphs and petrographs support the belief that man and art began their life cycles contemporaneously eons ago, then quickly diverged. Imaginative, generous, and humanly connected musicians like Matthew Aucoin seek to bring them back into consonance to perhaps rechannel our baser impulses into the creation of a better world.

Leonard Bernstein, shown here already famous as a young man, whose prodigious talents as a conductor, composer, pianist, teacher, and personality, made him the most renowned American musician of the latter half of the twentieth century.

Credit: Photographer unknown, courtesy BSO Archives

Part Two

CONDUCTORS

English conductor Harry Christophers. Photo by Larry Ruttman.

CHAPTER
7

Harry Christophers CBE: Chorister, Conductor, Everyman, and Special Man

Harry Christophers is Everyman as well as a very special man. That is the combination that draws you immediately to him, and keeps you there because of his *joie de vivre,* infectious passion for the music he makes, and his vernacular style telling you about that. Within a minute of my self-introduction to him among a crowd of well-wishers backstage just after he had led a concert of the Handel and Haydn Society at Symphony Hall in Boston I felt safe in jokingly referring to us with lilting voice as, "Harry and Larry," to which he responded lightly and laughingly, "Harry and Larry," a joke that has carried us through to this day. That experience is a metaphor for this wonderfully engaging guy and committed maestro which points back to his modest beginnings close to the other side of the railroad tracks despite his thin connection to Henry VIII. Giving the lie to that lineage, Harry's marital history includes no beheadings, and only one wife, whose acting skills and loving support have aided Harry in achieving early success as a master of period music, as well as bearing him three high-achieving daughters. Long before marriage and family, while growing up poor in Kent, Harry hooked onto classical music forever singing as a chorister at the Canterbury Cathedral. From that time on Harry steadily accumulated his musical chops at a series of renowned locales and groups, as a chorister at Westminster Abbey, then in the Magdalen Choir of Magdalen College, Oxford, and later joining the BBC Singers to continue singing and developing his talents as a conductor under the tutelage of a treasure house of world-class conductors. At that time he also sang with the early music vocal ensemble, The Tallis Scholars. Those stops constituted a quality trip hard to replicate for any aspiring musician. Harry's experiences and natural qualities of leadership prepared him at twenty-seven to form the now renowned early music group, The Sixteen, which has toured all over the UK and beyond for over forty years, bringing to him the fame and respect which impelled Boston's 175-year-old Handel and Haydn Society to reach out across the sea in 2006 to place Harry Christophers at its helm, a ship he still captains today. You can take the boy out of Kent, but you can't take Kent out of the boy. Or stated another way, Harry never really changed despite world success, retaining his love of pop music, football, taking it easy at home on a Saturday or Sunday, cooking up a storm, gardening, and having an all-around good time in the same ways he always had, an unreconstituted Everyman become a special man, lucky for us!

"We are here today in Symphony Hall with Harry Christophers, well-known English conductor, and the conductor of the almost 200-year-old Handel and Haydn Society of Boston. Today they are doing Handel's *Messiah.* Harry, you look a lot younger than your stated age (laughs)!"

"(Laughs) Very kind."

"Harry, I think my first question is, is it true you are related to Henry VIII (laughs)?"

"(Laughs) Oh gosh, no. Well, no, not really. My mother's quite well-known family went all the way back to the Welsh ruler Owain Glyndwr, the first Prince of Wales. She was one of four girls, so the family tree ended there because there were no boys in that family. I know that in my mother's family there were lots of well-known people who were linked to the Tudor family."

"Of course, the reason I ask is because when I looked you up I saw that Tudor was one of your names (Laughs). So I said, 'Could it be?' (laughs) Then I read about your wife and children. Obviously you haven't followed in the path of Henry VIII as far as disposing, beheading, and otherwise discarding wives."

"(Laughs) Oh no, far from that."

"While we are on the subject of wives, I have some questions about your wife Loni. I understand that she is musical and dramatic."

"Yes, she read music at Royal Holloway College, London. She is Veronica, Loni is a sort of nickname. Nobody really understands where that came from. We met, actually, via the very early days of the early music vocal ensemble, The Tallis Scholars. Since then she has followed her love of drama. Now she's a drama teacher. Hence a couple of our children are also in drama."

"Would you say you and your wife were drawn to each other by a mutual interest in music?"

"Yes, music and sport."

"What sport?"

"Football. I mean soccer, as you call it."

"Do you ever watch baseball in this country?"

"No, no, no. We were taken to a Red Sox game once. My wife loved it. It made cricket look interesting to me (laughs)."

"I've read that you and Loni come from different religious backgrounds?"

"Yes, Loni is a Catholic. I got married in a Catholic church. I was brought up in the Anglican Church and was a chorister at Canterbury Cathedral. I was a chorister at Magdalen College, Oxford. I sang at Westminster Abbey. I adore sacred music. You know, faith of some description or another is in everybody. I'm not a regular church goer. Quite frankly I never really think about it that much. I just I love the music. I support my wife's Catholicism, and our children have been brought up Catholic. Not all of them go to church regularly. But as I say, I don't dwell on the subject."

"What have you learned from Loni about music and about life?"

"(Laughs) A lot about life. We always got on terribly well together. She has always been one of my harshest critics, which is great. I'll put programs by her and get her thoughts. She is wonderfully supportive with her ideas. When I left Oxford, I sang for six years professionally. Then I remember deciding I really didn't want to sing anymore. Loni was so supportive of that. I look back and I think, blimey, we'd just gotten married, we'd had a tax bill every January and all sorts of frightening expenses, it was all quite hard, but she was very supportive of what I wanted to do through thick and thin and the early days of The Sixteen, the group I formed in 1977. We had years when things were going well and then years when we were facing real difficulty. We remortgaged a couple of times, but luckily came all the way through that. The Sixteen has come up to be a highly established choir and period instruments orchestra, particularly in the UK. Life with Loni has been good!"

"I can see that. I think you're a happy man. You laugh a lot. That's the impression I had when I met you the first time very briefly. 'Harry and Larry.' You probably remember?"

"Yes, yes."

"How would you describe what it was you wanted to do way back then?"

"You know, my whole life has been a lot of good fortune at the right time because I never really knew what I wanted to do. I love making music. I love having lots of friends. The way I'm shaped has been built on those. That is the way it's been with The Sixteen, and now being here with the Handel & Haydn Society. Developing a camaraderie is half the battle in music. If people get on really well together you make good music together. And the same is true in life to enjoy it to the full."

"Would you say that because of Loni's influence your musical style or your style of conducting has changed?"

"I think not. My style of conducting has to with what I've been doing over the years. When I started The Sixteen it was because of my love of sixteenth-century Renaissance sacred music. As I said, it was around that where Loni and I met. I have an interest in rock music. I've always had an interest in contemporary music. So my tastes went. In many ways Loni has been fascinated by that. She loves most all of music, but she doesn't understand why I like certain types of music. I drive her out of the kitchen when I put on Led Zeppelin, the Rolling Stones, or John Mayer, stuff like that. Over the years I've learned particularly from her love of drama. We have two children who are actors. I've now sort of developed more of a theatrical sense to what I do. Loni and I often talk about those theatrical aspects of music-making."

"I think Aisslinn Nosky, the concertmaster of H & H, is particularly dramatic, theatrical if you like, especially with her red hair?"

"Aisslinn is brilliant! But it's one thing to be deemed sort of flashy and flamboyant and having attention drawn to you by being striking. But it's another thing to also have an incredible gift for music. Aisslinn has an amazing gift. She's a really consummate musician, a fantastic leader, and a great people person spotting personalities. She concentrates on the pluses in people to avoid problems all the time. It's very important. And that's also part of my makeup. As a conductor over the years there's been far too many dictatorial conductors. That's not for me. Some of them make absolutely phenomenal music, but there are other ways to make great music."

"I think you'd say that the duties of not only the concertmaster but also the conductor is to make sure people are on the same page."

"It is, yes. The lovely thing about Baroque and paired music is that all these players know so much about their instruments. For me to be constantly feeding off them, as well as having my own input, means that if there is something that doesn't quite work for them, we'll talk about it and perhaps find another way to achieve whatever my vision is. I just love that interplay."

"Harry, how old are the winds and the other instruments your players use?"

"The wind instruments are copies of old instruments. You've got fantastic collections of old instruments here in the states. In England we have the famous Bates Collection, and the Fitzwilliam Collection, so we know exactly what people were playing in the sixteenth, seventeenth, and eighteenth Centuries. We've replicated those sounds. That is the lovely thing about Baroque music, hearing Bach and Handel played on instruments which sound like those the composers would have heard. To hear modern winds and brass is a completely and utterly different sound. We don't hear the tone colors which Bach absolutely intended. The first trumpet here is like an extension of the first oboe. It's honey sweet sounds, not a blasting instrument designed to go to the back of a huge concert hall."

"What is your instrument, Harry?"

"I used to be a clarinetist. That's what I was at school. I learned from a wonderful military guy, Mike Thatcher, because in those days there were wonderful Marine bands in Canterbury. Actually Mike sold me his instruments in the end. At Oxford I played a lot of clarinet, but then in my last year I had to make a decision whether to sing or play the clarinet. Sadly, I sold my clarinets to put a deposit down for my first flat. Well, not so sad, because I bought the flat."

"Handel's *Messiah* is a staple with the H & H at Christmastime. I guess it began its life for a small group, then expanded over the centuries to a bigger group, and now some people like you have brought it back to a smaller group. Is that the way you prefer it?"

"That is the way I prefer it. The first performance was in Dublin with a very small orchestra. As you say, I think it is lovely to hear it played by a smaller chamber choir and a smaller orchestra. First and foremost it is a phenomenal work, one of the few works which you can say had great popularity during the composer's lifetime which has never lapsed. Doing it here in Symphony Hall the audience will hear wonderful details which get lost in bigger performances. Probably many in the audience don't realize what dedication to detail goes into rehearsing and preparing it."

"Would you call it an entertainment, would you call it intimate, would you call it religious, which of those fits it best?"

"Every single one of those. Handel called it an entertainment to get away from the fact that in London he was being persecuted for even the thought of putting a sacred oratorio into a secular place like a theatre. It was fortuitous for Handel that the first performance was in Dublin away from the awful critics that were about in London at the time. It's a sacred work for the complete Christian year. That's what's extraordinary about it. It's not just for Christmas. It's a passion story about the Resurrection. Often the person that gets left out of the praise for it is Charles Jennens for supplying an incredible libretto in which every single word is from the Bible, be it the Old or New Testament. It is incredibly beautiful!"

"Let's talk about The Sixteen, Harry. I know that you've had fantastic success with The Sixteen for a very long time. What inspired you to take the course of forming them in your twenties?"

"Gosh. Well, it was right after university. Obviously there was some of the conductor in me that wanted to start doing things."

"Were you already a conductor?"

"No, I just did the odd concerts. I've never had any formal training as a conductor. I read Classics when I went off to Oxford. I changed after two years to read music. Classics was so blooming hard! I told Bernard Rose, my music tutor, 'I can't do classics anymore. I'm finding it far too hard. I'd like to change to music.' I remember him saying, 'Well, have you got any music qualifications?' O levels were the exams you took at age fifteen or so, A levels were the exams you took at eighteen to get you into university. I hadn't done music at either point, and so I was a real risk for Rose. He said, 'You know taking harmony and counterpoint and five-part chorus you have to really listen when you are singing it, and you'll be fine.' Anyway, luckily, I was in and I enjoyed it. In my formative year of conducting I was very lucky. I was in the BBC singers for three years and worked with some phenomenal people. I also worked with some pretty awful people. I did some pretty rubbish music. I did some fantastic music. I used to have a little black book and in the front of it were all the pieces I wanted to conduct and in the back of it all the pieces I never wanted to see again."

"(Laughs) Who were some of the phenomenal people?"

"In those days I worked with Pierre Boulez, Seiji Ozawa, Gennady Rozhdestvensky, and Roger Norrington. It was just brilliant. I learned so much from watching, particularly Boulez and Ozawa. Pierre Boulez was amazing. He thought the BBC singers were the bee's knees. Whenever any of his music was being done anywhere in the world, and the choir wasn't any good, he would ask for the BBC Singers. Ozawa had rhythm coming out of his behind. He was fascinating. Rozhdestvensky was an amazing showman with rhythm in his bodily movements. I watched these people like a hawk and I took elements from them. When I was sixteen I saw a performance of the *Verdi Requiem* from St. Paul's Cathedral, but it wasn't the piece that had an effect on me, it was watching the conductor. And this conductor was called Leonard Bernstein. I said to myself how can this guy be so immersed in the music, then feeding off the performers in front of him who were giving it back to him, and then somehow do something extra with his hands that was taking it to the audience behind him. It was kind of a three-way process. I found that absolutely fascinating! It was probably in my subconscious when I started The Sixteen."

"I'm really happy you said all that, Harry. I like the connection to my own hometown because Leonard Bernstein came from Brookline. Speaking of emotions, there were lots of people who said he was too emotional, he jumps up and down, he waves his arms, this that and the other thing, but it didn't bother you, and it never bothered me for the very same reason that it was all in service of communicating the music."

"Absolutely! I have an old recording of his of Haydn's *Creation,* and for somebody who was not a period musician, he got 99% of it right. It was in his bones, he felt it, and that's a lot, that is half the battle. I think here in America period music has got to go much further. I think what we are doing at H & H is absolutely fantastic, but it's got to spread much more outside of Boston. In most of the major concert halls here there is very little period music programmed."

"Seems like you carried that idea forward in England with The Sixteen, Harry?"

"I did. I thought I don't just want my singers to just sing the music on the page and make a beautiful sound. There are lots of people out there who are doing that already. I wanted something extra. I said we've got to communicate with the audience. I'll give you free range. I allow my singers to sing. I might have to rein them in sometimes, but I'm encouraging them as well. They know to watch me like a hawk because I'll do something different every single time. Everything has to be spontaneous in music. I also tell them how important the words are. There are far too many choirs in the world who have singers who don't sing the words. It's the text that has to live. I say to The Sixteen, just go back to Monteverdi, who said sing as you speak. If you do that, you are made. I get so much joy and happiness seeing these people do really well. For me that is the exciting thing about it. If I can be of assistance to any performer in front of me, and make them enjoy what they are doing and allow them to have fantastic careers, that's great! The wonderful thing about music is, it fires our emotions. The wonderful thing about sacred music for me is that it tests our emotions. It can do all sorts of things to us."

"The Sixteen is doing its part. You really get around?"

"We do. Every year I do a tour with a different choral program. We tour thirty-odd venues up and down the country. We love it, we absolutely adore it. It gets us to see England. You know, I had no idea of the cities. We are a small country but I hadn't visited most of the places we have been to. It's absolutely phenomenal. We meet people in these wonderful communities. People listen to us on CD or on the radio, but it is another thing hearing the music live. You've got to hear The Sixteen live to appreciate just what we are about. I think it's the exactly the same for H & H. Come and hear people live and see how we communicate with an audience. That is special."

"It seems to me that sacred music is played more in England than elsewhere in Europe or America?"

"We have a thing in England to try to get as diverse an audience in to hear Renaissance music, or music through the ages. One of the things that I always say to people is that we are taking the Renaissance music of Byrd, Tallis, and Monteverdi, for example, out of context because this music was then an accompaniment to the liturgy. It wasn't the focal point. But they are very great pieces. If those composers had lived later, they would have been orchestral and opera composers. It's just the fact that in the sixteenth century the only employment was in the church or the court. So when opera came in gradually through Monteverdi and his like, and singers started going more into the opera world, music started to diminish in church services. It's a great sadness to me that in places like Spain, France, Italy, and Portugal there is now next to no music in church services. It's bizarre! And it's strange isn't it that in England we had a Reformation all those many many years ago, and somehow church music has been preserved. Today it is in a very good state but needs to be preserved. We are very conscious of that in England with less people going to church to masses and things like that. The music has to be preserved."

"What must be done to make sure that is done?"

"I say it is now up to all of us to try and continue the phenomenal enterprising innovative work done by others, mostly in Europe. I'm thinking of people like Trevor Pinnock and John Eliot Gardiner in England, René Jacobs in Belgium, and the amazing late Nikolaus Harnoncourt in Austria. The list is endless. It is an exciting musical world that we need to preserve. Education is a vital part of it. We suffer in England in a big way with many of the state schools having next to no music being taught in their schools. It is an absolute tragedy. A few years ago the Conservative Minister for Education said there is no room for the arts in the school curriculum. What a statement to make! When the financial crisis happened, when there is any crisis, at those times people are depressed

Italian composer Claudio Monteverdi, muse of Harry Christophers

Credit: Portrait of Claudio Monteverdi, painting by Bernardo Strozzi (1581–1644), via Royal Opera House Covent Garden. *CC BY 2.0*

and they need the arts to give them a sense of reality."

"Same thing here. They had music courses in grammar school when I was a kid, but not anymore. The liberal arts in college are in the dumper too."

"Classics isn't taught. Latin is not taught in schools in England anymore."

"I loved Latin. I don't think I'd be writing books if I hadn't taken Latin."

"Every top spy was a classicist. Where is MI5 now (laughs)?"

"I can see in your face how passionate you are about this. Nobody is going to be thinking about what financier was terrific in 2017, but it's the artists who go on because the arts are so important. I know that you have been active not only in choral music but also in opera and symphonic music. Which means the most to you?"

"The Sixteen is the only choir I've ever conducted apart from being here with H & H. I love conducting orchestras. I've been very lucky in whatever I've conducted because it has always been for the first time, not having been to music college, never having been through a conducting program, or having gone through the repertoire in those early days. So the next Handel oratorio is new to me, I'm looking at it for the first time. I've never heard it, so that's nice. At home I don't really listen to classical music. If I've got time, I'm a big film fan. I love television series too. Loni and I both love the theatre, I love walking, I love getting out in the garden, I like cooking. The busy year of conducting, rehearsing, thinking up new programs, and looking at scores is incredibly time consuming. So I don't sit down and listen to CDs, which is probably a failure of mine. Maybe I should realize what everybody else is doing. But there is a part of me which doesn't like to be influenced by other people. I just like to have my own ideas. The single thing that has improved my approach to Handel oratorios is that more often than not I try and stage them at a smaller festival on a very tight budget. That gives me more insight into the characters. Particularly is that important in Handel, who always was a man of the opera. He defies the idea of oratorios. In so many of them he's got his theatre brains hard at work. We have just done *Saul* here, and the orchestra and chorus really enjoyed it because they realized that it is actually a drama."

"I didn't realize you didn't have a lot of formal training. It could very well be that not listening to a lot of the work of others, you bring your own pure and uninfluenced approach?"

"In the sense of formal training, I was a chorister at Canterbury, where I was trained to sight read music. To be a chorister at ages nine, ten, or eleven in Canterbury Cathedral you are doing a wide repertoire of music day in and day out. You have to get on and do it constantly. Then at Magdalen College Oxford, my love of Renaissance music began purely because of my celebrated tutor, Bernard Rose, then the Director of the Magdalen College Choir. I didn't really know much about it before then. When I went up to Oxford my loves were Mahler, Liszt, Britten, Tippett, and Brahms. At Oxford I discovered Byrd, Tallis,

Sheppard, Palestrina, and de Victoria, a wealth of music. Then it sort of went from there."

"Sounds like a great trip?"

"It was the trip of my life. I got into baroque music and took what I had learned from Renaissance music into baroque music. In a sense I was fast forwarding to life in the sixteenth century, life in the seventeenth century, and life in the eighteenth century. Before I arrived here in Boston, I did my first concert in 2006 with the H & H, their first concert ever in Europe, in Austria at Eisenstadt. For some reason, probably because Haydn had long served in the Esterhazy Palace there, they amazingly asked me to conduct Haydn, whom I didn't really know much about. Don't tell them that, Larry! So I had to do a lot of homework. I realized delving into Haydn that there was much more to Haydn than this person in an encyclopedia who was called, 'The Grandfather of the Symphony.' So your automatic reaction to that is he must be an old fuddy-duddy. Well, far from it. I soon appreciated the wit and emotions in his music. Now I regard Haydn as a greater symphonic composer than Mozart."

"Really, That's something!"

"There are so many symphonies, and so much in them. I think that is what is important. Somebody asked Zubin Mehta why he didn't conduct Haydn very much. He said it's too difficult for symphony orchestras because it is a discipline. I remember once doing a Haydn symphony with the BBC Philharmonic in Manchester in England. The concertmaster came to me and said, 'Harry we should be doing Haydn once a month.' It's just an incredible discipline. The strings were scared stiff of it, There is so much in the music to get. Mozart is much easier."

"Harry, before I get into some questions that sound simple which maybe you won't answer simply (both laugh), I want to ask you whether you are still attracted to rock and pop music concerts?"

"Yes, I listen to a lot of it, but not at concerts anymore. When the kids were younger, we went to hear 4 the Cause at Wembley Stadium. One of my big regrets is that I'd have loved to have been to a Stones or Led Zeppelin concert live. I lived as a schoolboy in Canterbury. My dad had a sweet and tobacconist shop in Castle Street. We lived behind it. It was really small. I was born in a little pub in the depths of Kent, so there was never really any money in the family. But I had a fantastic childhood, I loved it. Opportunities were blessedly given to me by someone which made it possible to have good schooling in Canterbury. I have a lot to thank Canterbury Cathedral for. So I didn't have any money to go to pop concerts, and pop concerts didn't come to Canterbury."

"How about later on?"

"When I went up to Oxford, I had an eclectic LP selection which my son rediscovered a couple of years ago while looking after the house for us. He texted me and said, 'Dad you've got an incredible LP collection up there, including Led Zeppelin, Genesis, and all sorts of things. But, Dad, I'm a bit worried about your

4 LPs of David Essex.' I'm a bit embarrassed about that as well. I love it. When I cook, because my wife decided she doesn't like cooking and actually I do enjoy cooking, that is my time to listen. On goes the iPod and it will be anything ranging from Ben Folds to Led Zep, to Chuck Johnson, to Bonnie Raitt. So my kids have kept me abreast of all sorts of pop things. The latest one they got me interested in was The Low Anthem. So my taste is eclectic there. Other than that, I'm listening to classical CDs. If I am at home alone on a Sunday afternoon, out will come the Mahler symphonies. I'll blast them. Or Stravinsky. I'm passionate about Stravinsky."

"You are definitely a man for all seasons, Harry."

"If I'm not listening to music on a Sunday afternoon, and Arsenal is on the television, then I'll be fixed on the game because I am a big Arsenal supporter. If I can get up to a game at the Arsenal, then I'll be up there. That takes priority, not going to a concert. There is an Arsenal supporters bar here in Boston on Boylston Street."

"A question often asked is whether classical music will go on? It is hard to draw young people in, but pop music draws these fantastic crowds. Why does pop music draw young people the way it does?"

"Pop is what young people want to do. It's not cool to go to classical music. It is not cool to sing in a choir at school, or to play sport, it is not cool to play in an orchestra. I think there is room for all types of music. Actually we've got ourselves to blame for the state of the industry, if you wanted to call it that, for not cultivating younger people. It comes all the way back to education, right to young kids at the primary level. When we've got the young kids at school, let them sing pop songs, but let's also be introducing them to a simple aria by Handel done well. It is how we educate young people that makes it possible for them to come to concerts, how we make them realize they don't have to dress up in a suit and tie. Let them come wearing whatever they want. I think Bostonians have accepted me for what I am, wearing training shoes and jeans most of the time. We do need to be breaking down those barriers, and it goes right back to education. There is no point in saying how are we going to present Handel's *Messiah* in Symphony Hall in a different way. We are not! If we added lighting, added all sorts of gimmicks, and had the ladies all dressed up in glittery dresses and the guys all wearing Red Sox tee shirts, that's not going to do it. That's just dumbing down."

"Let me see if I can gather my thoughts about classical and pop because I don't know that I'll get a chance to speak to somebody like you who came from the background you did. You hear people say classical music is so great, it's so inspiring, and pop music is a bunch of crap, some of it's good but most of it is terrible. Some will say it's not really the music, it's the beat, it's being with other people, it just doesn't compare. Others will say music is music and it doesn't matter whether it is classical or popular, there are great artists on both sides, and we will be listening to Mozart and Beethoven in a couple of hundred years and we may very well be listening to Mick Jagger and Elvis Presley then too. Probably the primary way that human beings express themselves across language barriers and national barriers is by music. So Harry, you're the perfect person to say which camp you are in, or is it all just music and let it go at that?"

"There is a lot of rubbish pop music about. Most of that rubbish pop music is geared to total commercialism, *America's Got Talent*, *Britain's Got Talent*, all those sort of things. That's the stuff that I despise. Ironically, sometimes a talent emerges from that is actually quite good. I suppose in a sense all the pop music that I like is from bands that have had total faith in themselves and have made it through thick and thin. It is staggering that groups like The Rolling Stones are still here, guys who were Hellraisers back in the 60s and 70s and now are pillars of the community. Another area in music that annoys me is classical crossover. I just don't understand it. It is totally commercial. You get people who call themselves opera singers because they sing opera arias, but they have never sung on an opera stage before. It is horrendous. The great thing about popular music is when it is good it reflects popular culture. Like the different rap music, Rastafarian music, whatever. There are all these different cultures, and there are some out there who are doing their own thing. I find it fascinating. My niece runs Music Introduction International in Manchester, England, which brings refugees together through music. Hearing their horrendous stories, be it from Serbia or Iran or anywhere on the news you don't really believe them, but when you hear the stories and music from people who actually had those awful things done to them, and see their different cultures coming together, you think how phenomenal that is."

"Would you put popular pop music on the same level as classical music?"

"It is different, very different. I don't put theatre on the same level as film. They are two completely different things. We can get enjoyment from both."

"Can humans live without music?"

"I don't think I can. I can't live without music. I can believe people who say they can."

"Is that living? Is music so central to being a happy person that human beings need it on a constant basis, maybe not three times a day like food, but often. Even cavemen had forms of music."

"I suppose the answer is, no, you can't live without music. I certainly can't."

"So what is music? Where does it come from? Where does it go?"

"Music is a sound; music is the silence. Some composers have changed their whole compositional style to go back to silence."

"To you, what is music?"

"To me music is beauty. Just the same as art is beauty."

"Where does it come from? You can say a composer composes it, but where does it come from?"

"It comes from the heart like performing comes from the heart, and the pulse comes from the heart."

"From the heart. From beating, the beat. Where does it go? I mean when you leave a concert?"

"It is with you when you leave a concert. When I have done a recording session, or some music has really moved you, those sounds are in your mind. You wake up the next morning and sometimes it could be an infuriating phrase that you really want to get rid of. When you hear somebody else singing it you think, oh no, please stop. Don't put it in my mind anymore. But most of the time it is lovely."

"Do you hear music in your head?"

"All the time."

"What is the main thing in music that speaks to you?"

"That's very, very hard (pause). Personality in the sense of the personal nature of music. Not necessarily delving into what the composer was thinking at the time, but for me trying to look at it and thinking you know this person. I'm thinking particularly of sacred music because that is what I've spent most of my life doing. I find it very exciting when you see a composer actually trying to put their own feelings across in the text that they are writing. I love seeing their personal touches, but I also like being able to put my personality onto it. That doesn't really explain it. I sort of know what I mean."

It would be presumptuous to say precisely what Harry Christophers meant in that last answer, but suffice to say he said enough there and previously to define the man and his music. He seeks to connect with those of times long before and with those of his own time personally across the bridge of sacred music, and to respond in kind with the warmth and power of his own personality. Musicians are collaborators, and Harry Christophers collaborates on a divine level, whichever meaning of that word you care to apply.

Swiss conductor Charles Dutoit and his wife, Canadian violinist Chantal Juillet.

Photo by Larry Ruttman.

CHAPTER
8

Charles Dutoit: World-Traveling Maestro

An inquisitive and intrepid visitor over his octogenarian lifetime to every country in the world, it can be said that Maestro Charles Dutoit has likewise visited a wide world of musical landscapes in bringing the joys of music to listeners everywhere. Born into ordinary circumstances in Switzerland, he learned his craft under the tutelage of master maestros like Herbert von Karajan and Ernest Ansermet, who likely were drawn to Charles as much by his unassuming persona as by his quick musical mind. Dutoit began his conducting career while still in his twenties and has gone on to become an octogenarian orchestral master who still leads a multiplicity of distinguished ensembles in the world's great music. One might ask how his travels to every land have influenced his thoughts about conducting and music-making, and his ability to deliver unusually arresting performances to his listeners?

My own view as to why Maestro Charles Dutoit has been impelled to visit all those countries, including both arctic regions, is because of his love of all people and his inborn curiosity about all things. His travels had nothing to do with how some people collect countries like trinkets. They have had everything to do with his world view, which has expanded exponentially over a lifetime as his experiences have been absorbed into his psyche in a way that has increasingly empowered him to make music so humanistic and so attuned to the feelings of his players, his audiences, and himself as to defy articulation. It has to be felt! Always popular as his repute grew, Charles Dutoit moving into his eighties was more popular and sought out than ever, a musician still with worlds to conquer, still masterfully communicating love.

Charles Dutoit suffered some bad press in late 2017, causing a temporary decline in his career which is now being reversed. Less than a year later he was appointed effective immediately as the principal guest conductor of the St.

Petersburg Philharmonic Orchestra. Previous to that in September 2017, Dutoit conducted three programs of the European Philharmonic of Switzerland at Montreux featuring renowned pianist and his one-time wife, Martha Argerich, spoken of in this story. Plainly Charles Dutoit has loyal admirers who recognize that his ripened and overarching talent should remain to enrich our lives.

A good place to start is in Switzerland, one of the smallest countries in the world, and Charles Dutoit's native land.

"Were you parents musical, and how old were you when you came to music?"

"Not at all. No, no, nothing. I mean my mother had a nice little voice and she probably sang in a church somewhere, but no, no music. When I was six or seven at school, I was tap-tapping like this (Charles taps), and somehow with good rhythm. Like a drum, and people noticed. So that was the first feeling I had about music."

"That was like Mozart."

"(laughs) Oh, Mozart had already composed. No, I started music very late. In fact, only when I was in college. When I went to the college after primary school, there was a band. I wanted to be in the band. They had the hat with the pom-pom, you know. But my father didn't like the trombone. He discovered that there were some violin lessons given in the college which were subsidized. So he sent me there. I didn't like it at all. But anyway, I practiced a little bit, but only until the time when a friend in college took me to some concerts, to some lessons, and to a music class on the history of music. I met people who started to wake me up to music. Then, frankly, I started to study a little better. I was thirteen already. Then it went very fast. I studied and I played in orchestras. By the time I was twenty-one I already had my diploma in conducting at the conservatory in Geneva. So in seven years I had to catch up on a lot of things."

"You learned fast! How did you get to the viola?"

"Because of my parents' needs. I wouldn't say we were poor, but very humble. I had to earn my living very early. There was a shortage of viola players, and I could earn some money playing the viola. And because I was studying and then conducting, it was easier to play the viola, which is less difficult than the violin because you don't have to practice six or seven hours a day. Also, I was a member of a string quartet, and the viola parts were very interesting. So that's how it was."

"There were some legendary musicians you were involved with early on, now passed on. First of all, the great Austrian conductor, Herbert von Karajan. What was your impression of him?" (Charles' answer shows how serendipity often figures in how our lives turn out, or maybe it shows how Charles' felicitous personality played a part in that, or maybe both).

"I played under von Karajan as a student. I was in a youth orchestra in Lucerne where he was giving master classes. I played second stand or first violin. Also, I was interested in conducting. I learned enormously from that experience. He had this incredible personality. His secretary was Mr. Mattoni, a very rich guy from the famous Mattoni mineral waters company in Czechoslovakia. Mattoni and I were sort of good friends. We were at a reception sitting next to each other. I said I was going to Venice, and he said, 'Oh, I'm going to Italy. If you want I can take you at least to Milan, no, in my car.' I said 'OK.' I had no money, so I was very happy. I went to Milan and there was von Karajan already, who also had been at that reception, and he was staying at the same hotel in Milan. He was going to Florence, and Mattoni arranged it so I could go with von Karajan in his car. He had a Mercedes 300S! So I drove with him two hundred or so kilometers all the way to Brescia. So OK, that was my first experience with him."

"I wish I had come along. That must have been an interesting ride?"

"He had yet to conduct Stravinsky's, *The Rite of Spring*, for the first time when he heard that I had done it. In 1964, it was still considered a hard piece. So von Karajan was very curious about this young man who had done it. So he invited me to come to Vienna, and there I made my debut at the famous Wiener Staatsoper doing *The Three-Cornered Hat* ballet by Manuel de Falla. That ballet was first given in London in 1919 with sets and costumes by Pablo Picasso and choreography by Leonide Massine, and conducted by my own mentor, Ernest Ansermet. So the whole thing just went. I saw von Karajan in every rehearsal possible of his operas. He was conducting a lot of things. He had an enormous influence on me in terms of my style, sound, and so on. That was one school of music, the German school. The other school, of course, was Ansermet, Berlioz, and the French school. Von Karajan was coming from the German or Berlin school of Wilhelm Furtwangler, Richard Wagner, and Arthur Nikisch. Two different schools. So for a Swiss like me it's important to know both sides because we speak both German and Italian. So our culture is mixed."

"Even earlier, Charles, I see you had made a mark. Tell us about meeting your first wife, pianist, Martha Argerich, making music with her, and like you, advanced from small beginnings in Argentina to world fame?"

"Yes, we were good friends from the very beginning. She was a little younger, five years younger. She had won the Geneva piano competition, which was very important at that time, and also fifteen days before that she had won the Busoni competition in Italy. She was living in Geneva with some friends, and I was studying in the *conservatoire* there. We became good friends. I had just been in Argentina for the first time, playing the viola and leading a chamber orchestra. We decided to tour together. We went by boat, eighteen days on the way down, had the long tour of South America, and came back by boat. Martha was very interested in what I had to say. We later became very good friends. She was my first soloist. She was studying the Ravel piano concerto. I said I have my first concert in a few months, my first contract, so why don't you appear with me? She said she had never played this piece in concert. She's not exactly the kind of pupil who would practice a lot of things. She liked to go all over the place with her friends. But she learned it and she was my first soloist. It was on the seventh of January 1959."

Thus early on Charles was demonstrating his love of the peripatetic life which would play such a big role in his advance as a man and a musician. "What was the most memorable of all of those countries you've visited?"

"That depends on your point of view. Is it for the beauty of the countryside, for the beauty of the city, for the culture, for the danger, or is it for the people? There are one hundred ninety-six countries."

"I'm curious as to why you came to be interested in WWII between the United States and Japan?"

"I came to America for the first time in 1959 when I was a student at Tanglewood. I went to Japan for the first time in 1969. I went there as a conductor in 1970 for the Osaka World Fair. Then was the first time Japan had opened up a little bit. I conducted the best orchestra there, the NHK Symphony Orchestra of Tokyo, often in the next ten years or so. I went there so many times that I conducted every orchestra you can think of. I have an enormous admiration for Japan, the culture, the politeness, the care of the people. But there also were some mysterious things going on during the war, a very strange attitude because the emperor Hirohito was considered to be God. I read a lot about the history of Japan. I love history. I wanted to see what happened during the Pacific war, why the Japanese were with Hitler, why did they attack Pearl Harbor, why all those battles? It is interesting to me to understand world history, but especially the history of Japan, the emperor, and General MacArthur. I had to understand the country. That was the reason."

"Did you study the war from the American side?"

"I did. I made the whole trip from Pearl Harbor all the way to Hiroshima, visiting every battlefield, including Guadalcanal and Iwo Jima. I wanted to understand both sides. I met many people in the islands of the Pacific where I traveled to understand WWII."

"We spoke of South America. Did you meet some interesting folks there?"

"A long time ago in Manaus in the state of Amazonas I met a Frenchman who had been a prisoner in French Guyana. He took me on a two-week trip in a small launch along the Amazon into the deep forest. The Amazon rises during the rainy season, and the whole area becomes flooded. We spent five or six days with Indians. I got very sick. But this man was incredible. People like that."

"Did you have any bad or scary experiences, Charles?"

"The worst place I have visited is Somaliland. I wanted to go to Mogadishu. I met a man there who was a native. He warned me, 'Don't go to Mogadishu. It's very dangerous.' Anyway, I went. I took a plane, and on the plane there was a superbly dressed Italian guy who said, 'You're going to Mogadishu? Do you have your bodyguards? Oh, my goodness be careful!' Still, I went there, and indeed it was frightening. Every five hundred meters there was a guy coming out of the bush with a gun. I had rented a kind of pickup. I was sitting next to the driver. After a few kilometers I said to the driver, 'Oh, my God, you know what? I forgot my passport and my money in the plane. Can we go back? I cannot pay you if we don't go back.' That was a trick, of course. So we went back. I gave him twenty dollars, and I went back to the plane before he left. This is the only place where I went back. It was terrifying to see these people come out of the bush all the time!"

"Sounds like the right decision to me, Charles. Better than being pirated away! On any of your many trips, other than that incident, did you feel that your life was ever threatened?"

"No. I've been twice to North Korea. I had no problem there. On my second trip there I met some fantastic musicians there who were crying because they had no contact with anyone outside. I played with them a little bit, and their sound was changing after only twenty minutes. Those guys had never heard themselves like that. I didn't give any concerts there. I was there trying to arrange a youth orchestra for a festival between South Korea and North Korea. We were well received, of course. I met so many people. Musicians are the same in every country, whether they're North Korean, American, or Indian. They play music. Twenty-five members of this orchestra with which I worked with for only ninety minutes came to the airport to bid me farewell. So it was a very touching experience. No, the only problem that I had was that one in Somalia."

"How do you prepare for your trips?"

"I read many books. Before every visit I was reading books. I never went to any country without preparation, and without knowing exactly what I wanted to see and do, and what to eat. I absolutely wanted to avoid comparing the country I was visiting with what I knew of other places, even with Switzerland. If you go to a place and you start to compare with what you have at home, it's finished, because we are spoiled and selfish and wealthy, and think we are the best. We think others cannot be better than we here in America or in Europe. We have the money, we have everything, and these guys don't. No, it's not like that! We have to understand why these countries are what they are. And there are many reasons for that. Sometimes they are in trouble because of us, because of colonialism. Colonialism has absolutely damaged Africa, and today we still are suffering, and they are still suffering, because of these conditions which were established during colonial days, and continued when we left the countries as they were. Then the tribes started to fight to get power. Unbelievable! We are responsible, you are responsible, America is responsible, I am responsible for many such things in the world. It's better to understand from their point of view what is going on there, and why it is like that. Everything we have represents our vision of the world. The world is not like that. There are other points of view."

"So would you say you are a citizen of the world or a Swiss citizen, Charles?"

"I'm Swiss, but when I say I'm Swiss I'm not proud of that in any exclusive sense. For example, I like and admire the Italian people. When you see an Italian person anywhere in the world, they will talk about the village they come from.

It's not that they are proud or pretentious, it's just the heart speaking. Even the Boston Symphony driver here, Peppino, talks about where he comes from in Italy. It's their roots, the village where they grew up, the language, the culture, the food. So that's it."

"What will be your next great travel adventure? Have you been to the North Pole or the South Pole?"

"Yes, and yes. I've been to Point Barrow in Alaska, the northernmost point of the United States. I've been to Antarctica. It's international territory, you know. I've done many concerts in Russia. Last year I was in Siberia where we played at the festival in Novosibirsk. I've been in Moscow several times, and I've traveled with several orchestras in Russia. I've been everywhere in Russia, including in the far east of Siberia on the Kamchatka Peninsula and in the Kolyma region which was made famous by Solzhenitsyn in *The Gulag Archipelago.* Yes, I was there."

"Amazing, Charles! You know, I interviewed Mark Volpe, the manager of the BSO, the other day, and I also had a conversation with him out in Tanglewood this summer. Both times, when your name came up, he said with wonder in his voice that you have been in every country in the world! How many people can say that?"

"Probably not so many. Many people have seen a lot of countries, but to have seen all of them, you must want to do that. I mean some of the countries in Africa are not so interesting. But I always found something interesting. Some people just go to the major places like Berlin and Tokyo, but some countries are very hidden."

"Charles, let's go on to your remarkable musical career. When you came to Montreal to direct the Orchestre Symphonique de Montreal in 1977, you were already forty years old. It seems to me that then your already successful career went straight up?"

"When I arrived in Montreal in 1977 the orchestra was OK, but without any special personality or color. So I had to build up what I thought was important. The reason is that I wanted London Decca, for which I was already recording in London and Los Angeles, to come to Montreal. They did come. I did build discipline into the orchestra, not discipline like a schoolteacher. No! Musical discipline, musical attitude. It took me two years. Of course, it was a bit like a drill to coach the orchestra to respond very quickly. Decca was very happy with our very first recording. It so happened that that time was the very beginning of the digital era when the first compact discs came out, ours being the fourth one ever published. It became heard around the world because of curiosity about the sound which we had really cultivated and learned. It was a huge success and the beginning of a long association with Decca, for which I did almost one hundred records with the Montreal Symphony. It's only half of what my total production is because I have recorded with many other orchestras. But with Montreal and we won many recording prizes, and we did thirty-seven tours."

Charles statement is modest when placed against the astounding numbers of his career: forty international awards and distinctions, including in 2017 the very rarely given Royal Philharmonic Society Gold Medal for "outstanding musicianship," been the music director of eleven symphony orchestras, recorded with 23 different symphony orchestras, won 87 prizes, two Grammys, nine Grammy nominations, and still counting!

"What personal qualities do you possess that allow you to be so successful as a world-class conductor?"

"It's very important to be brought up in a broad system of culture. You cannot be a musician just out of the blue. Some of the young people I see today, especially people coming from Asia, play music of the West, but they don't know much about it. So I encourage them always to be interested in the social values at the time of the composition, what was the economy or the politics, why is Beethoven who he is, why is Mozart who he is? Because there was the French Revolution in between those two, which influenced the mind and the writing."

Certainly a view of Charles Dutoit from a world-class violin player who has performed in an elite orchestra often led by Charles would be qualified to inform us of his unique merits as a conductor. That would be Cecylia Arzewski, who played for Charles during the years she became the Assistant Concertmaster of the Boston Symphony Orchestra under Seiji Ozawa. Later, she ascended to become one of the earliest female concertmasters, serving for close to twenty years at the Atlanta Symphony Orchestra in that capacity. Cecylia, well-known for not being over the top, but well-known for her directness, put it to me this way:

"Oh, Dutoit! Dutoit has his repertoire which is mostly French music. He has a wonderful flair for music which is something that Ozawa never did, and when he used to come to Boston during that time, it was great! Dutoit is very different. He is very spontaneous. When he came here when Ozawa was the music director the orchestra sounded great, just great, great, great! The orchestra always appreciated Charles Dutoit being here. It was a good match."

"I think your world view and your world experiences have had some sort of osmotic effect on the way you conduct and the way you present pieces of music?"

"Exactly. We are all the result of where you were born, what you have done, what was the environment in which you grew up, and what was your ambition growing up."

"As you look at musical education in the academy and in the conservatories do you think it could be done differently to bring out personal qualities in the way young musicians do music so that it comes more from the heart, and not mechanically?"

"I can. Many people are teaching an instrument as an instrument and that's it. But we are talking about a broader approach to music. There are some very good teachers in the world. But the average teacher is just concerned about playing the music mechanically. I'm talking about the broader world. If I had to open a class, I would insist that part of the education would be the relationship of musical education to other history. Not only that you know the technique."

"When we think of musicians, we think of all that practice. Did you practice a lot?"

"Another thing is the quality of work, the technique of learning. I have not learned at times because all my teachers were telling me to practice. But they never gave me a technique of practicing. No discipline. Practice, go and practice! One has to learn how to practice. One has to learn the rules of how to study a score, to study the musical forms, to study the orchestration. And for conductors, to learn rehearsal technique which is a very special thing. You cannot tell an orchestra 'we are not together, let's do it again'. Because everyone knows we're not together. One has to be like a doctor who makes a diagnosis of a problem to find the way to solve it. To find the remedy. This is what a conductor should be. All these things I think I've learned by myself digging into a lot of unknown things, and also by having an enormous experience as a playing musician. Also, by conducting in every field, chamber music, choir, modern music, super modern music, music from the old time. In Montreal in twenty-five years I have conducted 2,045 different pieces of 565 composers. I don't know if you understand what that means? It's probably three times as much as the Boston Symphony did during the same period of time."

"I was at the concert last night for the colossal Berlioz *Te Deum*. I observed that at eighty you have terrific energy and staying power. I can see it in all your motions. There was a good feeling among the players right to the end of that long piece. I love the way you defer to other people, like you did to the lead bassist, Edwin Barker. You did it backstage too. You tell people, 'no, no, no, you go first, you go first.' You show a certain respect for your compatriots, a word I use advisedly because you are a world citizen, whether the performers or the audience."

"Frankly, I never forget that a conductor is a piece of nothing without an orchestra. It's like a driver without a car."

"A manager of a baseball team without players."

"Yeah, you see! I was very grateful that Edwin did a tricky part in the piece so well. I was going off stage and had forgotten to call him out. So I went over to him and said, 'Oh, I forgot you.' We need the people. I mean you can be selfish if you're a violinist or a pianist. It's not only that you need them, but it's the whole pleasure and the whole satisfaction that you get. It comes from embracing all that. It doesn't mean you don't have to be tough sometimes. For instance, in Montreal I had to be extremely severe about discipline because the challenges were so enormous. I had to work them very hard. Some people resent that."

"What personal qualities do you wish you had had in greater measure?"

"Many qualities, who doesn't? I would say one thing is that I realize I haven't enough time. I'm getting older. If you are curious, and you are, and I am, we are curious, we want to know more. And once you want to know more, the more

French composer Hector Berlioz, muse of Charles Dutoit

Credit: Hector Berlioz de F.-X. Dupré (Petit Palais, Paris). Photo by Jean-Pierre Dalbéra, CC BY 2.0.

you know, the more you realize that you know very little, really. For me this is an extremely dramatic thing because I feel that I embrace so many things, but I know nothing or very little compared to what I would like to know. And I regret one thing, which is not having had that feeling as a young person when I had more time to absorb all these things."

"What single person affected the course of your life the most personally?"

"There are two. One was a man. He was the director of the Conservatory in Neuchatel, a small town in Switzerland. He was a very cultivated man. He read everything, every week one or two books. And I was young. He was a friend of the family. I saw him a lot. He was a pianist also. And he's the one whom I must thank for having opened up my mind to many things. Literature, especially literature, and the arts. And also politics. He gave me a paid subscription to *Le Monde*, an important newspaper in Paris, which he believed was the best written, best informed, and least biased newspaper in France. He gave me a one-year subscription to this newspaper as a Christmas present. I received it every day. I was only seventeen then, but it made a big difference."

"What was his name?"

"Roger Boss. We played piano together. So that's one. Of course, there are also my wives. I've been married several times and I must give credit to some of them, you know. Especially my last one right here! (Charles beckoning to nearby Chantal Juillet at this point) Chantal is fantastic."

"Yes, she's your business manager. Do you ever play music with her?"

"Of course. She has played all over the world as a violinist. She played here with the Boston Symphony two or three times as a soloist. But she has put aside her career for now because she doesn't want to travel alone and prefers to live her life with me. She doesn't play very much these days. She is on a long sabbatical."

"Tell us about your children, Charles?"

"I have two children. My daughter, Anne-Catherine, the daughter of Martha Argerich, is a very bright girl. She has a doctorate from Columbia University in literature and teaches comparative world literature at the University of Tempe in Scottsdale, Arizona. She has two children who are wonderful. My son, Ivan, is a successful producer in the entertainment industry. He lives in Santa Monica and has two great kids. I don't get to see them much because of scheduling."

"As a conductor, what do you find yourself prioritizing when you approach a piece, the composer's intent as you understand it, or just what you see in the score?"

"It's a mixture of everything. I mean the score is what the composer has left, so from there you have to go a little bit back to see what he meant. We know what he meant if he writes crescendo. But this crescendo concerns an enormous number of musicians. So the balances are important. If you write forte for a flute, or for a trombone, it's a different level, you see. So when you have a dynamic for the whole orchestra, you have to adjust all these things to make it sound good. It's a science. It's a real science. Now this is only the technical point. It's important to understand the score in the context of when the piece was written. Not just for whatever musical reasons there might be, but for the historical context."

"What might be a prime example of that?"

"Take Beethoven for example. Beethoven was shaken by the French Revolution. Mozart much less so because he died in 1791, only two years after the French Revolution. The French Revolution changed the context culturally and politically. It brought democracy to the people. The idea was that the people should have access to everything. So concerts were run for the people. Before that concerts were only for the Church or for the prince, not for the people. So suddenly and democratically new concerts had to be organized. That was the start of the symphony orchestra, the business of conducting, and also the repertoire. Before then music was written to be played on the spot and soon was forgotten. Bach had not been played much between 1750 and 1825. Practically nothing. Composers knew the music because of Bach's technique. But the people did not. So the repertoire started to open up to modern life. And where we are at now is actually the result of all that."

"So it's important for the conductor to know history, both generally and musically?"

"All this history is important for a musician to understand. More precisely, a score is the result of the mind of a person. What is hidden in the score? When you see a painting, it's a painting. I'm sure if you look at a painting and I look at the same painting, we may not see it in exactly the same way. A sculpture might be there, and you may feel one thing and I would feel something else looking at it or touching it. But music is a mystery because it's only a score, it's an abstraction. You have to take that and let it talk to you. So it's very different. Everyone takes whatever he can from that and sends these messages to the listeners. It's not the case for painting or for architecture. Those are made, they are there, they will always be there. But music is always changing. Styles have changed. Beethoven is not so much of the Furtwangler school anymore. He's more like this new school of British conductors like Neville Marriner and John Eliot Gardiner, who are musicologists, you see. So this has changed.

"Today, look at the young conductors. They all conduct Mahler, Bruckner, and the others at the age of twenty-five or so. I could never touch a Bruckner symphony at that age because it was reserved to the German school. It's not the case anymore. So music changes in a deep way. The score remains the same. Whereas the sculpture stays the same. You can look at it your way differently, but it won't be different. But music will never be the same because everyone plays it differently. That's it."

"In my own lifetime it seems that since 1960 or so there is a lot of Gustav Mahler being played. So it does change."

"Mahler was not played until 1960. A little bit was previously by a few conductors like Bruno Walter. The German conductors were not conducting Mahler because he was Jewish. Now Mahler is very popular. Suddenly it seemed that the world discovered Mahler for the first time in the seventies. It's really incredible that Mahler wasn't played at all. He said, 'My time will come.' And it did. But the repertoire has changed now because pieces by Mahler and others are so long. Most of them take up a full evening. Shostakovich also was not played, and now he's played everywhere. So many composers, in a way, have died: Hindemith, Honegger, Roussel, many composers who were played in the fifties are not played much now because there is not enough room for them in the repertoire."

"When you play classical music do you think that the audience is gaining something from the hearing, from the sound, from what's expressed, that makes them better human beings?"

"It should be yes, because I think the mission of the arts is to bring something greater to everyone. When you come to hear a Mahler symphony or a Beethoven symphony, obviously you want to have a moment at a higher altitude, so to speak. Then it's not only pure entertainment."

"What do you think is the future of classical music?"

"I think classical music will survive. But classical concerts are too expensive. Artists are too expensive, the orchestras are too expensive, and opera is unbelievably expensive. You cannot pay two or three hundred dollars to go to a concert, or six or seven hundred dollars to go to an opera. Young people can't do that. It's impossible. So even if they open concerts for the young people, they are busy doing other things to which they have access free of charge on YouTube. People of my generation, especially in America, wanted to be part of the community, and as a citizen it was important to support an institution which was growing and important for the development of a city. Today the people are too busy. They travel. They cannot buy a twelve-concert subscription because some of them will be in Alaska, or wherever. Life has changed so much."

"Are people like Elvis Presley and Bob Dylan going to be more popular in a hundred years than Mozart and Beethoven?"

"I don't think so. Mozart, Beethoven, these people are the crown jewels of our civilization. They always will be."

"What is music?"

"What is music? Oh no, don't ask me this question. What is music? I don't know. What is music? Music exists in sound. Sound exists in everything. You have ears for sound. The sound exists in nature. Music developed little by little combined with dancing. If you go to Africa, they still have these bongos, and they dance. Then you add the flutes, and the evening breeze. In old Egypt they already had flutes and instruments like that. And it grew up, it grew up, it grew up! Then came the band."

"You might also say, then came religion?"

"Very important is that Christianity has developed the arts tremendously because being the Church, they always had to have painters, sculptors. and artists to build these superb cathedrals and fill them with sound, to paint this, to put sculptures there. They had organs. Music was important in the cult. So until the Renaissance, music was there in the church. Palestrina and all those other composers existed because the Church needed them. They had a choir; they had an orchestra. The Catholic church always had instruments. Music went up and up, and up! The Christian religion allowed this development. The first music was always religious. Little by little music became more instrumental with Bach and the development of the keyboard. Then came the classics.

"What would life be without music? But maybe the better question is what came first the chicken or the egg? What comes first, music and then life, or life and then music? Would we be human beings without music?"

"It is hard to even answer this question because music existed from the very beginning. It may have been only rhythm, but they needed this kind of personal expression. This was the start of music. I'm talking about the physical necessity of having music (Charles starts stomping his feet here). And so music came to exist. Look at history from the very, very beginning."

That short quote tells us all we need to know about Maestro Charles Dutoit, his feeling for people, music, history, and expressiveness. It speaks of a truly cultivated man of the whole world, incapable of conducting boring or perfunctory music, always offering music which reaches into our hearts and minds.

American conductor Gil Rose. Photo by Julias Ahn.

CHAPTER
9

Gil Rose: Conductor and Impresario

Gil Rose could have taken an easy road to fame and fortune. He chose a more difficult one to fame to be sure, but the fortune part is still out of range. Most world-class conductors continuously program the warhorse compositions of dead composers like Mozart, Beethoven, Wagner, Verdi, Tchaikovsky, and others. Sure, their music is great, but do we need to hear it quite so many times to the exclusion of new music, and the forgotten compositions of the old masters, even some by the masters just named. Along comes Gil Rose, emerging out of Pittsburgh with no musical pedigree at his back, but a passionate desire to present to the public contemporary and new music, as well as those old masters. To prove what a lonely road Gil Rose chose you will be hard pressed to find elsewhere in the world many of the kinds of musical ensembles Gil has founded in Boston, making that city the capital of this repertory worldwide. Mention the Boston Modern Orchestra Project, known more affectionately as BMOP, and personages from Pulitzer Prize-winning composer, John Harbison on down, exult in praise for what Gil and his musicians have done and continue to do. The same goes for Odyssey Opera, Gil's other group in The Athens of America, which as its name suggests, ventures to distant shores to bring new operas to the boards, as well as neglected old ones of masters like Massenet, Dvořák, and Richard Wagner. Odyssey's predecessor, Opera Boston, where Gil was the Artistic Director from 2003 to its money challenged closure in 2012, presented many operas there, including Thomas Adès's acclaimed *Powder Her Face,* and the premiere of the Pulitzer Prize-winning, *Madame White Snake*, by Zhou Long, which blends the musical traditions of East and West. Such venturesome programming is Gil Rose's anodyne to the failing fortunes of classical music, and it has drawn a committed response and attendance from fans near and far. But what about funding these enterprises? Gil's great musical talent requires he supplement it with business acumen to keep costs down. This jack-of-all-trades is meeting that challenge so far, despite the fact that a jolt here or there could send it all into the trash bin. Gil is also committed and contributes to the long established Monadnock Music Festival in Peterborough New Hampshire, where he is the Artistic Director, finding time to belt out a cycle of Beethoven's nine symphonies. Gil Rose is a devotee of the Great American Songbook too. "C'mon along, c'mon along...." for the story of Gil Rose's, anything but ragtime, bands. For good measure, take a deep and revealing look into the facets of conductorial wit, wisdom, and musicianship which have brought Gil Rose to the pinnacle of his art.

"We're here today with Gil Rose, the well-known conductor of the Boston Modern Orchestra project, Odyssey Opera, and Monadnock Music. You're a busy guy, Gil. You are described as a champion of new and contemporary music.

"Were your parents musicians?"

"No, neither of them."

"So how did you get involved in music?"

"I did what a lot of kids growing up in a middle-class environment do, I played an instrument in the Pittsburgh public school system. I remember one day playing in a band in junior high school an arrangement of Wagner's *Tannhauser Overture*, and something in my head went off. That's what happens! Something will open you up, crack you open, when you least expect it!"

"That makes me think about teaching music in grade and high school in this country. It was when I went to school. I see it has fallen by the wayside?"

"It's a shame. We will suffer the consequences, not because we won't create great musicians because that will happen by itself. But we will not create great audiences which great musicians require."

"How old were you when you left Pittsburgh?"

"Seventeen when I went off to the College Conservatory at the University of Cincinnati. Then I moved back to Pittsburgh and hung around there for a year or two. I went next to graduate school for conducting at Carnegie Mellon School of Music in Pittsburgh, never having conducted before. So I stayed in Pittsburgh those four or five years, and that was it."

"At what age did it occur to you to become a champion of new music?"

"I think that for me it was not a matter of picking new music to champion, but the idea of picking under-preserved repertoire. I could have just as easily been an early music specialist or someone who specializes in romantic music that doesn't get performed very often. It was more a decision about how to bring to the world pieces that don't get played often or been left behind or forgotten. I think that led naturally to championing modern twentieth-century music and recently new music."

"What impelled you in that direction both in terms of events in your life and your own inner thought processes?"

"I think that it was some of both. When you start out as a conductor to make a career you have to have a reason for people to listen to what you have to say. I think that impelled me to explore alternative or niche repertoires. It was a personal decision too which went hand in hand with the practical reality. I was always more interested, fascinated really, in finding out why certain pieces disappeared, some undeservedly and some for good reason. So at the same time I wanted to contribute something that no one else was contributing."

"I think you're doing that. I remember in my twenties they did Mozart's miraculous opera, *Idomeneo,* at that time relatively unknown, now repertoire, and I walked away absolutely in seventh heaven."

"Yes, absolutely those things can be championed and can appear and then stick. That is always gratifying."

"Are there any particular mentors or musicians who were involved in your early development that you would like to talk about?"

"I had teachers like all conductors, but conducting is a little different than playing an instrument. Conductors are a certain type of person. I always felt that the best thing you can do for conductors is to mentor them. My training was a normal kind of path. I went through a university system studying conducting at a graduate level, and then went out on my own to seek my fame and fortune. I'm still at that. I think the old way that conductors were trained a hundred years ago is probably a better model then the university system which churns out conductors to go teach at universities so they can go churn out more conductors. The old relationship of conductors was mentorial. They served as mentors to younger conductors, not so much as teachers, but more as a model. You can teach people practical things about conducting. But I think in many ways it's true that conductors are born not made. They are a certain personality type. They have all kinds of needs, some of them positive, some negative. I try to concentrate on the positive ones if I can. There is a need to organize, there's a need to be in charge, some people need to be seen at the center of things, others not so much. I did have mentors, but I don't feel like I really had teachers. I learned more in my life as a conductor watching other conductors than I ever did talking with them. There was a time when I was a cover conductor at the Boston Symphony Orchestra. I would assist with various famous guest conductors who came through. Sometimes you learn a lot more watching them from off the podium than on the podium. I think that was one of the best learning experiences I've had."

"I suppose off the podium they interacted with the players and others?"

"I learned a lot by watching how they interacted with people. Conducting is a physical activity, a musical activity, and an artistic activity, but it's also a social activity. I think that I've always been kind of interested in that dynamic between people and conductors, especially orchestras and conductors. I'm still learning about that."

"What was most impressive to you about these conductors?"

"Both Christoph von Dohnanyi and the late Rafael Frühbeck de Burgos impressed me a lot with their complete knowledge of the score that they were conducting. All conductors are put in a position where they have to do a score that they don't know as well as a Beethoven symphony. Maybe it's a premier or you have a piece thrown at you late in the game. But I don't think I ever saw Frühbeck de Burgos conduct a piece that he didn't really, really know backwards and forwards and upside down. That gives you strength on the podium."

"Is there a difference between conductors who lead in a manner a little bit removed from the orchestra, and those that are more close socially with orchestra members? And which of those would describe you?"

"Both in a way, I always say that there two types of conductors. There are those who are interested in conducting and those who are interested in music. I prefer those interested in music. Conducting is an act in which there is no exact way to do it. Everybody has to make it work for themselves."

"Would you say your style is unique in conducting?"

"Me? No, I wouldn't say I'm unique. I'm a unique person. Maybe that makes me a unique conductor."

"How are you a unique person?"

"I'm not very interested in a lot of extra physical gesture. I'm interested in getting into a focused centered position as a conductor without a lot of gesturing. If you watch me in a concert and say that my feet never moved, I'll feel very good. For me the bigger the gesture the more diffused it is."

"So, Gil, how did you react to Leonard Bernstein who was effusive to a fault?"

"Bernstein made it work. He was a great musician and a great conductor. Every conductor has his or her own set of tricks that they bring because of their personality and experience."

"You're right. You have to be who you are."

"Yeah, orchestras can smell when you're genuine and smell when you're a fraud in a second. They don't have to know that, they can't tell you why they know that, they just can. They know who is there for the music and who is there for themselves. I'm there for the music as much as I can be."

"Do you have music in your head?"

"I think the best composers do hear music in their head. Their imagination hears something which they put on paper. When I look at a score, I don't hear the music in technicolor but I hear it in sort of a black and white version. That is the best metaphor I can make for it."

"Do you dream about music?"

"I've often dreamt about music, but not recently. There was a time in my life when I did dream about music a lot."

"Do you ever hear the sounds of music in your mind?"

"I do. I hear it, but not in the way I would hear it with my own ear. I think there's a difference. Mental hearing is different."

"Does music ever come into your mind unbidden?"

"(Pause) I don't think anyone has asked me a question like that before. I had to think about it for a minute. It's usually tunes that I have forgotten. I quite distinctly remember dreaming about a Sibelius symphony. I'm not quite sure how I dreamt it (laughs). I dreamt it from beginning to end. I didn't think I knew it, but evidently my brain had stuck it aside somewhere. It was a force. It was a strange experience."

"Do you have any strange or unusual experiences having to do with music which just come upon you during your very busy days?"

"I make time to listen to music every day. I do it first thing in the morning because it's before the heat of battle of the day starts. I'm also very calm at that point so I'm open for listening. I'm very methodical about what I listen to. I'm always searching to fill in my understanding of music by understanding repertoire, having a comprehensive understanding of basic repertoire as well as far flung repertoire. I'll start down a path and stick with it for months. One time, not so long ago, on a daily basis I listened straight through to all the Bach sacred Cantatas in a row by BWV number. You can't do that in a matter of days. I spread it over a six-to-eight-month period. It was a very interesting experience for me. I make these little listening projects for myself all the time. Sometimes I'll pick a piece and listen to twenty different versions of it. It's like the activity of a medieval scribe who just through the rogue act of tracing the activity of someone or something has incorporated it into himself. It's also like stamp collecting. It's a process. It's your granola or your roughage, something you need to do every day to keep your brain operating in a certain way."

"When you're preparing a piece of music to give whether it's a new piece you've never done before, do you listen to other renditions of it?"

"Never. If I have a question I can't figure out, I'll reference something. But never as an idea for choosing tempo. For me that just feels cheap. I will often afterwards take a listen to see what people thought about it. To conduct effectively, even if it's something you've never done before, I feel it has to come from within, that you have to make decisions that come from your own understanding of the score. That is where the mental hearing comes in. When you bring that to rehearsal then you have a whole different reality in front of you. You have to be able to adapt."

"Do you adapt in the rehearsal process. How does that happen?"

"On many occasions I've gone into rehearsal with some piece that I hadn't conducted before and thought, 'Wow, I really figured this out wrong! I have to do it differently.' You work making music with an orchestra. It is an active improvisatory thing. For me the best performances are the ones where the conductor comes to the table with an idea of what he wants and where he's going to go with it but is also open to the moment. My favorite concerts are ones where something special happens at an unexpected moment. I have to admit that I like the thinking of Sir Thomas Beecham who often said that an orchestra plays best when they are slightly under rehearsed as opposed to being over rehearsed where the mind wanders. Under rehearsed may not be as technically clean as over rehearsed but it's not as alive either. Players will often say I don't like to rehearse,

I like to play. I feel pretty comfortable going into a concert being at the 92nd percentile of readiness. It's exciting to go into a concert that way. Getting it too right is not for me."

"Yes, you want to be spontaneous. Your personality comes out and maybe the personalities of the players as well?"

"If you develop a trust, however you do it, the players will afford you that opportunity and go with you. You have to afford them the same opportunity back, take space, take a line. Leopold Stokowski talked a lot about the interaction of the conductor with players in the actual performance."

"Stokowski was a personality. He had lots of wives, like André Previn, another great musician still with us."

"It's funny you mention André Previn. I don't know André Previn personally, but when I was a boy growing up in Pittsburgh, he was the conductor of the Pittsburgh Symphony. He was the first famous conductor I knew. I went to his concerts and remember his music-making which I found very attractive, especially his interest in and quite clear command of English music, to which I'm drawn. I like his jazz and movie background too. Being an improviser, and also his very comprehensive and varied background as an arranger, makes him better, and can't help but inform his conducting style."

"His conducting style is elegant. Not a lot of motion. Did you like the way he conducted?"

"Previn used a lot of arms when he was younger. Physical style changes as one gets older. I think he became more economical than when he first became a famous conductor. He came out of nowhere. All of a sudden he was music director in Houston, then conducting the London Symphony and making recordings. In Pittsburgh he had that PBS television program, *Previn and the Pittsburgh.* He was much like Bernstein in the way he was a populizer and a communicator. He was a more extravagant and flamboyant conductor in those days."

"Gil, I've often wondered what it feels like to be a conductor, up there all by yourself on a raised platform with the audience behind you?"

"It's a funny position (pause). Someone once told me it's the only profession other than a priest where you have an audience on both sides of you, in front of you, and in back of you. You are being judged from all directions constantly. It takes a certain kind of personality to do it. Most conductors have a common thread although it manifests itself differently with each person. There are very flamboyant conductors and very reserved conductors, but they're all out there on the lip of the stage putting themselves on the line. It takes some bravery. It's a very vulnerable place to be sometimes."

"Do you feel vulnerable or comfortable?"

"(Pause) That's an interesting question. I do feel comfortable. I don't have issues of stage fright or conducting orchestras I don't know. Yes, I feel comfortable. I feel like I'm in the place where I'm supposed to be."

"Do you feel you're a person who has sound self-confidence or do you second guess yourself? You told me you second guess yourself on your interpretations."

"I don't know if I would characterize that as second guessing. There are many, many valid ways to interpret a piece of music, even something as standard as a Beethoven symphony. If you look at famous conductors knowing the arc of their careers, even just knowing how they interpreted Beethoven symphonies, they change their position on how they interpret the symphonies. There is no one way to play a Beethoven symphony. There is no bible on it. It's a mistake to think that a composition is not a living thing that changes, and continues to change, and will continue to change (pause). So I don't think so much about whether I'm second guessing myself. I feel like I'm there doing my job to the best of my ability. I will do some things right and some things wrong like anybody does any job, and keep pursuing my larger goals which drive me to do it. Being on the podium is not my goal. My goal is to produce music that is important for the public to know about and to hear in a vital way. if I could do that from the trumpet section I would do it from the trumpet section but I don't play the trumpet."

"But you were talking before about some people need to be something. How much do you need to be a conductor?"

"At different times in my life I've thought different things about that. If anybody needs to be a conductor, I would worry about that. I don't need to be a conductor. I could be a farmer."

"Do you need to be a musician? What if someone took that away from you?"

"I don't think I need to be anything."

"That's a good thing."

"Could be. Maybe it would be better if I did need to be something. Who knows? These are questions which get to motivation, the motivation being whether you're there to serve your own needs, emotional, personal, psychological, or whether you're there to serve the general good of music-making and its vitality, and what music-making brings to public understanding and public discourse."

"That means much more to you?"

"Yes, much more than conducting. I think it is important for me to make music, but there are a million ways to make music. You can be a player, you can be a conductor, you can be an educator, you can be a pedagogue, you can be a record producer, you can make music a lot of different ways."

"Gil, let's talk a little bit about dealing with composers. I can imagine that can be difficult at times? The composer gives you the score, you have to study the score in order to make the music. But then you have a lot of other things to worry about besides the composer."

"Each composer is different. I've dealt with a lot of different ones of different ages and different eras. Dealing with composers gets back to social management. Some composers are very hands off. Some are very involved. Some (pause) wish they were the conductor. Some are glad they are not. Everyone comes in a different package. So you have to immediately interpret them to be successful, and I haven't always been successful."

"You're talking now about living composers?"

"Yes. It's easier with the dead ones. The living ones you interact with personally are just like people. You get on with some, you don't get along with others. You take the assignment to do your best to bring their music to its best realization. You have to read each of them. After a while you have to help them help themselves sometimes because they have a different perspective then the conductor or the players, and so you're acting as a go between in a way between what they want and how to get to what they want. Sometimes you have to cajole them, sometimes you have to trick them, sometimes you have to listen to what they say because they're right. You make it up as you go along. Every person I've ever dealt with has been different. I've worked with some strong personalities, and some needed help to be the strong musical personalities they are."

"Do you have some rules of thumb you follow to accomplish that?"

"I wish I could say there was a rule of thumb. I think in conducting there are very few rules of thumb. There is a lot of dancing in front of the curtain where you have to know how to interact with people. Sometimes you have to be tough. Sometimes you have to be supportive. Those decisions are almost always instantaneous. The best ones come naturally. You can read the situation, read people, and that helps to get to the goal line which is the best performance or recording of the piece. I don't have any rules."

"What about the dead ones? Are they particularly influential when you're preparing the piece Do you ever say to yourself, 'My God, this is Beethoven, I have to follow his tempo markings'?"

"Actually, I say the opposite to myself. Tempo is a discussion that comes up with conductors all the time. Their primary function is the tempo function. They have other functions too. But the right tempo to make something sound properly is a result of the music, the space, the people who are playing it, and the humidity (laughs). There are a million factors that make something work or not work. Of course the metronome is a fixed point of reference."

"Mozart didn't have the metronome."

"Mozart didn't have one, but Mozart had something I think was better. Adagio meant something in Mozart's time, as opposed to andante. That meant there was a give and take in andante, and that meant there was a give and take in adagio, and in molto allegro and allegro con fuoco, and in whatever the marking was. They all implied something within probably a range of six metronome marks. That flexibility is very useful to making something sound right because it all depends on who you're playing it with, where you're playing it, what time of day it is, your own personal energy level, all sorts of things. If you give yourself a little leeway and not be too dogmatic about the tempo, I think you can make it sound. That's what I always try to get to happen, to make it pop and to make it sound. There is a sweet spot. Sometimes Beethoven's metronome markings are for me too fast. I understand the scholarship around them, and I applaud the early music people who have been instrumental in stripping away some of this heavy handedness in Beethoven symphonies that had become self-indulgent. Beethoven may have gotten a little too dogmatic in the sense that his markings may have restricted us from letting the music breathe. I think the dead composer leaves you the metronome markings as references to help you get started. I don't think they're rules. I don't feel bad if I take a Beethoven metronome marking slower then marked. I don't feel like Beethoven is staring down at me with a lightning bolt or something to give me the you know what."

"Mozart certainly wouldn't because even in the month or two between the time of the *Magic Flute* and the time he died actors were parodying that opera, and he was sitting up there in the balcony loving it."

"I have often experienced conductors who will cite a rule or a quote from Wagner or somebody who said this or that about how a Beethoven symphony should be played. I think that hiding behind the rules too much is a way of taking the spontaneity out of music-making. That is a security device for a conductor. I think you should feel free to find rubato where it is and not find it where it isn't."

"The remark you made about Mozart that fascinated me is that he never writes anything in an even numbered denominator. I interpret that as sort of laudatory of Mozart."

"I probably made that quote in reference to finding Mozart the hardest composer to memorize. It just drives me crazy! I can memorize Beethoven very quickly. In Brahms there is something about the logic in it that makes it easy. Maybe its linear, maybe its mathematical, or maybe it's something in the architecture so that it comes to me much more easily. But Mozart will do something for five bars, then change characters completely for two and three-quarter bars, and then change characters again for one and a half bars, then go back to the first thing, but this time it's not five bars, it's three bars."

"It sounds pretty amazing!"

"It is amazing and fabulous, but it's really hard to memorize."

"Gil, I made a list of some recent composers. It includes Lukas Foss whom you are featuring at Monadnock this coming Summer. I know you could talk about him all day. Here is the list: Harbison, Glass, Unsuk Chin, Machover, Babbitt, Foss, Carter, Schuller, Golijov, Bermel, and Rakowski. How would you categorize them?"

"Some of them are old and dead. For me they are either traditionalists or not traditionalists, they are either following out some kind of lineage of compositional thought, or reacting to it or against it, or ignoring it. Like Derek Bermel is not thinking about any of that. You mentioned the late Gunther Schuller who was following a certain lineage. David Rakowski is sort of making his own lineage. They all have their own perspective on how they are reacting to the twentieth-century canon."

"It seems to me Gil that you've been involved in all phases and all periods of music whether it's Baroque, Romantic, Wagner, the first part of the twentieth century, the second part of the twentieth century, new music, you name it. It seems you love all music."

"I feel really happy about that. Yes, all kinds of it. The last three years of my life I've been listening almost exclusively to Renaissance music. There's no conducting connected with that, but I find it very fascinating to listen to."

"What is your favorite form of music? Is it opera, classical, contemporary, chamber, or something else?"

"I don't think I have any favorite form of music. I don't have any favorite form of drama either."

"What is your favorite form to conduct?"

"That's a different question. It is just as varied as the repertoire eras as you were just mentioning. There are different kinds of conducting experiences. For me one of the things I love the most is working with a really good singer, and that moment when you are working side by side. Not side by side actually, you are quite far apart, but you are communicating back and forth. You know where the singer is going to go and the singer knows where you are going to go. There comes a moment when you really connect with each other. That is a really wonderful feeling! I've had that feeling a handful of times. It is rare when it happens."

"Mostly male or female?"

"(Pause) Both, both (firmly). Mostly female though."

"Have you ever fallen in love with one of your female leads? Others have."

"I'll decline to answer (laughing). I'll decline to answer on the grounds it may incriminate me (pause). I'm in love with all of them actually."

"There are some who are really nice-looking."

"Yeah, but I'm in love with all of them. In a way you have to be to be effective in opera."

"Mozart conducted his own operas and kept falling in love with his leading ladies, but they didn't necessarily fall in love with him. But you're better looking than Mozart, Gil."

"You do have to cultivate a special relationship with the leading ladies. The men stand for themselves. That is a different relationship (pause). I actually have fallen in love with all of them. Even the ones I didn't like."

"Would you say that BMOP is the major venue for contemporary music in the United States?"

"Yes. I'd say BMOP is the most important and most productive American orchestra dedicated exclusively to twentieth-century and new music."

"You have also said that performing new music should be the core of music-making. What do you mean by that?"

"I have a strong opinion about this. Beethoven would not recognize our symphonic or operatic culture today. The model that we've established at these major orchestras and big opera companies of staying with their subscription models doesn't really work anymore. Employing four employees for every orchestra member requires a certain safety in programming that will guarantee we play only to the lowest common denominator to our public. Beethoven would never have recognized that. Our system has developed to a point where a major symphony orchestra plays ninety-seven percent of its music by composers who died more than a hundred years ago. There is nothing healthy about that, nothing intellectually stimulating about that, nothing artistically viable about that. It's a shirking of the institution's responsibilities for the sake of safety. It's a dead end. It will be the death of us all. It will be the death of classical music! But classical music is like a cockroach, it'll survive an atomic war. Music will survive. But that model is going to take a lot of people down with it."

"So your model is a better model?"

"I think it's Beethoven's model. I think that orchestras, opera companies, and summer music festivals should be advocating for the best of what was, alongside the best of what is, and the best of what will be. To only program over and over and over the same repertoire is a mind-numbing gutless act."

"Do you see the future for BMOP according to the Beethoven model you just expounded?"

"We'll see how sustainable it is. The thing about that attitude is that it's not a lucrative one, it's not a safe one, but I believe it is the correct one. My orchestra is known for contemporary music, but it was not formed with the explicit idea of performing contemporary music. It was actually more formed on the idea of making a more flexible, less overhead driven orchestra model so that contemporary music and unknown pieces could be done. If you played the Lukas Foss First Symphony at a major symphony orchestra, you'd lose audience. I can guarantee you that if the audience had been there because you advertised it as the Tchaikovsky Fifth Symphony, but instead made an announcement from the podium, 'Oops, we can't play the Tchaikovsky tonight for whatever reason, we have to play Lukas Foss First Symphony,' and started playing it before people could escape, everyone would adore the Foss symphony. So why the hell do they have to hear the Tchaikovsky Fifth Symphony again? I know how it ends, there's no drama in it for me anymore. I know how it ends!"

"Do you ever go and listen to those warhorses?"

"Not as much as I used to. But I do play them."

"Do you play them in a different way?"

"No, the world will survive just fine if I never do another Brahms symphony cycle. I'm doing the Beethoven for the Monadnock Festival because it's about doing Beethoven beside Ned Rorem. The mission of the festival is more encompassing of all eras."

"How big a problem is monetary survival for what you do?"

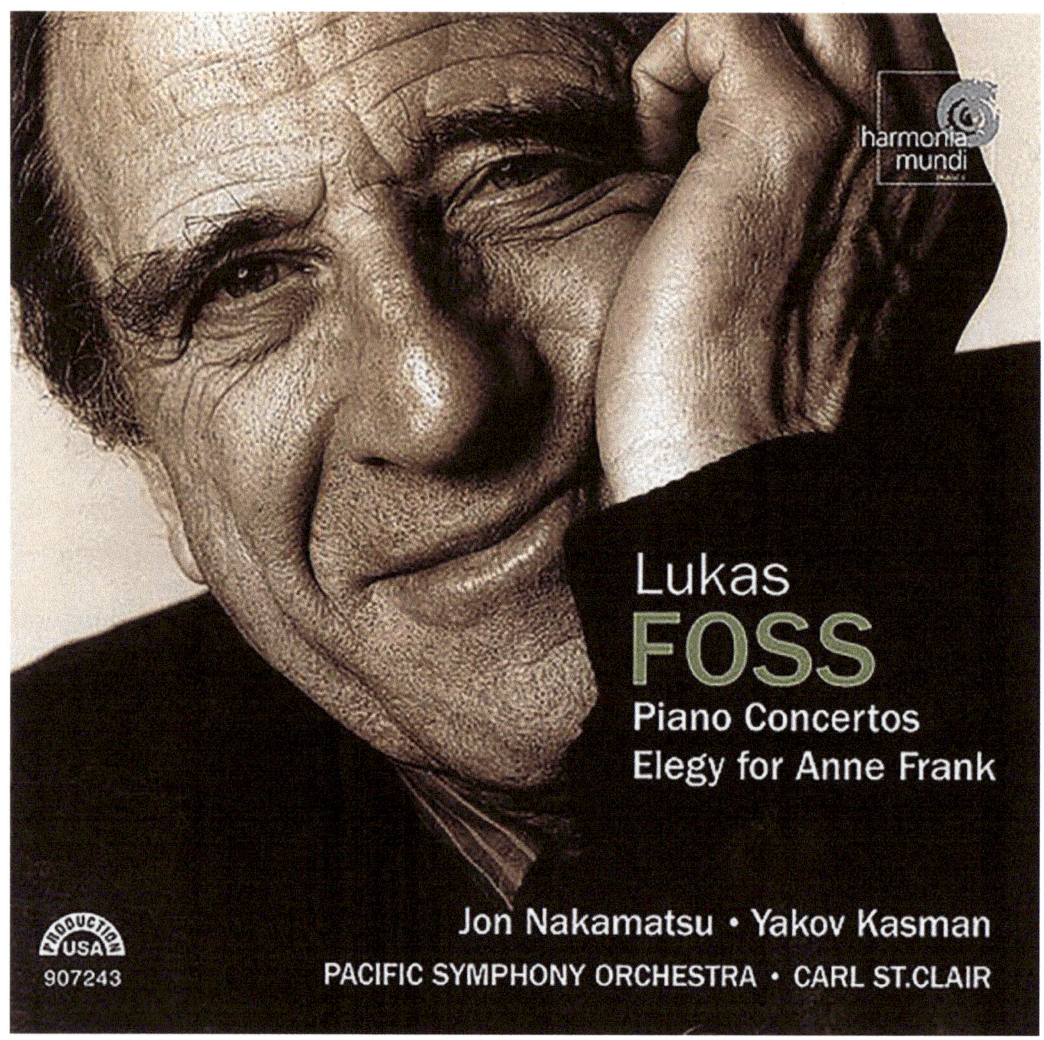

American composer Lukas Foss, muse of Gil Rose

Credit: Photograph of "Lukas Foss Piano Concertos Elegy For Anne Frank Jon Nakamatsu Harmonia Mundi" by iClassical.com, CC BY 2.0

"Keeping three nonprofits alive with progressive agendas is an absolute survival problem!"

"You are doing something that takes individuality. Maybe this is what you mean by the word 'unique.'"

"I think so. All three of the organizations I lead could be gone with a couple of bad breaks."

"I notice John Harbison said no other city has anything resembling BMOP?"

"That's true. There is a lot of new music in this country scaled for small ensembles. The financial support network that's out there for new music is for organizations that have a yearly budget of $150,000 or so. BMOP's yearly budget is $1.2 million."

"Does anything like BMOP exist in any other city?"

"There is a group in New York called the American Composers Orchestra that started under that model, but over the years they shrunk down into a much smaller model (pause). BMOP launched a record label that just released its fifty-fifth CD. No organization I know of in the world with a one-million-dollar budget has ever done anything like that."

"In this industry how many CDs would you have to sell to make one profitable?"

"You couldn't do it. BMOP has now produced fifty-five CDs on its own label and another sixteen or so on other labels, and not one of those projects ever came close in sales revenue to recouping the cost of making the CD. Maybe the most popular one has recouped up to one-third of the cost."

"Do you have some regular corporate as well as individual supporters?"

"More foundations. Not so much corporate, because corporate funding is so tied to advertising, and for advertising you want the big audiences, and for the big audiences you have to have the Tchaikovsky Fifth!"

"With the three ensembles you lead, I guess you have to be a lean and mean businessman to be an effective orchestra administrator. Do you feel comfortable wheeling and dealing?"

"Yes, for the same reason I feel comfortable on the podium, because I feel like I'm doing it in service of something important. Nobody likes to raise money for projects, but if you're doing it to raise money for something valuable and unique, like recording Lukas Foss's never-recorded symphonies, and you feel like they are important enough to be part of the public canon, it gives you the authority to ask for money. If you lead anything with the goal of producing something that is a value added to society all kinds of strengths arise from that."

"Do you spread the word on the road a lot?"

"No, we don't tour much. But we usually go somewhere each year. This coming year we are pleased to be playing some concerts at the Library of Congress."

"Gil, in what way are the workings of your mind different from other leaders that send you off on this quest for new and unknown music?"

"Who knows (pause)? I think the quest for alternative repertoire is one I've just always been on. I've always been a repertoire wonk. I have a big CD collection. If somebody releases some unknown Gounod opera that has never appeared on a CD, I have to have it. I might not get around to listening to it for a year. It's like a big tapestry of information. I want to fill out my knowledge. When you start to reject the premise that the standard concertizing world hands to us that these are the composers who make up the core repertoire, and that their pieces are the only pieces, the more you start to explore all the nooks and crannies of the repertoire. Then you start to realize what bull that is. All music of any era is interrelated. You could pick France in the 1880s, for example. To understand César Franck is to understand Wagner, and to understand Fauré and Debussy, and backwards to Adolphe Adam, is to see this directional way that music interacts, and informs your understanding of how music should go. For example, for me it's just always been of interest to listen to Bach's *B Minor Mass* one day and then listen to.... (pause) I'm trying to think of some obscure piece I've recently been listening to — oh, Paul Ben-Haim's Second Symphony, on another day."

"I've never heard of him?"

"Exactly! Paul Ben-Haim was one of the first famous Israeli composers. A fabulous composer, kind of like a cross between Bartók and Vaughan Williams, hard to describe. So I can listen to the most famous piece and the most obscure piece, and by knowing the history of those composers who wrote the lesser-known music I know that they were very relevant and well aware of Bach and Mozart, his operas, or whatever. They are part of it all, they fill in the gaps that our concert going life doesn't let us appreciate."

"What are the personal qualities you possess that allow you to be — if indeed it's true, which I think it is — a world-class conductor?"

"(Long pause and hesitantly) You mean different than other ones (laughs)? I think dedication, walking the walk, and working hard for the right reasons for the right goals."

"Do you have kids, Gil?"

"I have two kids. My daughter is about to turn eighteen and going to college in the Fall. My son will turn sixteen in February. My kids live with my first wife close by. I'm engaged now to a visual artist."

"Do you think music can solve all the existential type problems we have in the world now?"

"No. I was in a recent event a year and a half ago when a conductor of growing fame received an award I was also receiving. He made a flowery speech about how music could provide hope which could change the world and bring peace. I don't buy it. If that were the case it would have happened already. It's not the role of music. Music is not an all feel good experience. It's a reflection of man. Man is both divine and earthbound, so I don't ever expect music to change the world. I expect music to enlighten and show us more about ourselves, but It's not going to cure our problems."

"Gil, I know you have to go. it's been very enlightening talking to you. Thanks for a great interview."

"Thank you, Larry. I'm sorry it took so long to work it out. It's just a function of me. I always say I'm busier than a one-legged man in an ass-kicking contest."

My experience with interviewing great musicians is that almost to a person they say something pithy which reveals much more than the few words spoken. Take that last remark of Gil Rose. Right away we know he's down-to-earth, low enough to the ground to be comfortable using vernacular speech, colorful enough to pick the right metaphor to express the hard work and dedication required to succeed at his self-chosen mission of bringing underplayed, unrecognized, and new music to our ears, esteeming himself enough to bear that burden for the long haul, and high enough to respect his fellows.

American conductor Martin Pearlman. Photo by Larry Ruttman.

CHAPTER
10

Martin Pearlman: Boston Baroque Founder, Conductor, and Composer

There are a certain few lucky and talented people among us who have a head start in life because they always have known where they were headed. Lucky because that gives such a person twenty or so extra years to develop during childhood and adolescence when absorbing and learning is easier. In music, Wolfgang Mozart, who first composed at age four, is always singled out as the prime example. That is one key among others as to how it was that he composed so much astounding music by the time of his untimely demise at thirty-five. That has certainly played into the manifold attainments of Maestro Martin Pearlman, who began composing at age six, and quickly progressed from there to be a musician for all seasons as a conductor, harpsichordist, scholar, writer, teacher, innovator, and administrator. Still in his twenties, in 1973, Martin founded Banchetto Musicale, the first permanent Baroque orchestra in North America, now known the world over through its appearances and recordings as Boston Baroque, of which he is and always has been its music director and conductor.

Surely that list marks Martin Pearlman as a man whose talents extend to the limits of music and into realms more pragmatic and gives us a hint that behind his gentle and obliging persona lies a resilient and determined ambition to excel in whatever he attempts, as well as a person whose eye-opening ideas and opinions mark him as a man who thinks for himself.

It seemed fitting to trace Martin Pearlman's progression from the very beginning when I spoke with him in his quiet home in a lovely natural setting in a college town near Boston bespeaking his cultivated tastes. One wants to know what dynamics lie behind Martin's composing, conducting, and many musical endeavors.

"Martin, what are your earliest memories of listening to and playing music as a child?"

"I listened to records, and the radio too, since I was very small. And by the time I was three or four, I was able to put the records on myself and had favorites. I used to love to listen to the Khachaturian piano concerto. My parents had a nice collection. William Kapell was a very popular pianist I listened to. He died young in a plane crash. And Brahms and Beethoven, I used to listen to them all. My first concert was a children's concert at the Chicago Symphony. They played Bizet's *L'Arlesienne Suite*. I don't remember what else was on the program, but I remembered that. My aunt took me. I was about four or five."

"Were your parents musicians?"

"My mother was a very talented pianist when she was young, but, for complicated reasons, had to stop. When I was little, she would sit down at the piano sometimes and play Chopin or Beethoven. I remember listening and being able to tell what notes she was playing. My father was a very serious painter, but he grew up poor and decided he had to become some type of a doctor like his brothers. He became a dentist to support our family, but every spare minute he was painting. And when he retired, he painted full time. We would go to museums. He appreciated music, of course, but he was hard of hearing so he didn't turn in that direction. Here's one of his paintings (pointing). I've got oil paintings all around the house."

"You tell me your mother is still alive in her nineties. Is your father still with us?"

"No, he lived to be ninety-seven, but he died some years ago."

"It looks like you've got the right genes."

"Yes (laughing). He was eleven years older than my mother."

"So did you ever want to be anything else but a musician?"

"No, never."

"How old were you when you developed the idea that you wanted to be a musician?"

"I don't know. Nothing else occurred to me. I do remember being at somebody's birthday party when I was in kindergarten, and the father was asking us all on some kind of recording device what we wanted to be when we grew up, and I said a pianist, because I just didn't know. But it was always music."

"Did you always have confidence that you could be a successful musician?"

"You know, I never thought about it. It was just something I was going to do. I guess I was wired that way and it wasn't an issue as to whether or not. I didn't worry about how it was going to work out. I just was going to do music, and I've been very lucky. I've done music and people have supported it. I get to do a lot of concerts, but if it hadn't worked out that way, I think I would still be doing music, just be poor."

"Did you ever have a mid-career crisis when you thought you might not be able to continue in music?"

"Never a kind of crisis where I considered not doing music. Sometimes in music I would have to take a turn to the left or the right that I had to figure it out. For example, I didn't set out to be a conductor. When it became clear that things were heading that way, that the ensemble was getting too big, I had to stand up. I had to decide whether conducting was what I wanted to do. At that point I was a keyboard player and leading the ensemble from the keyboard. There were certain decision points, always within music. And also about composition because composition was always something that I've done. It's still the other half of my life, just a little bit less public, although some of my pieces are being played now. I've been composing since I was six, and it was my major in both undergraduate and graduate school where I concentrated in contemporary music. It was a question of which one I would do professionally."

"I know that you're considered very highly in several fields of music. As a conductor is the most obvious one. I know that you compose, you're a master of the harpsichord, you play the piano as well, you teach, you administer Boston Baroque of which you're the head. I would ask you what do you consider to be the major thing you do in music as of today?"

"I do all of those things, it's true. I mean I guess conducting and composing. The conducting is clearly the more public side of what I do."

"Which is the most important to you?"

"Conducting is important. I would say composition has always been central to my identity. So I wouldn't stop that. I value the time that I can spend on it."

"Well, you started out only two years behind Mozart."

"I'm a few years ahead of him now. Maybe not the music, but the years (laughing)."

"For the record, we just established that Martin Pearlman is ahead of Wolfgang Amadeus Mozart (laughing). When it comes to your compositional process, Martin, let me ask how you describe it. Would you say it's from the outside in or from the inside out? I'm thinking here of things like dreams, impressions, experiences you had in life, literature, light, color, whatever?"

"Obviously, everything in your life plays in, but I don't directly translate events into music. The music is a world in itself. I work the material and it comes out being emotionally me in various ways. It's not a one-to-one though, like something happened to me today or I dreamt something, and I put it into music. I don't do that."

"Gunther Schuller told of a piece he wrote in his latter years. He woke up from a dream in the middle of the night, he was a big dreamer, and he ran over to write it down because he knew by the morning he would forget. Would you say that in your particular case, no music comes from dreams or visions or imaginings, in that way?"

"Not in a direct way. I can be inspired by something. I wrote a piece, for example, called *The Creation According to Orpheus*. It's for three soloists, piano, harp, and percussion, with a string orchestra. It is influenced by some ancient writings I had read which inspired me. It didn't give me a specific musical idea, just kind of a general aura. I didn't go right from reading it to writing music.

These things gestate for a while, so it's hard to make a one-to-one correlation. It's not necessarily telling a direct story, where you might say this measure corresponds to this part of the story. It's a general feeling that builds. I also wrote a piece based on the text of *Finnegans Wake* by James Joyce. Obviously if you are writing on a text, you are very influenced by the text and what it is, but it's all filtered through your own personality."

"So the music comes from the text, or the music arises from your understanding of the text?"

"It's a complicated relationship. It works both ways. You can have musical ideas, and then eventually discover it works with a certain part of text, or the text might give you an idea. I mean it's a two-way relationship, I think. And then you might have different ideas for it and sew them together. It is working with material. It's like a sculptor."

"When you sit down to write the music are you reading off what you already have written in your mind, or are you working it out as you write?"

"A little bit of both. I do a lot of working it out. I'll write something and then adapt it so that the original isn't even recognizable anymore just in the course of working it out."

"Do you think you'll diminish one aspect of your career, like conducting and playing, and devote more time to composition?"

"I don't know. I think I'll always be performing. But I will be finding more time for composing. I've been doing more of it now than I was a little while ago. And I think it will increase with cutting out extraneous things."

"Do you read a lot?"

"I do read a lot. I read a great deal of classic fiction, nineteenth-century English novelists, like Trollope and Eliot. I've read Frances Burney's four books recently. She's a predecessor of Jane Austen. Her father was a famous eighteenth-century music historian. I've read Daniel Defoe who goes back even further, and some older things too. I like epics. I've read about Orestes, and, of course, have read Homer, Virgil, and Dante. Of the twentieth century, I just read a lot of Willa Cather. I don't read much modern fiction. Of course, I read some nonfiction. A good deal about music history, of course. I was just reading a book on seventeenth-century French music and their philosophy of music. I do a good deal of reading is when I have to research some musical subject, so that's not reading a book cover to cover but it's reading sections."

"So what composers do you feel akin to as far as your compositions are concerned, both people who are still with us and people who may not be?"

"Just last night I was listening to Pierre Boulez. His music has been a strong influence. I have always been interested in Elliott Carter's music."

"Who would you say was your prime mentor as a young musician, and now?"

"Well, certainly in early music and harpsichord it was Gustav Leonhardt, the great Dutch harpsichordist, who passed away several years ago. He was one of the

American composer Elliott Carter, muse of Martin Pearlman.

Photographer unknown. Courtesy BSO Archives.

shaping forces of the early music movement in the twentieth century. And one of the great performers. He was certainly a very influential person for me. Now, I don't have a mentor. Now I do what I do (laughs)."

"John Cage said that the spectator listener travels the distance the music allows in a work, and then alone completes the distance, thus allowing the spectator to bring his own interpretation to the work and make it his own. Do you believe that?"

"I do think that we all put ourselves into a work. Everyone experiences it differently. I'm sometimes asked, what do you want a listener to get out of this? I don't have an opinion on that. I want to play the work as fully as I can and let the listener bring to it what he or she can. So I guess that's true. I mean John Cage was a wonderful observer of and commentator on people's relationships to music. I've always admired him for that."

"In *The Magic Flute*, a kid can walk away with one thing, and the grownups can walk away with something else."

"That's the way it should be with any piece. I think it is true with any piece."

"What's your favorite form of music?"

"I don't have a favorite. It depends on the piece. If it's good, it's good (laughs). If it's an opera, or a symphony, or a piano solo, it just depends on what's a great piece. Same with composers. I don't believe in ranking them. I think it's meaningless to do that."

"How about pop music?"

"I like some. Not a lot. I like jazz. I was a Beatles fan back in college. I like Bob Dylan. but most pop nowadays is too produced, too calculated, too overproduced. Most of it doesn't interest me that much. There is certain folk music that I have enjoyed over time. Not only American. I love Indian and Indonesian gamelan music."

"So if the world lasts a couple of hundred years..."

"That's a big assumption (laughing)."

"That is a big assumption, But anyway, a couple of hundred years from now, are some of these pop artists of today going to be still around? And will Mozart, Bach, and Beethoven still be around?"

"Well, for the pop artists you can't really answer that. There is a filtering process that happens. I think most of it, no. Most of any kind of any music of any period is not going to survive. I mean there were people who were more successful than Mozart (laughing), to whom we don't listen anymore."

"Well, I think in popular music that's true. But when it comes to the greats that we have been talking about in classical music, they seem to have had a pretty steady survival rate."

"Some of them yes, some no. I mean look at the time of Mozart. If you go to a symphony concert or a chamber music concert now, normally you'll only hear three composers from the classical period, Haydn, Mozart, and Beethoven. That's it. Well there were more than three composers, there were hundreds of people composing music, and there were people getting very excited about operas that we never hear today. And wouldn't be very interesting today. And the same thing happens with any style of music from any period. And that to me doesn't devalue the stuff that gets lost. There is plenty of music that speaks to its time, it doesn't have that deeper thing that will speak to another time. So it doesn't last, but it's valuable to people at the moment. As to music, to me there is very little of it that I see having lasting value. But if I were alive in 1780, I probably could say the same thing about a lot of music I heard then. Yeah, that's popular, it's fun, but a hundred years from now, nobody will listen to it. But it doesn't matter, it's valuable at the moment, so I don't think it is an important thing to say this is going to last. You understand what I'm saying? It has value for the moment and that's fine."

"So do you think that pop and classical are on a par insofar as most of the music that is produced in either realm is simply music for the moment?"

"I do think that that's true of most music. Whether pop and classical are on a par, as I say, I'm not a good person to judge, because a lot of the pop music now is artificially produced in studio. It almost feels like it is done by committee, by what sells. That kind of music isn't worth hearing even ten years later."

"Is there any part of classical music that you would put into the realm of something that is so deeply entrenched in western culture that it will simply go on indefinitely?"

"Oh, I think so. I think that standard things we know, Bach, Mozart, Beethoven, Handel, certainly will go on. But these things also go in cycles. Bach wasn't played for a very long time. He was known to connoisseurs, and even they for a long time didn't feel it was normal concert music. When you go to a concert hall built in the nineteenth century, very often at the top of the proscenium there will be names of composers. Beethoven is always central. I think, personally, that Gluck is a very great composer, but he is not in people's consciousness on that level today. There was a big comeback for Mahler's music. I think he is a very great composer, but he fell out of fashion early on, There was a reaction against him. Beethoven never has fallen out of fashion. And Handel never has either, in a way. A lot of his works, like *Messiah* and a few others, have always been there. But a lot goes in cycles, I think. Today there are great many people who feel that Bach is the greatest ever, and that he's just sublime. And it is sublime music, and it is at the top level of what we have ever had, but I think that that exclusivity of Bach being number one doesn't make sense to me. How you can compare him to Mahler, or Beethoven, who are so different. I think that that grows out of our interest in our own time. I think it speaks to our time."

"Well, so what is it about popular music that gets those huge crowds screaming and yelling? Why does pop get such big acceptance by younger people, and why doesn't classical music connect in that way?"

"You know, it has a strong beat, and it's very simple to understand, and it speaks to people also through its words. Classical music never was a majority music. If you took the people in Europe in Mozart's time, I don't think that you would find that a majority of people listened to Mozart. First of all they didn't have the opportunity, there weren't recordings yet, you had to be in a royal court or opera house to hear it. It always needed support brought to it, unlike the most popular stuff. It might have been from a prince, and today it might be from a foundation, but it's always been music that is less popular than some other music. So that doesn't surprise me, and doesn't seem unusual to me in any way."

"Do you think that classical music has a problem with survival because of any inability to draw enough people to support the organizations?"

"I don't think so. I think that concern grows out of the fact that we live today in a democracy, we measure everything by numbers of people who vote for something, and that's not always the measure of value. And it is also not always the measure of survival. It might be the measure of popularity, but not survival. I think that what's at risk in classical music is not the music, but some of the institutions we built up during a time when things were going very well and were supported. Some of that can't be sustained. And so the people who are part of those institutions worry about the survival of classical music. The music itself will always be there, it will always be available to people, there will always be some institutions that can support it, but maybe not as many as we have had in the best of times. I mean these things go in cycles."

"Is Boston Baroque in good shape?"

"We are doing well, yeah, knock on wood. We have been doing recordings, we have our radio station that gets over 200,000 people listening a week, and we have sometimes gone outside. We were just in Poland performing. Going to Eastern Europe and to Poland and performing was great. The response was extraordinary. To get the meaning of music to these people was an extraordinary experience. We just did several concerts there."

You called your opera *Finnegan's Grand Operoar.* What do you consider central in this opera?"

"There have been a number of treatments of *Finnegans Wake* in various forms. It has inspired a lot of music, some just music, and some with songs with words from the book which are mixed and used in various ways. Even John Cage did a major work on it where quite intentionally you can't make out the words. What I wanted to do was actually to use the text presenting every word, every parenthesis, every digression for whatever passage I was doing, so that the composition had the flavor of the text. So that was what I set out to do. For that reason I had a speaker rather than a singer, because even normal language is hard to understand when it is being sung, I have a speaker who is speaking very precisely written speech rhythms so it lines up exactly with the music."

"Is *Finnegan's Grand Operoar* going to be presented again any time soon?"

"I'm working on it. We did the first act and we did the third act. Then I wrote the second act after that, so I'd like to present the whole thing, the speaker and seven instruments."

"I know you composed some for three Samuel Beckett plays. What did you seek to accomplish with that music?"

"Just to be true to the plays. Two of the plays had music as a character in the play, one of them was all the words and music. Obviously the words Becket could write himself, but the music was just *da da da,* so you have to create the music. One of the plays was not one that originally had music, so it was a matter of supporting the very slow action on the stage with music. They were commissioned by and then performed at the 92nd Street Y in New York at a series they have there. Then it was done again here at Harvard University."

"OK, so you compose, but also you edit. I'm thinking of the Monteverdi and Cimarosa operas, and Mozart's incomplete mature opera, *Lo Sposo Deluso*?"

"Yes, it was quite incomplete. I didn't write all kinds of music that Mozart never got to complete, but there were some incomplete sections that I did complete, and there was one section which didn't have any orchestration, so I did the orchestration. So it's not very much music I provided for *Lo Sposo Deluso.*"

"Speaking of Mozart, I read that you recorded his *Requiem* quite a long time ago using the completion by Robert Levin (noted composer, harpsichordist, composer, musicologist, and Harvard professor)? I guess the completion by Franz Xaver Süssmayr, who was Mozart's student, is the one that is played mostly. Do you prefer Levin's completion to Süssmayr's?"

"I do. I mean Süssmayr's is the best known just because it is from Mozart's time. He wasn't much of a composer himself. Some of his solutions aren't that interesting because the ending is a repeat of music that Mozart did earlier in the piece. He went quite far sketching the music, so some of the completion just requires filling it in and completing the movement. I think Bob Levin's completion works well. I like it. We did the first period instrument recording of it."

"What about period instruments as opposed to modern instruments. To me they sound really mellow and nice. Do you like them better?"

"I like them (laughing). You know, a good performance is a good performance whatever you play it on. But I prefer the sound of them for that music. You can more easily shape the music a little differently. The balances are somewhat different when you use the instruments that were intended. They blend in a different way, so I find I can do more with that music with period instruments. But I've heard some very good performances on modern instruments too."

"Do you like the harpsichord better than the piano?"

"For harpsichord music yes (laughs). Pianists shouldn't stay away from Bach. It's great music so they play it. I mean that a great harpsichordist should play it on the harpsichord. There is a good deal of harpsichord music, especially French music, that is just built on the sound of the instrument, so that music often doesn't get played by pianists because it just doesn't sound all that good on the piano. I figure the harpsichord is appropriate for a certain kind of music."

"Here's one, Martin. What is music?"

"I'm not sure that is an answerable question. Cage challenged all that. There is the question of whether silence is music? I mean it's a performance. There is a lot of theatre involved. I'm not sure what difference it makes. We put on a performance and we always have an experience. I don't think it matters what we call it. There are some people who listen to rock music and say that's not music. Well, I think it is (laughs)."

"Is it music when John Cage runs around the stage banging furniture about?"

"Well, that's the question. I mean Cage kind of opened it all up, and one reason he opened it all up was because he came out of the tradition of music. Even if it's a reaction, it's still related to previous music. I mean Cage studied with Schoenberg, he started writing music that we would consider normal music, and then this grew out of it. So it's related certainly. I've often thought about Cage. A lot of Cage is theatre. If you see it performed it's a whole other experience, and it can be quite wonderful. Whereas if you just listen to it on a CD, there is often not a lot there."

"Can the world get along without music?"

"We never have."

"What would the world be like without music?"

"Quiet (laughs). Obviously, it has been a central part of the human experience, but I have always avoided definitions. I find them retro in the sense that they're just defining things we have seen already in the past, so they close us off to new experiences. I'm not so concerned about that actually."

"I know now you don't like this kind of a question, but do you think that music is the greatest of the arts? Let's put it this way. What is it that speaks to you in music that you may not get from any other artistic form?"

"Music is more coded than the other arts. In other words, it's not as directly related to something in the world that we know, so in a way it goes deeper. In recent times that has changed a bit because we have had abstract art. Music is not a picture of something. We even had language, like in *Finnegans Wake,* that approaches abstraction. But music has that coded quality, which means that the things it is saying are not discursive, they're not about a specific thing. And they therefore allow interpretations, allow a person to be much more involved in what it means. I'm very moved by a painting, by literature too, so I'm not trying to diminish those, but the coding makes it very deep. Also, there is something about the way we are wired. People are wired differently for their responses to music. And musicians are wired in a way that music is like a native language, and things are always kind of forming themselves in musical ways. Most people are not quite like that, but they are wired to respond to it. Almost all of us do respond to it. I once saw a book that described something called tune deaf, which is different from tone deaf, meaning a person who couldn't tell the difference between an orderly arrangement of notes, like say the theme of Beethoven's Ninth, from just a random set of notes. Like somebody who doesn't understand any English wouldn't know if you're saying real English or just making up words. There are very few people like that. Most people do respond. It seems to be something in our wiring where we tend to think of notes. It's rhythm too. We are actually more sensitive to rhythm than we are to notes in that slight variations of rhythm are felt very strongly, whereas a note that is a tiny bit out of tune doesn't hit us as hard. So rhythmically, we have a certain sense of rhythm innate in us and I think it expresses itself in music."

"I think you are saying that music is the deepest of the arts?"

"I don't want to say that. I hate the questions that are asked about a great work of literature or about a great painting whether the writer or painter is a top-level artist. I'm not going to put Mozart above Shakespeare. They are both great. They both do what they do (laughs)."

"I've seen comments about saying that the three best dramatists ever were Mozart, Verdi, and Shakespeare. I don't know about that. But anyway, is all music all over the world on a par?"

"I don't know. There are certain cultures that have what we would call classical music. India has that. So what are you comparing a lot of times would be comparing our classical music, Mozart and Bach, to folk music in some other part of the world. That is a hard comparison to make. I can't say because I don't know world music enough to say that this is greater than that."

"I don't think I'm going to get you to say, oh God, there is nothing like Western classical music."

"It is what I respond to most strongly. It does seem like one of the greatest traditions there is. I'll say that."

"Do you go to many concerts of other organizations?"

"I go to something if it is particularly relevant to what I'm trying to think about. You have to understand that musicians can be sort of sponges with music. We take in the things that impinge on what we are feeling or thinking or trying to work out musically. We don't usually go to a concert just because we want to hear a concert. So I don't go to a lot of concerts. I may go to some. We take in what we need. (laughs)."

"In your role as a conductor during a performance, are you thinking more of how you're conducting the music as a conductor, or do you think more of how you are presenting the music of the composer?"

"I'm just involved in the music. I have always thought of myself as a musician, not as a performer, and (laughs) I'm just kind of doing the music, not aware of other things. It's interesting."

"Well Toscanini said he wanted to present a piece as truly as possible. And then there were more self-directed conductors like Leonard Bernstein, who put their own personal stamp on the music."

"He did, but he was very involved in the music. Bernstein was a showman, that's true. There are people who fit into two categories, performers and musicians. They're not mutually exclusive. You can get performers who are not great musicians, but are able to show the audience something important, but who are not deeply into the music, and you can get musicians who are really focused on the music but are not into the performance, not performing for the audience, but allowing them to listen. Then you get some who are good at both. Bernstein is an example. Yo-Yo Ma is an example to me of somebody who is a great performer in projecting outward to the audience, and he also has something to say about the music. You can get people that have that combination. There have been some very great people who have really just been involved in the music itself. Gustav Leonhardt, my teacher, was like that. He was one of the great twentieth-century musicians, somebody who really got the feel of early instruments going. He said something interesting once in a speech. He said he felt that to communicate directly with someone out in the audience was vanity. It was putting yourself there. Instead, you put yourself into the music, which is the medium, and then the person can relate music as they will. But the other to him was vanity. It was an interesting idea."

"When I watch you conduct the impression I get is that you are into the music because you're not very demonstrative, at least vis-à-vis the audience. You're into the music and the orchestra."

"Yes. In fact, I just got comments from the last concert about how they like watching me. They can see my gestures in the music and all that, and that's fine. I don't set out to do that. I'm just simply involved. One of the things about being a conductor is you have your back to the audience the whole time. So (laughs) when they burst out into applause or cheers or whatever it is, it's almost like an interruption, it's a surprise. It's a nice surprise. But my feeling is always I want to really do this piece, and I want to let you listen in. I'm happy to have you there and listening. But I'm not talking to you when I'm performing."

"Does the ego of the conductor separate the music as written from the listener? How does performance transform the music? In other words do you, when you present a musical piece, think to yourself, what did the composer really want to transmit to the audience, how can I help that happen? Because you hear about conductors who splice things, add things, accentuate certain things?"

"That's right. Well, I'll tell you, I don't think, *What did Vivaldi or Bach want to say?* What I do think is that the work when finished is independent of the composer. I want to say what's in this piece. And that's not the same as what was in Vivaldi's mind when he wrote the piece. He wrote this piece (laughs), and here it is. It's independent of him, he is no longer around. Even if he were around, here's this piece. I mean, a creator of any art often has the experience of a piece not being exactly what he meant. The better they are, the closer it is to what they meant. But my concern is what's in this music. So that's what I say, what is this piece, how do I get it across? How do I get at what's in there. Sometimes it depends on how great the composer is, how great the piece is, or just the nature of the piece. Some music takes more work to get across and hold together. Some pieces, like a Mozart opera, just kind of flow. Another composer, like the Vivaldi piece we recently did, required me to think about how to make the piece go in a long trajectory to keep it moving. So it takes a little bit more thought. It's about what I'm seeing in the work. I might add to it that when I'm trying to project this piece it is not totally arbitrary, just anything I want. I've come out of a world in which I have studied, not just that one piece, but lots of pieces like it, lots of that composer's work, lots of other composers' works, and studied performance, practice, and everything else. So it creates a kind of framework. And the freer you are the more you've been in that framework, the freer you can be without worrying about kind of bursting the bounce. I liken it to a small child when they grow up. You have to say don't do that, that's not right, that's impolite, blah blah blah, you know, all these rules. It becomes part of them and then there is a point in life when they just don't have to think about it, it's just what they do. So I think performance practice is like that. There is a framework."

"Well, you're a professional."

"Yes, but some people, if they're not oriented towards historical interests about the piece, or about the composer, then they're going to be beyond the bounds of what that composer might have heard or wanted, and it would be a whole different kind of a piece."

"Well, that's why the word scholar is applied to you as well."

"Yes, the scholarship for me has to be completely in the background and not thought about when I am performing."

"Right. That's a great background to have. What about preconceived experiences of music? You know, recordings? Does that impact your experience, and your practice, or don't you listen to them?"

"Not usually. I might if I'm thinking, for example, of a particular Vivaldi piece where it is very confusing, what did he mean by this, by these repeats written in this place. Should I repeat that part and then go back here? Technically, what to do? And I make my decision. And once I've done that, I'm kind of curious how other people decided it. So I might check it out. It usually doesn't change anything that I want to do, but it might be a particular technical point that I'm curious about how did these other people do it. Or when this month I did the Verdi opera that's up for a Grammy now, I had to do a new performing version of it, I had to write string parts, I had to make decisions where I was going to put the strings in. Once I did that, I was curious what other people had done. But I didn't do it before I did my work, I did it afterwards. I was just curious how what I did compared with some other decisions. So I do it pretty much on my own."

"I want to ask you some questions about your life as an educator. I think a lot of the best of the music students might say this curriculum is too over-directed, these people want me to go in the direction of what the school wants to teach, but I need more freedom to do I want to do. So how do you balance the interest of the student and the interests of the school?"

"I haven't had the school tell me anything about what I should teach. I do two kinds of teaching at BU. I have one course in performance practice, and I also have ensembles that I coach on their performance. You have to work with what the students bring. They can get up to a certain level, I make my suggestions, and usually we are compatible. There are certainly the people who are majors in early music who have grown up with recordings that we all knew. Sometimes they grew up with recordings of mine. And we are on the same page. I may occasionally get somebody who wants to do something different from what I like, but it's ok if they can do it. They'll learn if the audience will respond, or not later on. I have some students who are good musicians on the modern instruments and are just learning about baroque music and period instruments. That's a different kind of work. You show them things and they either take to it or may have trouble taking to it, whatever it is, and you work with them in a different way. I guess the answer is that over the years I have allowed a bit more latitude for what the student can bring to it. Some bring more, some bring less."

"Have you run into some brilliant students?"

"I've had some wonderful ones. The concertmaster of Boston Baroque, Christina Martinson, started in our department. And there have been some terrific singers. I have hired some of them."

"Have you run into any obstreperous students in the sense that they say no, no, this isn't doing anything for me?"

"Not that often. I guess I have occasionally but if somebody would be very, very strong in what they wanted to do, I can identify with that. I was sort of that way when I was a student, so (laughing) I give them what I can and they'll take what they can."

"Could modern classical musical education proceed differently or better?"

"I think the greatest education is when you are out there and performing. You learn more at that point than you ever did. Until then it's the technical and theoretical work which is very important. I, personally, am not at heart an educator. Let me put it this way. The professors that I learned the most from, such as Gustav Leonhardt, were people whom I admired. I was interested in their ideas, but they weren't necessarily trained educators, official educators. They were performers or composers or whatever, who did it, and I wanted to see how they did it. And that's been my attitude. I don't teach undergraduates generally. I teach graduate students who are more advanced and committed. It's not as much the kind of teaching where you have to reach out and pull them in and get them interested. They're already there. So my attitude is I offer them what I have and they can do what they want with it. So it's a little bit more by example kind of teaching. Does that make sense? So it's not like an educator who teaches younger people and has to bring them in."

Like Martin Pearlman's students, his listeners do not require being pulled into his concerts and compositions but are already committed to what he offers to us, and do what we want with his offerings, which is to enjoy the rare music which this musician for all seasons brings to us.

Ben Zander, with his former wife, family therapist, author, landscape painter, and environmental philanthropist, Rosamund Stone Zander. They co-authored the million-seller book, *The Art of Possibility*. Ben and Roz are shown here with young South Africans, during their fifth visit to South Africa for three weeks in 2008, during which they presented ninety-seven events. They inspired more than 15,000 people to think about South Africa as a country alive with possibility. A video made on that trip called: *South Africa, Alive with Possibility*, and introduced by Bishop Desmond Tutu, was placed in every South African school, and has inspired millions of South Africans since 2008. This video and much else about the Zanders' work together can be found on BenjaminZander.org. That trip and its effect on South African education was written up in a book, *Partners for Possibility – Stories of Impact* by South African social entrepreneur and founder of Symphonia, Louise Van Rhyn. *Partners for Possibility* is the compelling story of what can happen when you think in terms of possibility, instead of deficiency. It's the story of what happens when people say "Yes."

Photo credit: Symphonia.

CHAPTER
11

Benjamin Zander: Inspirational Conductor, Educator, and Author

Benjamin Zander is a charismatic conductor and teacher whose musical, communicative, and literary skills, formed by his extraordinary relationships with family and mentors from youth all the way through his life, have inspired musicians and non-musicians alike of all ages the world over in life's possibilities, most especially the teenage and younger musicians who have worked under his baton in Boston and internationally in the youth orchestras he has formed over his years in academia and later. Ben Zander's rare ability to transmit his own profound understanding of great composers like Beethoven, Wagner, and Mahler to these young players, empowering them to play with a sound far beyond their ability to produce without his mediation, in the manner of a mature great orchestra, is a wonder to hear. In so doing, Zander has inculcated lessons in collaboration, friendship, high values, and humanistic thinking so needed in our existentially threatened society of today. How does Ben Zander accomplish this miracle?

Later in these pages you will read at close hand about that miracle now continuing before our very eyes. To understand how it came to be, one has to understand how the absolutely unique individual known to us as Benjamin Zander came to be the person he is.

Part of that might be attributed to his constitutional makeup, but to my mind much more must be attributed to the one-of-a-kind circumstances and astounding influences of a host of gifted people all through his childhood, his teen years, and his vital and continuing growth to maturity of his adulthood. His father, Walter Zander, was one of Germany's best-known intellectuals before fortuitously fleeing with his family to escape the Nazis to England where Ben was born. Ben's amazing mother converted a loss to a win in a trice by somehow interesting famed composer Benjamin Britten in the disfavored competitive compositions of ten-year-old Ben. That resulted in Ben's long friendship and summer visits with Britten, his companion, notable tenor Peter Pears, and his amanuensis, and composer, Imogen Holst, at Britten's home in Aldeburgh. Many of Ben's teen years were spent being the student and companion to eccentric cellist and composer, Gaspar Cassadó, then one of the great musical figures in the world. During his teens he also attended two of England's most famous schools, Uppingham, where he was lost among a host of talented cellists, and St. Paul's, where his budding pugilistic career ended. His three siblings were then already reaching for the eminence each would attain in their later years. Ben continued on to London's renowned University College, where he won distinction and a major award in the literary field. Later Ben Zander found a spiritual friend for life in the music and wisdom of Gustav Mahler, and earthly and profound friendships with his two wives, Patricia and Rosamund, each of them women of great accomplishment in their chosen fields of music and psychology respectively, each of whom remained loyal and supportive of him even after the pain of divorce. Ben Zander suffered a major adversity in early 2012 when the New England Conservatory opted to relieve him from his forty-five yearlong professorial tenure, and his beloved leadership of its youth orchestra, because of their view that his judgment was faulty in a student security matter involving his choice of an employee. Significantly, later that same year, the conservatory recognized his contributions by awarding him the title of Faculty Emeritus. Ben stood up dignified and straight against the firing and responded with the establishment of the highly regarded Boston Philharmonic Youth Orchestra (BPYO), which he now leads there and around the world.

Plainly, Benjamin Zander has traveled a road nobody else has traveled, as these pages will tellingly reveal.

"The first thing I want to ask you is about your amazing father, Dr. Walter Zander. I think his bringing the family out from Nazi Germany, is really interesting."

"At the moment I don't want to talk about Dr. Walter Zander. I'm so riveted by what's going on in my life today. I don't have a single thought outside of that. I'm about to take 120 people on tour to South America. I've got a rehearsal on Friday and Saturday. This morning wrote a letter to my orchestra saying I completely changed the interpretation of the main piece. What I came in with was the idea we were going to do the same tempo for the whole piece. It doesn't work. So we're going to change the tempo depending on the mood of the piece. It is quite something for the conductor to write that to all the members of the orchestra. But we don't have time to rehearse it because the concert is on Monday, and then we go on tour. So on the tour we can develop it."

"Will you get any chance to rehearse them before the tour?"

"Just on Friday night. So my focus of the moment is on that. I'm seventy-eight, and most people when they're seventy-eight are looking back, but I'm not looking back at all."

"I'm eighty-six and I'm looking forward too. But it's like history. To know where you are now, you have to know what came before. Same with you and your history, Ben. I can understand you being very excited about what's going on now. What I'm asking you to do is step back and look at your life in the past to see who has been influential on you, how they've influenced you, and how musical institutions you have been associated with have influenced you, to tell us stuff only you can tell."

"Is this a history or an analysis? You haven't said what makes me unusual. You said I'm unique, but you haven't said what it is."

"I know you are unique from observing you and your work over the years. We have to concentrate on your life as it has been, on what you were like at nineteen, and twenty-nine and thirty-nine. Were you then the Ben Zander we know today? I promise you Ben that we'll cover what you are doing now, whether today or another day. This is the groundwork for that."

"Let's start with your father."

"My father was a huge influence on me. I'm very clear about that. A huge influence!"

"Was he the greatest influence in your life?"

"I don't know. I can't measure it."

"OK, you can't quantify it. Let me phrase the question differently to apply to those who were influential. In what way were they influential on you musically and as a person?"

"My relationship with my father was a complicated relationship, like all relationships. My mother was also an iconic lass. She was the force that got me to Benjamin Britten."

"That sounds like a story?"

"I wrote some compositions and we put them in the local arts festival. Michael Head, a quite well-known composer, came down to adjudicate the competition in the village. Head said my compositions were so bad that he could not consider them for the competition and that this boy should be discouraged from composing again. That's what he said, which is so ridiculous! What was my mother supposed to do, box Head's ears? Console me? Anyway, what she did is to send them to Benjamin Britten with the comments of Michael Head. Benjamin Britten called up four days later and said to my mother, 'This kid is nine years old, what are you thinking about, he's doing fine. Why don't you come to Aldeburgh to spend your summer holiday. It's beautiful, and you can live in a caravan, the kids can play in the sea, and I'll keep an eye on Ben.'"

"Benjamin Britten thought you had talent."

"Well, yes. Actually, Michael Head wasn't far off. I wasn't a good composer. But a nine-year-old composing is unusual enough anyway, and maybe Britten sensed some little thing. We spent a lot of time together. Was he a big influence in my life? I don't know. The experience of being with him was extraordinary! His friend, Imogen Holst, became my harmony teacher and she did have a big influence on me. She taught me everything about dancing. She danced through life, her body just moved like air, she was incredible. When I would do a harmony exercise for her, she would dance it through the room. Imogen was beautiful in a very simple kind of Botticelli way. I think I got the message that music was about dance, and that music was a lively art, not about writing common exercises."

"It's like you are describing your conducting style?"

"Some of that. Cassadó is there, Imogen Holst is there. I had a friendship with Benjamin Britten that lasted for some years. It was a fortuitous thing that suddenly I was spending my holidays with him. There are stories about him which I think are very illuminating I've told to people who have written books about him. But he wasn't really my teacher. I was too young then. But we would meet in his home and we would go over a composition I'd written. It was beautiful because Britten was a very loving person. He was already famous and became the most famous composer England has ever had."

"How about Britten's companion, Peter Pears?"

"Peter Pears was lovely and a very great tenor. I didn't know him well. My brother Luke became his doctor and knew him very well."

"Ben, your early life was unconventional, to say the least?"

"I have gone through life taking some very unusual steps. I went to prep school and then I went to public school. I was in the National Youth Orchestra as a cellist when I was twelve. Then I went to the famous Uppingham School where there were forty-five cellists. I didn't get into the first orchestra there, although I was already playing in the National Youth Orchestra, because there were so many cellists who were better than me. At Uppingham, they had a great music program and a fantastic cello teacher, Jane Callan. I'm sure she had a huge influence on me. She was wild, she was intense, and physically very free. I sort of went through life having these experiences and just picking up things along the way like lint on my clothes."

"Tell us about St. Paul's school, another very famous school you attended?"

"I was knocked out in my first boxing match there, literally knocked out. It was a very foolish thing when I think back on it. My brother, Luke, was a terrific sportsman, a fantastic cricket player, soccer player, rugby player, and boxer. When I arrived at school Luke said, 'Ben's my brother, he must be a good boxer.' So Luke put me onto the boxing team. The first fight we had was against the army, so I was fighting against a soldier. It was completely inappropriate. I was only fourteen."

"You were taking your life in your hands."

"Yeah. I was out only for a few seconds. But that was the end of the fight, first round KO!"

"Plainly your parents were big influences early on. Who else?"

"My cello teacher, Gaspar Cassadó, had a huge influence on me in every way."

"Tell me about Gaspar Cassadó?"

"Do you have three hours? He was a composer as well. Cassadó was the greatest cellist I ever heard. I played a tape of Cassadó playing to Yo-Yo Ma, and he said, 'I would give my left foot to be able to play the cello that way.' If I played it to you, you would understand immediately both his influence on me and why Yo-Yo said that. There is a facility and ease when he played. Just brilliant, breathtaking, a sense of beauty. It was a Chopin nocturne that he was playing. I think as a musician I'm a chip off that block. I see it when I conduct an orchestra. The sound I get is the sound Cassadó had."

"How would you describe that sound?"

"It's hard to describe a sound. The words don't seem to make any sense. Cassadó was extraordinarily supple and varied. You'd have to hear it. When I was recording the Mahler Second Symphony with the Philharmonia something very extraordinary happened. The Philharmonia Orchestra is one of the great orchestras of the world. We were about to record the second movement. I came in with the recording equipment and said, 'I would like you to listen to something very special which means a lot to me. It's my teacher playing a nocturne of Chopin.' And ninety hardened English musicians sat and listened for nearly five minutes riveted by it. Then we played the second moment of the Mahler and it was *totally* different than before. It was as if it was a different world, an old world, a world of ease and subtlety, intimacy, and flexibility, that simply doesn't exist anymore."

"How long were you with Cassadó? Did he influence you as a person?"

"Five years. He did influence me in lots of subtle ways. He was very free, detached from reality, around sixty when I met him. Didn't have children, didn't have a wife at that point. He would call me up at ten o'clock at night and we'd have a lesson until two in the morning. It was a very strange life. I could tell you lots of stories about the strangeness of my life as a teenager with Cassadó. I grew up with very little sense of barriers, very little sense of the restrictions of normal life. You never know what comes from what. But if you spend five years of your formative life in the presence of, beholden to, and in deep admiration of somebody who lives almost completely without restrictions, it's bound to influence you, but I don't know exactly how. But I do live today pretty much without restrictions."

"Can you tell us one of those stories, Ben?"

"Yes. I was in England because I was back visiting my parents. Cassadó had gone to Scandinavia to a conference. Instead of traveling with him which I usually did, he said 'Go back and see your parents. I'll get in touch with you.' I hadn't seen my parents in a long time. So I go back to England. I get a telegram from him which says, 'Meet me in Ascona, look for the Roman flood.' Now I'm sixteen years old, I'm in England, and I'm wondering where is Ascona, what is the Roman Flood? Is that a fountain? No idea! I take a train from London to Folkestone,

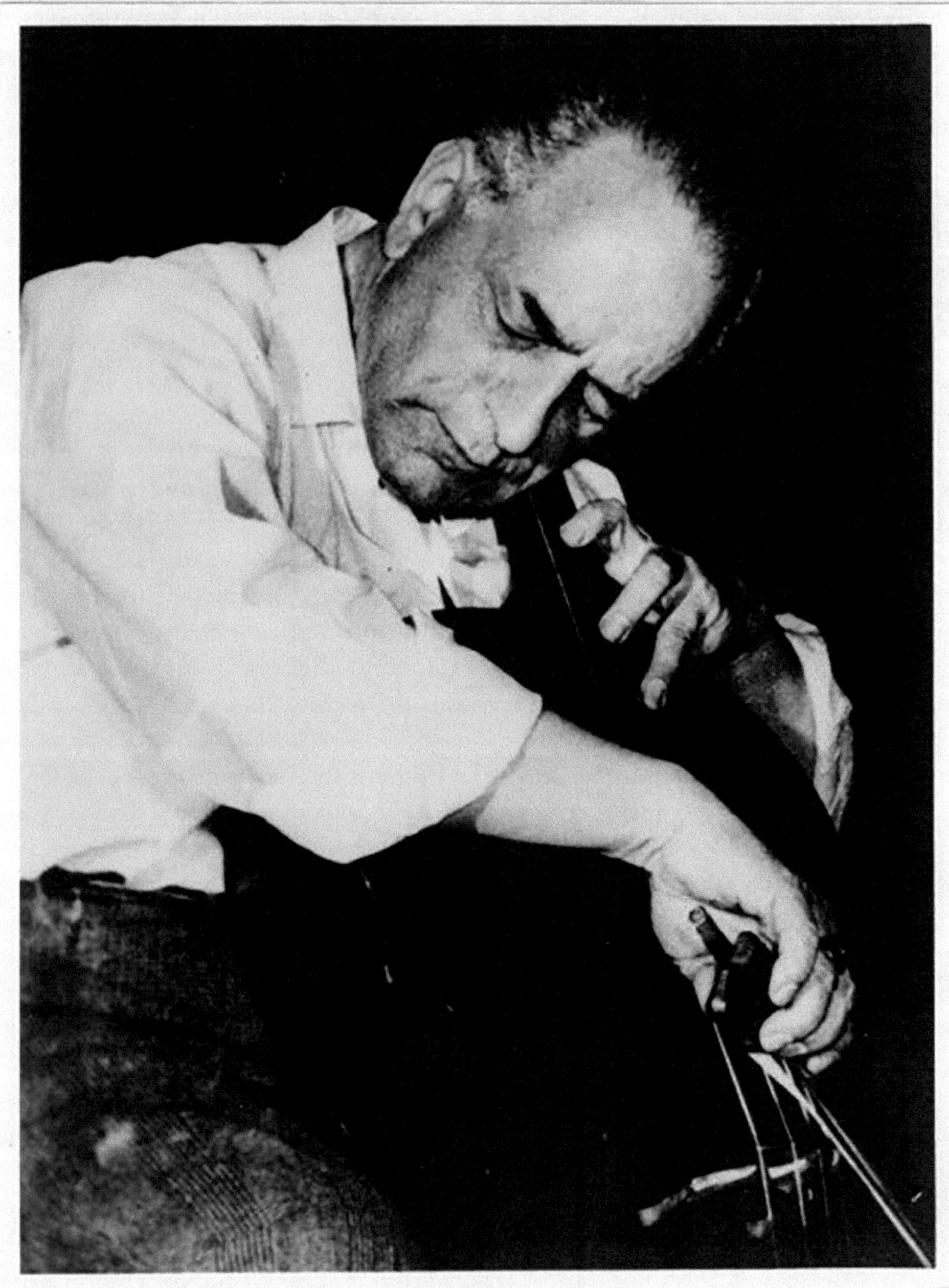

Intense, warm, and passionate Spanish cellist and composer, Gaspar Cassadó, whose profound influence on young Ben impels him to exclaim to this day, "God, I loved that man!"

Photographer unknown.

from Folkestone to Dieppe, from Dieppe to Paris. From Paris I take an overnight train through the Dolomites, and I arrive at seven in the morning in Ascona, which is in Switzerland. Gorgeous, beautiful village with a lake and mountains plunging into the lake. The most beautiful thing I ever saw. Seven o'clock in the morning. Now what? So I leave my case and the cello and I start wandering around Ascona, looking for what? I have no idea what Roman Flood is. Was it a hotel, a restaurant? I had no idea. So the windows come down very low in Switzerland. You can actually see into them. So I hear somebody playing piano, and I knock on the window. The window opens and I said, 'I'm looking for Roman Flood?' and he says, 'That's me!' He was a composer. Roman Flood says, 'Oh, you're the boy from Cassadó! He sent a message. He's stuck in Sweden because he has some concerts to give there. He says to find a pension and practice.' So I find a pension. No sign of Cassadó. I can't remember exactly how long it was, but it was probably nine days before he appeared. I was just sitting in the hotel alone, practicing the cello, alone in this beautiful town. And then suddenly Cassadó arrives."

"What happened then?"

"When he arrived, he didn't say I'm so sorry he wasn't in touch with me, or didn't call me up, *nothing!* Then he said, 'OK, let's have a lesson.' So I played the cello and he was very pleased that I'd made progress and learned the piece, whatever it was. But that was a strange life for a fifteen-year-old boy. And it went on for years. He didn't think, what's this kid going to do, how's he going to get to Switzerland, I didn't give him any instructions. I've got countless stories like that."

"That's a very revealing story. I think it directly relates to your character development."

"I'm sure it does. I can't tell you exactly what led to what, but I must have been influenced by being with him, and traveling with him when he went on tour."

"He was important for sure. What more might you tell about Gaspar Cassadó?"

"He'd call me at ten o'clock at night and say come for a lesson. And at the end of the lesson at 1 o'clock in the morning he'd say, 'Have you eaten?' I'd say, 'Well I ate at six.' And he'd say, 'Okay, we go eat.' And we'd go to some restaurant in Florence and have dinner. I was just fifteen years old and he treated me like a friend and an equal. Wow, an equal, and he was maybe the greatest cellist in the world! We had a very deep friendship. I did *everything* for him. Like an apprentice. He never charged for lessons in all the five years. Never! My father would say to him, 'How much do I owe you? How much I owe you?' Cassadó never answered. Then finally he said, 'If I charged for how much I thought my lessons were worth, you could never pay.' So now I never charge for lessons. I'm incapable of charging for lessons. People always say to me, 'How much do I owe you?' (Laughs). I don't take money. And that was inculcated by him. So there are lots of influences, really a lot. I've had a great life, a really great life."

"Here is a question I've always wanted to ask you. When you attended University College in London, you majored in English Literature, and you won the English Literature essay prize. What did you write about?"

"I won the King University Prize. It was about *Tom Jones* by Henry Fielding, a very popular novel from the eighteenth century. The essay was called *Irony in Tom Jones!* I was very passionate about literature. I didn't read voluminously, I read in depth. Shakespeare, and the epic old story, *Beowulf,* I knew from memory."

"So Ben, you were a literateur as well as a musician?"

"I was. I love literature. I don't read as much now because I'm so busy. I did then. I spent three years reading. I'm very glad I did. I have a very good acquaintance with poetry which helps me when I'm teaching Schubert lieder."

"Ben, we've talked some about your good life in England. Did you have any idea you would stay in America when you came?"

"I didn't. We had no intention of staying. I came with Patricia, my first wife."

"Have you ever lived in England again after that?"

"No. The plan was to stay for two years. Then I got an extension to teach at the New England Conservatory. I went back to England because I couldn't get a visa to stay in the USA while being here. I took a whole group of American students back to England and ran a school for them there while waiting for the visa. I taught nine high school seniors and some students who had just graduated. It was a fantastic school. I set up courses in academics and arts."

"I know that your second wife, Rosamund, has been a big influence on you?"

"I think the most intellectually challenging person has been Ros, my former wife, with whom I'm in contact constantly on a daily basis. Patricia, was a great person and a great pianist."

"You have had two amazing wives! I know that you gave a eulogy at Patricia's funeral. You are a remarkable guy to have been able to get along with your ex-wives so fantastically."

"(Laughs) I revere my ex-wives."

"Let's take Rosamund first. What is the major way in which she's influenced you?"

"Rosamund is a great painter. Her paintings are the only paintings I have. She is truly the most remarkable person I've ever met. I do think so. I don't know anybody with her clarity of mind. I don't know anybody who has more range. It's extraordinary! She writes, paints, and understands human relationships. There isn't anybody who fails to grow knowing Ros. I call her the Yo-Yo Ma of the human spirit. She has devoted as much attention and quality to her ability to create breakthroughs for human relationships as Yo-Yo has for the cello. She has that same kind of spirit. So she's been a huge influence on me, huge, huge, huge!"

"How would you describe that influence?"

"All of that is documented in the book we wrote together, *The Art of Possibility,* which became a perennial best-seller. Many of the stories in *The Art of Possibility* start off with me having a problem and going through the darkness of despair and conflict, and coming out with a new possibility. That's the shape of it."

"How about Patricia?"

"Patricia (laughs) was a very great musician. Actually, I think I had as much of an influence on her as she did on me. She came from a very weird background. There is a whole portrait of Patricia that nobody knows. Sanford Sylvan said Patricia Zander was far and away the greatest musician in Boston, bar none. That includes James Levine, and Gunther Schuller, and all of us. I really believe that. But what Sanford doesn't know was that her father was a gardener and her mother was a cleaning lady in England. There wasn't a single book in her parents' home. In spite of that she became one of the most well read, educated, phenomenally smart and informed people entirely on her own. Patricia was Yo-Yo's pianist and teacher for thirteen years."

"How did Patricia influence you?"

"I'm not sure I would talk about it as influence."

"Just freely associate."

"It's very hard to do that. You're asking questions that are profoundly rooted. You can't spend however many years I spent with Patricia — and I continued to be very close to her even after we divorced — and be able to quantify it. She was extremely refined. We played together as a duo. I can resent the idea that I would reduce this very profound relationship to a few words. It's like asking Mahler how his talented wife, Alma, influenced him (laughing)."

"How did Ros influence you?"

"Ros influenced me because she gave me a discipline I didn't have before. A new discipline called "the art of possibility." That is a very rigorous discipline. It influences the way you speak, the way you walk, the way you connect with people, the way you solve problems, the way you deal with disappointment. Everything in life is affected by this discipline."

"Can you expand on that discipline, Ben?"

"Well, teaching is what Ros does. We both do it. I give my students a way of thinking which is a discipline. It's not being more disciplined. It's a way of thinking which is *a* discipline or, if you like, a paradigm for living, which is a discipline in the way being Catholic is a discipline. You say, if you are a Catholic, this is how to live your life. These are the rules, these are the expectations. That's a discipline. Learning to play the violin is a discipline. You have to move your hands this way and move the bow that way, you have to learn to move your hands up and down, and you have to practice and practice and practice and practice, ten thousand hours, then you can say you play the violin. In that sense, Ros has invented and created, with my collaboration, to put into the world a discipline called "the art of possibility," which people can then follow in the same way they follow playing the violin or being a Catholic. It doesn't involve any religious belief. I'm actually anti-religious because I think it restricts people. But "the art of possibility" has many of the elements of religion in that it is of the spiritual world. It has to do with the elements of life which exist beyond one's temporal concerns and needs."

"Before you got to the point of being able to write a book with her, didn't you have to sort of catch up with her? Aren't there experiences related to that?"

"That's her profession. That's what she does. There are stories of my growth as a possibility thinker, like the times I had conflicts or overrode somebody's feelings. Strangely enough, we started on this path when we separated. During our short marriage the difficulties that were caused by the interaction of our two personalities were detrimental to her children. So Ros said, 'It's not good for us to be together.' But she also said something very profound, which I've repeated many times to many people. She said, 'Once you're related to someone you're related to that person for the rest of your life, so let's make the best form of that relationship that we can.' And we have done that rigorously."

"That's a great thing she said, really."

"Yes, it's a beautiful thing, it's one of many beautiful things she has said. She can almost be guaranteed to say something beautiful every time she opens her mouth. And that was one of those life lessons that come about when you break up with somebody. Normally, you do everything to portray the other person as wrong, and to tell lies in to make the other person feel worse, and so on and so on. So the rift keeps getting bigger and bigger. Ros did the exact opposite, she did everything possible to help me. For instance, she came to look for an apartment with me. When we found the apartment, she said, 'The red sofa would look great there.' I said, 'But Ros, you got that idea from your mother.' And she said, 'I don't care who I got it from, I want your apartment to look beautiful.' She was just as committed to my happiness after we separated as she was before. It made no difference because she felt we were always in a relationship, and to this day we talk every day. If there are things that are difficult for me to work out, Ros will work on it. She was working on this conflict I have with the orchestra today. So that's how she lives her life as a very disciplined person. Not that she's a very disciplined person in every single aspect of life, but she is always very disciplined in human relationships. Like Yo-Yo Ma is disciplined in playing the cello. It's the same thing."

"Were you the Ben Zander we know today any time before you left England?"

"Yes, I would say definitely. The only thing missing was the discipline and clarity I have now. What I had then was intensity, passion, a volatile character, and tremendous energy."

"I am asking questions that probe into your deeper mind, to the roots, the word you used. Is there any other musician in the world who has done all the stuff you've done?"

"Not the exact things. There are musicians out there who have done a lot of things."

"How about not giving a damn about what people think, and just doing it."

"I don't think I have ever thought that. I have always cared about what people think. I may give the impression that I don't. What I don't do is I don't stop doing things because I worry people might not think well of it. So I am not stopped. But if I do something and people don't like it, it does affect me. I am very affected by whether people accept what I'm doing."

"How were you affected by the big flap at the conservatory when your judgement was severely questioned about you hiring and retaining a person with a criminal record they thought bad enough to threaten student security?"

"I mean that struggle with the New England Conservatory, which led to my discharge, was extremely unpleasant and upsetting. It brought me into the public light in a way that I didn't want to be in the public light. I didn't say, 'Oh, fuck you, I don't care.' I did care. It got so bad that the TV trucks were outside the window here. I had to move out of my house to my daughter's house because every five minutes someone was knocking on the door wanting an interview. At various times I was depressed and anxious about all that. I'd love to tell you that I've completely had a life of joy and contribution, but that isn't the case."

"You've been involved in some very difficult problems. The life of an artist is intense to begin with. I think that a lot of great people have had big downers."

"Oh, sure, every five minutes (laughing). I would say now it is different than it was then, since then it was huge ups and downs. Now I have the discipline of the possibility way of thinking. Ros said something which is most valuable. She said, 'Possibility is always only one sentence away.' Isn't that great? That is a beautiful statement. That's a life-giving sentence. Because you realize that whatever you're suffering, whatever difficulty you're having, one sentence will take you into possibility."

"A short trip for a big problem. Sort of magical. Can you tell us of examples of that?"

"She's saying you have the power with one sentence to get to possibility. That's much more powerful than 'Oh, don't worry, time will take care of it' She's saying that at any moment, no matter how depressed you are, or however dark the circumstances are, all you need is one sentence to take you into possibility. And the example I give that is so powerful is of my father, who lost eight members of his family in the Holocaust, interned at a camp on the Isle of Man during WWII with 2,000 men who were all in a state of fear, many of them severely depressed. So he said, 'There are a lot of intelligent people here, we should start a university.' He founded a university at that camp in which there were forty lectures a week without books or paper. So that's a sentence that takes you from the greatest depression into possibility. The university flourished. And I use that as an example to contrast possibility and positive thinking. They sound the same, but they are not the same. Positive thinking is pretending things are great, when really they are shitty. Possibility is finding a new idea, a new way of being, a new creation, irrespective of the circumstances. So that is a very powerful distinction. That's the discipline of possibility."

"It sounds like Rosamund is the most influential person in your life?"

"In many ways, but she didn't influence my musical life. I influenced her musical life in that she's come to love and adore music and become an extremely perceptive listener to music."

"In 1974, when you conducted Mahler's *Kindertotenleider,* you said, 'Mahler's music entered my psyche and actually began to shape the way I was experiencing my life. It compelled me to explore the extremities of experience and be stopped by nothing.' Now that's really a strong statement, Ben. Please tell more about Gustav Mahler's influence on you?"

"That compelling force is what draws me to Mahler. That is what his music does. I am drawn to that. I think that I probably have a gift for realizing his music."

"As you go through life, even off the concert stage, is Mahler in your life? If we had to take your quote literally, 'compelled you to explore the extremities of experience and be stopped by nothing', that is like saying he's alive to you."

"It's very hard to tell whether he influenced me to think that way, or I thought that way and thus have a reciprocity with him as a result. I am drawn to Mahler's music both because of the extremity of the music, and how the youth orchestra sounds playing his music when I conduct. I've listened to the youth orchestra's recordings of Mahler, and think, 'Good Lord! How can these kids play this way, how is this happening, they don't have Mahler in their everyday lives?' Well the fact is that I can do that with my body. I can reproduce the extremes of emotion in Mahler's music from the most violent to the most tender, from the loudest to the softest, from the most extreme in its intensity to the most refined and delicate, by using my body. I can conduct it in such a way that the children who have very little direct experience with those emotions can reproduce them to sound like a world-class orchestra."

"I heard that when you did the third act of Wagner's *Siegfried* at Symphony Hall a few years ago. I was astounded. Everybody there was astounded!"

"The kids themselves at that very young age are open and they are feeling very emotionally alive. But they're not yet able to bring Mahler, Wagner, and Beethoven to life on their own sitting in their practice rooms. That's what I can do for those composers. I feel that there is something that speaks through me. I also find myself very at one with Bach, and especially with Schubert, Schumann, and many other composers, in fact. I don't feel particularly drawn to some modern composers, but with moderns like Shostakovich, Hindemith, Bartók, and Stravinsky, I feel completely at home. It isn't as if I only have that connection and that relationship with Mahler. Not at all. I don't conduct Bach because Bach didn't write for modern orchestras, and I conduct modern orchestras."

Austrian-Bohemian composer Gustav Mahler, muse of Benjamin Zander

Credit: Photo uploaded by user zthipn to last.fm, CC BY-SA 3.0

"Any other modern composers you have an affinity towards?"

"Szymanowski, and of course Britten, though I don't do a lot of Britten. But those composers speak to me, as does Ives. I'm doing Ives' *Three Places in New England* soon. I think it's a most beautiful piece."

"Have you ever done Britten's *War Requiem?* I think it is very moving."

"I think so too. No, I haven't done it. I should. Thank you for sharing."

"I know from the last time we met how well you get along with both the parents and the kids, and that they often write to you. You read one to me from a parent which is so expressive that I'm thinking of quoting it here."

"When you arrived I was writing a long letter to the orchestra. I gave a talk to them on Saturday. I'm taking 120 people on tour to South America. It's not a random group of people just wandering through South America giving concerts. It's a tour of possibility. It actually has a very clear intention. We are going according to some very clear principles of behavior which have a huge influence on everybody. I just got a letter from the mother of one of the kids this morning. It is very interesting. I'll read it to you because it encapsulates the idea of the whole trip in a very clear way. It is from the mother of one of the kids in the orchestra, fifteen, a great kid who plays the bassoon, from a high school here in Cambridge."

> Dear Ben:
>
> The talk you gave on Saturday about the upcoming tour really exemplified and underscored for me what is so special about BPYO. What I most appreciated was how you put the emphasis not on the performances, the peak moments of the tour, but on how the players conduct themselves during the ordinary moments and everyday interactions. This makes sense not only because there will be more time spent off stage than on stage during the tour, but because the vision of the orchestra is not just artistic excellence but learning how to become "part of the solution." From this point of view it's not just what we achieve or how well we perform that will make the difference, but how we conduct ourselves in our day-to-day lives, how we treat one another. Thanks for putting the emphasis on that in your talk. You encourage the members of the orchestra to continually pay attention to the way they interact with each other, to notice and interrupt any downward spiral in their thinking and behavior, and to be vigilant about their attitude when faced with life's inevitable setbacks and surprises. In this way the tour becomes as much about practicing a way of being in the world as it is about giving great performances. This is an inspiring vision. You also threw out a question to the players: "Why does the BPYO go on tour?" The group came up with a number of good reasons: to share their music with new audiences, to seeing new places, to represent the best of the United States, and to get to know each other better." I would like to add one more reason to the

list. To give people hope for the future, which the BPYO does so well with every performance. Thank you for everything you do and have a wonderful tour."

"So I took that beautiful letter from a mother, and sent it off to the kids, with a copy of the long statement which I had made about how we run a tour of possibilities, a fascinating document inspired by Ros' thinking, philosophy, and way of being. So Ros is a huge influence."

"That is wonderful Ben. We live in a time where we are threatened in various ways, existentially and otherwise, and I think the way you and Ros teach these kids to look for friendship, to respect one another, and to learn leadership values, is a great thing!

"I think we've done enough today. I'll be in touch, and we'll meet again soon to talk about your present pursuits."

....

"We were here a few months ago and this is a continuation of that interview. I am going to ask you this question, Ben, and let you answer it as you please. It's more in the form of a commentary then a question. The last time we met you said that you are very much more in the here and now than in the past. That is certainly attested to by the unbelievable letters to you from the BPYO orchestra members you sent me last night emanating from the South American tour a month or two ago. I'm so impressed by how much these young people love and respect you, and how much you teach them about music, life, and life's possibilities, as you and Rosamund Zander wrote in your book, *The Art of Possibility.* As Rosamund said the possibility of doing something is always only one sentence away. Like your amazing father who was interned on the Isle of Man in World War II forming a university out there fostering hope so much needed in those fraught times. The letter you read to me from one of the parents of a member of the orchestra prior to the trip the last time we were together about what she hoped the trip would teach has indeed become the fact. So Ben, what I want you to do today is to sort of freely associate on what it is you have been up to lately with the BPYO to which I believe your astounding musical and life experiences have been so well and effectively communicated, as well as your other pursuits."

"Beautiful, great question, thank you. Of course, I can go in many different directions. We shouldn't lose sight of two strands or maybe even three strands which are not included in the Youth Orchestra. One is the continuation of the recordings with the Philharmonia Orchestra in London. The reason that's important is that it is my one voice with an absolutely world-class orchestra on the international stage. I just completed a recording with them of the Beethoven Ninth, and two days ago a two-disc explanation of the Beethoven Ninth, which has absorbed me throughout the summer. It literally takes two CDs to explain the music. On the third CD is the Ninth symphony, and it's an absolutely amazing thing! I've done the Mahler cycle with them too that likewise is on the world stage.

"Then comes the Boston Philharmonic which is a local virtually all-professional orchestra on a very high level. We've produced a number of performances which are being turned into recordings which will be part of my legacy in the long-term future. I'm very proud of the Boston Philharmonic. It's grown from an essentially community orchestra into an orchestra which in almost any other town would be the prime orchestra. A critic in South Africa who knows every recording of the Sibelius Seventh Symphony said our rendition is the best performance of that piece in existence."

"I read that someplace."

"The BPO is a very important part of my life. It's forty-five years of conducting an orchestra, and it has actually formed me. It's not only that I've formed it, it's formed me. I've learned how to conduct from that orchestra, from those players who are my professional colleagues. I treat them with utter respect and deference because they are some of the finest players you can find anywhere."

"What comes next?"

"The third aspect is that I have a series of classes on the Internet called *Interpretations: Lessons in Music and Life*. Once a month I do a class. Sometimes I'll teach somebody who is on the brink of a major career, sometimes I'll teach a member of the Youth Orchestra who is struggling to become something more. Those lessons have an enormous reach. A few reach over 100,000 people. When I travel I meet enormous numbers of people who know me through those interpretation classes. I just got a letter from a lady in Argentina who said she has changed her whole way of piano teaching as a result of one of them."

"I'll have to tune into those, Ben."

"What will be left when I can't conduct any more will be the interpretation classes which I can go on doing until I drop. I intend to keep teaching young musicians and fully fledged professional musicians, as well. All of these are now being collected together into something called the *Zander Media Center*. It's going to be launched online where you'll get rehearsals, coaching sessions, classes, and lectures, along with all the recordings which are getting to be quite a body of material.

"For instance, I'm hoping the explanation I've just completed of the Beethoven Ninth — maybe it's a grandiose notion — will be in every library in the world because it deals with the issue of how do you interpret the Beethoven Ninth. This is the only recording that does that according to Beethoven's specifications, with explanations of every section. It's certainly the most significant piece of work I've ever done. I've been working on it for over forty years, so it is my life's expression. So all of this I've talked about is a terrific body of activity without even mentioning the Youth Orchestra. I say all that because people get so excited about the Youth Orchestra that the other things which I'm doing are sort of pushed aside. I don't think you'll make that error because I've now told you where my heart is. If I were to choose among those five activities, I wouldn't be able to because they are all of extreme significance."

"What I do see is that folks love your pre-concert lectures."

"The Boston Philharmonic concerts are all preceded by a lecture. In London I gave a lecture before the Beethoven Ninth and about nine hundred people came. The ushers said they had never seen anything like it. The place was full for a lecture (laughs)! They said 'We've seen concerts in here with fewer people!' So that to me has become a tremendously important thing for ordinary music lovers. I take care of their anxiety and their lack of knowledge and provide them with excitement and insight. That is all they need because classical music is available to everybody and anybody can love it. They need a little guidance, what the background is, what the history is, and what was going on in the composer's mind. Then they have something to listen for."

"You are a multi-tasker for sure, Ben. I see you as a conductor, and a teacher of music and life for adults and for kids, whether musicians or not!"

"Actually, there's nobody out there who is functioning at that level who is also conducting a youth orchestra every week. People are either doing one or the other. So that gives me an immense range from the highest level. To have access to an orchestra like the Philharmonia, and to a lesser degree the Philharmonic, gives me an outlet for my musical capacities which is all I could possibly want. So given those different parameters of my life, add the Youth Orchestra which is extremely important to me for two profound reasons. One is that my advisor, Mark Churchill, Managing Director, Elisabeth Christensen, and myself have managed to attract some of the best young musicians in the country who happen to be studying in Boston at NEC, Harvard, MIT, or in high school. I just finished auditioning 150 people of whom we took 110, ages twelve to twenty-one. Three of them are twelve and a large number are twenty-year-olds who are there because they are extraordinary players who won their positions as a result of their high accomplishment. The younger ones are there because we see something in them that we believe will eventually come to a flowering on a very, very high level. So the body of the orchestra has enormous potential. We see huge possibility in all of them. I treat them all as equal, not in their capacity, but in their possibility."

"The Art of Possibility, as you and Rosamund titled your book, as we touched on last time. I would like you to tell in detail how you teach music, life, and life's possibilities to these young people?"

"Right. In the world of possibility they are all equally worthy of our deep concern and attention. Secondly, they are so good they actually can sound like grown-up orchestras because they do it at the edge of their capacity. Have you heard their recording of the Mahler Eighth? It's pretty amazing because that music is very difficult and demands the highest preparation not only on my part, but on the part of the coaches and the students themselves who take it very seriously because they're playing in Symphony Hall. It's wonderfully satisfying for them to do that! There's a third part too, and that is teaching leadership, meaning that they learn to speak and live and act so that they and the people around them flourish and make a difference. That is something we take on from the very first rehearsal. I start off with a one-hour lecture about this philosophy which is essentially the 'art of possibility' in action. It is something we talk about every week."

"So, as I said, you are teaching these young people about life. How do you proceed from there?"

"Then we start the rehearsal, but we don't start by playing. We start by explaining to them what we're up to and why we are up to it. In the background is the sense that we live in very troubled times in which the values that all of us have taken for granted, like telling the truth, treating people equally, justice and freedom, freedom of the press, and respect for the Rule of Law, are being called into question on a daily basis. Rosamund and I take that on as part of our job. She makes sure we have a suitable assignment every week which we use for the leadership work. One tool of that is the so-called white sheet which gives a voice to every member of the orchestra so that if they have something they want to draw my attention to they have a voice to do that. Everyone who submits a sheet has to sign it so I can respond, if necessary. The idea is to use the voice of every member of the orchestra so that they feel powerful. Usually in an orchestra the only person who has a voice is the conductor."

"Do most of them use it?"

"That's a very good question. Most do not use it in the Youth Orchestra although many more use it than in any other youth orchestra. I get maybe thirty papers after a rehearsal out of one hundred people. I remind them they'll never have another chance to do this because no other conductor allows it or invites it. Secondly, they will develop writing and listening skills that they wouldn't if they were just sitting thinking about their own part. If they're thinking about the whole world, and wondering what they would do if they were the conductor, then they'll start developing their sense of the whole. The other tool we use are the assignments which are devised by Roz and me to open them up to break through the barrier of how they're normally running their lives by making them step out of themselves in order to do the assignment. It moves them into that unconscious part of the brain, which is not logical, doesn't make plans, or look forward to the future, that unconscious part which impels them to live with spirit and love."

"Can you give us an example of that?"

"I can. Ros told us a lovely story yesterday of spirit and love. The assignment she gave was to get in touch with somebody who is lost to you. The client got in touch with a roommate that he had in high school many years before with whom he had an argument severe enough so that they broke off relations. The years went by and there was no contact. So he picked up the phone and found his roommate in Colorado. He got on a plane and went to Colorado to meet him. They went camping for three days under the stars, sharing stories and memories, and love and hugs, and they came back together. Now that is in the domain of the unconscious. He went because he took it on as a project. It changed a very important part of his life. It resolved an old wound and gave him a new friendship. It is beautiful."

"It is beautiful. It seems the white sheets and the assignments have a very powerful positive effect."

"When the students leave the orchestra invariably they talk about the assignments as being about their growth as human beings. The evidence is in the white sheets."

"That's what so impressive to me."

"The players learn to write better and better and to trust that first of all. They know that I will read the letters. I almost always respond to them. I write back so they know the sheets are being read. That is the leadership aspect. Then comes getting on the plane. One thing they all talk about is the amazing companionship of being in an orchestra with 110 other like-minded people."

"You spoke of a kid who really came out of himself. I think his name was Zack."

"Zack came from Philadelphia. He said his family was going to move to Boston so he could play in this orchestra, and that his father was going to get a new job here. That didn't pan out so he drove up and back every weekend. Zack was the boy who said he came in shy and nervous and thinking he had no ability. Joining a group like this and touring with them changed Zack's outlook altogether!"

"These trips sound personality forming. Go on, Ben."

"Now we come to the social aspect of it. Unless a kid is in an arts school, they are in a regular school with people who don't understand or value what they're doing. That is heartbreaking for them because they care so much about the music and work so hard on it. They come in on Saturdays and are making friends with kindred spirits talking and being passionate about music, not about football which they would be talking about otherwise. Why is that important to the touring? One reason is that we've got this fantastic Saturday afternoon event every week for four hours. In addition we play three concerts a year, two of them in Symphony Hall, we make recordings, we have the friendships, we have the learning and the wonderful coaches. Isn't that enough? For some orchestras it would be enough, and for some it's all they can offer because to tour is staggeringly expensive. Imagine taking 120 people to South America, arranging flights, hotels, and concert halls. On and on. The reason we do it is because it adds a dimension that none of the other things that I do — the Philharmonia, the Philharmonic, the Youth Orchestra, and the interpretation classes — do. None of those have the penetration into and the reception from other cultures which is life changing. They get the experience of seeing what those young people down there are going through. There they make friends and receive insights into the culture. They may not have the language in common, but they find they don't need the language."

"So they are affected not only by the culture but by direct contact with the people?"

"Yes, with the people tremendously. South American people are particularly expressive. That adds to their experience of life and what it means to be a human being. We have a Korean trombone player who didn't go on the tour because he has a job back in Korea in the summer playing substitute trombone player in a great orchestra in Korea. He didn't go on the tour but said he would go on the tour next year. I said, 'You know we can't have you go next year unless you go on this tour because it's part of the total experience.' Just think of the decision that he made. He's never been to Europe, never been to south America, never met any European or South American people. He only knows Korea. He'll go back to Korea and he'll play trombone for the rest of his life until he's sixty-three and then retire. That will be the end of that. We offer them a life experience that they can't get for love nor money for free. I mean the whole thing is free."

"How do you pull that off, Ben?"

"How is that possible? We do it and we go on doing it even though the strain is enormous on me personally as a fundraiser. I work constantly on fundraising. It's the main part of my life. I just got upset before you came in because I was on the phone with someone who has given us a nice donation for $50,000 for our endowment. We don't have an endowment; we need the money to pay for the orchestra now."

"You need current-use gifts?"

"We need both current-use and endowment gifts. When I'm dead, let somebody else do it. But we're not having people give us money now for something twenty years from now. It doesn't make any sense to have an endowment right now. I told my manager to call the person back and tell them we don't have an endowment presently but we can we use the money for the youth orchestra tour fund. The parents help by giving donations to the orchestra, and we have a very wonderful sponsor who gives generously."

"Where do you like to go more personally, to Europe or South America?"

"It's very interesting that you ask that because there are two sides of my love of touring. When we go to Europe, which by the way is twice as expensive as touring South America, we play in the major concert halls, the Berlin Concert House, the Concertgebouw in Amsterdam, same in Budapest, and other venues, and that satisfies my great joy to be able to bring great interpretations by the youth orchestra to the people for whom the music was written. But that kind of a tour isn't about interacting with children, it's about getting and giving concerts in major concert halls. When we go to South America it's all about interaction, interaction, and interaction. All the kids talk about that, and they all love it! So they're very different experiences, but I think it's healthy for the orchestra to go to the World Series every other year and play with the big boys and get reviews about how well we played!"

"It takes a lot of energy to do this at your age, Ben. Where do you get the drive?"

"The answer is I have a passionate desire to bring music into the lives of as many people as I can before I die. The other part is I have a passionate desire to bring along as many young people as I possibly can to be fully effective, expressive, and contributing human beings. I believe I have the capacity to do those two things. As long as I have that capacity I also want to leave some great interpretations behind."

"I think that is a lovely statement, Ben. You know what you hope to achieve. I think those ambitions which you're fulfilling are great ambitions!"

"I feel that, I feel that."

This story began with the idea that Benjamin Zander is a unique individual and musician, formed by a conjunction of influences unlikely to be repeated, which have given the world a man able to carry out the three passions made in the above statement far beyond the point most other great musicians and teachers have been able to do. Ben Zander is a rare man, misunderstood by some, envied by others, but admired by most, for continuing to realize the passions which daily drive him forward.

American violinist, Hilary Hahn, whose combination of technical mastery, emotional expressiveness, and adventurous repertoire, have brought her to the pinnacle of the world's appreciation.

Credit: Phineusphoto, CC BY-SA 4.0 <https://creativecommons.org/licenses/by-sa/4.0>, via Wikimedia Commons

Part Three

INSTRUMENTALISTS

German violinist Anne-Sophie Mutter. Photo © Harald Hoffmann / DG

CHAPTER
12

Anne-Sophie Mutter: Master Violinist and World Citizen

One might think that a child prodigy championed by Herbert von Karajan, the famed maestro of the Berlin Philharmonic Orchestra, presented by him to the world at age thirteen, exempted from school to devote herself to music because of her prodigious talent, then feted across the globe ever since, would turn out differently. At worst she might have become some sort of ever-present *enfant terrible,* and at best a somewhat opaque individual seen clearly only when shouldering one of her two Stradivarius violins in concert. Not at all. Anne-Sophie Mutter is beautiful in her person and persona, attuned to the society of the world which reciprocates by embracing her not only musically, but as a concerned human being. Once away from the demands of her art and audience, this amazingly talented artist partakes of life fully, whether as a mother, daughter, and friend, or as an advocate of issues in which she is passionately interested, all the way from the protection of flora and fauna to her belief in how our commitments to togetherness and finding solutions will lead us away from existential threats. Indeed, as I sat with Anne-Sophie Mutter amidst nature in the Berkshires, she responded to the birdsong all about, as had Mozart on hearing the song of a bird in his famous remark, "Das war schon" ("*That* was beautiful"). What you see is what you get. She presents herself elegantly attired and looking elegant when she appears on stage, but away from the footlights Anne-Sophie Mutter easily greets you as the friend you want to have, talks to you about the problems you want to talk about, listens attentively to what you have to say, smiles broadly, laughs with gusto, and soon dispels any notions about the distance of celebrity. Her words in this story give us insight into an artist at work on her art, and a person at work on improving our world. Listen, if you will.

"The first thing I want to talk about is do you have a dog at the present time?"

"I have two dogs."

"What are they?"

"Bonnie and Clyde, teckels. I've always had teckels, dachshunds. They are small, I can travel with them. They are fit. They are dogs who have great character and they are stubborn and funny and independent. Everything I am looking for in a dog."

"Sounds like the dog we have — a standard poodle."

"They are supposed to be super intelligent."

"She is. She is super nice; she never gets in anybody's face. She is very pleasant."

"Time with animals is important to connect with nature. It is very important."

"So how do you connect with nature?"

"I mountain climb."

"Where do you climb?"

"In the Austrian Alps between Austria and Italy. I really like long hikes. These are nice paths. And you have a goal. Basically a goal is what you need when you are walking. We walked from Florence to Assisi last year. This year we want to walk about 240 kilometers. We already have a plan to walk from Porto to Santiago de Compostela. We are making about 35 kilometers per day. This is what I mean connecting with nature. I need the silence. I need to hear the trees."

"We're hearing them right now (Anne-Sophie and I are having lunch *al fresco* at the famous Blantyre Hotel in the Berkshires at her invitation)."

"Exactly. I need to look birds in the eye. I recall a book from early on that told of a dog called Argos which was the only living creature remembering and recognizing his master, Odysseus, after an eighteen-year absence? I was very touched when I came to that point in the book."

"Tell me about your kids. Are they musicians?"

"No, my son, Richard, is studying law. He is going to become a lawyer like his late father. My daughter, Arabella, is in the arts."

"Anne-Sophie, let's go back to the beginning to the famous maestro, Herbert von Karajan. Would you say that he was the biggest mentor in your life?"

"No, I wouldn't say that. He certainly was the most prominent, and well-known, and influential mentor I had, but already my first violin teacher was an extraordinary mentor. Erna Honigberger knew how to strike a chord in a small child's ability to learn, how to learn, how to be playful to learn, how to keep this child concentrated and focused. Erna was quite a pedagogue. My next great mentor was Aida Stucki at the Winterthur Conservatory in Switzerland. She was my main violin teacher. I had many mentors. I'm a very fortunate person because at many junction points of my life I was really fortunate enough to have people there for me."

"How old were when you studied with Honigberger and Stucki?"

"I started at five and a half. The first lessons were with Erna Honigberger. I had to change because Erna died. She was already quite an elderly lady. At the age of nine I went to the Conservatory in Switzerland to study with Aida Stucki."

"I know your first husband, Detlef Wunderlich, was a lawyer. Was he a musician as well?"

"No, but he loved music and he was von Karajan's lawyer and advisor. That is how we met. His great passion was opera. We would always go to opera performances. He was very close to most of the great opera singers."

"Was he a mentor in life to you, so to speak?"

"No, no. He was much more than that. He was my husband. That is much more than a mentor. There was no mentoring whatsoever."

"How about André Previn, your second husband. He's a great musician, and you have worked with him a lot?"

"Yes, absolutely. He is here having lunch in the music room."

"Oh he is here right now. That's wonderful!"

"Oh yes, we are spending the vacation together. We are still very good friends."

"I guess maybe you would you call him a mentor even though he was your husband?"

"He is a wonderful musical inspirer, a great inspiration."

"He wrote things for you like that violin concerto for the Boston Symphony."

"Yes, various compositions. I've lost count. We are going to premier a new piece he wrote for me for violin and piano once again. It is called the *Fifth Season.* We will present it next year at Carnegie Hall. There are innumerable pieces André has written for me."

"It's great that he is still writing music?"

"He is composing like mad."

"Is there a prime mentor whom you have now?"

"I think life is a mentor. As to a person, it depends on your definition. How would you define the word 'mentor.' Your question asks for a certain definition, so I need to know how you define the word in order to properly answer your question."

"I think of it as somebody to whom you would turn to help you find the answer to musical issues you might have, just like I turn to literary friends to test things out, so to speak."

"Hmm. When it comes to that it is very difficult to say because I'm playing all year round with wonderful musicians, some of them very experienced, others inexperienced. In every musical conversation there is something which touches you, which changes you, so life is a mentor. But I do not have a person I go to with my musical issues. I haven't had one since I left music school. That was at the age of sixteen."

"Still, it is interesting hearing you talk about meeting so many people in your travels around the world."

German-American composer André Previn, muse of Anne-Sophie Mutter.

Photographer unknown, courtesy BSO Archives.

"Yes. With every visit you talk about life and you make music together. Music is not in a vacuum, we all live together, we exchange our political views, and you learn from each other, sometimes by disagreeing."

"There are some people, some major artists, who are known for being alone. They come, they perform, they go, they don't really talk to people, they don't interact. Sounds like you are the opposite of that?"

"I am both of that. I suddenly am a person who needs quietude. I'm happy alone. I'm not someone who is lonely when I'm alone. Because I like silence, and sometimes you can have a great silent time even with people around you. I like people. Generally, I like people a lot. Young people, old people, interesting people. People with passion."

"Well, you like silence. That could be a description of how I feel. Do you like the dark?"

"Yes."

"Do you like the wind? I think you told me you like the wind."

"I do. I'm not so much a fan of storms because I have lots of trees where I live. It seems every time I'm in Austria there is a storm. Of course, with global warming the weather has become so severe in Europe that even now we have things like tornados which we never had before. In the mountains, sometimes the storms are so strong that I can see the trees leaning towards my house, and most certainly I don't like that. If I can avoid it I do not want to be hit by a falling tree."

"Obviously, you believe in global warming."

"I have seen enough scientific evidence to be convinced that global warming is here. I see the bees die. I see that in my small environment. I see drastic changes in nature which are very concerning."

"You say you talk politics with your fellow musicians. We here in America are living in tough times politically. Do you as a European think the United States is losing its way in the world?"

"I think it is very difficult for the countries of the world to stay in an open dialogue. It is difficult for Europe to live with needing to unify so many different countries. America too has many different cultural roots to foster to be able to live in peace and respect. In Europe we started that experiment with the European community not that long ago. We have some very right-wing countries about which we think we cannot agree with what is happening from a democratic viewpoint. In Turkey freedom of the press and speech are threatened, people get arrested and disappear, thousands of journalists and teachers have been imprisoned along with people who speak up, artists, you name it, the man in the street! In such circumstances It is very difficult to still keep an open dialogue, to try to find common ground, and to try to talk reason into relationships. Also, Hungary and Poland have a different viewpoint from the rest of Europe as to how things should go. We need to keep a dialogue and we need to work together. Only when we work together can we survive. Look at plant and animal life. If we let it alone there is the perfect symbiosis between live and let live. I let you live, and you let me live on the surface of your skin and clean it. There are thousands of examples how nature works that way. So that's my answer."

"Can Europe work with the United States anymore?"

"Well, Mrs. Merkel is very open minded and happy to talk. I cannot speak on her behalf, but I know that all of Europe, of course, as we have seen at the G20 Summit, is really trying hard to keep it a G20 Summit, not a G20 less one. There are huge differences like the Paris Climate Accord with which Mr. Trump doesn't agree. I think one sad outcome of that position will also negatively affect the United States because all those many jobs offered by the alternative energy development sector will be diminished. There are a huge number of jobs in solar power created in the States which will now go to China. I don't know if it's really in the interest of any country to isolate itself. Climate is a global thing and we all exist on the same planet. If the air in India is bad, that is bad for America, that is bad for Germany. We all have to ultimately face the fact that whether we like it or not our only chance for survival is to work together."

"Are musicians better at working together than most people?"

"On stage for sure (laughs). Yes, seriously. Look at the East West Orchestra Gold idea of an orchestra which is now flesh and blood and existing! I'm thrilled to bits that I will be part of a tour of the orchestra in 2019, appearing at the Chicago Symphony Center, because I have always believed in the idea. Oh yes, such diverse groups have fierce discussions before and after the performance about their different political viewpoints, but in a respectful manner. They might shift their positions a little, but then you make music together and you share emotions and you realize, 'Wait, this person next to me is from Palestine, she has feelings, she has a mother, she has children, she is weeping, she is in pain when something horrible happens to her people.' Just on a hands-on level you realize that we all have the same needs."

"We are all just people."

"We are all humans, we are all frail, we all have flaws, and we all have to work together. We have to reach out to others."

"So Anne-Sophie, given that musicians have to work together, maybe musicians would be better at running the show. Maybe musicians would be like Angela Merkel and would be better at leading. What do you think?"

"I wouldn't go that far because for politics you need certain skills. It is not a business. First of all, you really need historic knowledge to know where the world comes from, what cycles we go through, what to possibly avoid. That doesn't mean that politicians will necessarily avoid going in the wrong direction. I think music could contribute positively, just because of the climate of having to live with each other, and could perhaps ultimately result in a different political climate, especially if we were to have music education early on. We would then be taught discipline and passion and listening, and to be happy being a member of the group. Happy too to be the leader of the group when it is needed to take a stand, but to be able and comfortable to switch roles, and to listen as much as to lead when appropriate. Music is a character school, and a way to bond culturally with different heritages."

"How about women as politicians?"

"I don't know. I don't mind, women, men, as long as the person has a decent character."

"How about you as a politician, Anne-Sophie?"

"No, I think I would be totally unfit as a politician. I'm much too impatient. I'm very impatient. I am happy and able to make compromises, but I also have very high goals (laughs) and between these three it seems to me it's very difficult to bring them together. Of course, I would like to implement a really proper musical education on a national basis in grammar schools. Maybe one day I might go in this direction, bite the bullet, and just do it so it is done, and then of course immediately leave (laughs)."

"Do you think if young kids have a musical education, they grow up differently, even if they don't become musicians?"

"I think it opens a window on a different kind of thinking because it will also make them more susceptible to read literature and, ergo, to be able to contemplate more about different ways and philosophies of life. We need to read the philosophers. If you look into musicians' lives, they are very often connected with authors, even if it's only for the lyrics. It opens a whole different world away from that world in which one has to learn such and such to become such and such and to be successful at the money game and be able to buy a Mercedes. It would be great if we could bring our children up to pursue the practical aspects of life, because for sure we have to survive, but to also ensure that they are (long pause)..."

"Humanistic?"

"Yes, humanistic. Exactly. Their humanistic side is developed. That's what makes them human. That's what will make them more empathetic, more open minded, more interested, and more neutral towards prejudice."

"Well, Anne-Sophie, they whisked you out of school when you were a kid because you were so talented. You didn't have a childhood like other people, you never went to university like other people. But, obviously, you are speaking like a liberally educated person. Liberal arts have gone down the drain lately. I mean it is computers and numbers and these people are well educated but they don't know anything about life, they think the iPhone is life, and virtual reality is life. How did you get to be that way?"

"Probably growing up in a time where the virtual world didn't exist."

"You talk like you graduated from a liberal arts college and got a real grounding in literature, language, history, politics, and what have you."

"I have a school degree even though I never went to school. I never went to school physically, but I went through all the stages needed to finish school. I just turned fifty-four. I have a life of reading behind me and in front of me. I have fascinating friends who are very well read, and live very thoughtfully, like Lambert Orkis, the pianist I have worked with now for thirty years. Lambert is very inquisitive. He is my very close friend. I've had some great trips with Lambert, his wife, and my children in America to some of your most wonderful national parks like Yellowstone and Sedona. Those places were just absolutely breathtaking and brought me back to my childhood passion, American Indian art. I have always just loved Indian art, Indian pottery. Of course, it is a very sad story because we basically took their identity away, but still their art is existing. It was very important for me to go to the Hopi reservation to connect with the Hopi people because that had been one of my great treasures from my childhood."

"So would you call yourself a small-town girl?"

"Definitely! I grew up in the little town of Rheinfelden at the foot of the Black Forest in no man's land. The great thing though was that part of Europe borders with Switzerland and France, so the multitude of cultural influences there in literature, in music, in the arts, in food, in language, was just tremendous. I think that is what really makes Europe so wonderful! It is so small, and you have these different languages and old ancient cultures. I do think that reflects on and affects the people to let them go through life with eyes more open."

"We spent a summer in Geneva which is similar in that it borders on France."

"Geneva is very slick, isn't it?"

"Slick? (laughs)"

"Maybe I'm not the greatest friend of slick cities. I am a country girl at heart. I love New York. I find it the most exciting place on earth. But after two weeks I am exhausted (sighs). The noise, you know. God, please silence. Give me a meadow. Boston is much more European, and for me as a European it seems to be a place much easier to take."

"Yes, Boston is much easier to take. Brookline where I live borders on Boston. Symphony Hall is like a stone's throw, but Brookline has lots of green areas, and no shopping malls."

"That is wonderful. Who needs all these shopping malls anyhow? Sometimes I go there and I am amazed, but then I'm so overwhelmed by the amount of choices, I don't buy anything. It is just too much. Like a plate full of food I just cannot eat because there is too much choice."

"You said in a couple of places that you didn't want to make the same mistake with your kids that your parents made with you, that they were too strict. Can you tell me something about that?"

"I don't really want to go there. Let's just say that I think all parents can be too strict, particularly when it is the first child. I was the third one."

"Are your parents still alive?"

"Yes. They are a bit insecure. They try their best and they make big mistakes sometimes, other times smaller mistakes. But we all make mistakes. I fear I did too. I love my children to bits, but it is so difficult to be a parent, you know (very quietly and seriously spoken). To say the right words when they are needed, to be strict and give them guidance when they need it, is difficult. A wonderful thing happened two weeks ago. Arabella sat next to me and suddenly out of the blue said, 'I'm so grateful you are my mother because in the difficult years you were strict with me when needed, while some of my friends' parents were not with them. They just didn't seem to care.' I was very grateful for that. But I'm sure you can only try (again spoken quietly). You have to forgive your parents too if you can. I hold no grudge against my parents."

"Anne-Sophie, you are. as you say, a small-town girl who suddenly at a quite young age became one of the greatest violinists, if not the greatest one in the world, and also a very stunning and glamorous person. Some people who have that metamorphosis in their life sort of lose focus, but you don't seem to have lost any focus. So how did you make that transition?"

"Do I look like a stunningly glamorous woman eating my chicken? I don't think so."

"You can't be stunning and glamorous all the time."

"Can't I? (spoken emphatically with humor) I'm disappointed.... Being in the public eye is one thing. I love aesthetics, I love beautiful things in life, flowers, butterflies, and it comes also down to a nice concert dress. And that's that. The concert dress puts me in the mood for the performance. It is what the horses in the circus feel when they get their feathers on their head. I guess they know that it is time to go into the arena and that's that. And I guess every woman wants to look decent."

"Yes, right. So you don't think of yourself that way at all. That's good."

"The artistry is always first."

"Oh yes, absolutely."

"And everything else is whatever it is."

"Listen, I'm happy with that answer because now I think that there wasn't a real metamorphosis. You're the same person you were then."

"In all of us there is a metamorphosis when it comes to your understanding of life and your purpose in life, how you behave towards others, how your goals in life shift when you are a grown-up. Then comes everything else. I guess who you are as a person shines through anyhow. You cannot get away from that."

"What's wrong with looking — I don't know whether glamorous is the right word — but what's wrong with looking terrific and coming out in a nice dress?"

"Exactly. As long as it is not in the forefront of your thinking."

"I like to sit up in the balcony looking down. And close to the stage. I'm watching you play the Tchaikovsky violin concerto, and I'm incredulous at your manual dexterity, but also how you get to the heart of the music."

"It is mentally and physically not an undemanding profession, let's put it that way (laughing)."

"Well where did that technique come from? Would you say that that the manual dexterity you have is athleticism of a sort?"

"It is a tool to bring music to life. You cannot separate it out. It is as if you would ask Roger Federer the same question (here Anne-Sophie enthused about Roger Federer, then about to win Wimbledon for a record eighth time at an advanced age for a tennis champion)."

"You cannot separate one from the other. I mean technique is an exclusive tool, and Roger's technique is a tool of his art. So athletic, non-athletic, yes, of course, being a musician has an athletic component because you cannot eat and drink what you want and then go out on stage. You have to be in good shape to do that. So that's the athletic component. But playing has no athletic component to me, it is just crafting the music which is there in the appropriate architecture of the piece with, of course, your skills being in top-notch shape."

"Would you say that you have the ability to control the violin technically on a higher level than some very high-level violinists around the world?"

"There is always room for improvement. No matter which acoustic I play, like when I play in the shed here at Tanglewood, you basically have to start from scratch again. The acoustic in the tent is a tent acoustic, even though we are reinforced. The big problem here is that the humidity has such a great impact on the size of the sound of the violin because it muffles everything. So the skill really is to be able to play under any circumstance, hot, cold, humid, dry, night, day, upside down or standing on your feet, to bring out the best of what is in you. We can only try. So I guess on the high level on which all the great violinists are, we only try to succeed, and take that as a jumping off point to the next performance."

"I'm not going to ask you a question like who do you think are the greatest violinists in the world besides yourself, but I will say that some people affect me more than others, like Leonidas Kavakos today, and Jascha Heifetz and Yehudi Menuhin in the past?"

"I guess every sender has also receivers. Not every listener can tune into every player. We do relate to some players differently than to others. It is true though that hopefully the aim of us artists must be like the aim of the great Maria Callas. Who wouldn't have been thrown by her singing? We must develop such overwhelming intensity that it is unavoidable not to be hypnotized. Very few of us reach that."

"I wrote a book about baseball. I read someplace that you like hot dogs and baseball. Is that true?"

"Hot dogs, yes. I have not the foggiest notion what baseball is all about, but I love the atmosphere, the people there."

"Oh, you have gone to games?"

"Yes, I have gone to Yankees games, and my son is a great Yankees fan. It seems to be such a friendly atmosphere. If you go to a soccer game in Europe, it is not so friendly. That's what struck me when I first went to a baseball game. It is a family occasion and people really relax, they walk in and out, get hot dogs, the whole thing. Very unprofessional answer I know."

"Anne-Sophie, it is not. It is a very astute answer because even though football, in terms of popularity in the United States, now is considered more popular than baseball, baseball was and still is called the national game. Nobody remembers their first football game or who they went with, but everybody remembers who they went with to their first baseball game. I first went to a Yankees versus the Red Sox game in 1936. My father took me by the hand when I was five years old."

"That's cute." (Anne-Sophie is amused by this).

"Here's a change of subject, Anne-Sophie. When and where did you first learn about the Holocaust?"

"It was very early on in our school curriculum that we were taught about the Second World War, and, of course, the Holocaust was a big part of that education. *The Diary of Anne Frank* was a book my mother gave me very early. And there is another serious book called *When Hitler Stole Pink Rabbit,* which tells in an amusing way about the trip of a young Jewish girl and her family escaping Hitler and the Nazis to Switzerland. My mother was deeply touched by the return of the great violinist, Yehudi Menuhin, to Germany as the first Jewish artist to come back after the Second World War. She told me about that when I was a child, and also about how wonderful it was when the GIs came and threw down care packages. I have this image my mother implanted in me of the great American savior, which has also been passed on through my generation to the generation of my children. I still see my mother's face when she gave me that image. What a great moment it must have been to be liberated by those obviously nice America soldiers! So that is an early memory which is very much in my mind. Reading *The Diary of Anne Frank*, and hearing about the return of Yehudi Menuhin at ten or eleven years gave me a sense of what music really can mean for people."

"I know you do some teaching. Do you carry that idea forward to your students?"

"I try to remind my scholars, and groups like the very nice one yesterday of young music students with whom I had a question-and-answer session, that, of course, we want to hit the right notes and do justice to the score, but that what really counts is that we connect with the listener. That we show that music is more than just an arrangement of sounds. It is really a present from the composer to the listener because it is not only an outpouring of very cerebral work from the composer, but also an outpouring of the soul of this person who has composed every single note in the music. If you look into the lives of artists in general, and in this particular case composers, their lives are not easy, their lives full of obstacles, full of despair, hunger, solitude, and the absolute need to deliver the message they have in them to an audience, and to get a response from that audience. To get a silent response where the audience is just in awe of what they have heard, or an ovation, whatever. It can change the world in a small way!

"Perhaps in a bigger way for some people who don't have much music in their lives?"

"Absolutely. You can do benefit concerts. Not only can you go into refugee camps as Menuhin did, playing for soldiers who have to go to war, you can play for the elderly, you can play to aid children's villages in Aleppo. Someone has to do it, and many of us are doing it. Music can create an atmosphere in which people are more open-minded and open-hearted to donate not only their time but also their money. But it is not all about money. It is about standing still for a moment, contemplating going to an evening where there is a benefit concert being held, and thinking of other people who are not as privileged as both of us are. I guess you have grown up in peaceful surroundings, and have probably been able to choose the profession you wanted to. That is a huge privilege compared to the two thirds of people on our planet who live in warlike circumstances, or those in places where every few seconds someone dies from hunger. That is why we in music have to pull forward and insist on doing good, doing the right thing."

"Anne-Sophie, to whom is your main duty as a performer? To the composer, to the audience, to yourself, to your fellow players? What would you say?"

"To the composer, then to my conscience, to my compass as an artist and a human being. They guide me to what repertoire to play, which sometimes is forgotten or not yet written. I need to play it because someone has to do it. And the other part of the compass is towards my benefit work, but, of course, as a musician, it is first to the composer.

"Then what else can I do in order to help music forward into the future? I do that in the work I do with my foundation, which is now in its twentieth year, to provide for young string players education, contact to great colleagues, to conductors, and to discovering music. We give commissions, we buy instruments, we play together, I tutor them, I take them with me to auditions where they have to play. I help them with anything else I can."

"You seem to have the really good idea of helping them according to their needs, and not on a formulary basis."

"Absolutely. The life of a musician has become even more difficult. It has never been simple. The demands of the media, the fact that music education has basically disappeared from the young generation's life, make it problematic."

"Here it has. I didn't realize so much in Europe, but there too?"

"Yes. Still there is more than here, but the tendencies are clear."

"Why?"

"Why? Because it is considered not to be a necessity. You have to focus on the necessary curriculums in order to have a profession later, and being an artist has always been looked upon as, well, if you must do it, then try, but if it doesn't work out, then after that you can still do something else."

"I know you do a lot of modern music, but let's take the old masters, Beethoven, Bach, Mozart, Schubert, and others. Which of these older masters do you feel close to?"

"I feel close to all of them. Once I study them for the first time, or re-study them, there is no difference. They are all under my skin. One of my favorite jazz songs, *I've Got You Under My Skin,* says it perfectly."

"Let the record show that the wind just blew some of my notes off the table."

"And we have caught them. I'm faster than the wind, now it's official! (heartily laughing)." Anne-Sophie moved in her super athletic way around my bag and retrieved the notes off the ground before they blew away.

"On your website, you mention among your favorite books Marcel Proust's *In Search of Time Lost.* In relation to that you said, 'Only now do I understand my own consciousness. It helps the dark sides of my life, as well as to make my memories become brighter, and it helps me to continue.' Your comments there make it sound like you had some really bad times? Certainly it was dark when you lost your first husband to cancer."

"I think we all have losses. Because I grew up with so many musicians, I grew up with many older people around me. That is just the way the cookie crumbles, you are young and inexperienced, you find teachers and mentors who are obviously more experienced and older than you are, and then you lose them. Loss is part of life, but that doesn't make it any easier. Yes, we all have dark places."

"When you perform any work, especially a new work, do you have a private conversation with yourself about how you are going to interpret and present it?"

"I look at the score. I'm looking for the road map and eventually I will find the road map. Where the theme is, where the development is, what instruments are more prominent in the musical dialogue. Therefore, I have to listen to it, I have to relate to it in changing the tonal quality and character of my instrument. I need to find where the bigger narrative of the piece is, which, hopefully, even if the piece is written in contemporary language, still has the parameters of a classical score. Like John Williams' *Markings*, his new work I'm playing here this week. You have the theme, you have the development with this wonderfully exuberantly joyful and vibrant middle part, and then it goes back in the recapitulation to the theme. So you look at that, you grasp that, you understand that, then the question is how you color it, what tempi you use. If you're lucky you can ask the composer. Sometimes one tempi doesn't agree with another, so you try different tempis. Sometimes the composer has already set a tempo down, and he himself at the first rehearsal might say, 'It doesn't work, let's try it slower or faster,' and then you take it from there. Then the piece has been born, it has been played for the first time, like *Markings* tomorrow, and then it will develop a life on its own. It will be played differently every time by me, and differently, definitely, by violinist colleagues who will have a different perception of it."

"I saw you a couple of years ago conduct the Boston Symphony Orchestra in the five Mozart concertos."

"Oh yes. God, was that humid! I remember that. I thought, *I'm going to die* (spoken with feeling). Seriously, I hope tomorrow is not going to be that bad."

"When you did that, I realized you are a conductor only occasionally."

"I'm only leading."

"Whether as a player or a leader you have to make a lot of decisions?"

"I'm making the decisions. Then too, I have to inspire my colleagues."

"Did Mozart put tempo markings in those concerti?"

"Oh yes, absolutely."

"Did you follow those?"

"Yes, but you know back then he didn't have a metronome. Since Beethoven we have the metronome. Even with metronome markings there is quite a broad street. You can go in fast, but fast can be fast, or just only fluent, or it can be rather hectic. At the end of the process of thinking about an entire piece, let's say a three-movement piece, the relationships between the movements have to work. That's the first parameter. And then you can lean towards a slower allegro or a faster one depending on the acoustic, also your mood a little, and the abilities of the orchestra. Some orchestras are wonderful in slow movements, others don't have such a beautiful tonal quality that you really want to have them play largo, so you move the tempo forward. But the proper relationship between these three or four movements has to be observed."

"I think the last of your favorites here is, *Letters to a Young Poet* by Rainer Maria Rilke. You talked there about the question of what is important in life. Isn't that essentially the question of existence?"

"Do I live in order to play or do I play in order to live? Of course, I live in order to make music."

"What if it was taken away from you, God forbid! Say you suffered an injury."

"That would be very very sad, I think part of my soul would die, but I would still be a very happy mother with two wonderful children. That is a great, great, great gift in life to have children. I think I would be very fidgety listening to my colleagues, but still I could be useful as a musician."

"What about the life of a traveling artist. Do you get lonely or jumpy, or do you have friends everyplace to keep you occupied?"

"I do have friends, but I must say traveling is not as exciting as it used to be."

"No, I wouldn't think so."

"Here at Blantyre it is just totally gorgeous, but generally I am also looking forward to coming home."

"I think everybody does, home is home."

"Home is home, and if you are very rarely home then it makes it more precious. People who don't travel don't understand. They think traveling is the greatest thing. Traveling is important because it is invigorating and teaches you open-mindedness. But there comes a time when if you travel two-thirds of the year it is particularly nice to come home, shut the door, say hello to the kids, and make food for the dogs."

That last statement by Anne-Sophie Mutter says it all about who she is. You can take the girl out of Rheinfelden and into the great world beyond where she lights up the planet, but you can't take Rheinfelden out of the girl who remains a woman for all seasons as adept at making food for her beloved teckels as she is at reaching an impossible high note for her millions of followers.

American mezzo-soprano Susan Graham. Photo by Larry Ruttman.

CHAPTER
13

Susan Graham: Diva and Texas Lady

The word *diva,* related to the expression *prima donna*, both derived from the Italian, did not become words in the English language until late in the nineteenth century when opera became soundly entrenched on the American stage. It applies to female opera singers of overarching vocal ability, as well as to singers of testy disposition who are difficult and hard to please. It applies to Texas born and reared, mezzo soprano, Susan Graham, strictly for her ability, and not at all for her temperament, which is that of a liberated, confident, feisty, but agreeable Texas Lady, much as depicted by transplanted northerner become Texan, as played by Elizabeth Taylor in the 1956 big screen classic, *Giant.* I used the phrase "overarching vocal ability" just above to describe a diva. Let's parse the word "overarching" to discover why Susan Graham is a diva, and others who can sing with equal volume, sometimes beautifully, are not. A sports analogy might help. In football a man who can hurl the football downfield for stupendous distance does not a great quarterback make unless he is accurate on most of his throws. Nor in baseball does a batter who can send drives great distance beyond the boundaries of the playing field on occasion a great batsman make unless he combines that with a certain frequency of safe and timely hits. Nor in opera does a singer with volume and craft a diva make if their singing is not matched by the "overarching" expressiveness required to fully deliver the transcendent beauty and meaning of the aria to our soul. That is the distinguishing factor which determines why so few singers win the accolade of "diva." Obviously, Susan Graham is blessed with an astounding singing voice. As said, that alone is not enough. The following pages will allow you to get to know Susan Graham, and why the manner in which she has lived her life has brought her to that station. It all starts with her family, which you will meet. It is one that might be described as an American family of which any of us would be proud, and which supports her every day to this day. You will experience her own natural persona, which greets each person as an equal while looking every inch the diva whether on or off stage, with no hint of looking down on anyone because of her attainments. You will feel her respect for her musical collaborators, both those with whom she performs music, and those who create it whether here or gone. Her words on issues personal and public will convey to you her good sense, skeptical and keen intelligence, and unwillingness to accept popular opinion against the test of time and her own discretion. Perhaps most telling is Susan Graham's ongoing sense of the improvement of her art by studying the conductors under whose batons she performs, by her creation of the characters she plays with her own ideas superimposed on her study of past practices, her self-examination of what it is she wants to convey to her audiences, her humility confronting the works of the composers she interprets, and her wonderment before the power of music.

"We are here with Susan Graham today on January 19, 2018. Susan, how are you today?"

"I am feeling very fulfilled."

"Why do you feel fulfilled?"

"Lucky enough to sing Mahler 3 with the fantastic BSO."

"Mahler's view of the symphony was it should be about the whole world and that one is."

"It is amazing. I feel like my contribution is a drop in the ocean and then the real thing happens after I'm finished. Sitting through that sixth movement is just incredible."

"I was sitting up in the balcony and I thought that your body language last night was very modest. The feeling I got from you was like I only sang a part here, what about all these couple of hundred other people performing."

"That's exactly how I felt (laughing). By the time the applause comes my part is long gone. We've been to a whole other universe since then."

"During the curtain call you even went so far as to sit down and watch it like you were in the audience."

"Well, I was in the way. The conductor, Andris Nelsons, was standing up the brass section and I was blocking the audience's view of them, so I had to get out of the way. They had already seen me."

"Had you ever performed with Nelsons before?"

"I did *Der Rosenkavalier* with him last season."

"He has risen to the top. What is your impression of him in this go-round?"

"The rehearsal was kind of perfunctory. He seems to be a person who wants to get the nuts and bolts ironed out at rehearsal. Then once the performance begins he brings in the magic. On stage we were in a whole other realm than at the rehearsal the day before."

"How soon did you realize you were in another realm?"

"I don't come on stage until right before the movement I'm in. From the first notes of my movement it already was very different than it had been the day before at rehearsal."

"What is his magic?"

"Deep feeling and great risk-taking with tempo and dynamic. I observe that he is completely unselfconscious. He is a shy person one-on-one, but once he gets into the music-making he completely transforms. He becomes someone else who isn't at all worried about his enormous gesture or his lunge at the first violins. I'm afraid sometimes that I'm going to get my eye poked out with an errant baton. It's like he is in a trance. It's quite astonishing."

"Would you say that is able to make music that is more beautiful or more feeling than a lot of other conductors?"

"It is hard for me to compare. I've done Mahler 3 a lot and other conductors have equally deep interpretations. Everybody is different. He's quite young, I think he is not yet forty. For a conductor that young to have such a depth and fearlessness of interpretation is extraordinary."

"Did you feel differently singing last night as opposed to this afternoon's performance?"

"I hoped I was in the right place because sometimes when Andris is conducting his beat becomes sort of amorphous. That is part of what makes his music-making so great. The part that I have to sing is sort of very tricky rhythmically. Typically, Mahler is very irregular, and so is my part. So I'm just sort of watching him and waiting for him to look at me and kind of invite me to start my phrase (laughing). I was tiptoeing a little bit cautiously last night. I mean just in my head, not musically. Today it was a little better because we did it last night, so today we had one under our belt and felt a little more comfortable with it. I feel like tomorrow it will be even better."

"Is that what you mean about his taking chances?"

"Yes, because there are people who want to do it right and there are people who want to do it musically, and sometimes those two are not mutually exclusive but sometimes one can preclude the other. You can be metronomic, you can go by the beats, you can do everything that the composer wrote, and do it so it's not flat, but it can be less profound than someone who sort of just squeezes every ounce of expression out of every beat which I feel is kind of what Nelsons does."

"Speaking of conductors of the BSO, we lived with Seiji Ozawa for like thirty years. I thought he was great, but there are other opinions out there. I'm just curious about yours?"

"I've always loved every minute with him. I had no problem ever."

"Are you able to discern the conductor's idea of what he wants to convey to the audience, especially those who don't talk much?"

"The best conductors don't talk, they show with gestures, but don't talk much about it. They show with their body, show with their hands. Lots of times in those beautiful more lyrical moments you'll notice Andris wasn't even using a baton. His hands were like he was molding with clay. He was molding the music."

"What do you think of Mahler as a composer?"

"Nothing gets to my soul like a Mahler symphony. He just taps into so much of what being a human being is. There is this very human rise and fall in his music which makes your heart pound. The sheer musicianly creativity of the composition is awe inspiring. It's all about how it gets you in the gut."

"We'll talk more about Mahler a little later. Susan, is there such a thing as a Texas personality? Do you have one? What is it?"

"Everything in Texas is bigger than life. I come from a city that's called the tall city, and the motto of the town is 'the sky's the limit,' so that, coupled with my upbringing in New Mexico which has the biggest skies in the world, allowed me to grow up feeling that I had no limits on me. That I could do anything I tried to do. A Texas personality is someone who's generally, to my way of thinking, friendly and affable and open and not pretentious and just sort of welcomes everybody, the more the merrier, and easygoing."

"You're talking about me (laughing)."

"See, you're an honorary Texan."

"How about your ability to self-evaluate as a person and musician?"

"I know pretty much what my flaws and my strengths are both personally and musically."

"Are you good at taking criticism?"

"If I feel it is justified I'm very quick to be able to say, 'I'm sorry you are right, that was my fault.' It is also very easy for me to say 'You screwed up (laughing).'"

"Right, hey, tell it like it is."

"I've gotten in trouble for telling it like it is because sometimes, in the interest of brevity and succinctness, I don't sugarcoat it the way some people might like me to. I used to be very concerned with being friendly and being liked. It is very important for me to be liked, so that's part of my gestalt, I guess. But the older I get the less filters I have."

"Wait until you get into your eighties. You really won't care. You'll let it all hang out."

"I know, I'm in my fifties and it's already there. I'm getting there."

"You'll figure how long can it go on, and who will remember anyway (laughing)?"

"What do you have to lose?"

"What would you say your parents' big effect on you was? Are they still around?"

"Unflagging support. My mother is still alive. My father passed away in 2000. He was my Rock of Gibraltar. She used to come see me perform. My mother is not able to travel much anymore, but when I appear in Texas she can make the car trip."

"What would you say is the main thing you got from your parents that has allowed you to progress the way you have?"

"They were always just so proud of me, always so happy when I had success. All three of us, my sister and brother and me, are great achievers in our own fields, and we all were encouraged to be the best that we could be. There was a real work ethic instilled in us by our parents, and a real priority of being kind and respectful to people, no matter who. Oh lord, if I had to leave you with one impression it would be that I owe so much to my family. My siblings and I have never had a fight, my parents were married for over fifty years, we don't squabble, we just have such harmony. I grew up in a *Leave It to Beaver* household, very harmonious, not affluent, but always enough. I feel very, very lucky that I had the kind of parents who appreciated everything that came their way. I think that is one of the reasons that I'm perpetually surprised and astonished when I look at what my life is. This wasn't supposed to happen to a little girl from Roswell, New Mexico."

"It is a very American answer though. What you've just said, Susan, is what we hope that somebody will say. It expresses great family values."

"It's 'the American Dream,' I guess."

"Can you trace your ancestors, or even family you have known, back to another part of the country?"

"My grandparents on both sides were ranchers in eastern New Mexico. A tradition of hard work came from them. In those times in that part of the country it is just what you had to do. There wasn't anybody to do it for you. My grandfather on my mother's side was born in 1896 and came as a little boy in a covered wagon from North Carolina. I don't know how they got to North Carolina. He became one of the biggest ranchers in southeastern New Mexico."

"I never was terrifically interested in genealogy, but the New England Historical Genealogical Society, which is close to 175 years old and through which Harvard professor Henry Louis Gates produces the television program *Roots,* collected my papers. I don't yet know what my genealogy is, but if you ever want to find out about yours, they would be delighted with you, Susan. Maybe you would be interested in that?"

"I'm always interested in that. What I know is that on my mother's side they were mostly English and on my father's side were mostly Scottish because Graham is a Scottish name. What was discovered thirty years ago was that the little boy who grew up to become one of my great, great, great grandfathers came over on a ship from Scotland. He started the journey as a 'Collins,' his parents died in transit, and the Grahams who were on that trip, adopted him. So he spent the rest of his life as a Graham and we therefore are Grahams, but apparently we originally were Collinses (laughing). Isn't that weird? So maybe genealogically we are Irish."

"Wow, that is fascinating. They could probably uncover the whole story. Maybe Professor Gates would be interested in it?"

"That would be interesting. Yeah, that would really be interesting!"

"Are you married, Susan?"

"I married Clay Brakeley, a Californian, recently. That is my first marriage. Actually he grew up in Texas with me. We went to college at Texas Tech at the same time. He has lived in California for thirty years, so I guess that makes him a Californian."

"How is it going?"

"We are still together after a whole year (laughing)."

"Are you able to spend a lot of time with him?"

"No, that's probably why (laughing). He works on the road too, but we will be together in Los Angeles next week. We're both just extremely self-sufficient. We've been on our own for a long time."

"Susan, I guess the two people that The Met prefers for backstage interviews are...."

"Renée Fleming and me."

"Yeah, right. Both of you are very charming ladies. I remember one you did with Russian soprano, Anna Netrebko. She seems to be a character as well as an astounding singer."

"Yes, she is. She was doing *Don Pasquale* and had beautiful costumes for the opera. On camera she lifted up her skirt to show her brightly colored stripy tights and her high-top boots and very beautiful stockings. I remember that. I also remember Dolora Zajick who is a particular personality although she's not real talkative on camera."

"Oh, yes. She's been with the Met quite a while."

"Yes. She's from Reno, Nevada, a low mezzo soprano, now in her sixties. She has a shy personality, but when she says something, it will get your attention. I was interviewing her and thought I've got to make her feel comfortable so she will talk to me on camera. It was the occasion of her twenty-fifth anniversary at The Met. So I said, 'How does it feel to be here on your twenty-fifth anniversary and doing this amazing role of the witch in Dvořák's *Rusalka?'* At the time she had her teeth blacked out, wore a big fake nose, and looked like a witch. She looked hard at me and said, '***My*** twenty-fifth anniversary! You're no spring chicken yourself, you know (laughing).' I remember that one. I remember interviewing the Latvian soprano, Elina Garanca, who was in Mozart's *La clemenza di Tito*, singing Sesto. I had sung that role and now she was singing it. Normally the questions they give us are kind of generic, so sometimes I tend to go off script and mix them up a little bit. I said to Elina, 'What was really impressive to me having done this role in this production before is that you came down that long staircase, and you didn't look down once at your feet even once.' Elina actually jumped up and down and said, 'You noticed, you noticed. I counted every step beforehand to make sure that I would not trip. I did not have to look, because when you are singing you don't want to be looking down at the steps.' She was very excited that I noticed. So that is a backstage secret."

"What would you say is your most memorable live in HD Met performance?"

"My last performance of *Der Rosenkavalier* with Renée Fleming in 2010. I remember it for two reasons. In the first scene when we are on the bed, my character, Octavian, jumps off the bed to close the window to keep the morning sun out to prolong the evening. I had to run across the stage to do that and instantly got a terrible charley horse like an ice pick going through my leg, with live HD cameras filming me all over the world. I had to act like nothing happened. So I started skipping to take the weight off of this painful leg. Then I went back to the bed singing with Renée. I had my leg up here and was massaging it secretly while I was singing. It was painful the entire day. You can still watch that video and can see the moment when it happened. For me that was the most memorable performance also because I knew it was the last time I was going to be doing that role with Renée. It was all very touching."

"Susan, I'm interested in the creation of operatic characters by an opera singer. What goes on in the singer's psyche as you prepare the role? Where does the inspiration come from? Let's take three roles you are famous for: Cherubino in *The Marriage of Figaro* by Wolfgang Mozart, Octavian in *Der Rosenkavalier* by Richard Strauss, and Marguerite in *The Damnation of Faust* by Hector Berlioz. Respectively as to age, I judge them to be maybe fifteen for Cherubino, eighteen for Octavian and early twenties for Marguerite. Those are not far apart in years but they are very far apart in the development of a person. So I ask you to at this moment to look inside yourself to your memories of creating these roles to tell us the inner dynamics you experienced to create these roles. Did you create these roles from reading, coaches, the score, the music, your own life, your own experiences at those and other ages? These are really interesting characters. Cherubino was...."

"Hormones on a stick (laughing). A hormonesicle."

"And Octavian is a little older...."

"Not much older. Well, a serious consideration is the gender of the character because I play boy parts and I play girl parts. First of all, the age of a trouser role that I would play is not as important to me because they are all quite young, even Sesto is young. People have always asked me about the physicality of playing a male character. It's not that I'm thinking I'm going to be male, it's not like an artificial butchness that you superimpose on the character, it's more of a youthfulness. I have five nephews that I've watched grow up, five different young men in all stages, all in their thirties and forties now, but twenty years ago they were adolescents when I was learning these parts. I had five to choose from, so I could pick the youngest one for the fifteen-year-old, I could pick the middle one for the eighteen-year-old, or whatever. I was able to watch the physicality of young boys who are kind of like big puppy dogs, their feet are too big, they don't know what to do with their hands, and they are awkward in certain ways. That is something I've always tried to incorporate physically, a sort of physical verisimilitude. As far as getting inside the mind of these characters all of the things you listed go into the formation of an idea of a character for me. I do read about them, I do have lots of coaching, I do talk to people who have done the roles before, I seek advice, I listen to recordings a little bit but not a bunch. That is because what is most effective for me is to come to it with kind of a blank canvas. I have all this information in the back of my head, but the actual character, the personality, what the character thinks, the choices that he will make or she will make, come to me spontaneously. It grows throughout a rehearsal process, but even in a performance it can be spontaneous because the character is the one making the choices not me. If I'm going to go to a table and pick up a glass of water, it's Cherubino deciding to do it not me. So how Cherubino would pick it up might be different than how I would pick it up, or Octavian, or Marguerite. At the same time it all has to do with my own perception, my life, my way of looking at things and there's a lot in the Marguerite that you heard a couple of months ago that has grown up with me as I've grown up as a woman. The way that I sing a certain phrase has to do with some of my own experiences, some of my own breathlessness at being in love, which is different than it was twenty years ago. The important thing to me is to make it as organic and as honest as I can in the moment. That requires a lot of preparation beforehand so that you are free to make the choices in the moment."

"How about the composers speaking to you, so to speak. Do you hear Mozart's voice or Strauss's voice or Berlioz's voice?"

"No, just what the composer puts on the page. The score speaks to me, that is his voice really."

"I know you love to play the piano. Is that a help to you in learning a role?"

"I play as much as I can. Whenever I have music to learn I learn it on my own at the piano. I save a lot of money on coaches (laughing). With a new role, I certainly find a coach to help me fine-tune and memorize, but I don't have to have anybody teach me the notes. I have been a musician since I was six years old. I've studied piano my whole life. I've had a very rich musical life. I think that the musical language of the composer is something that becomes pretty quickly evident to me, the kind of phrasing, the kind of articulation, the kind of expression within a phrase because sometimes when you have text and you've got the music, they are not saying the same thing at the same time. The text is saying one thing but the music might be saying something else so you have to decide which one you are going to play at that moment. The text can be saying I'm so happy but the music can be saying I'm really sad (laughing). You have to find a way to make that work."

"What is your favorite musical instrument?"

"I can only play one, and that's the piano. But I love a good English Horn. A well-played violin or cello may be the most beautiful instrument."

"How about the human voice?"

"I have to believe that. I'm a singer (laughing)."

German composer Richard Strauss, muse of Susan Graham.

Credit: Rijksmuseum, CC0, via Wikimedia Commons.

"In every other situation the instrumentalist plays the instrument, but the vocal cords are the person himself or herself. Could it be that the human voice in the hands of a master is more expressive than any instrument?"

"Absolutely. Absolutely. I mean all violinists try to play like we sing."

"(Laughing) They can't do that."

"They'll say it, they'll say it."

"You've played these roles, dance roles, other roles, all roles. Of the characters you've portrayed which ones are the most like you?"

"They are all a little like me. I've never played a character that is nothing like me."

"So does that mean that human beings are a little bit of everything?"

"Yes. Octavian is like me because he's very loving, he's funny, and he kids around. He is also very ardent and passionate. Cherubino is the same. Marguerite is lovesick and breathless. Didon in *Les Troyens* by Hector Berlioz is probably the one that I identify most with at this point in my life because she's a queen and beloved by her subjects, but then falls madly in love and feels like a sixteen-year-old. Then at the end of the opera she is betrayed, and she is heartbroken and furious. I've been through all of those things and I can relate a lot. I've never thrown myself on a funeral pyre. Not yet. Probably from a human and female standpoint she would be the one I closely identify with."

"What singer has affected or inspired your singing the most?"

"I was very inspired by my slightly more senior peers who were having the big explosion in their careers when I was just starting out. The people I was lucky enough to sing with like Thomas Hampson, certainly Renée, are of the same age basically. I also I studied with singers older than me who were inspiring, like Christa Ludwig, Tatiana Troyanos, and Placido Domingo. Flicka inspires me in music and life (laughing). I used to say whenever I had a hard time in a rehearsal or some personality conflict, how would Flicka handle this, how would Flicka do this. Flicka is the nicest person in the universe so she has always been a beacon of good behavior when I was tempted to do otherwise."

"Flicka? I must be missing something. Sounds like a Wagnerian character."

"Flicka, Frederica von Stade, sorry."

"I understand Frederica von Stade and James Levine had a lot to do with your career taking off?"

"Oh yes. When Frederica had to cancel singing Cherubino in *Figaro*, she told me that as her understudy even before she told Met management so that I could invite my parents to come up from Texas to see my debut in that role. I feel like that launched me because up until then I had just been doing understudies and small roles. Jimmy Levine was in the pit for the performance, looking up to me, blowing me kisses, and being so supportive. After that he assigned me better roles. I got to sing Octavian in *Rosenkavalier* the next year."

"You also made the remark that that is why we love Jimmy. He certainly was very helpful to many singers who idolized him."

"He invented the opera world we live in in this country. I don't think that's too strong a statement. And certainly at the Metropolitan Opera."

"I was fascinated with Tatiana Troyanos and I was really upset when she passed away. Was that sudden?"

"She had cancer, but she didn't tell anybody."

"What was it that was so arresting about Tatiana Troyanos?"

"She was a tortured soul. She was nervous and neurotic and fearful. Every time she opened her mouth you felt like she was really on the edge because basically she was. That made her very, very exciting as a singer. Audiences sensed a tension and an energy that is very compelling. I sang next to Tatiana in a production of *La clemenza di Tito.* She sang Sesto, and I was the sidekick, Annio, so we sang Mozart duets in thirds. At the end she vibrated, just vibrated. She was not a real happy person. Early on in rehearsals, even though I had just met her, and was only twenty-nine, she was not very nice to me. The only reason that she was ever nice to me was because she got to know my dog and loved my puppy, Libby, the poodle who lived for eighteen years. Libby was brand-new then, six months old."

"We talked some about Renée Fleming. You and she are special friends. Tell us whatever more you want about Renée because she, like you, is one of the most famous sopranos around, divas, if you will."

"We grew up in this business together like sisters. She's a very down-to-earth mom who happens to be a very glamorous world diva (laughing), but she's shy and like all of us she has her own insecurities She wants to please people, she always has her audience first in her mind, she wants to give people what they want, and she has a voice that is touched by God. Just the most beautiful voice I have ever heard."

"What makes her a good friend?"

"She's very loyal, very honest, and genuinely very generous. Renée sang at my wedding."

"I got a kick out of reading about you spending last Thanksgiving at a karaoke bar. You described it as like a circus. Tell us about it?"

"That's where opera people go to let our hair down. We don't do it often. It's just the chemistry of all these people together who had never been all together before. it was mainly our cast from *The Merry Widow.* Paul Groves is a great tenor and a party animal, and when he and I are doing a show together, because we are such great friends, we like to have a lot of fun. So that always kind of bubbles up and we gather everyone around. Paul is like the Pied Piper. He can just say 'Come on y'all,' and everybody goes OK let's go (laughing). There is always fun around Paul."

"Susan, what is music?"

"Life. Music is life. Music is a reflection of who we are as humans. Music tells us things that words can't, it ignites feelings in us that we didn't know we had, and it can reach a depth that nothing else can."

"That is quite a statement! Is it the greatest of the arts?"

"Yes (here singing). Yes, says Richard Strauss who believed music is a Holy Art. My character, The Composer in *Ariadne auf Naxos,* sings that: 'Musik ist eine heilige Kunst…'"

"Could we live without music?"

"Why would you want to?"

"Where does it come from and where does it go?"

"I can only think it comes from God because I don't know."

"Are you a religious person?"

"Not really, but whatever the definition of that is, I'm sitting there today and listening to the sixth movement of a Mahler symphony. I'm surrounded by it, I'm in the middle of it, it is going through my body, the vibrations are blowing my head up and it is overwhelming. I was crying by the end of it. I'm thinking how does this come out of someone's head, how can a human being hear this and put it all together in this way that makes water come out of my face, how does that happen? Bach! How is that perfection possible? Beethoven, Mozart! It's unfathomable to me that someone can just be like, 'Oh I think I'll sit around and write *Don Giovanni* today. I don't understand."

"I used to think that *Don Giovanni* was the greatest opera, but now I think it is *The Marriage of Figaro.*"

"It might be. I don't know. I think that there is a divine inspiration that wants to be heard. And where does it go? It goes into our hearts, it goes into our souls, and it goes into making us who we are."

"We see that the North Koreans are going to send a symphony orchestra down. Is music a path for understanding among the contesting nations of the world?"

"Yes, I think so. I'll tell you a funny story. When I was very young back in 1988, I was invited to go to Shanghai with around six other artists by the San Francisco Opera Center which is the young artists branch of the San Francisco Opera. We and the conductor, Patrick Summers, did a cultural exchange with the Shanghai Conservatory and the Shanghai Philharmonic Orchestra. We also joined with them to do a production of *Tosca* with two of our American singers and some of their Chinese singers. Part of that week was also a gala concert including the final trio from *Rosenkavalier.* There were old Chinese men playing in this orchestra whose instruments had been buried under floorboards during the Cultural Revolution. When we started the first rehearsal for that *Rosenkavalier* trio, it became clear that these men had never heard it before and were playing these old instruments with tears coming out of their eyes. They had grown up during a time when hearing this music was forbidden. That was such an eye-opening experience for me because it is something that we in this country take for granted. I grew up listening to *der Rosenkavalier* ever since I was a freshman in college, but here these older professional musicians had never heard it before. And the power that it had over them was so moving that it made me believe in the power of music. And so yes, I think that if musicians in their musicianly heads and musicianly hearts from different cultures can come together, then it can work miracles."

"That is great to hear, Susan. I want to ask if opera is headed in the right direction to survive at a time when it appears looks have as much importance as talent in getting the role."

"I read a review today of Seattle Opera's *Così fan tutte.* The first line said it was a lovely cast of attractive young singers, and I thought OK, but what priority does that have in casting. I think it has a very high priority."

"Should it?"

"I don't think it should be a priority over voice, but there are some opera companies which have to market any way that they can. And if they have to put young movie star good looks on the stage to get people in their small town to come, then that's what they'll do."

"So what do you think the future of opera is? Do you think it will remain a viable art form?"

"I think so because I looked out today and last night, we are doing Mahler's Third symphony, and virtually every seat is taken. I think opera is the same way. We do a lot more performances, so it is harder for us to sell out every house. Our challenge now in opera is to find ways to attract new patrons. At one of the performances I did of *The Merry Widow* at the Met recently, the audience was laughing at every funny thing we did. There was a guy in the second row laughing out loud. They were hollering and just really in the spirit of it. Backstage we were amazed because normally our Met audiences are quite serious. This audience was going crazy. We found out that out there was a group called Fridays Under 40. They give them free booze before the show starts, free champagne. They come in, they are ready for a good time, and it was the best show that we had done because the audience was giving us so much we gave them back more. And we thought if we could have audiences that happy and excited every time, what fun that would be."

"So what's the moral of the story, younger audiences, champagne?"

"Free booze. I think it's the free alcohol (laughing)."

"When singing in an opera what is it you want to convey to the audience? You have been quoted as saying I'm giving a gift from my heart to the audience."

"I just want them to understand what the character is going through, what the character feels. If I can convey that then I'm happy."

"I would ask you the same question as to recitals?"

"Similar. It's a little less concrete because a lot of art songs are poetry which is sometimes more vague in its meaning. I do have to have a viewpoint. I have to establish what my viewpoint is on that song and then how to actively communicate everything that I think it means. It's really about arousing feeling."

"Do you do many song recitals? Do you like to do them?"

"When I'm doing them, I like doing them. They are daunting to think about, and it's really daunting to create new programs. I'm touring a program right now that I really, really like, but I've done it nearly everywhere in the world, so now everyone is clamoring at me to do a new program. I don't want to do a new program. I want to keep doing this one, but you can't do the same thing forever."

"Whose songs do you like to do?"

"Mahler, Berlioz. I like to dabble in songs that people don't know very well. I like to do some Tchaikovsky songs now and then. And I've got a group of Scandinavian songs. I sing in Norwegian and Danish and Swedish."

"Are there composers you especially like?"

"Mozart, Berlioz, Mahler, and Strauss. Those are the big four for my singing. I love Prokofiev songs, even though I don't sing any of them. I love Beethoven symphonies too. I believe in music every day, and whenever I hear those composers or, for example, Tchaikovsky, Bach, Handel, Bruckner, I am truly mystified by the miracle!

"The last one is the same question of what it is you want to convey to the audience, this time as to singing something which is like the Mahler 3 you did last night, in which you have a part but there is a huge chorus and a big orchestra. It could as well be *The Damnation of Faust.*"

"Well, there is quite a big difference, I think. *The Damnation of Faust* is not called an opera by its composer, Hector Berlioz, but it is an opera. It's a story with characters and very specific events going on, and very specific feelings. But the text in the Mahler 3 is pretty esoteric. I have to decide at certain points whether I'm just another instrument in the orchestra or whether I'm delivering some very profound message from God. I mean that's Mahler's whole thing. Mahler is struggling with trying to be godly. But this is Friedrich Nietzsche poetry and writing in the Mahler 3, and it's kind of difficult to define exactly what it's all about. In the Mahler 3, I say something in one place, and then 45 seconds later I have two notes. So there is not a lot of development. I think I'm kind of another textured instrument in this case. Because I have a lot of duet moments with the principal violinist. I say something and then he says it back to me, and I say something and he says it back to me, and that's sort of musical interplay there."

"So is that different than communicating with the audience for the other two forms?"

"Yes. A piece like Mahler 3 is quite unusual because it's kind of piecemeal. For me there is not a big through line in the development. There is not even a proper song, whereas in the Mahler 4 there is an actual song. Mahler 2 has a little more concrete text for a soprano and a mezzo. Mahler 8 is the *Symphony of a Thousand,* so you've got a whole bunch going on, eight soloists and a giant chorus, so that is a unique symphony. It's particular requirements, particular demands. So my point is that my expressive tool is not necessarily the text but vocal color. Vocal color is my main preoccupation in the Mahler 3."

"So what do you think your relationship is with the audience? What do you owe them off the stage?"

"My gratitude. Meeting them, seeing them, talking to them. I always do that."

"I was very affected by your performance of Marguerite couple of months ago under Charles Dutoit in *The Damnation of Faust.* How do you rate Charles Dutoit as a conductor?"

"Top. Certainly I've done quite a bit of French music with him. He's an institution. He has a way with French music that is wonderful. He's just the real deal. That performance of *Faust* was fantastic."

"I suppose that a lot of the things that have come out against Charles lately in this 'Me Too' time may have an element of truth to them?"

"It's hard to know. I think that generally speaking, not just of Charles, there could be misinterpretation, there could be exaggeration, there could be an axe to grind, there could be bitterness, there could be any number of things. I'm not out and out doubting the veracity of what people have felt or alleged, but I do think it is a shame when a misplaced flirtation leads to the end of someone's career. There are gradations."

"God, or whatever the force is out there, put men and women on the earth and made men and women the way they are."

"I think in the performing arts generally, and especially speaking about conductors and performers in music, there is an undeniable sexual energy that drives what we do. For instance you can't listen to a Mahler symphony, particularly the sixth movement, of the third, without thinking that there are some very basic primitive depictions going on in that music. You cannot deny it. To be able to fully, no pun intended, flesh out everything that's there, there are many, many different kinds of energy one has to tap into. I think on an opera stage it's the same thing as in symphony, or chamber music, or a Schubert song. All music has sex in it. Take *Der Rosenkavalier.* Oh, my God, hello! That opening scene is so graphic (making a musical noise)."

"What about the allegations against James Levine? Are they going to stop his career?"

"Oh yes. He's done. I fear he's done."

"Do you put those allegations in a different category than those against Dutoit?"

"It is hard to say. I think no one should be made to feel that they have no choices. No teenager, male or female, no young woman, no older woman, no one should be made to feel that have no choices. However, I feel quite strongly that there are situations in which a woman or a man has choices, whoever is on the receiving end of these advances. And they make choices. I've been on the receiving end of flirtations before, and I made choices. I made choices to turn around and walk out the door. It didn't harm me. It didn't change my career. And I never lost work over it that I know of. Maybe I did, but I don't care. There comes a point where some of those choices might be difficult for some people if they say to themselves, 'Oh you know the casting couch will give me opportunities.' But that's a choice you make."

"Why do you say that Levine is done?"

"Because the people who are making allegations against him were young people who felt like they could benefit from him. When you are underage, that is another discussion. But everybody has a brain and the ability to use it."

"How do you see your future? How much longer do you think you want to sing opera?"

"Maybe five more years. Then, still singing if I can, doing recitals and orchestral concerts."

"How about administration and stuff like that?"

"I'm not really that interested. I'm the Artistic Advisor to the Los Angeles Opera Young Artists Program. I mentor them and coach them. I impart my experience and try to pass the torch to younger singers. I don't fancy myself a voice teacher and I don't want to go into an academic situation."

"So what do you call that?"

"Coaching, mentoring. That's probably the direction that I'll go. I like being sort of the fairy godmother who flits in and waves her magic wand, sprinkles fairy dust, and says you're wonderful, then goes away and comes back in a couple of weeks and does the same thing. That's really what this program is now for me. So yes, I do want to have some involvement with young singers."

"The coaching can make them a lot better, right?"

"Yeah, my goal is to help them figure out what is inside of them and help them unlock it."

"Yes, because that's the only way they are going to be able to communicate with their audience?"

"And at a certain age they are just out of school, they haven't really started working professionally yet and being exposed to so many great conductors and great directors around the world. They haven't had that experience yet that hopefully, God willing, they will have. To prepare them for that I like to give them permission to dig deep for expressiveness, because when they come out of school they are very preoccupied with doing it right, and doing everything by the book. Because all they receive is criticism in school, in conservatories. You are just criticized, that's all anybody ever does, nobody ever says you should have an original thought, and let's expand on that. That's really what I want to help them start to discover."

"Absolutely. Well, you will be happy to know that even though I have a lot of other questions I'm not going to ask them all (laughing), but there are a few that I'd like to ask."

"I'll give you two more (laughing). Choose wisely (laughing). I'm going to a concert at NEC tonight, at Jordan Hall."

"Social media is with us to a fare thee well. Is that good or bad? What is your stance on social media?"

"I have mixed feelings. I don't believe in giving everything away. Not every private thought that I have needs to end up on social media. Facebook is a private thing for me. It is only for people that I'm related to and people that I consider my good friends. Have you read my three criteria for whether I'll be connected with you on Facebook? I have three criteria. The first is I have to know your name. The second is I have to recognize your face if I see you. And the third is I have to give you a hug and mean it when we come in contact. If any of those three criteria are not met, I won't friend you on Facebook, and that means most fans. After today's performance I get ten Facebook requests and I turn them all down because that's not what Facebook is for me. It's a way for me to stay in touch with people that I know and are in my life outside of Facebook. I have colleagues who have a thousand friends on Facebook because every time they go anywhere they'll add thirty people from the orchestra who they may never see again. I'm not interested in that. I'm too old to be trying to convince people to love me. If they can't love me through my art then I'm not going to go on social media and tell them to love me. I can't be bothered."

"What's your greatest unrealized ambition going forward in your life? (pause) I like it when I ask a question and you have to think about it a little."

"Unrealized ambition? Well, let's see, I won a Grammy, I've been in a movie, I have held the *Mona Lisa* in my hands, I've sung for the queen, I've met a lot of movie stars, (laughing). It's a real unrealized ambition, to act in a straight play. I'd like to do that."

"Well, you'll get to do that! Susan. This was a delightful interview. I love talking to you. I knew I would have fun talking to you, just from hearing you perform and hearing you talk on the Opera America program you did a few years ago."

"Well, I'm glad you think so."

It's anybody's guess how all these facets of Susan Graham's life have combined to make her the diva and human being she is. About all we can be sure of is that they have so combined. The alchemy of that remains a mystery never to be solved, just as we wonder about how the greatest composers who ever walked among us came into being. Susan Graham's own words spoken above bear repeating here: "Music is life. Music is a reflection of who we are as humans. Music tells us things that words can't, it ignites feelings in us that we didn't know we had, and it can reach a depth that nothing else can."

American violist Kim Kashkashian. Photo © Silvia Lelli / Lelli e Masotti Archivio.

CHAPTER
14

Kim Kashkashian: Master Violist, Committed Pedagogue, World Citizen

Everyone into classical music around the world knows that Kim Kashkashian is one of the great violists of our time. As such she travels the world. But she stays home a lot too because she is devoted to family, her daughter, her important work as the founder of the growing organization, *Food for Music,* and her devotion to her teaching. One might say she is a happy medium between the world virtuoso who is always on a plane and the stay-at-home musician who teaches, plays locally, coaches at the conservatory, gives to good causes, and is a contributing member of her community. Kim Kashkashian dons many garbs: a lovely gown performing before the public, ordinary attire teaching a class, business dress from time to time to address a large gathering or a small group on feeding challenged populations, or on the history and workings of the viola. Or Kim may discourse on how music is a tool against existential threats, or on how her Armenian background has equipped her to translate the folk music of that land into the songs of today, or about her mentors who are among the greatest of present day composers, or about sonics and the production of the sound played by her and others to the pleasure of her audiences, or how we should react to soloists who move about on the stage as opposed to those who stand and deliver, or about the values of reading, or on diverse other subjects crowding her alert, interested, and loving persona. Is Kim a metaphor for why the rest of us love musicians, whether classical or pop, and throng the venues where they perform? To take it a step further, is Kim a metaphor for the notion that life and music are one, and that to attend a concert is often a transcendental experience which reaches deep into our soul.

"Kim how are you today?"

"I'm very well thank you. We are trying to stay cheerful on this gloomy and icy day."

"Kim, one of my favorite compositions and perhaps the best one that Mozart wrote before he left Salzburg for Vienna was the *Sinfonia Concertante for Violin and Viola.* The other night I listened to a very enchanting performance of that by you and Gidon Kremer, led by Nikolaus Harnoncourt, who recently passed away."

"Yes he did. It is a great great loss to the music community."

"Yes, he was really a committed conductor. I want to ask you a few questions not only about that performance but also the piece itself. Do you remember your thoughts as you were doing that piece with Gidon?"

"Well, we performed it maybe thirty-five times in the course of a couple of years. It was a work in progress as is any set of performances. I think an active performer never feels that they have reached their ideal goal with a piece of music. Mozart is certainly untouchable that way, as is Bach. You never feel like you have gotten even close to the structural balance and the phrase balance and the emotional balance that the text provides. So we are always constantly working towards that."

"What do you think Mozart was trying to communicate to us with that piece?"

"I think a very meaningful dialogue, and therefore a dramatic and emotional positioning."

"What emotional positioning?"

"I would not want to lay out anything that would influence a listener. I think that one of the great things about sonic artistry is that it will be and should be a different experience and have a different meaning for everyone who listens. In fact, for one person who listens six months later it will again hopefully have a different context, a different meaning, and touch the heart in a different way."

"Does that composition fulfill that for you?"

"Yes, very time it means something different, but I have to say that in a broader scope that is true of listening to any music, or even imagining it in my head. If it is the same as the last time, something is wrong. It has got to be changing, it is a changing art."

"As to imagining music in your head, do you actually hear music in your head?"

"Yes, I do hear music in my head. I see colors and patterns and gesture that go with the sounds in my head, so let's say it is a multi-level art experience. It is not an external sound; it is an internal sound. That is the closest I can come to describing it. I suppose I am creating it. In that sense it is imagination."

"What do you hear, classical, popular, viola?"

"I hear voice, classical, and folk music, not American country folk, but folk songs we call origin music, mostly Hungarian, Armenian, and Korean folk music."

"Just now you mentioned sonic artistry. What do you mean by that?"

"It's interesting to talk about the imagination of music and how our active imaginations, performers' imaginations, turn the material into the sonic experience that a listener in the concert hall might have. I think that it is a fantastic, exquisite area of mystery that happens between the vision and the execution. In other words, how does our craft of playing the instrument go through the instrument so that the sonic experience we imagine gets to the ears of the listener. That is the thing that continues to occupy all performers on one level or another for the entirety of their professional lives. Maybe even beyond that, because what happens when we retire is that those sounds are still with us, how we produce them, for whom we are producing them, why we are doing that. This is the fascination of the execution of the sound of music."

"Have you ever composed?"

"No I haven't. If I were to invite original activity into my life, it would probably be in the world of visual arts because that is another area I find fascinating. My mother was an artist. So my brother and I grew up with the smell of turpentine as well as the sounds of our practicing."

"So you grew up among the arts, so to speak. Did you live in Detroit very long?"

"I didn't stay long at all. I went from Detroit to the Interlochen Arts Academy as an eighth grader, and did my high school years up in Interlochen, Michigan, about four hours from Detroit due north. I never went back again except for holidays."

"Was your mother a musician?"

"No, my family were not musicians. My father was a schoolteacher and a writer. He taught history. My mother became an art teacher after he passed away which was when my brother and I we were quite young. My mother is gone now too. They were both teachers which probably gave me my teaching gene."

"We are going to talk about that. I know you've always loved teaching."

"My father sang and that refers back to these Armenian folk songs that we were talking about. He had one of those great Armenian baritone voices that you actually hear quite frequently in Armenia and not so frequently elsewhere. It was just a great natural voice full of resonance and full of love, I have to say. He sang every day so my music background was really inspired by his voice."

"Do you ever go to Armenia? Do you have family there?"

"The history of the genocide which occurred between 1915 and 1920 approximately is a sad story. Most of what was then called Western Armenia was destroyed and the people either fled or were massacred. Both sides of my family came from Western Armenia and some of them were able to immigrate to this country. So my father was a young boy when his mother was able to get him and his sister out. That's a story in and of itself because he was hidden under a hay wagon. With a great deal of risk they met in Greece and there got on a ship to here. He was brought up in Boston from the age of twelve. My mother was born in Boston a few months after the arrival of her parents during the same period of time. In our twenties, my friend Marci Rosen and I drove across the country in my first car. Our goal was San Francisco where I was to play in a group that no longer exists called Chamber Music West. We had cousins in the San Francisco area so we headed for their homes. When I got to my cousin's home at midday they came pouring out of the house. My older cousin, who was my father's age, was crying, just tears pouring down his face. I looked at Marci and I said, 'Oh, my goodness, what did we do wrong. I don't know what is the matter here.' He embraced me and said, 'You know, you are the only living, you and your brother are the only living people from our entire village.' That was it. Everybody else was killed during the massacres. So it is quite an extreme story."

"Have you played in Armenia?"

"Yes, I've been back numerous times. We were invited to go and play by their orchestra in Yerevan the year of the dissolution of the Soviet Union. I took my mother with me because she had never been back to Armenia, so we visited for the first time then. I've been back every couple of years since then and although, as I just explained, we have no family, no direct relatives there. I do have friends whom I consider to be family there."

"Do you have siblings?"

"I have one brother who is two years younger than I am. We both grew up playing the viola. He was probably the more talented of the two of us. Everyone thought so. He attended the Curtis Institute of Music for one year and then quit cold turkey saying that he didn't want to commit 100% of himself to music because there were too many other things that he loved. Now he is an environmental scientist in Colorado working on water rights. He is very happy. I think he made the right choice for himself. He would have felt stifled by just concentrating on one thing. A musician ultimately has to give all his or her energies into that one channel. At least you do until you're of middle age and you've got control of your craft to a certain degree."

"How about your daughter? Is she a musician at all?"

"My daughter studied clarinet and had that beautiful Armenian sound and ability to phrase. But one day when she was about fifteen she came home from school and said, 'Mom I want to talk to you. Would you sit down?' I thought, 'Oh my goodness, what's wrong. Something horrible has happened if I have to sit down.' She said, 'Mom, I don't want to hurt your feelings, but I have been watching how you live, I don't ever want to live like you do traveling all the time, so I'm not going to be a professional musician, I hope I'm not hurting you.' I said, 'Honey, this is probably the best decision you could make because as my teacher used to say, only those who have no choice should become musicians because it is a hard life.'"

"I met your daughter coming in today. She is very nice. After all those years living in Europe has coming here to Boston been positive for her upbringing and your music?"

"What I can say is that Boston seems to happen on a human scale. So there is more than enough stimulation here to go around, and you aren't in the horrible position of having to pick and choose which of many fantastic events you might want to go to and experience in person. Eventually they all come to Boston. You might miss some premieres that would happen in London or New York or Paris, but in the big picture, I don't miss anything."

"I think so. You're a major artist in the world but you don't feel as though you are out in the sticks here."

"We are certainly not out in the sticks. New York is not very far, and in fact London isn't very far. You take a five-hour plane ride and you're there more quickly than you can get to Los Angeles. So I don't really feel isolated in any way. Boston was also a great city in which to bring up my daughter. When we moved back to the States she was ten years old and I wanted a more human size environment for her rather than New York. I think it was the right choice."

"Have you played in Turkey?"

"Yes, actually three or four times now. Always a difficult first step to make. I realized when I got to the border that I had been unconsciously inoculated as a child by the horror stories my grandmother told us every Sunday. I was a little bit nervous and I realized there was no need to be at that time about twenty years ago. I think there is more need to be now because of the present regime."

"This guy Erdogan is not a particularly nice guy."

"No. But for many reasons. I have also accompanied other Armenians who were returning for the first time to the place of their family's origin. Let me say it is never an easy trip. But a very worthwhile one, worth the pain of doing it. The last time I went I was going with the family of Tigran Mansurian, the composer who had written a sonata for viola and piano at the request of and commissioned by the Turkish Arts Council. Tigran has written a lot for me. He has written two pieces for viola and percussion, two viola concertos and this sonata. He is Armenian and he lives in Yerevan, although his family grew up in Persia, then immigrated back to Armenia, so the trip was his first actual return to what he considered his homeland. It was a very, very emotional and difficult time for him even though he was surrounded by family."

"I've read that lots of composers favored the viola?"

"That is true. It goes back to a combination of environmental facts, and stylistic facts musically. If you look back stylistically to pre-classical times, you have a very strong bass line and you have in choral music equality above that. But when you look at the first string music, for example at Handel or Telemann, or moving forwards towards Haydn, you see that the bass line and the soprano line take precedence over the middle voices. And for string instruments that then became the norm where the inner voices were in fact the inner voices supporting those other voices. The viola was seen that way with certain exceptions based on the love of a composer. Basically it stayed that way until the very, very late Romantic and Viennese school composers where you see the middle voices having equality. If you look at a Schoenberg or a Berg string quartet you see total equality among the four voices. But that was a development that took a couple of centuries to unfold."

"So that's not true in Beethoven, Mozart, Haydn, Schubert, any of those?"

"No, it is not. So this is a gradual development towards parity that has a stylistic basis. Does that make sense for you?"

"Yes. Do you think that will continue?"

"Well it has continued. Absolutely still going on. Today the viola is considered, as many other instruments are, equally valuable solo instruments or equal in an ensemble."

"I've read where you have thought that the viola was more recognized in Europe than in America. Is that changing at all? Here it is sort of like missionary work is what I think you said."

"(Laughing) Yes, but that has a different environmental context which is that American orchestras historically have been supported by private funding, whereas most European orchestras have had government funding. Government funding in Europe provided for a more diverse and perhaps more challenging programming which resulted in more new music, more contemporary music because the ensembles were not dependent on a Board or on ticket sales for their audience. So the fear has existed here that if too much contemporary music were programmed the orchestra would lose its support. Maybe it is starting to turn the corner, but that was certainly true until twenty or so years ago. They still think that way a little bit, much less than before."

"So does that open up engagements for you?"

"As you and I both know most viola concertos are twentieth- and twenty-first century, and the principal violist of the orchestra, of course, should and does take dibs on the once-a-year occurrence in a symphony season of a viola concerto, which means that outside violists such as myself don't get hired frequently in America. That is not the case in Europe because the orchestra is not limited to one contemporary viola concerto per season. So that's the difference in the orchestral setting between here and there, and that is why it is the way it is. It's completely understandable given the environment and the set of circumstances."

"Kim, I think that some people say the viola is sad, but I don't think you would agree that it is sad."

"No, I don't agree that it is sad although it is very good at expressing melancholy. It has wonderful uses to express other emotions, as well."

"Is it more expressive than the violin?"

"I wouldn't say more expressive, but it seems to be closer to the human experience. A viola is not as perfect as the violin or the cello because the length of the string and the pitch don't match. So when you try to make a viola speak well and articulate well, it's more like dealing with a human partner than an instrument or tool that does what it is supposed to do. So in that sense it is a little unpredictable and goes through more fluctuations than a violin or a cello and therefore creates the expectation of vulnerability which I think is a very human characteristic. So the viola is not necessarily more expressive than the violin, but more human."

"You must get very close to your viola?"

"I've been through a lot of violas in my career. I've played on some very very beautiful older instruments, and I've also played on one relatively new instrument by Peter Greiner which served me very, very well for years. The search for the perfect viola is an unending search. I've been playing on the Greiner close to twenty years."

"Even though, as you said, that the viola has been underutilized as far as composition is concerned, maybe you believe it is the prime string instrument of all? Maybe that's why Mozart loved it so much."

"It might be why certain composers seemed to have loved it for particular tasks. The viola has a unique role for sure."

"I read about one of your main teachers, Karen Tuttle. Who would you say has been the prime teacher in your life?"

"I'm going to have to divide that up and answer it in three parts. In terms of making me able to be friends with the viola and making me able to understand how to use my inner voice with the viola it would be Karen Tuttle. She appeared in my life in the middle of my sophomore year at Peabody Institute as if an angel had come down from Heaven, truly, because I had no idea of any of the concepts that she espoused. For example, the fact that resonance in the instrument was dependent on resonance in the body, and that the body needed to be part of what you were doing playing an instrument. There were ways that she actually had codified and could teach even the most hopeless and tied up young lady like me, how to relax and find my power. So I lay at her doorstep the fact that I learned at all how to be a good performer and how to play the viola and how to have a sense of integration between the viola and other parts of my life. I lay all of that with great, great thanks at her doorstep."

"That is a lot, Kim. Do you try and teach the same thing to your students?"

"Absolutely, of course, in my own way. All of her students have taken on her teachings and made them our own, and we all teach it in our own ways now, but absolutely, yes. It is extremely important that the instrument is seen as an extension of the body and that there is a degree of good health that can pervade that system, that ecosystem of instrument and body."

"What are the other parts, Kim?"

"Well, the next thing I'm going to mention is the Marlboro Music Festival which as a concept of European music-making was also a very, very strong influence for me. In particular, Felix Galimir because he took me on as a young musician and helped me gain power, courage, and strength, made me stand up for myself, and taught and showed me things that were unique in his understanding about the Viennese school of Berg, Webern, and Schoenberg.

There are many of us who remain very, very thankful to Galimir for those teachings.

"The third category, which happened later on in my life, were my encounters with György Kurtág. He was my middle-aged mentor, let's say. I encountered him first when I was living in Freiburg, Germany. By that time I had been teaching for years and had a professional career. The first day I went to play for him I realized that there was a whole new page of expectation and experience that had been just made available to me. It took me the next ten to fifteen years to come to terms with that. I'm very grateful for all my painful and frequent encounters with his teaching."

"That's great. You won your Grammy in 2013. I see here your album *Kurtág / Ligeti: Music for Viola.* You just told us about Kurtág. Of course, Ligeti is documented to the nth degree. Did you know Ligeti at all?"

"I never had the chance to get to know him, but I did play that sonata for Mr. Kurtág. Kurtág and Ligeti were extremely close all of their lives since their student days until the day that Ligeti died. I would choose to say they are still close. I think that Kurtág has an ongoing relationship with him. The Hungarian influence in my life has been strong. Also Peter Eotvos has been influential. He is kind of the younger composer generation who has taken over from Ligeti and Kurtág."

"Tell us about the Hungarian influence, Kim?"

"The flavor of the Hungarian language has meant a lot to me over the years in learning to work with some Hungarian musicians, and in particular Peter Nagy, who teaches at the Liszt Academy in Budapest, who shared with me the Bartók archival material which has all of the songs that Bartók collected. These are treasures which informed my understanding of the Ligeti sonata and of the Kurtág pieces as well. An important aspect of my later training was to work with those folk songs and translate them into modern music, just as I translated the Armenian folk songs into the modern Armenian setting."

"Would you say that the Armenian background and the Hungarian influence are the chief ethnic contributors to your musical development? Or are there others?"

"I guess one could say that except for the very strong Viennese influence in the Marlboro tradition that was also a big influence for me. I think part of what we do is to channel the architecture of the score through the vessel of our personality. That can be done in many different ways. What Rudolph Sirkin always said was that he gave himself a minute before he walked on stage every time to just say to himself, 'Please let me be an empty vessel for the music.' So this is what I think we all aspire to. Let the architecture of the music, the text, resonate through who we are on a deeper level than on an ego level. The fact is that the empty vessel that the music resonates through is the person. No person will play a composition the same way as any other person. The same person will always play a composition a different way."

Hungarian composer György Kurtág, muse of Kim Kashkashian

Credit: By Lenke Szilágyi - http://www.muzsikalendarium.hu/muzsika/index.php?area=article&id_article=3847, CC BY-SA 3.0, https://commons.wikimedia.org/w/index.php?curid=45098951

"Is Bartók a big influence on your music?"

"Yes, through the same prism of folk music. Bartók, of course, talks about country music and city music. So one has to see everything that he wrote through that prism of the archival material that he collected."

"Kim, you are the founder and artistic director of Music for Food, sort of a takeoff on Shakespeare. Please tell us about Music for Food. I know it has to be close to your heart."

"We formed Music for Food for a triple purpose. I see it as a triangle of energy exchange between musicians, audience, and the food pantries. What we saw was that our students, in particular, who were heading towards a professional life, needed to be able to sense, in the words of the great Arnold Steinhardt of the Guarneri Quartet, their place not only in the world of music but in the world at large. We believed we could set up a model and a vehicle for these wonderful and talented young people to give of their gifts that they had worked so hard to learn to use on the concert stage, to use them to reach the audience with a dual purpose to inspire the audience to reciprocate by giving back. The idea is to inspire the audience to be responsible and active in their role, and to give concretely to a food bank in response to what they were hearing. So what I believed I was setting up, and I know this remains an ideal, is a situation where the intangible beauty of music creates through the activity of the audience in response to the musicians the tangible result of food for a food bank. So it is a three-way energy triangle."

"How has it worked out?"

"We are in our eighth season and we are growing and learning as we go. We don't have the kind of budget that would allow us to grow exponentially, but I believe that we should remain grassroots and grow as musicians are inspired to take it on. The reason that we are this way is because it is totally a volunteer organization. Everybody volunteers, the musicians volunteer, the audience volunteers a donation, we don't sell tickets, so 100% of any donation goes to a food pantry. That means we don't have an operating budget unless some wonderful foundation decides to fund us. So far we have been very lucky with an anonymous private grant which keeps us surviving, but it's not enough that we can plan to become big. Actually, it is interesting to see that every year we are growing anyway, and on this grassroots operating basis of not needing to be a big footprint in the world, which I like and was my original intention, I think things are going more or less as we had hoped. In fact, more and more of the conservatories are taking this on as a possible curriculum model. For me is fantastic because it means that young musicians in schools other than the New England Conservatory are being exposed to the option of music for food activities in their lives. Like this year conservatories in San Francisco, Cincinnati, Cleveland, and the Curtis Institute of Music are all taking on music for food, their students are going to food pantries and playing and performing in concerts with faculty. So it is spreading as I had imagined and hoped on a grassroots basis."

"That is wonderful, Kim! There are so many things that can happen through music. That leads me to another question about music and the many existential threats in the world. Musicians have to learn to get along with one another to play together. My question is do you think musicians could be an answer to helping to eliminate any of the threats that face us as far as human existence is concerned?"

"Absolutely! First of all let's back pedal a little bit. It has been documented that in conditions where there is a threat to life, music is one of the greatest hopes and conservers of energy that we have experienced. We have seen it in the concentration camps, we have seen it elsewhere. I want to say that *Music for Food* acts just as a piece of chamber music acts on the musical stage. *Music for Food* can be acted out in the world in a way that connects and inspires audiences, food pantry clients, and those who directly serve the needs of food pantry clients. It can be acted out to make us understand that the privilege that we have had to be able to study, learn, and concentrate on music is a great privilege, and that we can share that privilege, so that the power of music can turn into actual concrete things that people out in the real world need. So yes, it is an extremely powerful life tool."

"What can music do concretely to prevent an existential threat like war or a nuclear holocaust?"

"I don't know if there is a concrete measurable phenomenon I can cite, but music has the power to soothe the spirit and move the heart, and any direct musical event that moves the spirit and heart of the listener has the chance to be a catalyst for motion out there in the world."

"I think that is a great answer, Kim. I think that's better than trying to reach for something concrete because it expresses the power of music."

"One of the musicians you have worked with strikes my eye. I have always loved the way Leonidas Kavakos plays. I just think he is a wonderful violinist and a very serious individual. I don't know whether you communicate with him."

"Oh, I do. We are old friends. We played together a lot when I lived in Europe."

"Really! Please tell me about playing with him?"

"Leonidas personifies a fantastic and integrated balance between intellect and heart. One could say he is a good balance between Apollo and Dionysus if you want to put it that way. He would understand that right away. Very few musicians have such a balanced perspective that way. I love working with him for that reason. He also has complete command of the instrument; he can do anything he wants without thinking. Leonidas is a wonderfully balanced musician with a very deep heartfelt perspective as well as the intellect to back it up."

"I watch him standing and delivering, almost motionless, and then watch some other violinists who move around a lot. Just something about Leonidas' physical presence and the way he plays that just seems on a higher level to me."

"I think it just speaks to a different part of the human psyche. Moving about can be fully emotional. That is the interesting thing. I think that what we are talking about here is the very essential and valuable element of the energy being catalyzed and visualized on stage. That is a way that a lot of artists do express and it's genuine. I would never say it isn't. It is a choice for some like Leonidas not to do that. And it is a choice for others to include that in their expressive repertoire. And then for others it is not a choice. That is the way they are and that is the way they do things."

"Look at Yo-Yo Ma."

"That is another person who is a great example of the integration of all aspects integrated into the whole. It is a valuable tool and it has its place as do all of these tools. Any way that we can reach out and move the hearts of our listeners is valuable and not to be rejected."

"What you are saying, Kim, is a valuable lesson for me to remove any prejudice I have, because when you say it to me it is meaningful and carries a lot of authority."

"As we shape our young students to become professionals that is something that comes up over and over again. It is the issue of how much of what you are doing needs to be seen to be properly heard, and that brings up many areas of artistry, for example the whole Glenn Gould idea that he wasn't going to perform in public but only produce CDs. He was one of the first to say the artistry is purely sonic. Is that really valid for everybody or is the physical manifestation of the energy and the deeper meaning of the piece also important. I think for many artists it is and is a genuine expression of the music."

"Do you move around a lot?"

"You would have to ask somebody else. I have no idea. I do move as I was trained to by my teachers in ways that allow for optimal resonance of the instrument. I don't know if I move to express the emotion of the music. That I don't know."

"It is certainly understandable that some people will feel better doing as you do, just as others like Leonidas have no trouble choosing the way he does it, sort of straight up and not showing a lot of emotion."

"This is a big subject, not just for musicians. If you go back to the works of Carl Jung and the four types of personality he posited, you see that we all have elements contained within us, but one always comes out on top."

"I've heard of that, thinking, feeling...."

"All of us contain the four stereotypes. It's just a question of how is it balanced in one's character as to how do you choose to present it to the world. They are all valid elements."

"It is sort of related to Mozart and Verdi showing us a mirror as to who we really are, as opposed to Puccini who is showing us stuff that's melodramatic, albeit he is a great melodist and musician."

"He is more stereotypical."

"I can sit there and cry when they do *Madama Butterfly,* but I'm saying to myself come on."

"It is like any button pusher. In the movies we describe certain films as being button pushers too."

"Could anybody do anything better than *The Marriage of Figaro* for a day in the life of real people. It touches on everything."

"It would be hard to choose. I would take one of the Schubert trios myself (laughing)."

"As among solo, chamber and orchestral music which do you like best?"

"(Laughing) Well, I like to listen to all of it. I like to play chamber music depending on the partners. It can be the most heavenly way to make music. I'm also very happy up on stage completely by myself, just playing Bach or Kurtág, or even improvising Armenian folk songs. There are different ways of expression, and depending on the situation, the audience, and how you feel, I would have a hard time choosing between one and the other. My experience playing in an orchestra is extremely limited. I paid the rent when I was a student at the Peabody Conservatory by substituting in the Baltimore Symphony Orchestra. I learned a lot because Sergiu Comissiona was still the conductor at that time. It was a great musical experience, but since then I have had very little orchestral opportunity except when I was allowed to play in the symphony that followed the concerto that I had just played. That's always fun, but I don't do it enough of that to be able to say what it is really like."

"Kim, we know how close to your heart is to teaching. Why do you love teaching so much?"

"Two basic premises here. I believe that I inherited the gene from my parents. Secondly, my actual first choice of career had I had the opportunity would have been psychology. I would have probably made a pretty darn good clinical psychologist, so I love working one-on-one with students. I take them on for a four-year period if they come as undergrad and a two-year period as a grad student. I watch them and hopefully help them stretch and grow and develop a broader picture and framework for how they think and feel."

"Musically?"

"Musically and otherwise because it all goes together. I cannot separate musical training from what happens to the person because as a performer you are on the line, your whole person is on the line, whenever you walk on a stage. You are making all of yourself vulnerable, so you need to know how to present it without falling apart, but staying vulnerable at the same time. These are things that need exploration and work. So beside teaching about music and how to understand style, phrasing, shaping, and the craft of making music, I'm also teaching how to understand yourself as a person, how to understand your own strengths and weaknesses, so that you can successfully walk on stage and present music."

"Here is a question, Kim, related to that. Try to cast aside modesty and stand outside of yourself and tell me what you think of yourself as an instrumentalist and a person as you have developed this far in life from your teen years?"

"I would like to say something that I say to my students at the very moment when you feel that you have actually done exactly what you intended to do, and that is, 'Be very careful because it can't possibly be true or you would be dead.' I think striving for what we envision, what we can fantasize as possibilities, striving in a dedicated and honest way is the best that any of us can ask of ourselves. And to do that with that sense of vulnerability I spoke of, but also the sense of being safe, that you can strive as much as you may choose to stretch your envelope without affecting the essential you. Those things are things we come to as we grow up, if we are lucky.

"I would say that being a mother helped me enormously. It helped me make huge strides because it shifted my perspective away from myself and towards this little being whose needs were enormous and without end. Without question I needed to shift into understanding the rhythms and needs of another person. That actually helped me very much to understand where I could feel secure in myself and where I could push myself."

"It seems you have striven hard. That seems removed a bit from being able to shift your perspective, even towards motherhood?"

"Well, I never was and never will be a natural performer. I have learned to do it well but it is not my nature. My nature would be to be hidden one-on-one with someone and I think my best energy exchange and best use of my ideas and power are in a one-on-one situation. I think that remains true today."

"What does that mean, one-on-one?"

"Like we are today, one-to-one. I think I've given my best performances in a very, very small setting, probably for the same reason, because I treasure the intimacy of it. As you said, putting aside modesty, I have taught myself to play well, so it seems natural, but I am not a natural performer. There are plenty of violists out there who have a much better command of technique that I ever did or ever will have. I can say that what is unique for me is the production of sound and what can be transmitted through sound, because that was always my primary interest. That is probably because of the richness of my father's voice. So these things come full circle in a way that you inherit what is ingested on a cellular level, and that is also what you end up with when you are much older. You learn to balance it out. Probably those are my strengths and my weaknesses. Because there is a stubborn streak in my personality, I just never gave up trying to be comfortable on stage. But if I am deeply honest, I have to look back and say, 'Well, I tried, but had I given up earlier by saying it is just not natural for me, so go do something else that is more natural, I might have had a stronger effect in the world.'"

"I kind of doubt that, Kim. I think you are doing way better than OK. It's said that you have a really beautiful tone and that you produce great sound."

"For some people it's very affecting which I am grateful for. I'm doing fine. I'm trying to be objective here. I'm pretty sure that I have been an extremely effective teacher. I'm pretty sure that I can be an effective performer, but not on the highest level that I could imagine because my limitations are much bigger than my imagination."

"I'm impressed by the way you speak about music, the world, and yourself. Why is it that I find that musicians, especially ones of the quality of people like you, are so articulate? Many of the musicians I have spoken to have the command of the language required to give an informative answer."

"(Laughing) I don't know about anyone else but I have been a reader most of my life. One of my dearest memories of my father is our weekly visits to the library. We would fill the trunk of his car with books, his books on one side and mine on the other, and off load and reload them every week. At home I had my chair and my table stacked with the books for the week. I think that habit, that sense of richness in life and my inner life takes place with the printed page. Well I've just dated myself haven't I (laughing). I read a lot. I always have, and I always will."

"Reading is a form of one-on-one."

"Absolutely. It absolutely is. It's a real part of life and of conversation."

"So do you prefer music to reading?"

"I can't say I prefer one or the other. Each have their place in my life, but don't ask me which I would give up because (laughing) I don't think I could answer that."

"Could you imagine yourself just stopping giving concert performances, or flat out not playing the viola?"

"Oh, absolutely. If you mean not playing the viola on the concert stage, absolutely. If my singing voice were better, then yes, I could imagine giving up playing viola, but my singing voice isn't as developed as my viola voice, so if I want to express with sound, I think I would still grab the viola. I have a completely untrained, reasonably good potential voice, but (laughing), I can still express more differentiated emotions sculpting sound on the viola. So the viola might be hard for me to give up."

"Kim, what is music?"

"That is a question we all try to answer in different ways throughout the development of our lives. That which is essential cannot be put into words. If you think of it that way, as color, motion, any form of energy including sonic energy, those are the things that you actually cannot fully put your finger on and describe. The fact is that composers take sonic energy and give it architecture, structure and duration, vertical and horizontal understanding, and create these fantastic structures for us. What is the difference between seeing it on a page and hearing it played. That's a big question too. And I would have to say that music is both things. It's the structure and the potential that the structure gives us, and then it's the manifestation of that structure in sound."

"That's great, Kim! it is always interesting to hear what some terrific musician is going to answer to that question. I wouldn't want to stop you there if you've got more to say about what music is."

"On a more personal level music is comfort, courage, the expression of tragedy, and gives us a way to understand all of the human emotions in sound. On a more visceral level, music gives us an understanding or translation of the human condition, maybe even more so than visual art or the written word."

"How do you think music arose? Do you think it was part of the formation of humans or do you think it came later?"

"I think it was the first form of communication, stick on rock (makes a banging sound), a way to call people back from a hunt, a way to celebrate together with rhythm, body motion, and making noise. I think those things are absolutely elemental and arrived at the same time as humans. Music is part of being human, of being in the world."

"Sadly the younger generation is not educated in music in general. Listening on the internet is far from listening by attending concerts."

"There is a huge difference between experiencing a live event in a real space than it is to hear an electronically recorded event through headphones. I don't know if I can quantify what that difference means except that part of what we understand as the art of music-making is that combination of the space time continuum. If you eliminate space you've taken away part of the meaning and experience of the transmission of sound."

"Could we survive without music?"

"I think you are asking an impossible question because this world is a concrete world and not a spirit world. It has color, it has kinetic energy, and where there is kinetic energy there is (makes a banging noise) sound."

That last remark personifies the world of master violist and world citizen, Kim Kashkashian. It is a concrete world in which Kim puts her energies to our service, whether with food, learning, or music. It is a kinetic world in which Kim knows sound and thus music will always be there to serve and lift humanity and all living creatures. It is a real world in which Kim lives every minute of every day to the advantage of all of us.

CHAPTER
15

Laurence Lesser: Master Cellist, Pedagogue, and President

Perhaps Laurence Lesser, master cellist and honored teacher, is the musician whose life can teach us the most about why some instrumentalists, like famed cellist, Yo-Yo Ma, travel the world forever, and others like revered French pedagogue and pianist, Nadia Boulanger, stay in one place for a lifetime. Larry Lesser was favored with the company of and played with masters like Jascha Heifetz and Gregor Piatigorsky in his youth, was a top prizewinner in the iconic Tchaikovsky Competition in Moscow in 1966, and appeared then very ready for a prolonged international career. Not long after the competition he married another of its winners that year, great violinist, Masuko Ushioda, who had already embarked on a world journey as a violin virtuoso. At that point, no one would have been surprised if both Larry and Masuko each won world renown and a massive audience in the tradition of other master instrumentalists. However, it did not turn out quite that way, and one wonders why? What did ensue is equally impressive and meaningful in its own way. Larry became an honored teacher, first at the University of Southern California and Peabody Conservatory in Baltimore, and then, in 1974, at the New England Conservatory (NEC) in Boston, where he and Masuko chose to live for life, both lured to the Athens of America by NEC's then president, honored American composer, Gunther Schuller. There Larry continued his virtuosity as a cellist and teacher, somewhat interrupted by unpredictably becoming the president of NEC, and the man who guided the 1995 restoration of Jordan Hall at NEC, one of the most acoustically perfect concert halls in the world. More predictably, Larry instituted at NEC a free concert series, now celebrating its thirty-fourth year, which he named "First Monday at Jordan Hall," where he, faculty colleagues, and wonderful alums have brought to its expanding audience, chamber music classics, mostly known and some relatively unknown, over its long history, each concert

American cellist Laurence Lesser. Photo courtesy of Laurence Lesser.

preceded by Larry Lesser's own quiet, loving, and erudite remarks. Meanwhile, Masuko continued her performing career while concentrating on family, children, and teaching. She became a popular and beloved teacher at the New England Conservatory of Music, so close to her students that she would admit only them and family to her presence in her untimely declining final days. Larry's own story, and Masuko's too, is perhaps a metaphor for the balance in life that is so sought in music. For sure it sheds light on a way of living a musical life whose benefits to music are a match to those provided by the equally talented and inspiring artists who constantly circle the globe.

"Larry, I think where I want to start is back there in Los Angeles where you grew up. Were your parents musical?"

"My mother was a conservatory graduated pianist. She was in the middle of seven children of immigrants from Eastern Europe. She was born in Indianapolis but she grew up mostly in Dallas, Texas. By the time she moved to Los Angeles, which is where she met my father, she had lived in Dallas, Fort Worth, Indianapolis, Chicago, Denver, San Francisco, and Los Angeles. Her father was a peddler by trade, moving from place to place. Yes, she was a pianist. People would ask my father if he was a musician also, and he would say, "No, I pay for the lessons." He was a tax attorney from Fall River, Massachusetts, who grew up dirt poor, was ambitious, found his way to Washington D.C., entered Georgetown University for their two-year diploma program in international relations, finished it, but understood immediately that he would never get a job at that time in the State Department because of anti-Semitism. He went back to school at George Washington University and got a law degree. He stayed another year and got a bachelor's degree because he loved learning. He worked for the IRS and was sent by them to Los Angeles in 1926. He left the IRS and started his own law practice there. He lived the rest of his life in LA. I'm the youngest of three boys. We all had music lessons, and, indeed, my father paid for them. My oldest brother became an architect but played piano better than any of us. We all had piano studies when we were very young. He continued them. He learned the French horn then too. My middle brother played clarinet more than anything else, but of the three of us he probably listens to music for pleasure more than any of us. As for me, it is my profession. Anyway that's how it all began."

"Larry, I have noticed that you go way beyond music. I think you are not only a musician but you know a lot about music history, and you are broadly educated in the liberal arts. Where does that come from?"

"My father loved learning and hated the law, but that was what it was possible for him to do. He loved history very much."

"I'm interested in your experience playing with the Manhattan Concerts Orchestra in your college years. Was it a classical orchestra? Tell us about that, Larry?"

"It was essentially a pops chamber orchestra. I took a year off after my freshman year at Harvard and enrolled at USC which was where my cello teacher from high school was living. By the time that semester ended my father had no money with which to help me. I had decided I wanted to be back at Harvard. A pal of mine told me the Manhattan Concerts Orchestra was looking for players. I signed on. The only thing Manhattan about it was three days of rehearsals on 57th Street near Carnegie Hall. That was all for Manhattan. Then we got on a bus. It was a social education. The places we played were maybe 30 or 40,000 people, it was a Community Concerts type thing. The biggest place we played was Baton Rouge, Louisiana. We went down the eastern seaboard as far as Waycross, Georgia. I learned Waycross is the gateway to the Okefenokee Swamp. We went as far southwest as Mercedes Weslaco, Texas, we went to Juarez, Mexico, across from El Paso, we were in Carlsbad, New Mexico, we were in Dodge City, Kansas, all of these small places. That was a wonderful education!"

"Probably became part of your persona?"

"Probably did. It was fun. You had to get up at 7:00 every morning, be on the bus before 8:00 having eaten your breakfast, be on the chartered bus to the next place which was a few hundred miles away, get there late afternoon, check into a fleabag motel, go to the concert hall to try a twenty minutes use of the hall, play your concert, go out for a beer afterwards, and on to the next one, fifty-three concerts in sixty-three days."

"The only difference between that and Class D baseball was that you played the cello and they played baseball. I notice that when you went to Harvard you were sort of torn between mathematics and music. Do you still find math useful in your profession as a musician?"

"I'm sitting upstairs right now finishing my tax returns. My father was a tax attorney. I've been doing my own tax returns for sixty years. It's fun, it's a game. I don't do mathematics anymore though. I studied with Gregor Piatigorsky who was very much affiliated with and close to Jascha Heifetz. There were these chamber music parties that they had. At one, somebody asked me if I was a mathematician. Mr. Heifetz (no one was permitted to call him by his first name except a few people, like Gregor Piatigorsky), whom I knew very well, was standing right there. I said, 'No, but I studied mathematics.' Heifetz said that was a good distinction. I think that's true; I studied mathematics. I don't do it anymore but I'd like to think that most experiences you have in life are useful eventually in some form. So I would say that it was when I became NEC's president. The foremost thing I would say I learned about my study of mathematics is organization and structure, how things relate to one another, how you find patterns. I also was pretty quick reading budget pages, and I could have a talk with my CFO that sometimes made her uncomfortable because I could see into the numbers quicker than she could."

"Well, maybe it informed some of your policies?"

"I don't know. I can't speak to that. I would like to think my policies were grounded in reality but informed by imagination and love for what we were doing, education and art."

Russian-born American cellist Gregor Piatigorsky, muse of Laurence Lesser

Photographer unknown, courtesy BSO Archives.

"Larry, you had a lot of great teachers but a couple have hit my eye. One is Gaspar Cassadó because when I interviewed Ben Zander he told me about his life with Cassadó in his teens. He described him in glowing terms. What might you say about Cassadó?"

"Cassadó was a very great cellist, a very interesting man. Ben Zander studied with him before I came on the scene. I studied with him for one year in Cologne, Germany on a Fulbright, 1961 to 1962. He had some very important technical information he taught me about playing the cello. I thought he was very unconventional, very different from all the others, very creative. I would say probably of all of the great cellists of our time he was a real composer, much more so than Pablo Casals or Gregor Piatigorsky, or any other cellists of our time. He wrote some good pieces for cello, orchestra, and chamber music. Most of it is not paid attention to anymore. Cassadó had a very solid musical background. In life he was a colorful guy, built a little bit like Casals but bigger, with a boxer's kind of physique and very much a ladies' man. He was a grown-up little boy."

"That's the best thing to be (laughing). How about your time with Gregor Piatigorsky?"

"After I studied with Cassadó, I finally studied with Piatigorsky, who was my greatest mentor. He was not a pedagogue in the traditional sense. He was a very philosophical person who saw life in the big picture, and music as a part of that. He was a very, very wise man, and very funny, enormously naturally gifted for the instrument. I learned most of what I know about technique by watching Piatigorsky, not by listening to the instructions he gave about put your finger here or hold the bow that way. I watched him playing when he would demonstrate, and I would figure out things for myself. I think that is the cornerstone of how I approach my work as a teacher because I think that if the person who teaches you the instrument doesn't do a good job of giving you the tools to know how to use the machine that you're using, who is going to do it? It is not going to be your pianist friend! But there is no reason to have technique unless it is serving music, unless it is for a musical purpose. Actually, Piatigorsky, in one of his great lines — he had lots of them — said, 'When it is hard technically that is the time to become very musical.' It sounds very funny, but he was right. If you find a musical motivation for a technical solution or a technical solution for a musical thing, they work together."

"I want to talk about Masuko. I found her to be a really fascinating musician. I always felt when I watched her that she was the leader of the ensemble. There was something about her playing that reached the heart. I just loved her playing. You said that 'her playing was incandescent, deeply musical with a rare beauty of sound and profundity of expression.' I know you met her when you were both winners of the Tchaikovsky Competition a long time ago back in the 60s, but could you just reflect about her as a person and a musician and a mother?"

"Masuko was a great artist. She was a great human being. She was very smart about people. She was a very centered person. She hated the music profession and was madly in love with music. Piatigorsky felt the same way. They didn't like the business part. She was very, very good at the business part of it, not in the business sense, but in knowing how to talk to conductors and management. She was so fresh and vibrant that it was easy for her. She won the most important competition in Japan when she was fifteen, so arguably at that point and for the next several years she was the most famous violinist in Japan. She played a lot at a very young age, she went to the Soviet Union to study, she lived in Europe, she was constantly on the go. We got married in 1971, and in the twelve months following that she had ninety-three concerts and she was gone cumulatively half of the time. We married when she was twenty-nine and I was thirty-three. That wasn't so awful because each of us had already lived separate lives."

"So how come Masuko didn't become a traveling virtuoso?"

"Well, she had been for more than a decade. Then we became more close to the point that she said she wanted to stop playing. She wanted to have a dozen children. She wanted to have a life. I mean she did have a life, but she didn't stop playing, and she didn't have a dozen children. I think they are both great things. She played for the rest of her life. And as the children grew older and they needed less of her, her students became her children. So she was deeply devoted as a teacher. When she had this terrible diagnosis of acute leukemia in November of 2012, it was just like being hit by lightning. While she was in the hospital she wanted to see the immediate family but not the family at large. She didn't want to see any of her professional friends, she only wanted to see her students. They would go one by one to the hospital and have a lesson in her hospital room."

"That's amazing."

"It was like they were her kids. She was very smart, very, very deeply intelligent about people, she could read people, just the opposite of me. I'm a little bit face blind. She could remember anybody she had met in her life, even if their hair was different, or their color, or they were wrinkled or whatever, she knew who they were. She may not have remembered the name that went with the face, but she knew the face. Everybody liked her. She was so warm and so quick to respond. She was interested in people. She never learned to drive. She was direction blind. She could remember faces, she could remember how things looked, but she couldn't remember if something was right or left. We would travel a lot whether to play concerts or just because we enjoyed traveling. We would get to a hotel, come to the floor we were on, and I would let her go where she wanted when she got out of the elevator. One of two things happened. She went in the wrong direction to the room or she stood there for a second and said, 'Well, I always know I go in the wrong direction, so I'll go that way,' and she was wrong! She knew where it was supposed to be but had trouble going in the right direction. She didn't want to drive. She grew up in Tokyo where at that time not so many people drove. They have great public transportation. She loved taking public transportation. When we lived on Bellevue Street in Newton, she would walk down to Newton Corner and take the bus. She loved to look at people."

"Larry, your background is thoroughly Jewish. How did you happen to marry a Japanese woman?"

"Why did I marry a Japanese woman? I fell in love with her. I talked to Piatigorsky at the time that Masuko and I were getting serious. Piatigorsky was Jewish. I said, 'I'm thinking about getting married to her.' He was like my father; I could talk to him more openly than to my own father about some things. I said, 'What do you think about that?' He said, 'What do you want to know?' I said, 'Well, you know my family is Jewish, Jewish people marry Jews, she is Japanese.' And he said, 'I don't think that is an issue at all. The biggest issue you will find, if it happens, is if the two of you have competing ambitions, and that you can't work well together. It has nothing to do with her race or her country.' And he was right. Masuko wanted to become a mother, she was a great artist, she never stopped playing, and that made a balanced existence which was very satisfying to her. I see other cases of conflict in marriages in music where people are trying to outdo one another or becoming jealous of one another. We never had that problem."

"There are various subjects having to do with your long tenure at the New England Conservatory of Music, including your tenure as President of NEC from 1983 to 1996. Let's go back to 1974 when Gunther Schuller, a very famous musician and another president of NEC, appointed you to the faculty. What persuaded you to come Boston?"

"Well, first of all I had a taste of Boston from my Harvard years; I was teaching at the Peabody Institute in Baltimore from 1970 to 1974, a town I still like very much. But when I was offered a position to come to NEC in 1974, I was enthusiastic because that would mean I could live in Boston."

"Let's move ahead until when you became the President of NEC. How did that come about?"

"My predecessor as president was a very kind, warm person named Stanley Ballinger. Stan failed as president because just like later on with me, his wife died of cancer, but while he was president. Stan was so traumatized by the loss of his wife that he was not able to function sufficiently well as president to raise the money required for the continued existence of the conservatory, so he was let go. A new president had to be found at that crucial time."

"You put that in a very existential way for the future of NEC. So what happened next?"

"In January of 1982 there was a very fine Vice President for Finance at NEC, Andy Falender, who really had saved it from financial ruin because he knew how to run things. The Trustees decided that he alone couldn't run the school while the search for a president went on, and that there should be some musical and educational function in the administration until a new president came. I shared that task with two other faculty members. When the spring semester was over in

1982, no president had yet been found. The Trustees asked if I would do the job alone until a president was found. One of the conditions was under no circumstances could I be a candidate for the presidency. At that point, I was not interested in the position. The trustees said we'll call you 'Acting President.' I said, 'I don't want that title.' I settled on the title 'Artistic Director.' It appealed to me. It was consistent with what a music school should be. So I was the Artistic Director of the Conservatory. In November, a very good candidate for the presidency, whom I had recommended, decided he wouldn't accept the job. Andy Falender said, 'You know, Larry's doing a very good job despite having no administrative experience. Maybe we could find some kind of a structure that would enable him to keep doing what he's doing.' Well, by the time March of 1983 came, I was named President and Andy Falender was named CEO, and we were jointly reporting to our caring and sympathetic Board of Trustees. It worked out very well because Andy and I really got along. We had a stack over here which was mine, another stack over there which was Andy's, and another stack we both worked on. We worked very, very well that way."

"How did the chores of the presidency affect your playing? Did you have enough time to do both?"

"I would say that for the entire period of fifteen years until I left the presidency in December of 1996, the biggest loss for me — I never stopped teaching or playing in all that time — was that I didn't have time to learn a new repertoire. So I lost fifteen years of growth in what I did. Later I tried to catch up, but you can't do everything in life."

"How did it come to pass that you assumed the presidency alone?"

"After five years of doing it with Andy, he came to me one day and said, 'It's like the movie *Godfather*. It's like I've just been offered a contract by the Mafia and I can't say no. I've been offered the position of Executive Directorship of the Appalachian Mountain Club.' Andy was not a musician; he was an outdoors and conservation person. And then he did that gig successfully for more than twenty years. So the Trustees took a chance and said I could be president by myself."

"Did you have any reservations about going it alone?"

"No, I had on the job training for five years. So in 1988 Andy left and I was then fully President until I retired from the job in 1996."

"One thing I remember during your tenure is the restoration of Jordan Hall which all of us love because it's one of the great music venues in the world. Did you have a big hand in that, Larry?"

"It is the thing that I'm proudest of. What happened was we knew we needed to raise money. Any administration, any president, of any kind of an organization not for profit, has to raise money. We had a very dynamic Vice President for External Affairs, Nancy Perkins. Nancy, along with Anne Hawley and Holly Sidford, were at the Mass. Council for the Arts and Humanities before coming to NEC at that time. Anne Hawley became the Director of the Gardner Museum, and Holly Sidford became the Program Director of the Reader's Digest Fund.

Nancy was terrific. We had a lot of talks about the need to raise money. Everybody knows Jordan Hall, but what was terrible at that time was that people didn't realize Jordan Hall was part of the New England Conservatory. There has been a lot of controversy since the time the sign at the back of the stage was put up saying, 'NEW ENGLAND CONSERVATORY.' People got all up in arms and said how can you put the name up there. I said, 'Of course we need it up there because we need people to know this great concert hall is us.'"

"How did you raise the money?"

"At that time the decision was made to mount a capital campaign with a goal of thirty million dollars. We decided to make the restoration of Jordan Hall the centerpiece of the campaign because there was so much emotion toward its restoration that enabled us to raise the money. The restoration took a long period of planning. The work actually started in 1994, most of it was done in 1995. It was not a renovation. I said, 'No, you are not going to use the word 'renovation, It is a restoration.' I'm happy and very proud about that. It was a restoration, and the main thing we were going to preserve was the acoustic, and to try and make it look as beautiful as it was when it opened in 1903. We succeeded and did things that couldn't be imagined in 1903 — complete HVAC, complete wiring for sound, update in handicap access, completely new lighting, wiring, everything was brought up to date. Most of the stuff you can't see, but what you can see is that glorious space which is one of the greatest concert halls in the world. That Boston has Jordan Hall, and Symphony Hall only one block away, is almost kind of unfair."

"Surreal! But tell me something Larry, did the acoustic in your estimation change at all from what it had been?"

"A little bit, but almost not at all. What we did was several years after Carnegie Hall had that scandal about pouring a slab of concrete under the floor of the stage during major work there. I said we are going to do two things. First of all, we have to find out how Jordan Hall was built. So we had a little archeological dig, as it were, and the first thing they found out was that when Jordan Hall was built in 1903 it had a poured slab of concrete under the stage from the beginning. That kind of turned peoples' heads. Then I said, 'I think we should redo the floor of the stage a year before the restoration to see whether that has any impact on the acoustic.' The floor was made out of southern hard pine from the Carolinas. Then some others and I had the idea to get the same kind of wood. Sure enough we found out we could not only get the same species of wood that the floor was made of, but we could get wood from trees that were one hundred years old that had been cut down and made into factory beams. A lot of factories had gone out of business, so that wood was reclaimed and made into planks or strips. We put the new floor down in 1994. Didn't change much of anything, it was constant. So everything we did in the restoration was geared toward that goal, not changing the acoustic, don't throw out what's good."

"What about the new stuff, like HVAC?"

"Of course we knew we had to put in HVAC. The engineers brought in this firm to design the HVAC. We had an acoustician, Larry Kirkegaard, who was the acoustician for Ozawa Hall at Tanglewood and similar work at Symphony Hall later. Our architect was the esteemed, Ann Beha. The engineering firm came in and they made their presentation. I loved all of that stuff because my oldest brother was an architect. I said, 'Can you hear this air conditioning?' They said, 'Not very much.' I said, 'Start all over again, that's not acceptable.' So they went back to the drawing board and they designed a system which really is virtually silent. And the way they found they could do that is to make ducts that are huge so that the air moved at a very slow speed, lower than audible pitch. So that was one thing."

"An adventure! What came next?"

"The next thing were the seats. The seats were famous for tilting, I'm afraid some of them are tilting again. But at that point I said we have to keep those seats. We have to refurbish those seats. There were only two places in the United States that were equipped to still do that kind of a job. The one we chose was in Michigan. The hall was closed on May 2nd, 1995, and reopened the next October. The first thing that left were the seats. They were dismantled and sent for the entire summer to be rebuilt. Those seats had been designed for Jordan Hall, and the design was patented. So all of the drawings and plans for how they were built were on file at the Patent Office in Washington. That meant when they had to be restored we had access to know how they were built. We were very careful about all that stuff. It was a mammoth project to finish in a short amount of time."

"I would think so. I remember going the first time, even before a concert, just to look at it."

"One of the critics at the *Boston Globe*, reviewed the opening concert, and said it was, 'Murder on Gainsborough Street.' Well, the cause was that the paint hadn't dried, so it was too reverberant. Larry Kirkegaard came back in and said, 'I see what the problem is.' The problem was that we now had more exposed wall underneath the balcony and upstairs because we took out some rows of seats to put in the handicap seating, so there is more bounce back. I said, 'What are we going to do about it?' Larry said, 'There is a solution.' Next time you go into Jordan Hall you can find out what the solution is, and I'll tell you what it was. Underneath the balcony all the way around the wall is now lined with felt. What Larry said was that the thicker the felt the high frequencies will go down and down. So he designed exactly the right thickness to alleviate this harsh brilliance of the high frequencies. Next time you go into Jordan Hall touch the wall underneath there, you will be amazed! It is the same color as the paint."

"That is really a terrific story about Jordan Hall. It makes me think to myself, basically you are a musician, but here you branched out into to something akin to being a CEO of a business because of all the decision making and things that passed your way were of an administrative nature to which it appears you took enthusiastically. What is your feeling about it, Larry? Do you feel as though that was an important experience in your life? Did you derive satisfaction from being something other than but essentially, if not intimately, related to being a musician?"

"You asked me a little while ago how it happened. I told you historically why it happened, but I think the reason it happened was because I love being in Boston and I love the New England Conservatory. It was a moment of crisis, so to speak. I said I want to help. I would say that the years of my service to the school were because it's my home, because it is the place that I care about and I still do. And, of course, I learned how to do all those things. I'm not stupid, I had some training in math and organizational thinking, and I learned on the job. It was a very worthwhile thing to do. I will say at the other end of it though, my wife, in the later years of it, was quite unhappy that I was president."

"Why?"

"Well, she knew me as a musician. She said, 'I didn't marry a president.' She was unhappy with it. I was gone, very, very busy doing all of that. We had young children. I was not absent, because I came home every night to have dinner with the family. And then I would go back to school to listen to a concert."

"Did it cause a dangerous tension in your marriage at that time?"

"No, my wife was very wise, very smart."

"Larry, I think that one of the great things that you have established at NEC is the chamber concert series, 'First Monday' which I guess was your baby entirely, and still going very strong. Please tell us about 'First Monday.'"

"Monday night was an ideal night to do it because the Boston Symphony is not working on Monday nights, and NEC didn't use Jordan Hall very much on Mondays. So I got the idea of doing Monday concerts at the beginning of the month and calling the program 'First Monday at Jordan Hall.' It is now in its thirty-fourth year, and the audience has expanded over time. A couple of months ago we had nine hundred people there. It is free. Nobody on stage is paid. The Conservatory gives the hall and administrative support to run the series as part of its mission. We are playing here because we like playing with one another, and we like playing for people who like listening to us. The people are not coming for society reasons, they are coming because they love music and they want to hear it. That is a social compact which started at the very beginning. From the start we did use NEC alums playing in it, as well as professionals and faculty, some of whom are in the Boston Symphony Orchestra. In those 34 years there were more than five hundred different people who performed at First Monday — 500 different people. That is a great satisfaction."

"It sort of mirrors your early days with Heifetz and Piatigorsky."

"It is a kind of passing of the torch, and that is what we are doing when I invite younger people to play with us. I had that same experience when I was a young pup."

"There are lots of free concerts of various types at Jordan Hall I've attended over the years!"

"Yes, you have to give concerts played by your young people because that's what you are teaching them to do, and they need that experience in a safe environment. And, of course, they are spoiled because they have Jordan Hall. Most of them come back and say how much they appreciated the acoustic then, but now they are playing in a hall where the acoustics are just inferior and, wow, you are so lucky to have Jordan Hall. We are lucky, you the audience is lucky."

"Larry, I like the talks you give for a few minutes before every First Monday concert. You fill in the gaps in what we're about to hear in a nice low-key way."

"Well, I know you asked about my dear wife, and as to that, she said, 'Why do you talk so much?'"

"That's what my wife says about me."

"So your wife thinks I talk too much before the concerts?"

"She doesn't like me to talk, she loves you to talk."

"She is tired of hearing you talk."

"Larry, I want to talk about your teaching career. You have said you don't want your students to sound like you, you want them to sound like themselves. What do you mean by that?"

"When I am teaching there are two teachers in the room. I'm one of them, the young player is the other one. There are one hundred and sixty-eight hours in a week, and all we have is one hour a week to be together. It is half a percent, it is nothing. So my duty in that one hour is to set them up so that the rest of the week they teach themselves. They have to learn how to teach themselves. I am well known for saying at everybody's first lesson that my ambition is to get rid of you."

"Yes, you say that if they haven't learned from you after a while, maybe they ought to go somewhere else, maybe even do something else."

"It's sort of like that. The goal is to set them up so that they can continue their journey of learning without me, and to take on the role of being the main source of their own inspiration and growth. They are always going to be influenced by the world around them, by other players, by whatever, as I'm still influenced. So I think it is very important to show them how to make the machine work, I think it is very important for me to teach them how to hear their own inner voice. I make them sing out loud a lot, sometimes I make them sing and play at the same time so that they connect their voice with the muscles that make their sound. It is amazing how often that doesn't happen."

"Larry, when you invited me to one of your lessons I thought it was an amazing experience. I wrote a memo of it later that same day, saying that 'Larry's main message seems to be to forget about yourself, commune with and have a conversation with the composer, dead or alive, and play his music, not merely the notes, but as the composer would like through your own interpretation.'"

"Yes. You look at a page of music and it is black dots on white paper. That is not music. Those are instructions. The music is the sound you make. There is no way a piece of paper can ever capture everything you need to know or do to make that music, so you have to learn how to expand upon the fundamental information you have been given based upon life experience, based upon some sense of who the composer was and his or her culture, based upon who you are, how you react to those things. What we depend upon when we listen to performers is that they bring themselves to the music they are playing and present both of them to us so that it's a three-legged stool. It's the music, it's the composer's vision, it's our reaction to it, and it is how it is received by the audience."

"As the lesson that day I recall you had Brannon Cho, an Artist Diploma candidate, playing Frank Bridge's cello and piano sonata. It was one thing sort of flat — when they played it through the first time, and totally different the second time. In between, what I saw you do was use your singing voice, your articulate ability with words, your own personality, you were playing the cello as you felt required, you kept stressing, as you just did, notes are not music. Then, lo and behold, the second time that they played it, I felt that it came alive, it sang and became a real piece of music that one could respond to. I saw before my eyes what your teaching technique brought about in a very short time."

"I hope every one of the lessons will be the same. I've seen Brannon since many times and every time it is some version of that. That's what I do."

"Would you say that teaching is the jewel of your career?"

"It is easiest to say teaching because I spent more time doing that than a lot of other people, and I'm known for that. I'll tell you something. A student of mine from Korea, Jiyoung Lee, is playing a recital tonight. She did her bachelor's degree at Curtis, she did her master's degree and Artist Diploma at Juilliard, and she came to me after that. She's doing a doctor's degree. We were talking a little bit about that earlier because today I got a call from another student, a brilliant cellist from Rochester, who, like Jiyoung, had been admitted to Curtis and Juilliard, and whom I very much wanted to teach. She called to say she had indeed chosen to come study with me this coming September, turning down full scholarships from Curtis and Juilliard, despite NEC not being able to match the Juilliard offer. I said to Jiyoung, 'What is different about me?' She said, 'Well, I liked everybody but you have an instinct about what I need, and you express it before I even know I need it.' I guess that's pretty good, something I like to hear people say about what I do. That I have a sense. These are all extremely gifted young people that I teach. I'm very, very fortunate, and it's a good kind of partnership. They come to me because they think I have something that I can give them, and I invite them to come to me because I think they are worth spending time with.

"Apropos of that, there was a wonderful English chamber music player, a violist named Cecil Aronowitz, and somebody told me a small story about him that just made me feel so good. Apparently a group played for him, and they said, 'Thank you Mr. Aronowitz, thank you so much for what you have done for us,' to which his reply was, 'I'd like you to know that the pleasure was not all yours.' Isn't that sweet? That's the way I feel about my students. It feeds me."

"So maybe teaching is the thing in your career that has meant the most to you?"

"You were at the 'First Monday' concert the other night. Playing that Mozart quintet for me was sublime. It's all the same thing, Larry, it's communicating through sound what you feel, whether it's performing or working with young people to get them to do the same thing. Teaching is like parenting."

"It seems your students look at you that way."

"I want the people who study with me to be a big family and to support one another. The first people I taught was when I was a teenager teaching kids younger than me. When I was at Harvard I had a few students. I look back on my teaching career now. I started teaching in 1974 at NEC, and now it is 2018. In that long period of time each year some came to stay and some left. It's an overlapping thing, like a baseball team. You know baseball, Larry. It's never the same, it's not the same team, they always morph. But I can tell you that in my NEC years I have taught more than two hundred fifty people. I'm now trying to make them into a community on my website where they can find one another. With the help of some of my students I'm reaching out to them and saying, 'I'm playing this concert at NEC on September 26th in celebration of my eightieth birthday, why don't you come?' That community is important to me. I would say if I add the people that I taught at USC and Peabody, it's about three hundred people, all told."

"Last question, Larry. A sort of philosophical one, if you will. What is music?"

"Sound in time."

"Can you expand on that?"

"That answer is meant to be extremely broad, covering everything from tribal drumming to modern 'classical' music. It is intentionally vague and can be interpreted in endless ways."

So what is the difference between the world-girding virtuoso and the stay-at-home master teachers like Larry Lesser and Masuko Ushioda? Really none musically. Obviously, there is some difference in personal choice of lifestyle, and in the multiplicity of roles some, like Larry Lesser, take on. But both perpetuate the pinnacle of their art by "communicating through sound what they feel," the former to rapt audiences everywhere, and the latter to the students of today becoming the artists of tomorrow, 'parenting,' to use a word in Larry Lesser's lexicon, the ever-expanding concepts of classical music, and those of us whose lives will be forever altered by them.

Polish-born American violinist Cecylia Arzewski. Photo by Maya Press.

CHAPTER
16

Cecylia Arzewski: A Musician Is Who I Am

The best metaphor to reveal the unusual and engaging personality of Cecylia Arzewski, a foremost world-class violinist and one of the first female concertmasters of our time, is that she put aside forever her violin when she recorded for posterity the last note of the chaconne in Johann Sebastian Bach's seminal sonatas and partitas for solo violin, thus fulfilling a lifetime dream. How many top-drawer instrumentalists have ever done that? There might have been a few, but I can't think of any. As Cecylia says, "I'm done. That is exactly how I feel. I'm living the life I choose." She has chosen well. Cecylia spent many days writing a children's book soon to be published, "to entice children to want to listen to music" to experience the good life, in which Cecylia's dog, aptly named, Gustav, has discovered music, and tells children to listen as he has listened. She also spends quality time raising her adopted daughter, caring for her dogs, Mikey, Duke, and the aforementioned Gustav, with her professor husband, in a house perched near the top of a hill affording a broad and scenic view of the restful Berkshires near Tanglewood, where Cecylia often played and now listens. In her singular way, Cecylia explains it by confessing, "I never felt that playing the violin was who I was — a musician is who I am." And a sentient human being, one might add, who has negotiated the shoals of professional music-making equipped to dispense pungently and revealingly in these pages the depths and heights of that occupation, and the profound place music occupies in her life. She has emerged living life in full in the company of her own and other species, not being limited to the relatively narrow perspective of an instrumentalist. So how did Cecylia Arzewski's life unfold from her early days in Poland, not long after the conclusion of WWII, where she sat under the piano at which her father burnished his talents as the keyboard player of the Krakow Philharmonic Orchestra, to become the woman she now is?

"Cecylia, before we started today you really surprised me by saying you've put away your violin for good. You look young, you look slim, and physically there is no question that you could play the violin if you chose to do so. Why did you decide to do that?"

"Yoga, it's all about yoga. That keeps me young and in good shape. First of all I never felt that playing the violin was who I am. I always thought that playing the violin was what I did to begin with. What I will never stop doing is listening to music and being interested in music because I primarily consider myself a musician. That is who I am. What I did was I played the violin, and the violin to me was a tool of expression, an instrument that can sound very beautiful when played well, but a very difficult and demanding instrument. Violinists have more injuries than any other musicians because of the counter pressure that happens when you play the violin where the left hand holds the violin and the right hand is pushing it down with the bow, so that your body is sort of divided in half where the right side is doing something contrary to what the left side is doing. When I began yoga, I remember my teacher asking me what is it that you want to achieve from yoga. My answer to it was integration of the right side of my body with the left. My dream always was to record the Bach sonatas and partitas for solo violin. I said many years ago I would probably stop playing when I did that which is exactly what happened. Ten or so years ago I decided that at close to sixty there had been a tremendous amount of wear and tear on my body playing in the orchestra for so many years. I felt that if I waited another four or five years to record the Bach sonatas, I would not be able to do it physically. I resigned from the Atlanta Symphony and worked towards this recording for three years. When I finished the recording the last thing I recorded was the chaconne. When I played the last note I felt I was done. I put the violin down with tremendous sadness. I'm not going to tell you that this was easy, but I really that I had nothing more to say. I never had a particularly big ego even though I suspect my colleagues saw me that way. They saw me as competitive. I felt that competition was never really on my radar. I never went out and played an audition or a competition against someone, I just wanted to do my best. If that's competing, I guess I'm a competitor. In terms of ego, I wanted to experience and play certain concertos, I wanted to learn certain pieces, I wanted to perform them. Yes, I wanted to be a concertmaster, and I also wanted to record the Bach Sonatas. So I did all that. I honestly don't know any musicians who sit and say I think I've done everything that I wanted to do on my instrument and I'm done. But that is exactly how I felt. I have never picked up the violin after that."

"So what do you do to keep busy?"

"When people ask me what I do now, I usually answer by saying I practice witchcraft (laughing). But the real answer to that question is that I'm living very nicely and so grateful for not having the stress. I'm grateful for waking up in the morning and not feeling that I must get to the instrument as soon as possible because I'm a morning person in terms of practicing. I love to work very early in the morning because that's when my mind is very clear, so I'm doing that with my writing now. I start writing at 7:00 in the morning. I feel like I am living the life that I choose, not a life chosen for me. I do whatever I want to do. I make my own schedule (laughing). It is one thing if you have a job from nine to five, but it is another thing when you have a job where the schedule changes almost weekly, and you constantly live by that schedule, and you fit everything else in around it."

"I'm lucky to be able to do that now as an author, but I couldn't as a lawyer. Let's go back to your childhood in Poland, Cecylia. I think you have a story about a little radio your parents told you not to touch?"

"Yes, they told me not to touch the radio, so naturally I pushed up a chair and I climbed up on it because the radio was up high. I turned the knob and there was the Bach Chaconne played on the violin. First of all, I didn't know the Bach Chaconne, second of all I had no idea that what I was listening to was Bach, but Bach I did know because I used to go to church with our housekeeper, instead of her taking me to the park like she was supposed to. She would take me to church and threaten me so I wouldn't tell. I kept saying to her, you don't understand I want to go to church, I don't want to go to the park. Why? Because there was an organ that would be played in church, and when I heard the Bach Chaconne on the radio, I immediately connected it to the music from the church. And I thought, oh, my God, I don't have to play the organ, I can play this piece on the violin. Not so bad. That was a huge moment."

"How old were you?"

"Probably five, five and a half, shortly after I started the violin, but I was already playing the piano."

"So is Bach your favorite composer?"

"No, I wouldn't say my favorite, but I think of Bach as the Buddha of music. I think that without Bach there would be no Chopin, there would be no Mozart, there wouldn't be other composers. Just like I believe that without Beethoven there would have been no Brahms."

"Tell us a little about the piano and your father."

"I really don't know what came first the chicken or the egg. Probably I heard the piano first, before I heard the organ. So I used to nap under the piano while my father practiced when my brother was at school. I remember the smell of the rug because the rug was made by my grandmother. I had a whole world, my secret world, under the piano. I would put objects there and occasionally they would rattle. My father did not like that very much. I grew up mainly in a pianist household. My brother practiced; my father practiced. We had what I call one and a half pianos, a concert grand and an upright. Sometimes my father would practice on the upright if he was learning a piece, but when he wanted to play it, he would go to the grand piano. I went to rehearsals and concerts early on because my father was the keyboard player for the Krakow Philharmonic."

"Was your father a big influence on you?"

"Probably the biggest. He taught me to listen. I inherited his perfect pitch, his ability to perceive musical tones as higher or lower in relation to a melody. People say it is a blessing and I say it is a curse (laughing). He had the most unbelievable ear I ever came across. He could hear an orchestral chord and say the second trombone is flat. I've never come across an ear like that, never."

"Another guy that I was interested in talking to you about is Eugene Kavala, your teacher when you were a very young girl in Poland. How big was he in your life?"

"Huge, because I didn't want to play the violin and he knew it. Eugene Kavala was my first violin teacher. His specialty was teaching children. It is a specialty; it is something I've never been able to do. I've tried but I'm not good at it. I love teaching and I think I'm pretty good at teaching grownups. What he would do is he would come to the house a couple of times a week in the very beginning, and everything we did together he changed into a fairy tale. First, he gave Polish names to all the four strings on the violin, E, A, D, G, which were never misbehaving. Then he would make up other stories about the forest, the gnomes, the elves, and contrast them in terms of dynamics, that is softness to loudness of the music. There was always some tree that would fall down and make a huge sound or thunder. There were lots of references to nature which I put into in my children's book that I wrote but haven't published yet because I'm going to have to travel once I do publish it. It is told through the voice of my dog, Gustav. It got to the point where I looked forward to Eugene's coming, and once he came I was just so happy he was there because it was more like a play time for me. Of course, I was very connected to music, so I could have an emotional connection to that as well. I saw him the last time about twenty years ago for the last time. He has passed away since. He was just a sweet gentle soul, very modest, very soft spoken. He had a nickname for me, and after a while there was never a time when I would see him when I wouldn't wrap my arms around his neck because he was just such a wonderful warm human being."

"I remember so clearly Joseph Silverstein, who was the concertmaster of the Boston Symphony Orchestra for many years. I know he was a prime mentor of yours. I guess he wanted you to be his concertmaster when he conducted the Worcester Symphony Orchestra. You drove out there together and talked about music or listened to music. He was a heck of a guy in your life. Tell us about your relationship with him?"

"It is hard for me to talk about Joseph Silverstein to this day because I feel like I'm still in mourning. He is buried here in Stockbridge and I go and I visit him, sometimes a couple of times a week. He was one of a kind. Other than my father, he was the main mentor in my life. His death was two years ago. I am still in shock. I still cannot believe that he is dead. It is hard for me to accept it."

"What made him such a special person?"

"He was special in every way. He was special as a husband, he was special as a father, he was special as a teacher, as a concertmaster, and as a violinist, of course.

Maybe that should have been the first thing I mentioned. His father was a violinist, a maker of violins too, and Joseph's first teacher. Joseph Silverstein was also incredibly generous to me. He spent time with me. I don't really feel like I ever stopped studying with him. I was always running to him all the years we were together in the Boston Symphony asking him about this and that. I listened to a lot of music. I am a very curious musician. I like going to concerts; I like comparing recordings. What was interesting in my relationship with Joe Silverstein was that he had this vast knowledge of the violin and violin music, and he realized about five or six years ago that I had that kind of knowledge too, only mine was on the piano and pianists. So he would make copies for me of old recordings of violinists like Eugene Ysaye, and I would give him these recordings of pianists that I had. It was a very special relationship. He had such amazing stories about conductors and violinists, about studying with this one and that one, and about his experiences. He was a brilliant, brilliant man. There wasn't a subject you couldn't discuss with him, extremely well informed, well read. He was patient and kind to me."

"I understand he was your teacher at the New England Conservatory of Music even before you joined the BSO?"

"I came to study with him first in 1967 at NEC. I was not an easy student at that point because I had just come off a seven-year stint with Ivan Galamian. I wanted to get away from Galamian. It was seven years serving the great master. I think it was enough. But because Galamian was the most famous teacher in the world, I thought there wasn't anything that anybody else could teach me after those seven years. Joseph Silverstein transformed me as a violinist. He changed my approach to the instrument, he changed my style of playing, he explained to me how things worked, which is something Galamian never ever did because he didn't feel like he had to because he was Galamian. I don't know what there was about that man. I didn't really care for him. I just wrote about it this morning how he was tall, dark, cold, and scary. At times he could be very cruel. Silverstein was the opposite. It took me a while to adjust. Joseph threw me out of a lesson one time because he knew I didn't practice. He said to me to go home and practice, and if you come back next week and you haven't practiced, that will be your last lesson."

"Primarily, how did Silverstein change you to be different than you had been before?"

"One way was that I listened to more violinists. I was brought up on David Oistrakh and Nathan Milstein. I remember one time when Joe Silverstein was trying to show me something on the violin. I started doing it, and I said to him this sounds so different. He said, yes it does. I said I don't like that style. He looked at me and said you learn that style first and then you'll choose, but first you have to learn it. He also introduced me to Jascha Heifetz, and Fritz Kreisler, whom I had never heard. To tell you the truth in the very beginning I didn't like what I heard because it was so different from Oistrakh. Silverstein said that there is a certain sizzle in the sound of Heifetz and Kreisler that you don't hear in other violinists. I hear it now in Hilary Hahn. She is the best. It's not the sound, it is the approach to the instrument. It is organic playing."

"You spent a couple of hours with Jascha Heifetz, maybe the most famous violinist of the last century. I think you made the remark he taught you more in two and a half hours than Galamian did in several years."

"Galamian didn't teach me anything."

"What did Heifetz teach you?"

"It was like being in the presence of God, so if God tells you to go jump out the window, you go jump out the window. So when he would ask me to do certain things that I was never able to do, suddenly I did them. And I was even surprised myself (laughing). I didn't just surprise him, I surprised myself. He would ask me to play certain phrases over and over again in different ways. He taught me certain technical things too. He actually complimented me one time. He said that I had good intonation. And I thought to myself, yeah, paid a dear price for it. I met with Heifetz a couple of times."

"Did he have a Jewish sound? Do you think the Jewish violinists play differently?"

"No I don't believe in that. The only reason we have so many Jewish violinists is because they were not allowed to go to medical school or law school. Music was a profession, it was a way for them to make a living."

"Cecylia, what about this reputation you have for outspokenness? How would you describe your own personality?"

"I knew lots of male musicians, violinists, who were just as outspoken as I was and probably more so, and they were never talked about as being so outspoken. I think it is a gender thing."

"It was said that you were outspoken about Seiji Ozawa, your conductor at the BSO?"

"That had a great deal to do with Joe Silverstein. Let's put it this way, Joe and Seiji didn't exactly like each other, didn't exactly get along. That was one of the reasons that Silverstein left the Boston Symphony. Seiji hurt a lot of people in the Boston Symphony. He made some very poor decisions about hiring, and then he would fire them. I feel that he was a very vindictive man. This is aside from music, and on a personal basis. I saw this daily where he would decide to go after a musician in his orchestra, whom he didn't like for whatever reason, and go after them and go after them until they couldn't perform anymore. The usual thing with conductors is that it is either too fast, too slow, too loud, too soft, so if you start saying this over and over again to a percussionist, for example, eventually he'll lose his cool and not be able to play at all. And this happened with several musicians in the orchestra."

"Go after them as people or as musicians?"

"Well, both. Conductors are notoriously very intimidating when you think about just the physical aspect of it. The conductor is up there on the podium, and your job is to please the conductor. He becomes a father figure. So when you get this negative response, you basically unravel. We all knew why it was happening, and it was very sad. He didn't just go after certain people in the orchestra but he also went after certain people who had close connections with Silverstein."

"Did you ever speak to Ozawa about this problem?"

"Yes. Before I left the orchestra, I asked him to take care of the older players. He had it in his mind that he was going to listen to everybody in the first violin section and rearrange the whole violin section to put people in different places. There was talk that he was going to form a new first violin section that way. He couldn't do it with people like me whose seats were protected, but he could do whatever he wanted to with the rest of the section."

"Did he demote some people?"

"Yes. I don't want to name names, but yes, there was somebody in the violin section, there was somebody in the percussion section, there was somebody in the viola section."

"I was surprised when first chair violist, Burton Fine, left the orchestra."

"I don't know very much about that situation. I was not close to Burton. Burton kept to himself. He was a loner. He was a thinker, a very bright man. A great violist. I wasn't in the orchestra when he left, but I saw what was happening before I left. I saw that Seiji Ozawa had designs on Burton Fine. Everybody knew it. Everybody."

"What was making Ozawa do this?"

"I don't want to sound like Sigmund Freud, but I always felt that he had a tremendous amount of aggression towards the western world. Does it surprise me? No. He was born in Manchuria during the war. He is Japanese all the way through."

"How did he retain his position as the Music Director of the BSO all that time, around a quarter of a century?"

"Japanese corporation money. Money, money, money, how do you think that hall was built. The Seiji Ozawa Hall at Tanglewood. It was designed by a Japanese architect. Everything about it is Japanese."

"Richard Dyer, the former longtime critic of the *Boston Globe* wrote about you to the effect that you were the outspoken, colorful, and gifted player of the Ozawa years. My impression is that you do say what you think. We need people who tell it like it is. It's a quality that sometimes makes it harder to get along with that person. Cecylia, do you see yourself as benign and nice to get along with, or in a more nuanced way?"

"I'm not easy to get along with."

"Well, OK, that is telling it like it is. Why not?"

"Because I like things my way. I'm a perfectionist. Extremely obsessive-compulsive."

"How about the orchestra members in Atlanta where you were the concertmaster for close to twenty years? Did you have problems or conflict with them as the concertmaster?"

"Well, think about it. In 1990 a woman arrives in the South and she becomes the concertmaster."

"Jewish concertmaster."

"A Jewish, Polish concertmaster, there you go. A *woman* Jewish, Polish concertmaster. Didn't go over very well. I had conductors coming up to me asking me, 'How would you like me to refer to you, what should I call you?' And I said, 'Well you can call me Cecylia, which is what my name is.' And they would say, 'Would you like to be called concertmistress?' I'd say, 'No, not mistress. I'm nobody's mistress, never have been, never will be (laughing).' The most difficult one was the conductor Robert Shaw. He didn't know what to call me, he really didn't know what to do, and it took a long time."

"I saw him conduct once. He was a great chorale conductor. Great, if not the best. I remember he pointed his finger at the chorus, and I said, 'My God, it is the hand of God.'"

"It was the hand of God. When he came out on stage before the rehearsal the chairs had to be lined up a certain way, there had to be no more than one inch of space between the chairs. It was a whole production. He had to have seven pencils next to him lying down, he came in with a suitcase full of stuff to every rehearsal."

"But you considered him a great musician?"

"I considered him a great chorale conductor. I remember members of the Cleveland Orchestra telling me how when Shaw was the chorale conductor there, George Szell, the director, would want to hear the orchestral balance, so he would call Shaw up on stage to have him conduct. Szell would go to the back of the hall to hear the balance. The members told me they would all laugh because when Szell was up there the orchestra sounded great, and when Shaw got up there the chorus suddenly sounded great. He had a way of communicating with that chorus, I've never seen anything like it. He used to write weekly letters to them, he had a personal relation to the chorus. That chorus was his baby, his thing."

"Did we finish with conflicts with the orchestra members?"

"Yes, there was conflict about the fact that I was a woman. One time I had a meeting with one of my music directors, and one of the orchestra principals (laughing) actually said to the music director, 'Well, I don't understand why she is the one who decides on the bowing.' Just like that. I sat there. I said nothing. I said to myself, 'This is going to take care of itself. This is the most ridiculous statement I ever heard.'"

"The concertmaster does that, right?"

"Of course, it is part of my job."

"Do the other violinists follow your bowing?"

"They have to (laughing). It is their job."

"How important is tuning the orchestra prior to the piece? Do you have to make it happen correctly every time?"

"Extremely important. I can't make it happen. I can offer them an A from the oboe which is what I do when I stand up. They have to take it, but whether they do or not is really up to them. If they don't take it and they play out of tune, I can hear it, so yes, it is very important. It is not just the violins, it's the rest of the orchestra. Everybody has to match the oboe."

"Did you speak to the orchestra to convey the conductor's wishes?"

"No, the conductor asks the orchestra for something, whatever it may be. If I feel that's where the bowings come in to give him what he is asking, and I feel that the bowings cannot provide him with what that is, I have to change the bowing in order to provide it to him. So it creates a conflict in the sense that suddenly in the middle of the rehearsal I take out my pencil and start rearranging things. The principle second is sitting right there, he can see what I am doing and he is copying, copying, copying. Then I have to convey it to the principal violist and cellist."

"It seems like one of the main things you do between the conductor and the orchestra is to adjust the bowing?"

"Yes. I can also suggest technical things. You might say that bowing is the art of using the bow to achieve the proper tone quality of the music. If he is asking for a particular tone color and he is not a violinist, I can turn around to my first violin section and say please play that passage on such and such a string and it will give it a different color. So then we do that passage again and we play it on a different string, and yes it gives it a different color. The conductor hears it and he looks at me and gives me a big smile and it has been a good day."

"Is it your responsibility to carry to the orchestra the intentions of the conductor in communicating the meaning of the particular piece to the audience. Does he usually share that with you?"

"Sometimes he does it verbally, sometimes it is just done with motion."

"Then does it become your responsibility to get the orchestra to do this?"

"It is my responsibility to get the string section to do it, but as to the rest of the orchestra it is the conductor's responsibility. Sometimes there are issues of articulation, directions in the score as to continuity on a single note or group of notes, where the violins are articulating a passage, and suddenly you hear the woodwinds articulating the passage completely differently. So I would wait until intermission to go up to the conductor and say, excuse me, we are playing it like this and the woodwinds are playing it like that. Do you want us to play it differently or do you want us to play it the same. I think perhaps we should have the same articulation. Oh yes, I agree. And then he would fix it. But that's their job, not my job, That is why I waited until intermission."

"In your long career as the concertmaster of the Atlanta Orchestra would you say that overall it was a positive experience?"

"Yes. Musically speaking, artistically speaking, it was a very pleasant experience. It was a wonderful experience."

"Do you think you were successful there as the concertmaster with respect to the success of the orchestra?"

"In terms of the success of the orchestra, yes."

"Cecylia, what is music?"

"What is music? Where is that quote when I need it? Here it is. I'll read it. *Music is a moral law. It gives a soul to the universe, wings to the mind, flight to the imagination, a charm to sadness, and life to everything. It is the essence of order, and leads to all that is good, just, and beautiful, of which it is the invisible, but nevertheless dazzling, passionate, and eternal form.*"

"Who said that? It is so apt, so all embracing."

"Some people say it is Plato. I love it because of the idea that music is a moral law."

"Are you deferential to the great people you've met over a lifetime?"

"I have met great people, but I never thought of them that way because I worked with them, and so they didn't represent the same thing to me as they might represent to you. In other words, to me we were all equal."

"Right. My feeling, even meeting great musicians, is that we are all just human beings, so I don't put any of them on a pedestal. I do very much admire and appreciate their talent. I think what you are saying to me in another way is that you are yourself in their company."

"We are all people. That's really the bottom line. And music is something that we do, and some of us do it better than others. That's the only way that I see it."

"Was there anybody out there that particularly impressed you?"

"In 1957 when I moved to Israel, we were all playing for the Israeli American Scholarship Foundation. In the group was Pinchas Zukerman, Miriam Fried, and Itzhak Perlman. It was the first time I heard Itzhak Perlman play. I was nine years old. I was sitting there and this boy with shorts walks up onstage with crutches. Someone handed him the violin and he starts playing. I thought, oh my God, what's the use. Why am I playing the violin, this is unbelievable. I could see the talent, I could feel it, I could taste it. it was incredible, it was something beyond anything I had ever imagined!"

"I felt that same way when I first heard Anne-Sophie Mutter play years ago when she was fifteen."

"Do you know her pretty well? She was nice to me."

"I do know her pretty well. She is a lovely woman. When she first came to America you couldn't talk to her she was so shy, and I thought how can somebody go out there and play a Max Bruch violin concerto the way she did and not be able to talk to people? Anne-Sophie has flowered and matured and opened up. She has even changed her style of playing, but not for the better, I think. It is a bit on the hysterical side now is the way I would put it. Then it was very similar to how Hilary Hahn plays today, just like that."

"Cecylia, you've played under a great many conductors. I've read that you loved Bernard Haitink, Claudio Abbado, Colin Davis, and Leonard Bernstein as conductors unreservedly. You've spoken about Seiji Ozawa in different terms. Given that account, would you say that most conductors because of their position of relative autonomy over the rest of the orchestra fall into a greater or lesser category of taking things out on the orchestra or lording it over them?"

"It really depends on the personality of the particular conductor. You've heard stories about George Szell, who led the Cleveland Orchestra for a long time. He would show up at a rehearsal, didn't like your tie, and dismiss you."

"Charles Dutoit?"

"Oh, Dutoit! Dutoit has his repertoire which is mostly French music. He has a wonderful flair for music which is something that Ozawa never did, never had, and when he used to come to Boston during that time, it was great! You know what is interesting is to see the different conductors who come throughout the years. Of course, Ozawa was here for a long time, and then the same conductors will come who came under Ozawa, and now let's say they come under Levine, and then they come under Nelsons, so it's very different. We had Seiji who did not have a lot of musical flair, or just feeling. It was mostly old choreography and was like the Kabuki theatre. It was very, very choreographic, and you played the piece with him over and over and over and over again and he would do it exactly with the same motions in particular pieces. I would look at my staff partner because he would make a funny face somewhere, so I would look at my staff partner and he would look at me and we would look up and go 'umh umh' there it is again, the same motion over and over and over again. Dutoit is very different. He is very spontaneous. When he came here when Ozawa was the music director the orchestra sounded great, just great, great, great! The orchestra always appreciated Charles Dutoit being here. It was a good match."

"Lorin Maazel?"

"Maazel, I only worked with him one time many, many years ago. I even remember what we did. It was the first time I played Schumann's second symphony. Yoel Levi reminds me very much of Maazel from everything that I have heard. Levi was his assistant in Cleveland and I'm sure he picked up on a lot. And one of the things that remained with Yoel is that he does everything from memory. When I say everything, I mean everything. Piano concertos, violin concertos, you name it. The score is never in front of him, never."

"Cecylia, Yoel Levi was your conductor in Atlanta for many years, so you must have lots of thoughts about him?"

"An extraordinary talent, extraordinary! Personally, he could be somewhat cold."

"Wasn't there some sort of flap when Levi left Atlanta?"

"My relations with the players there had ups, and downs mostly to do with the political situation that happened with Yoel Levi's firing. He was basically fired. I was very much for him because I went to Atlanta feeling enough confidence in

Yoel Levi's conducting that he could and would transform the Atlanta Symphony into another Cleveland Orchestra, where I had been the Associate Concertmaster. I feel that he was on his way to doing that. We were the only orchestra at the time in the country that had a recording contract with Telarc. We toured to Europe; we played in Carnegie Hall almost every year. It was a good time."

"Kurt Masur?"

"I think Masur was an extraordinary musician. I don't believe that a great conductor has to have a great stick technique. It's all about here (Cecylia pointing to her heart). When I think about the concerts we did with William Steinberg at the BSO, he had no stick technique at all. You couldn't tell one motion from the other. His stick was all over the place. We would all imitate it. But the music, what he felt in his heart, that's what poured over to the orchestra. There has to be that chemistry, it is all about that. In that respect I remember the Dutch conductor, Hans Vonk. Do you know of him?"

"The name sounds familiar."

"Vonk died about twelve years ago. The best Beethoven Fifth Symphony I ever played was here in Tanglewood when he substituted for Bernard Haitink. Many years later he came to Atlanta. I went up to him and said I still remember that performance of Beethoven's Fifth at Tanglewood. He said that was a very special day. What was wonderful about his comment was he was not taking credit for it. He complimented the Boston Symphony. Haitink did the same thing. It's a certain modesty that European conductors have that I think American conductors don't have. When he came to Atlanta to do the Beethoven Seventh Symphony, Vonk had a neurological disease which was quite advanced. In fact, this was one of the last concerts he performed. His beat was so small that you could barely see it. That Beethoven Seventh was the greatest Beethoven Seventh I've ever played. It was tight, it was together, it was done with conviction."

"André Previn?"

"The best thing I heard from Previn was at a prelude concert thirty years ago here at Tanglewood. Previn played a Franck sonata with Joe Silverstein. It was exquisite, absolutely exquisite! I remember listening to his piano playing and thinking to myself, why doesn't he conduct that way (laughing). I don't think he was the conductor that he was the pianist."

"Simon Rattle?"

"I love Simon Rattle! When he came here for the first time it was a shock for the orchestra. We never expected him to be that good. Wonderful person, sort of like Colin Davis. I subscribe to the Berlin Philharmonic Digital Concert Hall, and occasionally they do interviews of Simon. He reminds me so much of Colin Davis."

"John Williams?"

"John Williams. Again, a man I love! He is kind, he is completely unassuming, and an incredible talent. I heard his early jazz recordings many years ago. I don't understand what possesses somebody who can play jazz piano the way he did, same with Previn, to go and become a Hollywood composer. I don't understand that. He doesn't seem to me that way. He lives in a suburban neighborhood in LA, he doesn't have the space that I have here, his house is here, next to him there is another house, and another house. You wouldn't think that this is the billionaire he has to be by now."

"Michael Tilson Thomas? Did you play with him?"

"Yes, he is a friend of mine. We got into the Boston Symphony in the same year. What a talent! A talented musician who probes and probes. Somebody who is very interested in music and somebody who is interested in supporting living composers."

"You have taught individual students privately. What is it you like about teaching?"

"If you know how to fix a problem, that is instant gratification for the teacher. Nothing gives me more pleasure than someone coming to me with an issue or a problem, and to be able to say, well, why don't you try dropping the elbow, or why don't you try this, or why don't you try that, and they pick up the instrument, they play, and they go like they can't believe it and I am in heaven. I'm happy that I've been able to help some people out in that way."

"You've played orchestral, chamber, solo and have taught. What role do you like best?"

"Chamber music is the most intimate form of music. There is no question about it. Orchestral playing to me is like listening to an organ. I love to be surrounded by that sound. Solo, when I play alone it is very much like being a pianist (laughing). I like that too."

"So that leaves us with teaching. You didn't say which one you like best. You like them all. I know that."

"I love them all."

"When you play solo, what is it you want to convey to the audience?"

"By myself, all by myself. Well Bach comes to mind very easily. I have always thought of the different voices of Bach. Voices, different people sitting around talking, and each one has his own or her own opinion."

"That is what you want to convey?"

"I feel that each one of the voices in Bach is a different character, a different personality, and each voice has to be conveyed in a different way."

"What are you conveying?"

"What they are feeling when they say something."

"Do you think Bach had this in mind when he was writing the music?"

"Probably not. I don't know. I doubt it. I don't know how he wrote what he wrote, I don't know how any composer writes what he or she does."

"That's what I'm trying to get at. You can ask composers about that, and I've gotten some ideas from them. When you are playing a particular composer's concerto what is it you attempt to or want to convey to that audience?"

"A feeling, a verbal feeling that is transmitted through sound, an expression of what he is trying to convey."

"Cecylia, what does music mean to you personally?"

"I don't think that without music I would be alive today. Music has been my constant companion. It has been the longest relationship I've had. It has supported me through good times and it has supported me through very bad times. I have always used music and turned to music for healing, for inspiration, for imagination, for everything in my life. You know when you asked me that question about what is it that I'm trying to convey, in the course of a day I listen to different music. I listen to the music at a particular time according to what I am feeling. I never listen to jazz in the morning, it is always after five, six o'clock that I will put on a jazz recording. But in the morning I tend to listen to Bach, sort of clears my mind, clears my head."

"Do musicians hear music differently than the rest of us?"

"The way I listen to music is very different. I do think musicians listen to music differently. For example, when I am listening to music the first thing I do is to identify every note I hear. To me different notes have different colorings and different shades and represent different expressions to me. Just the notes themselves. Very often I have one favorite note in a particular piece of music. I don't know where that comes from, but it is the way I respond to hearing that note. So I'm a musician."

"Can music affect the fraught political scene we see in the world today?"

"Do you think I could put on a Mahler symphony and strap Trump into a chair and make him listen to it? If I could, do you think he would walk away from that experience feeling differently than he did before he heard it?"

"Probably not."

"This is why I think that music is so important in schools."

"Do you think it can change a person?"

"I have no proof of this, but I do believe that if children listen to music at a very early age, and if they have music in their house and have music in their lives, they would be very different people."

"I think so too. Should musicians be involved in administering politically or otherwise the nations and the world?"

"That's not our job."

"Cecylia, you may have something you want to add that you think it is important to say in light of what we have already talked about?"

"I like questions (laughing)."

"Well, I'll ask you a question. We are here in the company of two other human beings, and the three dogs who ran out to greet my wife, Lois, and me. I myself feel that my dog is entitled to just as much respect as any person, that I should be nice to my dogs and nice to people. You have great feeling for animals. So my question is I guess music is very important as are animals, and I suppose you could extend that into all nature. But let's take animals. Are animals important to human existence and the viability of life?"

"Oh, completely. Totally. I didn't grow up with dogs. My mother to this day, she is one hundred years old now, hates dogs. She really, really hates dogs. She is afraid of them. Basically that's what it is. My first dog was fourteen years ago, Gustav, whom I found in the middle of the Chattahoochee Forest in Georgia. I think he changed me as a person."

"How?"

"Well, it is all give, give, give, and it is a tremendous responsibility. My brother has the perfect description of a dog. He says dogs are like children who never ever grow up. And it is so true. They don't grow up. You can train them, you can take them to obedience school, they can be very well behaved, but they never really ever grow up and become independent. They are always dependent on you. They are always acting out. What goes on, especially between my two dogs, is like children, no it's mine, no it's mine. I would love to get more involved in an organization that addresses cruelty to animals. I'm a vegetarian, I do not eat meat for that reason. The longer I live the more conscious I become of what it is that I buy, what I wear, such as leather shoes. I try not to buy them. Leather pocketbooks and fur, forget it. Doesn't exist in this household. Animals are very much like children in the sense that they're tortured by people who have no business even looking at them. Finding Gustav really opened up my awareness to the cruelty that animals go through. Things are done to children the same way. Children experience abuse and animals experience abuse and it's horrible."

"You named your first dog Gustav after Gustav Mahler. Why?"

"I took Gustav in because I found him starving in the forest. I was going to find him a home, but even before I got home to Atlanta I had already named him. When I think about all the abuse he had suffered, and the early months he was with me, I realized it took a particular kind of person to bring him back to health, to take care of him, and put up with his neurotic phobias. Gustav is such a different dog today than he was thirteen years ago."

"Did you tell me why you named him Gustav?"

"Of course, because I fell in love with the dog and I love Gustav Mahler. The children's book that I wrote, I wrote for one reason, and that is to entice children to want to listen to music, to want to go to museums, to want to travel and to experience a good life. This is done through the voice of my dog, Gustav, where he talks to these children ages seven to twelve and explains to them about his sudden discovery of music and how they should listen to what he listens to because it is so special. And it is put into children's language like the oboe becomes the duck. There is a very clear violin solo in the second movement of the Mahler second symphony, where the violin makes a sound that sounds like a cat."

"Have you completed this book?"

"Yes."

"Is it the only children's book you have written?"

"Yes. I'll publish it after my daughter is in college. I believe it will find a good publisher."

Cecylia Arzewski may have put down her violin for good, but in its place, she has dipped her pen in the inkwell, as it were, to find a creative way to bring her love of music and God's creatures, to all of us.

Author's Addition to the Above Story on Cecylia Arzewski

Indeed, Cecylia Arzewski dipped her pen in the inkwell to author *Gustav's Gate*, as you see on the next page. Her book, which came out on November 11, 2021, a day known as Armistice Day, appropriately devoted to peace, received five stars, and universal plaudits from its readers. It is well worth quoting Cecylia's last paragraphs in that book which capture its essential love of music, animals, and nature, as follows:

> "Mom and Dad have lots of music CDs. They play them throughout each day as they go about doing chores or reading. I love hearing music throughout the house. Music provides me with the love of nature. When I listen to music, I feel unafraid. I like listening to Bach in the morning, Beethoven's symphonies in the afternoon, and Mahler in the evening. I especially love Beethoven's *Pastoral Symphony* in the spring. Because there are lots of birds in this music, sometimes I don't know whether the birds I hear are on the recording or outside at the feeders. Sometimes I find myself rolling on my back and pretending to conduct while listening to the music in the house. I wonder whether I could really learn — go to a conducting school and become a famous doggy conductor. I have to ask my mom whether there is such a thing as a conducting school for dogs.
>
> "You see, big cities have culture to offer, and the forest has nature to offer. I like having them both in my life, and I would be sad to lose one or the other. Maybe it is important to have both culture and nature in one's life to achieve balance. I feel very fortunate to have parents who feel the same way as I do. I wouldn't want to change anything in my life—yes, including my brother, Mikey."

Cecylia Arzewski's children's book, published in 2019. Her dog, Gustav, was named after Gustav Mahler, Cecylia's love for whom makes Mahler her muse.

Credit: Gustav's Gate cover used by permission of Cecylia Arzewski.

Japanese-American pianist Aiko Onishi. Photo by Larry Ruttman.

CHAPTER
17

Aiko Onishi: Pianist and Pedagogue

One day in Tokyo in early 1946, only six months or so after Japan capitulated on August 15, 1945, two officers of General Douglas MacArthur's occupying army strode purposefully up to the entrance of the well-to-do home where the then-eighteen-year-old Aiko Onishi had lived a somewhat cloistered, protected, and relatively peaceful life with her mother and father, Teiko and Kazumi, and her two brothers, Koich and Eiji, before and even during most of World War II, from Pearl Harbor in 1941 to Hiroshima and Nagasaki, days before the war's end.

The end had been preceded by the horrific firebombing of Tokyo on the night of March 9, 1945, which had obliterated sixteen square miles of the city, killing an estimated 100,000 people, making homeless another 100,000 people, and destroying hundreds of thousands of homes, which earned its reputation as the single most destructive bombing raid in human history.

The event was dubbed by the Americans with the utilitarian-sounding name of "Operation Meetinghouse," and by the Japanese with the more descriptive name for the fiery and deathly vortex as the "Night of the Black Snow." Those days, of course, marked the end of the Onishi family's peaceful existence in a home filled with music made by Aiko and her mother. No words can tell of the horror that befell them that night better than Aiko's own words:

"The March firebombing is still very vivid in my mind. It was so close to my home that my mother, older brother, and I, along with a maid, decided to take refuge, leaving behind my younger brother, Eiji, and a cousin who was living with us, since they insisted that they could save the house from the fire by hosing water to the roof.

I can imagine how terribly my mother must have felt. Everywhere we headed, there were fires. We took numerous zigzags, and finally ended up on a railroad truck on higher ground where many people took refuge. We left home about midnight and stayed there until 3:30 or 4 o'clock in the morning when many fires had subsided and it felt safe enough to head home. We were more than grateful to find my brother and cousin safe.

The houses around our block were mostly destroyed by fire. Since my brother and my cousin hosed the roofs, our house was saved along with a few small houses facing the back of our house.

One of my cousins was living more towards the center of Tokyo. She had a very young baby. She with her baby and her in-laws set out to escape from the fire, but they all perished together. Her husband was away on business. He was a cameraman, I believe, for a Japanese newspaper. It took him a few days to find their remains. Sad story!"

So one viewing the officers advance on the Onishi household might well have thought the officers were on a military mission. In fact, they were on a friendly, even social, mission, perhaps one of the first in that fraught period following the bitter struggle.

A request had come to MacArthur headquarters from Marietta Wilkins, the mother of Justice Raymond Sanger Wilkins, then of the Supreme Judicial Court of Massachusetts, and later its greatly respected chief justice, inquiring into the survival of the Onishi family during the war. One might not expect such a request in the clouds and smoke of that horrific war. What was behind it?

It turns out that Aiko's mother, Teiko, whose family had joined the Universalist Church of America around the turn of the last century, had come to America to study piano in 1917, in the midst of another great war, at the New England Conservatory of Music. Teiko graduated from there in 1920, with transcontinental support from Mrs. Patterson of Pasadena, California who underwrote her tuition, and Mrs. Marietta Wilkins of historic Salem, Massachusetts where she resided while attending as a family member. Both gracious ladies were members of the Universalist Church of America. During those years that Teiko was in the Wilkins home, Marietta and her husband, Samuel, then the mayor of Salem, treated her lovingly as a daughter while she commuted almost daily to the conservatory in Boston twenty miles distant, making many friends in both places, and bringing happy memories of America back to Japan. Teiko emerged from her years of study to become a noted pianist, concertizing in Japan for some years after her return from America. She met her future husband, Kazumi, an aspiring and ultimately a very successful businessman, on the steamship that brought her home from San Francisco, marrying him two years after her return. In turn, under Teiko's generous and kind tutelage, Aiko became an accomplished pianist, even in those war-torn days.

Indeed, the family had incredibly survived the war without casualty. That good news was reported back to the Wilkins by the officers who soon learned of the musical background of the Onishi family, and Aiko's budding talent. The meeting grew into shared friendships and visits to each other's homes. Aiko would occasionally play at home when the officers and their wives visited. No doubt Aiko's talents acted not only as a salve to the remnants of bad feeling on both sides, but to the growth of Aiko's artistic reputation among Americans in Tokyo.

In fact, the impression Aiko made at a recital attended by both Japanese and Americans, where she played Chopin, was so great that her music fell movingly on the ears of music-lover Harry Marsh, one of General MacArthur's closest associates, who then was traveling back and forth between Japan and America on official business of the occupying army on a regular basis.

So taken with Aiko's playing was Harry Marsh that he sought and obtained a meeting with Teiko and Kazumi at the Onishi home to ask if he might be an emissary to Teiko's Universalist friends in Boston to see whether he could ignite their interest in helping Aiko to come to America to study music. With some discussion, it was soon agreed that Harry Marsh might pursue what he plainly considered a mission.

Not long after that, Harry Marsh met near Boston with the highly influential Universalist minister of the Arlington, Massachusetts, Universalist church, Minister Ayres. It might be said that a minister of war was meeting with a minister of peace to quell the fires of war with music! Dr. Ayres was persuaded and took up the cause.

He spread the word in the Universalist world. The able minister of peace, Dr. Ayres, applied the *coup de grace,* when he located a source of money in church coffers as yet unused, suggesting that a Universalist fund originally set aside for missionary work in China by the Women's Association of the Universalist Church be converted to a two year all expenses scholarship for Aiko to study at the highly regarded Eastman School of Music in Rochester, New York. *Voila!* The scholarship was duly awarded to Aiko in 1950 by the Association.

This mirrored her mother's experience before her, to the point where Aiko was welcomed as a daughter into the home of Mr. and Mrs. Ruth and Louis Cartwright, the City Manager of Rochester for thirteen years, and then its Postmaster. Aiko drew close to their daughters, Eleanor and Martha, with whom she still corresponds.

Ultimately, as will be related below, Aiko chose to live, occasionally perform, and become an iconic teacher of several recognized pianists, at San Jose State University in California, where she taught for well over twenty years, becoming a full professor, and the chair of its music department. Aiko also became a naturalized U.S. citizen, albeit returning regularly to her native land to share her pedagogic talents with students there as a guest lecturer at the famed Toho Gakuen School of Music, her own studio, and other cities in Japan for more than thirty years.

Aiko Onishi is admired in both countries for her widely recognized pianism and teaching skills. She also authored a classic treatise in Japanese on the art of playing the piano, later translated to English, aptly entitled, *Pianism* (2009), in which she describes tone production, pedaling, and the different physical movements required to produce many different kinds of sounds.

This account, and the story of Aiko you are about to read, reminds us yet again that war and the arts, the latter often glamorizing war, and only lately in history debasing it, have been two of few constants throughout man's recorded and pre-history, and pose the existential question of which of these essentially opposed constants will ultimately prevail, if either, since it appears both reside deeply in humanity's genes.

Does the story of Aiko Onishi, now close to ninety, give us a clue to that conundrum? Maybe, maybe not, the reader will be the judge.

It is, at the very least, a beautiful story worth telling of a uniquely gentle and loving person devoted to peace, music-making, music teaching, and beauty.

Since the time of Mozart it has been customary to start off by asking talented musicians at what age they first took to their art.

"I don't know because I was too young. My mother was still practicing then. The story goes that I was held on my grandmother's lap listening to her practice. She was called to the telephone and left the room. My grandmother asked me if I wanted to play the piano. By the time my mother came back I was seated at the piano and sort of playing around, and she saw that my hand position was very good. She wasn't going to start me until five or so. I was then three and some months. That is when I started. Of course, I don't remember any of this."

"Aiko, that's a Mozart story (both laughing)."

"I wasn't a genius at all, but I imitated her hands so that is how I knew how to position, I think."

"Tell us your favorite memories about your mother, Teiko?"

"My mother and I were so very, very close. I had a protected life. I went to a private school and for the first year, a maid came with me to school, back and forth. My home was very loving, peaceful, no raised voices, and we normally had three or four maids. We were beautifully taken care of. Very much love. I have wonderful memories of childhood. If anything happened that made me unhappy, when I came home and saw my mother, it was gone. She was very musical. My friends at school admired her as well. My father called her 'angel.' Unfortunately, she only lived to sixty-seven."

"What was it like coming to America for the first time?"

"When I first came to this country it was a great adventure. My mother encouraged me that I could leave home. That was only five years after the war, and I thought maybe I'll meet some people who don't like Japanese. Then I got on the boat and I saw the moon and thought, 'Same moon.' A Universalist member met me in San Francisco, where I was warmly welcomed and given a tour of the city. So many ladies wore hats, gloves, and heels. Union Square was beautiful with flower stands on every corner. Then I took the train to Chicago, where I was met by another Universalist member. In Chicago I heard dogs bark and thought, 'Same dogs.' Since I was a female and a pianist, I was beautifully cared for."

"Aiko, you are a famous teacher of music on both sides of the globe. I suspect the quality of your teachers had something to do with that. Tell us about your teachers?"

"I've been very lucky. Especially to get one of the finest teachers, Cécile Genhart, who was so interested in me, musically as well as personally. She was like my second mother. Coming to study with her and being taken into her care at Eastman was a life altering event. I was surprised by her. She was so graceful, beautiful, such a wonderful pianist, and so caring. She said we had a similar *upbringing." (Cecile Genhart, noted Swiss pianist and distinguished pedagogue, who taught at the Eastman School of Music continuously from 1926 to 1971.)*

"Who else did you study with?"

"Mrs. Genhart was wonderful and gave me all the fundamentals, how to listen, how to pedal, all about touch and phrasing. After six years with her it was time for me to return to Japan. However, Mrs. Genhart suggested that I study with Mr. Frank Mannheimer during that summer after graduation at his home in Duluth, Minnesota. She thought he was the best teacher. It was an extraordinary experience for me. He excelled in applying vivid imagination to music." *(Frank Mannheimer (1896-1972) was a noted concert pianist who rose to an esteemed status in London as one of the few Americans to teach at the famed Tobias Matthay Pianoforte School, where he trained many American and British pianists, and became close friends with Matthay, a famous pianist, and author of the encyclopedic, The Act of Touch (1903), and his associate, the iconic British pianist, Dame Myra Hess).*

"How did the summer go with Mr. Mannheimer?"

"After a wonderful summer with him, Mr. Mannheimer arranged a few recitals for me on my way back from Eastman School in Rochester, New York via San Francisco to Japan. About ten days before the opening recital for a big music convention, I hurt the tendon in my right fourth finger. I was told by a doctor to either cancel the recitals or get a cortisone shot before playing. After consulting with Mr. Mannheimer, I decided not to practice with my right hand, but to perform. Mr. Mannheimer gave me the healing book of the Christian Science Church, saying, 'This may help you,' even though he was not a Christian Scientist. I read it very seriously for two days and prayed throughout. As always, I rested on the afternoon of the recital. I dozed off for a short time, which was unusual for me. When I woke up, my hand felt warm and comfortable. I started to move very slowly and realized that the finger was completely cured. I played that night almost in a trance! I have had some other spiritual experiences since then."

"That's a great story, Aiko. Sounds almost magical."

"I was in awe of Mr. Mannheimer for his extraordinary extra sensory perception. After meeting a person for the first time, he could sense his personality and background. He would know who was calling before picking up the phone. It took me quite a while to feel comfortable to be with him. After coming back to this country from Japan, he took me under his wing. He would arrange concert tours every spring and send gifted students to me from all over the United States."

"What has been the single most inspiring experience, musical or otherwise, you've had in your life?"

"At my first lesson with Mr. Mannheimer I played the Prelude, Chorale and Fugue by Franck (*César Franck, renowned nineteenth-century Belgian-French*

Noted pianist and teacher, Frank Mannheimer (standing), muse of Aiko Onishi, discusses musical points with noted church musician and composer, Leo Sowerby.

Credit: Photo of Leo Sowerby and Frank Mannheimer courtesy of The Leo Sowerby Foundation, Kilgore, Texas.

composer, pianist, organist, and teacher). For the opening of the prelude he would suggest, 'Think of being in a mist not knowing where you are. For the beginning of the chorale, imagine a monk burdened with guilt and sadness walking slowly towards the altar.' With these imaginative suggestions, I knew exactly what kind of mood, tone quality, and expression to imply. He was also very sensitive to coloring, especially in French music. His imagination was extraordinary. It was a great privilege to study with him."

"How long did you stay in Japan?"

"I remained in Japan from 1956 to 1964. Besides concertizing there both with orchestras and in recital, I started to teach at the Toho Gakuen School of Music in Tokyo in 1959. I took a leave of absence and returned to America in June 1964 to Mr. Mannheimer in Duluth. I studied with him again all that summer. It was great! He asked me, 'What are you going to do now?' I said probably go back to Eastman with Mrs. Genhart during the winter. And he said, 'No, I have a better idea. I'm going to London in October and there I can introduce you to Dame Myra Hess. So why don't you plan to come?' So I went to London. He always went to London in October and came back to Santa Rosa, California, every spring, where he had a beautiful house surrounded with wildflowers. He also spent summers in Duluth."

"Dame Myra Hess was a great pianist. I have listened to her recordings. How did your lessons with Dame Myra go, Aiko?"

"Very well, but by that time, she had had a slight stroke and arthritis, and couldn't play anymore. She had only one student a day. I went to her house at 11 AM. I would play a piece. And she would suggest many changes. Then she would ask me to play the whole piece through again. I was normally there from 11 to 2. Once I was there until 3 o'clock. Both of us enjoyed working together as long as required for the pieces I had prepared. It was wonderful! Then I'd go back to Mr. Mannheimer, who would ask, 'What did she say, what did she say?' And then he would prepare me for another lesson with Dame Myra. It was a most memorable winter in London." (*Dame Myra Hess (1890-1965), already a famous pianist, won a special place in British history when she organized and played in some of a series of over two thousand lunchtime concerts over six years to raise morale during and after the London Blitz of WWII, held at the National Gallery in Trafalgar Square in central London. The effort won for her the Dame Commander of the Order of the British Empire (DBE), conferred on her in 1941 by King George VI.*)

"Aiko, allow me to ask you some questions about your philosophy of music, so to speak. What is the main thing about music that speaks to you personally?"

"When I listen to music I can be transported. to another world. It is a spiritual communication. When I study a piece, first I look for the hidden message of the composer. Then I try to find beautiful coloring and nuance. It is almost like a treasure hunt. There is no end to polishing. When my students and I work together, finding more beautiful details, it is very exciting! We are just the means to give the message to the listener in the audience. Play as beautifully as one can, seeking and always tuning into the hidden inspirations and images of the composers. Many performers use the scores only to show themselves."

"What is music?"

"What is music? It's everything to me. I don't know. It's like being asked who God is (laughs). It's so vast. It is imagination, emotion, communication. Music has been such a big part of my life. I don't know how to define it. Music-making and listening to music take me completely to another world, perhaps unreal to some people. I listen so intensely to every note being played. I don't drive listening to piano music, especially if played beautifully. It can get too dangerous!"

"Do you still perform?"

"Nowadays I don't perform. So I play for my own pleasure. It's wonderful to find more beautiful things. You keep finding little precious details you weren't aware of. It's like magic."

"Can music do things that other art forms like painting and literature cannot do?"

"I think music is more emotionally involving than painting, literature, and the other arts. It can express a deeper emotion. I think it's more direct than novels, poems, or painting. It's immediate communication."

"Do all people appreciate music?"

"Some people cannot fully appreciate music. It must be a gift that you are born with. I think you might appreciate it better if you have more knowledge or some training. My father came from an artistic family. His hobby was painting. He was a wonderful painter. My mother was a musician, of course. At the beginning my father didn't understand music as much. By listening he gradually learned to appreciate music. He came to know right away if the performance was good or bad. He couldn't tell you why. But he knew exactly how good the player was. So I think it is a sensitivity that you are born with or not. It can be cultivated."

"Could humans live without music?"

"It would be a boring world (both laughing). I think music goes way back to the very beginning, even before David, who played a harp. So I'm sure music was there. Native tribes have festivities with dancing, probably accompanied by music. It's expression. Perhaps some tribes had never heard what we call music. However, they could be more aware of the sounds of nature, such as bird songs, forest murmurs, and the ripples of brooks. I believe that music has always been there, perhaps singing to start with."

"Aiko, there are some more earthbound questions I'd like to ask you. For example, should musicians govern the world because of their traditions of collaboration, cooperation, and community, whether in chamber music or orchestral music?"

"I don't think so. Music is a full-time job. More than a full-time job. To be a musician is a 100% job. And you shouldn't do both."

"What personal qualities do you wish you had in greater measure?"

"I'm still shy in some ways, but not in music-making or teaching. I think shyness comes from the very protected upbringing of my childhood. Sometimes I don't fit into a rather aggressive American culture. I could have been a little louder."

"I think that in your book *Pianism* you talk about the different ways to produce many different kinds of sounds. Maybe you could speak briefly about that."

"Piano tone is produced by string vibration caused by the hammers. If you would imagine harp strings, for the gentle tone, one would pluck lightly and slowly. For a louder tone, one would pluck more deeply for a bigger vibration of the strings. For a brighter tone plucking needs to be quicker. We should treat the key descent on the piano the same way. We should touch the key for the best control and play the key applying the same speed as you would in plucking the harp strings. Just know that the sound is made when the key descends two thirds of the way down. This is called the tone spot or key spot. By the time the key reaches the bottom, it is after the sound is made. The finger should be completely released, so that the spring would bounce the finger back to the tone spot. Even many professionals make this mistake of going all the way to the bottom of the keys and sticking there so that the sound is not as full or ringing. It becomes harsh."

"Does the playing of your countrywoman, Mitsuko Uchida, meet your standard for tone production as expressed in your book?"

"Yes, I think so. Mitsuko Uchida is a uniquely beautiful artist." (*Dame Mitsuko Uchida, world-famous Japanese pianist and conductor, acclaimed for her interpretations of Mozart, Beethoven, Schubert, Chopin, Debussy, and Schoenberg*).

"Aiko, you are here in the east to teach a master class. What do you try to teach in master classes?"

"I try to teach how to read the music score very carefully. To listen to each note one plays. Most students are not very careful to choose the right sound. They must use their imagination."

"What would you say the differences are in the way European and American piano players play as opposed to players from Japan and the Far East?"

"In Japan, or in China and Korea, the pianists work very hard at a young age because their mothers make sure that they practice. Even the little ones practice three hours a day. So they develop wonderful fingers. But it's like a computer. They can play all the notes correctly, but music-making is not taught. These days it's all just technique. And that's why when I go to Japan I'm talking about what it is to make music using imagination, mood, and color."

"Aiko, when I was a kid in Brookline music was taught in grammar school. Now they don't do that. Do you think they should do that?"

"They should, because they grow up without knowing a thing about classical music. That's really a shame."

"What is it that all these younger people like about pop music? What is that draws tens of thousands in audiences screaming and yelling. Is it the music or is it the togetherness?"

"I think it's the togetherness and the rhythm which creates excitement. Sadly, as I said, the younger generation is not educated in classical music. Even listening on the Internet is far from attending concerts. However, there are some very gifted performers and conductors. I do hope that classical music will continue to exist!"

"Aiko, have you ever stopped having students and teaching?"

"No. My former students often fly in for the weekend for two days, three days, sometimes longer, and stay with me. We work together. We have great time. I'm very grateful that I still have a lot to give."

"Why is it you have and still prefer teaching to concertizing?"

"Teaching is much more gratifying for me. It's wonderful to help students develop not only musically but as individuals. Since we share so much, we become lifelong friends. Many of my friends have told me that they know of nobody who has so many children!"

Indeed, Aiko Onishi, who grew to womanhood amidst the bombs and fires of war, sets a moving example of peace and beauty for her students and anyone who comes into her orbit, and, by extension, for all of us through the magic of music and the example of her quintessentially loving life.

American soprano, Renée Fleming, who can aptly be described as the world soprano of our time, and whose daring and talent have taken her into realms of popular music beyond the operatic stage. Photo by Andrew Eccles.

Part Four

BEYOND GENRE

American pianist Ran Blake.

Credit: Photo by Brianmcmillen - Own work, CC BY-SA 3.0, https://commons.wikimedia.org/w/index.php?curid=18266596

CHAPTER
18

Ran Blake:
Pianist, Teacher, Composer, Sage

There is nobody in the world like Ran Blake. Nobody. The world knows him as a pianist with a dark and dreamy style that only he can play, as a teacher whose students idolize and love him, as a composer whose music defies notation but lives in the soul. Ran is a one-of-a-kind individual whose persona can't be explained and becomes reality only when you are in his company, hearing his seemingly scattered pattern of speech and never repetitive music, long enough for them to ultimately coalesce enough for you to get a glimpse into his remarkable psyche and what goes on in the mind of a true genius. Ran is an elusive person to interview for a story. That is not for the usual reason of being non-responsive. Just the opposite. Ran is super responsive, but often hard to follow because the processes of his mind are so quick and so eccentric that he often digresses to another thought or topic before he returns to the answer to the question, if he ever does. I've interviewed lots of people, many of them very bright, some eccentric, but none of them are remotely like Ran Blake. So the writer is faced with a conundrum. How do I convey this man to the reader of a book? Often, faced with the usual repetitions and wanderings of an ordinary conversation, the writer will tinker with the words to render a readable and reasonable level of literary quality without destroying the sense or tone of what the person said. Too much of that in Ran's case would rob the reader of the feel of Ran's presence and could impinge on the thrust of Ran's words. A somewhat delicate task, to be sure. So, dear readers, what will follow is what I hope is the real Ran, not just his *sui generis* personality, but also the wit and wisdom of his thinking.

"We are here with Ran Blake today. I'm sitting in Ran's apartment in Brookline, which is a famous place because many people have talked about its grand piano crowded in a room whose floor to ceiling shelves are crowded with his lifetime collection of a multiplicity of musical and film noir items. How are you today, Ran?"

"I'm a little bit sleepy but doing not too badly, thank you (wry smile in his voice). And I'm going to do much better when I have that Lois applesauce."

"(Chuckling) Ran is talking about my wife, Lois, who is a great cook and a great person and makes great applesauce. And she sent some over to Ran today because she loves him. Ran, what are your earliest memories of listening to or playing music as a child?"

"I know I can remember when I was three and four, living on Union Street in Suffield, Connecticut at what was called the Fulton house, and thinking that Bing Crosby was a very safe singer. And I wanted it more seasoned but I couldn't express the word. I didn't know what hot pepper meant. That was a two-family house. I know supposedly a year later my family moved a block or two further down the hill. We, at one time, had three uprights. But I do remember thinking about nighttime and (pause), secretly putting the radio on when my parents…. But that probably is back at the other house. But I know that I was told that I would get up at all hours and go down and play the piano."

"Was there ever a time after that, that you doubted you could have a successful career as a professional musician?"

"Oh, that was probably all the time. And did I really decide? I mean, we're jumping now to adolescence. My father wanted me to get into the paper envelope manufacturing company. He felt that would be very secure."

"But how about your inner feelings? Did you feel you could make it? Did you always know you had it within you?"

"(Quickly and quietly) No. (short pause) And am I making it as a performer? It's the New England Conservatory. It's their salary, a tenured salary — not tenure, we don't have tenure. It's their salary that keeps me alive. I only get to perform three or four times a year. I can't make a living that way. It's not quite jazz, it's not quite pop, it's not quite classical. It probes different philosophical issues. I also just go back to Gershwin and Ellington. I have these film noir plots but that's not… (sort of quietly drifts)… I've got some reputation, but I don't fill symphony halls."

"I think that you're a self-effacing and modest man, especially for somebody as famous as you are. So beyond the question of livelihood, do you have confidence in your talent and genius, if you will, for making music whether by composition or playing?"

"I don't know if I've ever been asked that question. I'm not sure I can address this. I see you're going to make me work today. I think in many ways I don't have confidence. I mean, I've gotten some nice awards. I just am flabbergasted by the question. But I really don't know if I have confidence or not. I don't know (sounding somewhat surprised). I think maybe I don't."

"Well, here's an anomaly, Ran. I'm way less smart than you, and I have way less to offer the world than you. But I have much more confidence than you. You're saying you don't have confidence. How do we explain that?"

"Well I wouldn't put up a fight. Maybe I do have some confidence. It's just never occurred to me in all my eighty years. I don't think I've been asked that question. So you better send me a copy of that. But I know you'll want to keep part of this as a surprise. But I mean the jury's out. I just don't know what to say! I mean, I have confidence as a person. I love my stepbrother, some great friends of Dorothy Wallace, Jeanne Lee, Gunther Schuller. So whether I do or whether I don't, I'm not sure I have too much to say about it. (Chuckling and coughing lightly) Maybe I'm very assured once a year on Halloween Eve or something. (Chuckles) Good one!"

"I suspect it may be your modesty that keeps you from saying, 'Yeah, I know I'm terrific.'"

"I guess it could be."

"Do you ever say to yourself after a performance, 'Boy I really knocked 'em out. Nobody can play like that'?"

"I've never said that second sentence. But I remember in 1979 knocking people out in Paris. I went back with confidence a year later and let's say there were a few walk outs. Someone said, 'Where did the jazz go?' (pause) And then I know I wowed people once in LA. But no, I don't. I usually think after a concert, 'Where will my next dream be? Who was that that said hello to me?' And 'I know I've seen that young lady before. Where was she? She wasn't Nancy Drew, she wasn't Ethel Barrymore, she wasn't Abbey Lincoln, she wasn't Michelle Obama. Where did I see her before?' So I might be doing Sherlock Holmes in my dream, wondering who spoke to me. But quite often, I'm not really aware. More and more, when I'm playing the piano, I'm just seeing these scenes, whether it's Sister Bernadette, Jeanne d'Arc, Mother Teresa, a vamp, an Edward G. Robinson villain. And I just am dreaming out loud with the lights off. I start a piece, but then the plot will change. Now there may be an Old Man River... always a feeling of Ray Charles in blues... But will there be a hurricane in the Mississippi? Will there be rain? Will it be calm? Will Mark Twain be on the boat below me on a little raft? I don't control the plot. I'm there, on a Regattabar stage, if you call it a stage, maybe not. I know that I'm going to play a particular piece. I may have worked out a little introduction. I know the melody and the piece takes off. I will do it, but I'm uncomfortable doing it with a rhythm section. You have metered things; you must stay in focus. I mean with Jeanne Lee or Christine Correa there is a little more flexibility. When I'm solo, I tend to go in and out. In noon-time when I teach a class, the lights are on, it's bright out, I'm talking, but I don't suddenly start dreaming. It's not the same as playing in the dark. Often, I might even be closing my eyes when I talk to you. Of course, once a year I might fall asleep. But basically, I don't like light. But It's very nice to have light when you are reading a book."

"Maybe you're meant to be alone playing, rather than collaborating. It sounds like what you're talking about is improvisation. You really don't know what's going to happen."

"Playing alone is what I really like. I do often return to a melody, but I don't want to follow the chords or the rhythms. I want to follow my own dynamics and my plot."

"Can you remember what you played afterwards? Could you notate it if you wanted to?"

"Oh, no. I did the required course at Bard College, getting a rather mediocre grade. But, it's not just the lack of ability. There are so many changes. People can follow some kind of a melody. I'm not just going off to the deep blue end all the time, but again, I keep seeing these things, I would have no memory afterwards. I don't have memory of the audience. I know there are intrusive bright lights, but I don't remember much. I'm in some kind of a dream."

"You like dark, I have a feeling you like quiet too. Your own world?"

"Oh, very much! Do you hear background music on now? Aaron Hartley, a very good trombonist manager of mine, has put together a cocktail with Stevie Wonder, Chris Connor, Gunther Schuller, and the New York Philharmonic. Gunther with the ragtime, Ornette Coleman, and then something rather relaxing and easing. And I hear this all through the night, I can adjust the volume. It comes in above my pillow. Some nights I keep it off. And I can hum come the morning and sing it back. Not always. I can't always find the note on the piano. And sometimes, if it is sophisticated, I have to hear it again and again. In my teaching I just love the subconscious, but it's really a lot harder to do that in the classroom. You're right, I am well known, but Hankus Netsky will tell you I'm not always the favorite teacher."

"I know that Gunther Schuller was so much of a mentor to you. Who else were your prime mentors?"

"That answer would be very easy. Dorothy Wallace of Brookline was a great patron of the arts and a mentor in my life. There were teachers like Mal Waldron, Bill Evans, Janet Wallace, no relation to Dorothy, Ray Cassarino. But really, Claude Chabrol, Alfred Hitchcock, Chris Connor, Thelonious Monk, Abbey Lincoln, Billie Holiday, Mingus, Messiaen, Charles Ives, Shostakovich. If you asked me this tomorrow, I would add one, I might subtract one. And I left out George Russell, who is very important. And you know, I would add a filmmaker like Carlos Saura of Spain, or the late Claude Chabrol of France. There are probably writers — think of Wilkie Collins, Willa Cather, Toni Morrison. These really serve as my mentors. Thelonious Monk was so important and is still. He is our most treasured pianist in the world. What a storybook he has. Nobody like him."

"Let's take Gunther Schuller. What would you say is the single most important thing you learned from him in terms of your musicianship?"

"Learning how to listen to myself. Learning when to shut up and not to tell your story too long. How to format it. How to invert it. How to really examine it with a microscope. But not so thoroughly that you lose the feeling of the moment. To have respect for music all over the world. To know there is a great deal of mediocrity. But how fabulous to explore a Stravinsky, to dig into Schoenberg, the Charles Ives Fourth Symphony, second movement, Honegger's Fifth Symphony, brilliantly played by the BSO with Roger Voisin on horn, Monk's 'I Should Care' and 'Brilliant Corners,' 'Criss Cross' by Charles Mingus, 'The Portrait' and 'Driva Man' by Max Roach. My love for the singers! And the joy of Al Green, Stevie Wonder, as well as the very tragic Billie Holiday. I think that great appreciation comes from learning to listen."

"I listened to *Dreamscape* by Schuller the other night. As he described, it came to him in a dream, and when he woke up, he ran over and wrote the notes down because he wouldn't have remembered them by the next morning. I understand he called you that morning?"

"Yes, Gunther called me in the morning. It was amazing. I've never forgotten the telephone conversation. He was a sophisticated man in his eighties. He was kidding me, saying, 'Ran, what have you dreamed about? Your world is getting into mine. I had the most wonderful dreams, and I don't know whether it was a series of nights or all one night? I think it came in different compartments.' I wish I had taped that phone call. He said it all came clear. He was able to hold quite a bit of it, but he didn't trust himself, so he kept his manuscript paper right by that big bed of his, with his treadmill close by. He had his homemade supper at seven. Never call him then. And at eleven he'd settle down for the evening to dream. He was *so* excited! I can never forget his voice, his enthusiasm."

"Let's talk about Eden MacAdam-Somer, and the Contemporary Improvisation Department at the New England Conservatory of Music, I know Gunther Schuller brought you to NEC many years ago, that for years you headed that department, and still teach there. Now Eden co-chairs that department with Hankus Netsky. I know that you are close to her and to Hankus, and that she was the first doctoral student in the CI Department. Tell us about that."

"Hankus calls her one of the greats. And she does a great deal of her own music, Jewish vernacular. She also does old American pop folk music from English folk music. She does sort of a modern jazz with Aaron Hartley, her fiancée, on trombone. Eden is so versatile. But there's always Eden, not a nameless robot. Some people that do thirty types of music don't have her character. Her flexibility does not destroy her soul as it does with some people. She's on the airplane to Afghanistan as an educator. Eden will be the star of tomorrow. As an administrator, she is now really running the department with Hankus. Only time will tell whether she gets famous, but when you hear her play there is just something she has. She has a world vision. Her defense of Judaic music while also acknowledging the other religions in the Middle East shows her accepting nature. I think Hankus Netsky is fabulous too. His understanding of string ornament, his loyalty through the years to other administrators, and his endeavor that George Russell get more acknowledgement shows how terrific Hankus is. So there are great great people at NEC. Eden says she can't do it without Hankus, and he said he can't do it without Eden."

Ran Blake and Gunther Schuller, Ran's muse, at Gunther's seventy-fifth birthday concert at Sanders Theatre, Cambridge, Massachusetts. Photo © Kathy Chapman 2022.

"Absolutely. I like talking to each of them."

"Eden's students love her. Plenty do me (laughing), but they absolutely adore her. If she walks in the corridor five times a day or in the same room the students would ignore her and go on with their poker game, but you just see the radiation as she walks in. Her charm is really quite something. It's quite magical."

"Ran, let's just take the CI Department. You're producing composers that write differently because they are from different places?"

"Yes. Let me give you an example. Ilona Tipp. She was my teaching assistant in the fall. She is in the graduate program with Dominique Eade and the assignment was, 'What music do you like but don't know? And will you blend this with the music that is in your system? I'm going to assign to you a student who knows the music you like but you don't feel, who is also interested in the music you like but he doesn't feel it either, he feels shallow at it.' So Ilona and a young man, Christopher his name was, worked on an Irish Ray Charles collection to see if they could achieve that blend. My dream is that to make great third stream music, music that blends, you really have to know both parts. My way is to hear Bartók, Ives, some Stravinsky, some Schuller creeping in, and gospel, the blues, pre Bach, pre bebop."

"Is the teaching style employed in the CI Department of the primacy of the ear and making people listen and remember before they get into composing and finding themselves, a novel way of teaching?"

"We think so. There are really good things at Juilliard but I don't think it is quite so comprehensive as what we are doing with the ear. I can't tell you how many bad days I might have where I'm not clear, and sometimes the students haven't worked. But I think it is very new at times. But, of course, we are going to be chauvinist and say we are doing things that nobody else is. I don't know everything that is happening. I know in Afro-American studies wonderful things are happening at Berklee and elsewhere."

"We know that pop music, whether we are talking rock, rap, country, or many other forms, draws huge crowds and has a tremendous following, especially among young people. What appeal does it have that draws the younger people and such huge audiences to it?"

"Some of it can be very good! The answer is still pretty much two things. Melody and the beat. Harmony doesn't matter. In certain kinds of rock or electronic music, if it has that beat, that's even more important than melody. The feeling of dance. That is what is loved. People right now might like to dance profanely from *The Rite of Spring* by Stravinsky. People do get to like that piece, it has grown. But they really want an even beat. Our jazz and African friends might want it layered with different beats. Roy Rogers on a banjo and a little bit of riffing, if it's got that beat, it probably swings. Maybe not in the sense of Tristano or Miles Davis. That is what they want. And much classical music does not have a continuous beat. Minimalism does, Philip Glass, Steve Reich, but mostly not. Now a Mozart minuet may be in ¾ time. That would be way more preferred than a dark sonata by a rather serial-induced twelve-tone piece without any rhythmical punch, although it could have rhythmical punch to some of us. I think it's those two things, the rhythm, the beat, the danceability."

"Does that beat exist in all of pop music?"

"I would say it does in ninety percent of it. Also there are people who love singer songwriters where the beat is much more laid back, like Joni Mitchell. Like all the people who sing at Passim's. Then there are the lyrics. So singers are loved. So we could say the beat is singable, hummable melody. Even a hit one, like Gershwin, often goes back to the melodies. You can change a key. Ella Fitzgerald can play with the beat if the band right behind is straight. But what people don't like are the old standards of Ellington, or Gershwin songs like *S'Wonderful.* People would rather hear about Abraham Lincoln cut a tree down, there was a white dog called Puppy who loved Lois, and maybe 'Mr. Tambourine Man' by Bob Dylan. That's got a beat, a simple melody, but a far out group of lyrics. So lyrics are very important. There are people that crowd Passim's to hear somebody tell a story."

"OK, the beat. But why does it mean so much to them? I mean is it only musical or is it something to do with their lives or personalities or identification. They go crazy over things that are almost intolerably noisy and not particularly valid?"

"There is one answer I can give you that is not deep. I have said this before. They don't have many ears for it. Take a very quiet Debussy piece, which could have an inner rhythm but doesn't blare out. Some students can't hear in their ears. They want it louder and louder. I damaged my ear going to that block behind Fenway Park where all those dance clubs are. I tried to keep up, but I came home with a splitting headache. And I'm sure, when you speak very quietly, I don't hear things. People want a thing called noise music now. Noise music! John Cage started it, but this has gotten bigger and bigger. No real pitches or chords. Lots of screaming. And, of course, if you put it together with cleverness, good electronics, it can be well done. Many people like so-called house music. It has no words; it has nothing to do with the Passim's type of modern-day folk. It's just continuous. Some of it can be clever. You might even change the key. But is there a key in the first place? And people get rather high, enjoy it, get in their own world. And that throbbing (clapping insistently) is very, very important."

"So Ran, what is the big appeal of classical music?"

"Classical is very fashionable, or at least it was fifty years ago. We'd go to the Boston Symphony on Friday afternoon. I think people go because they genuinely love it, not to be seen. *The Rite of Spring* is now entering in the repertoire, but basically the appeal of classical music is the seventeenth to nineteenth-century music. They somehow feel the counterpoint of Bach. That quite often has an implicit beat. It doesn't hit you like some rap. Everybody knows some of the themes of Beethoven's Fifth Symphony. It's familiar. There are certainly dynamics. There can be a grandiose moment. There are subtleties but you're comfortable in your own bed. I think that you really would not get a half-full Symphony Hall for an evening of Arnold Schoenberg. People can't relate to it. Young people can relate to Philip Glass because of the beat."

"Is the beat rhythm?"

"Yes it is... There is another kind of rhythm, a melodic rhythm like Charlie Parker, who's great at invention. With 32nd-note runs, then duple to triple time, and then silence. But underneath that is a beat, whether it's Philly Joe Jones, Max Roach, or Kenny Clark. That beat in early jazz was loved. Benny Goodman could put it in. Now that would be old-fashioned for our listeners. They want it really out there with a very virtuoso drummer screaming. I used to think that young people would never like twentieth-century music. That was wrong. When minimalism came in, they liked Glass more than Mozart. It certainly is not chromatically dissonant. It doesn't have the strange tones that Cecil Taylor, a great jazz virtuoso, used."

"Are Mozart and Beethoven and Bach slipping away from us?"

"Will there be a Glass a hundred years from now who will kick the crap out of the young people? Bach and Beethoven will be famous, but will they be as famous? I don't know. Will there be concert halls?"

"Yeah, will the Boston Symphony fade away from us?"

"I think seasons will get shorter. I think there will be less classical. I think there will always be a Boston Symphony. I hope it doesn't fade away, but I wonder. You will probably be able to go to concerts, but CDs are fading away already. In fact, will there even be CDs to buy in the next ten years or so? We can download and get something so quickly now on the internet. How many people are really hearing Louis Armstrong now? His solo on 'Muggles,' 'West End Blues,' everybody knows who he is. I think he's going to fade away before Bach and Beethoven. Their music is written and there will always be people playing it. I'm really so sorry about the early jazz. Monk will remain a legend. There will be a new Dylan, but he will be remembered. Elvis' name will be known to people."

"But will people listen to their music?"

"Yeah, and it's certainly nice music, but does it compare with Howlin' Wolf, Muddy Waters, John Lee Hooker, Robert Pete Williams, Robert Johnson, Bessie Smith, Ma Rainey? It's too tame."

"Do human beings get more emotional kick from classical music or from pop music?"

"They do from pop. It's rhythmical. But it depends. A priest might get a lot from Messiaen. So we could say that's deeper. Right at that moment there is quite a frenzy as people are hypnotized by pop! There may be people who will ruminate some after a Bach concert. I don't know. The verdict is out. I would say Beethoven will be loved. Will Benny Goodman be remembered? The name will be, and even the deeper jazz of Thelonious Monk. It will be the music of the era. The written music is one good thing about classical. I might sneer at that, but that will preserve it. So pop will be the music of the moment, with the exception of some opera and classical music. And that only gets 8% of the audience."

"Ran, a singer might not have a terrific voice, but people will love her. Billie Holiday didn't have a great voice. What is it that made people love her?"

"The passion. There are rhythmical things. She may not have a great voice because of its diminished range. It is her enunciation and the color of her voice. I'm told that I have quite a piano technique, yet there are things I can't do. I don't have speed, and quite often that relates to technique. But people find a touch that they like. Sarah Vaughan had all the technique in the world, but her sound had the color that only she had. It's a personal thing. I think Monk had a great technique, but he didn't do a couple of things that Oscar Peterson, Horowitz or Rubinstein did. We are in the middle of two conversations about what is my taste and what is the taste of the world?"

"You say that you're not popular sometimes with your students because you don't have that beat in your music. On the other hand, your music is entrancing. Why do people like it so much?"

"Well some students do like it, but some just don't like the teaching of *The Primacy of the Ear,* the title of the book I wrote. When you came in just now, there was music playing. I'm trying to memorize it fully, to really get it in. It's stuff I haven't heard until a week ago. That takes a week or two. I'm supposed to have good ears. Maybe at eighty they slow down a bit. So you really learn something and only then do you embellish it. Today's young people don't want to do that... I think I've changed the subject. I think the reason my music may not last is that I don't have a body of real compositions that are notated."

"Is there anyone else who plays like you? You get lost in your music. You don't notate what you played, so you can't reproduce it."

"I don't know of any but why would I be the one to know? When I was fifty, I was out hearing music a lot. I didn't hear anybody like me. But how do I know there is not someone now?"

"How can you be a great pianist if you don't have a personality to match?"

"There are still good student pianists who don't have personality. Maybe they're like a drone. On the other hand, you're right because the personality is so important. Gunther said you're playing for somebody, you are also playing for yourself, and for some kind of a God if there is one, but don't be redundant and scattered. We've got to build into you that you don't have to do an ABA form of Beethoven, but we have to build in. You still want to be musical. He knew that I could go to many keys, use different positions, change chords immediately, and that it wasn't important if I remembered it. I just can't seem to do straight jazz or straight classical. I think maybe, Larry, what makes me better than many is that I will try to play freely. Tomorrow when I am alone, I will do my own type of stuff, but then I'm going to practice, even if it is the easy Mozart thing.

American jazz pianist Thelonious Monk

Credit: Portrait of Thelonious Monk, Minton's Playhouse, New York, N.Y., ca. September 1947. Photograph by William P. Gottlieb, Library of Congress.

I'm going to go and play blues and say, 'No, Ran Blake. Now for a minute use triplets, then go on and do the basic straight blues. At the end I can do what I want, but can I, for a minute or two, do pre-bebop?' Being able to do it helps my free playing. By wanting to go back, observe, and grow, whether it is a Muslim piece or Icelandic piece, or a tango, occasionally be authentic to the style even if you fall flat on your face. Do it again, pick yourself up, then stop and go back to your dream world. Doing that once in a while does bring me a bigger canvas of colors. I don't want to just sink in. Anyway, that's quite a ramble round the forest I went."

"Can humans function without music?"

"Well, we know a few can, maybe a thousand in the world (laughs). I can for a day once in a while, when I've been in the elevator a lot, and around things that make my ears tired. I think that if you live alone in the woods... to have music you have to have recordings. But yes, can I function an hour without music? A little, but, no I couldn't. I can't imagine life without music."

"Do you think music has a humanizing force?"

"I wish I could say so, but we do know that there was bad military music in Hitler's army. But Shostakovich humanized the brutality of Stalin. He was great. I love Shostakovich."

"What is it that speaks to you in music that you can't get from any other artistic form?"

"I guess film is my only other art, like you like baseball as an art. Rapture, I do get it from music and film. *Taxi Driver* is a very good study of melodramatic disintegration, but without Bernard Herrmann's music, I wouldn't see it again. There are probably a few film noir films I would see again. It only becomes sublime if there is great music, whereas music can work without film."

"So if you saw these films and they didn't have music would the films entrance you?"

"Probably Fritz Lang's *Dr. Mabuse the Gambler* would. Of course, I have the original score, which is great, and now the new DVD has the raw score. Yes, I could see that. I could see *The Cabinet of Dr. Caligari.* It would be intellectual, it would entrance me somewhat, but it wouldn't overwhelm me."

"Where does music come from?"

"I think it comes from our soul. Louis Armstrong could be in the field playing music alone and it comes from the soul. Billie Holiday too. I guess Monk needed a piano that was made by mankind. The harpist, Ann Hobson, played from the soul. It really comes from within. Their instruments are made by man and have evolved. They are very important, of course. Maybe they had a soul enterprise or soul manufacturing. I mean people made Strads. There is soul in that. And then there is crafts manufacturing. But I think it has to come from the soul just as does our great painting and sculpture."

"Is there music in silence?"

"John Cage says so. I think it is a very important part of music. I have been told I use too much silence."

"Is there music in the air?"

"Look at that mammal. He is breathing. I'm glad I'm not waking him up so he doesn't come over and get you an allergy. I think it is an exaggeration to say there is music just because the streetcar is going by. There is the environment, there is beauty, it's great we are not out in Times Square with all the yelling tonight."

"(Laughs) Is music mysterious?"

"I don't think the *Star-Spangled Banner* is, but it is music. I think I am. I think Gunther is. I think Thelonious is, I think there is a mystery in Billie Holiday that Ella doesn't have, but Ella is a virtuoso with a three-octave voice span. I feel Billie Holiday is deeper, but there is nobody quite like Ella. Sarah Vaughan's voice grew, and she got more humanity."

"Does music exist on the notated page? Or does music come into the ear and into the brain and into the heart while it's playing, and then does it just sort of disappear into the ether?"

"I think that the printed page is what is going to keep the music of today alive, unfortunately. There are too many recordings, and people can be entranced at a symphony. Their cells phones are off, you might be looking at a very beautiful woman two aisles away but you're not going to say to her, 'Could I see you for just an innocent drink after the concert? I'm not going to try to seduce you, but Mademoiselle, you might have tomorrow's grocery list, and you are right there in the audience.' We don't spend the evening with our recordings at home. Gunther did, maybe you do. I do, but only two nights a week during the school year because a film noir is easier at the end of the day. Having taught people, my ears are tired. But that's a very leading question. Some people can remember concerts they went to. One thing Seiji Ozawa did so well was Toru Takemitsu's music. There are great moments. People still talk about *The Rite of Spring* conducted by Gunther at the Conservatory."

"Can you hear those moments in your head?"

"Yes. I now can oralize the first 4 minutes, not hearing a hidden bassoon, but I can close my eyes and hear the first four minutes of Shostakovich, as well as I can 'Stardust.' I can only do it for three or four minutes. I better say three minutes."

"If you could tell classical musicians what they could do to draw more people into their concert halls, what would you tell them?"

"One is to serve some not-dainty large sandwiches for students. Give them a free subway ticket home. Beethoven they like, but also they like Glass. What we have to do to get people to concert halls is to support music. People in school do not have a chance to hear chromatic music. People who have gone four years to the conservatory to study Schoenberg would rather hear Beethoven or Madonna. They don't want things that go out of key. Everybody would rather hear *Clair de*

Lune by Debussy than a number this wonderful pianist is going to play tonight which leaves the key. And were there so many audiences? Weren't the Mozarts in court with delicate little food, little bits of coffee, tea, brandy? People would be sewing in the background if it was more family. Sometimes they need stories. They really made a big adventure of my birthday concert. Yet two weeks later, when I charged ten dollars a ticket, only twenty people came to Lilypad. Of course, a free meatloaf sandwich wouldn't make you or Lois go out on a snowy night. You've got food in your ice box. So how to attract bigger audiences? Theatre might have, but it has some prohibitive prices. We read the reviews in the *New Yorker*. How many sit down to read even a detective book? Video games are in. People need the visual. Even free tickets don't help. The number of concertgoers is very small. We can say we are busy. I can say now that I'm eighty that I'm a sage. If Lois plays *Madame Troubadour*, I would go. If she was going to be in a Bizet opera, one that might have been discovered taking place in Nice, and Puppy happens to be a sister visiting here from Venice, I would go to that. We don't feel like going out much now. So that's a big question."

Now that is an answer that is vintage Ran Blake. I spoke before about his wit and wisdom, as well as the challenge of following his train of thought. In that long ramble, Ran gave us an original, funny, and pointed reply to my question about how more patrons might be drawn into concert halls. Along with it, he pronounced himself on several other issues, some more serious than others, such as where modern society is headed, what might be the music of the future, why music should be taught in our schools, what he thinks about the youth of today whom he teaches, the distaste by the public for musicians who like himself employ out-of-the-box chromaticism, a taste of history in the drawing rooms of Mozart's time, how reading books has gone out of style in modern America and replaced by video games, his wry take on his own sagacity, the warm personality which characterizes him in talking about my wife Lois, and his essential modesty in confessing he can't really answer the question. All that delivered in a style impossible to duplicate, and without you readers having heard his even greater sagacity when he takes his place in near darkness at the keyboard of our dreams!

CHAPTER
19

Eden MacAdam-Somer: Musician Extraordinaire and Person Extraordinaire

---

If then-deeply-in-debt super talent agent and concert promoter to be, the late Jerry Weintraub, had not been able to come up with a cool million in less than twenty-four hours, and fly from New York to a Las Vegas casino to press it into the hot palm of Colonel Tom Parker, Elvis Presley's longtime manager, to impress on him his novel notion for Elvis' first ever national tour, would those millions of fans who loved and locked with The King on that and many another tour to follow have ever existed? If Johannes Brahms at the height of his fame had not told the world that an unknown Czech composer by the name of Antonin Dvořák was a great composer in-waiting, would we ever have been gifted with his stirring Symphony from the New World, or his heart piercingly beautiful cello concerto, and countless other moving compositions? Maybe not.

Where, then, is that manager or promoter who will recognize and become excited by the incredible multiple musical talents of Eden MacAdam-Somer, truly a musician extraordinaire, take them, fly with them, and accept the challenge of marketing them to an awaiting public in favor of the time burdened Eden, who recently delivered her first child, and at this writing is soon expecting her second? This amazing woman is composing and performing as time allows, while serving as the co-chair of the eclectic Contemporary Improvisation Department of the New England Conservatory of Music, and also, in her composer's hat, blending different genres to create a new classical music. This then is the story of an American Original who incredibly excels as a composer, instrumentalist, dancer, singer, lyricist, educator, writer, and social activist, and whose humanistic, empathetic, and inspiring personality may have distributed her talents so well in so many directions that, ironically, their effect has somewhat inhibited to now her impact on a wider audience. Eden is indeed a musician and woman extraordinaire. Her persona radiates love for her fellow humans and for her music.

American musician Eden MacAdam-Somer. Photo by Larry Ruttman.

Her many musical talents allow her to inhabit the music world completely, and combined with her personal traits connect her to people in every part of her life from the very private to the very public. Maybe that dream promoter has missed the boat. Ultimately these qualities and talents would have brought Eden wide notoriety and adulation. Maybe they still will. Maybe marriage, motherhood, and teaching will replace fame and keep her grounded in one place, while her plethora of talents make her a world-class musicians' musician!

"I'm with Eden MacAdam-Somer, who is an amazingly versatile musician. I'm not sure where to begin because you do so many things musically. I'll begin by asking you to tell me about your parents, Eden, and growing up in Houston?"

"Yes, Houston, but I was born in New York. My mom's from New York, grew up on Long Island, and I was born in Manhattan. When I was two, we moved to this tiny little town in Ohio in the middle of nowhere where my dad is from. So my mom is Jewish from New York and my dad is Lutheran from Ohio. They are both physical therapists, now divorced. We lived in Ohio for about four years, and then we moved to Houston when I was six. I lived there for twenty years. So that's mostly where I grew up."

"I understand your mother is interested in music?"

"Both of my parents love music. My mother grew up playing recorder and studying flute. She was also a ballet dancer. She never played or danced professionally. Probably the love of music comes mostly from my grandfather because he adored opera, musicals, and every kind of music. He and my grandmother were out every night in New York listening to music. I would go to visit them. They began taking me to the Metropolitan Opera when I was six years old, and to plays and all kinds of musicals."

"What was the first opera you ever heard?

"I think it was Mozart's *Così fan tutte*. I still like it, but when you're six you just appreciate the colors and the sounds."

"How about your father's musical interests?"

"My parents both loved folk music. We went to a lot of bluegrass festivals when I was little. My father really loved folk singer-songwriters, and he likes to sing and play the harmonica. His mother and her brother both played stride piano, and his uncle was also the church organist. So there's music in my family from both sides."

"Do you have siblings?"

"I do. I have three siblings, and we're all musicians. I'm the oldest, and the sister after me, Adaiha, is a professional cellist and viola da gamba player living in San Francisco. My younger sister, Batya, is a violinist in San Diego specializing in contemporary classical music. She also plays in a jug band, which she recently got into. My brother, Ilan, is a cellist as well, living in Santa Barbara. He plays bluegrass and other styles of music, but he just decided to go back to school for environmental science."

"How did you get the name Eden MacAdam-Somer?"

"When my parents married, they hyphenated their names. My dad is Tom MacAdam and my mom is Karen Somer. So they put them together. And when they split up, they divided their names again, so my siblings and I are the only four people on the face of the earth with that name (laughs) as far as I know, so that's pretty cool. As for Eden, my parents chose Hebrew names for all of us when we were born. They liked that one and thought it was unusual."

"Were you brought up Jewish?"

"Yes. My mom is Jewish, and my father converted to Judaism when I was four. He was really interested in philosophy and religion and studied Judaism. I think now he just practices general Christian spirituality."

"Do you still follow Judaism?"

"Yes, but I'm not observant. We grew up in a household where we celebrated the Jewish holidays and maintained the general traditions, but I wouldn't say we were a very spiritual family. Then when I was twelve I started studying for my bat mitzvah. I really fell in love with the music. We had a wonderful cantor at our synagogue in Houston, Cantor David Propis, and he was just a fantastic singer. I loved going to services because I got to sing and hear him sing. My favorite part was studying with him. When it was time for me to lead the service, I was really excited that I got to do that and got to read and chant the Torah."

"Do you partake in Jewish religious services to this day? You could be a cantor."

"Not really. I love the music. I sing with the Klezmer Conservatory Band with Hankus Netsky, who I work with at the New England Conservatory of Music. I sing and play a lot of Jewish music and because of that I'm also studying Jewish culture now. I'm kind of getting back into it, interested in it, and wanting to learn. When you grow up in a tradition you don't always learn the ins and outs of it, you just sort of go with it. So now I'm going back, I'm reading, and I'm saying, 'Oh, that's why this is the way it is, that's why I feel this way, because I was brought up this way, but I never knew why.'"

"What was Houston like for music?"

"Houston is an interesting place, a fantastic place to grow up as an artist. As a child I got to study with wonderful teachers in Houston, including Judy Offman, who gave me strong foundational skills through her approach to the Suzuki method, and Kevin Kelly, who introduced me to the fun in playing music. At thirteen, I began working with Fredell Lack, who was one of a few American women violinists in her generation to have an international touring career. Born in Oklahoma, she studied at the in New York with Louis Persinger from the age of 14, and debuted in Town Hall at 21. She moved to Houston when her husband, an eminent epidemiologist, was offered a professorship there, and began teaching at the University of Houston. Fredell became my prime mentor and teacher and inspired me in so many ways. Over time we became good friends.

American musician extraordinaire, Eden MacAdam-Somer, and her young son being held by noted American violinist and Eden's teacher and muse, Fredell Lack. Photo by Aaron Hartley.

She played a lot of cutting-edge music in her day, started up numerous music education programs in Houston, and was a staunch human and animal rights activist. During the Cultural Revolution in China she sponsored many young Chinese artists to come to America to study. This is something I have been thinking about a lot lately in working to help bring young Afghan musicians to study here. In New York, the equivalent would have been studying with someone like Dorothy DeLay, but I wasn't that 'serious' as a teenager, and likely never would have been able to get close to someone like Dorothy DeLay, you know. My sister studied cello in Houston with Laszlo Varga who had sat for ten years or so as the principal cellist with the New York Philharmonic Orchestra – her working with him would have been much less likely to happen in New York."

"You wrote on your site that he just died recently?"

"Yes. He was like a grandfather to us. We grew up playing chamber music at his house. He would call us up and say 'we're reading Debussy tonight, come on over.' We would go and we would play, doubling parts. It was a beautiful way to learn the music."

"How long has it been since you completed your formal education? You went to the Shepherd School of Music at Rice University in Houston, then what?"

"I graduated from Shepherd in 2004. Then I went on the road with a folk band for a bunch of years until I was feeling stuck musically. I had new directions that I wanted to go in, but I wasn't sure how to get there. I wanted to be in a place where I could focus on music of all kinds in connection with improvisation and history and current changes in the world. I was interested in ethnomusicology, but I really wanted to be playing a lot, not studying from afar. I had talked with some friends who had attended the Contemporary Improvisation Department at NEC and who loved the program there. So I called up the school and asked if they were offering a doctoral program. But the administrative director said they weren't. Apparently, just after I called, Hankus Netsky, who is the current chair of the department, walked into the office. Our administrative director said, 'Somebody just called about a CI doctorate.' And Hankus said, 'Well, we used to offer one. Call her back (laughs).' So they called me back two days later and said, 'You should come check out our program.' I was shocked – what are the odds of getting a call like that – but really excited. I went back and met Hankus, started working on my doctorate at NEC in 2009, and finished in 2013. Hankus Netsky is one of the most amazing teachers I've ever worked with in my life!"

"I know you now work together a lot, and now you co-chair the Contemporary Improvisation Department with him. Please tell us more about Hankus?"

"Hankus has a way about him – he's truly an exceptional educator. He's very honest with students. He never gives false compliments. But he's always very enthusiastic about what they want to do, and really supportive of that. Even if it's not his vision for what music should be, he really helps them get to where they want to go. He gives great criticism but he's never cruel. I really appreciate that about him because it's difficult as a teacher to strike that balance of being very honest with students but not shutting them down. He's also got incredible ears. Hankus is just fantastic!"

"Eden, the way you got to Boston was providential for sure, maybe even surreal. One might think you would have headed for New York?"

"I was actually aiming for New York when I left Houston. But I spent about a week in Manhattan and I just realized I couldn't do it (laughs). I'm just not a big city person, really. I need a lot of green space and quiet. I was touring a bit, and spent some time in Massachusetts doing a recording project. I really liked the Boston area. It felt like a city I could manage. I loved that there was so much green space."

"Nice that you could see the green. The rest of the country sees only blue (both laugh). So now that you are firmly ensconced at NEC as the co-chair with Hankus of the Contemporary Improv Department, do you think you'll make Boston your permanent home?"

"I think Boston is a great place to be. I don't know how long I'll be here but for now it's great. I love the Contemporary Improvisation Department at NEC, and the people I get to work with there. So this feels like a really good home base."

"There are great musical cities in the world, like New York, Vienna, and London, but Boston seems to be growing in that regard. Do you think of Boston as a world center of music?"

"I do think it is a world center of music. Right now there is an incredible influx of folk musicians into the city. There are houses full of young kids who are coming up here to study at Berklee or at our Contemporary Improvisation Department who are really interested in getting deep into folk traditions and wanting to work on it as part of their academic studies. So that's very exciting. There is a huge bluegrass scene in Boston, and a nice old time scene too. There's a great folk dance scene in Boston from contra dancing to different sorts of folk dance which is wonderful. I think there's also a growing community of young jazz musicians here. They are staying in town and that is exciting too. A lot of times jazz musicians finish whatever they're doing here, and then go to New York or somewhere else, but now there's definitely a core of folks who are staying here. And there's a core of young contemporary improvisors who are staying here!"

"That is wonderful. I don't think I knew the extent of it. Why are they staying?"

"They like the community. They like the fact that there's maybe a little bit more room for growth here than in New York. New York is so saturated. I think that it's sometimes hard to start new things there, whereas in Boston there might be a little bit more space for that. So I think some of the younger folks here are finding opportunities to do that here."

"Eden, tell us how your teaching style evolved?"

"I'm learning all the time. I've been teaching since I was fifteen. I was at the Aspen Music Festival and my first violin teacher, Judy Offman, had a student whose family was vacationing there. They were interested in maintaining weekly lessons for their daughter, and when summer ended I continued acting as a weekly coach for her back in Houston. It was a good intro to teaching, following the lead of a really experienced educator, and eventually I began developing a studio of my own. I love it, it's challenging! I always try to be very honest with myself and with my students. And I try to just remember that we're all trying to grow as creative artists; we're all trying to shape things. I try to be respectful of that."

"You wrote about the things that you felt a teacher should always be aware of: musical awareness, personal style, and technical facility. Might you expand on those words a little bit, Eden?"

"I have really been inspired by studying the Suzuki violin method as a little kid. Shinichi Suzuki's philosophy was that if a child is surrounded by music from the time they're born, that they will speak it as a language and it will enrich their lives. This is really true for any musical language: folk music, or old-time fiddling, or classical music, or jazz. If you grow up hearing it all the time every day, after a while it just sinks into your body. So at the conservatory level we have students coming in who might be new to jazz, for example, and they might really want to learn how to play jazz. In an academic setting, one often finds students learning jazz by studying and memorizing licks, or patterns. Having that technical facility comes in handy, of course, but if you actually look at the way that many 'great' jazz performers have learned music, their focus was on listening to their favorite artists play. Charlie Parker did that by taking a Lester Young record and learning every single solo on it over the course of a summer, and that's really how he started playing jazz. Lennie Tristano had the same philosophy with his students: learn the solos, sing the whole thing through before you even touch your instrument. I think that until you do that kind of intensive work you really can't speak the language, any musical language. But it takes time. It takes time and it takes patience and you just have to do the work, there are no shortcuts. And that's the challenge about it."

"Everybody is different. Do you find that your students are going off in their own directions under your tutelage? Do they surprise you?"

"Oh, absolutely, they're always surprising me, introducing me to new artists, taking off in new directions. They'll start working on an idea, sort of be pondering it and working on it. Then all of a sudden, a month later they'll come in and say, 'Look what I figured out!' And it's just this brilliant new direction in which they're taking their musical voice. It's really exciting."

"It seems like a happy place to be?"

"It's wonderful. It's really, really great. And it's a fantastic community. Our department really is a community. We have all these interesting students coming in from so many different backgrounds. Everybody is really listening and learning and collaborating and getting excited about what everybody else is doing. In our department we have about fifty-three students now. That's as big as we want to get. It's a good size."

"Is it your take that players with less than the best technical facilities really have trouble being able to say what they want to say in music?"

"I think it depends on what you want to say. I think the greatest artists out there figure out how to do whatever they want on their instrument. That's what I mean by technical facility. If they want to play something, they figure out how to play it. Sometimes students want to go the other route where they'll say, 'That's really tricky so I'm not going to play that, I'll take a shortcut and go around it and do something else.' I think that they're cheating themselves out of the opportunity of really speaking their mind, because if their idea originally was to go all the way up to this high note, but they're like, 'Oh, that's too hard, I'm going to just play it an octave lower,' that's not good. There's a way to do it, there's always a way to do it, but you have to really push yourself to get there. And that's where technique and really knowing your instrument comes in. I never want the technique, or the lack of it, to drive the music. The music should always drive."

"Didn't you, Ran Blake, and your husband, trombonist Aaron Hartley, go on a trip to play in Europe?"

"We did. We were in Italy and Spain last spring together for three weeks. It was really amazing! We did three concerts, including a concert in Milan which was fantastic. It was a sold-out hall of over a thousand people."

"Wow! That is something."

"We played a mix of duo, trio, and solo repertoire. Ran did some solo work, we did some music as a trio, Ran and I did some duos, and then I did some solo work as well. So it was really, really nice. And I got some wonderful reviews from the European newspapers. Somebody called me 'the Eastern European Joni Mitchell' (laughs). It was exciting to get to be there, and to see how much support there is for new music in Europe. After the concert there were throngs gathered just to meet Ran and shake his hand, have him sign their arm, or people brought every record of his they had collected and had him sign those. Just wonderful. Then we played two concerts in Santander and Huesca in Spain, both incredible experiences."

"Eden, I think your blogs are terrifically literate, meaningful, and thoughtful. I think you have a mastery of the English language. Do you think of yourself as a writer?"

"I love writing, and I've always been a prolific reader and writer. Actually, I almost went to the University of Rochester on a scholarship for creative writing when I graduated from high school. University of Rochester is affiliated with the

Eastman School of Music, but at the time there wasn't a teacher there that I wanted to study music with, so I didn't go (laughs) because music was still my priority."

"Looking at your blogs on your aptly named website, Fiddlegarden.net, it seems you are a social activist extraordinaire, as well. I see you've gone to Kabul a few times, where danger lurks everywhere, to teach peace through musical education to Afghani children at the Afghanistan National Institute of Music (ANIM)."

"One of the most wonderful parts of my life has been the experience of traveling around the world and getting to connect with people from so many different cultures. Wherever I've been, I've always seen music create community. Even today I was at home with some folks from Columbia who are helping us with repairs. It turns out they are musicians, so we spent half an hour today just talking about music. Music can be used as a means of expressing trouble that is going on in other people's lives anywhere in the world, as a means of ameliorating things to make people's lives better, or to better understand each other. For me, reaching out to others through music is an imperative."

"How long have you felt that way?"

"You know, I don't know. Maybe always. From the time I was a teenager I was interested in folk music and started connecting with people from different walks of life and different parts of the world. I can't stand to see anybody hurting, so when I see somebody who needs help, I just want to make it better. The more that I can help through my music, the better."

"In your blogs you speak not only like a social activist but a social activist leader. I can see your leadership qualities when you perform on stage. People seem to follow you. You say in one of your blogs, 'Artists, speak up!' That is exhorting people to do something. Do you see yourself as becoming a social activist and a leader going out into the streets like, for example, Joan Baez? Seems to me you're already doing that by going to Kabul. Are you ready to put your safety on the line like that again?"

"I guess I don't really think in terms of what's safe and what's not safe. I decide what feels important and what I need to do, and then I just do it."

"Would you become a social activist if that would bite into your time as a musician?"

"If it felt important enough, sure, I would go in that direction. I don't think I could ever not play music — music is so much a part of me that it will go with me wherever and whatever direction I go in."

"It's a wonder to me you can do all the stuff you do. From my looking into it I'm sure I'm missing a few. You're a composer, violinist, violist, an instrumentalist on other instruments, a teacher, an administrator, fiddler, singer, percussive dancer, conductor, editor, lyricist, and musician extraordinaire. Who came up with that last one?"

"I came up with that. I've been using that for years, since I was a teenager."

"You don't lack in self-esteem. That is good. A person should know who they are."

"(Laughs) Yes, I know myself. But I don't use the term 'extraordinaire' in a prideful way, truly...I know that I don't fit the 'norm' as an artist, and I feel lucky to be extraordinary in my way."

"Oh, yes, I added some other things you do: musical theorist, writer, social activist, player in symphony, chamber music, jazz and swing, klezmer music, American folk, and other music. What don't you do in music?"

"(Laughs) Thankfully, music is infinite. The more I know the more I want to know... the incredible thing about music is that one never comes to the end of it."

"Eden, I know you play a lot of instruments. I know about the piano, the violin, the viola, the voice, dancing, and stamping your feet when you dance. Are there any other instruments you play?"

"I play the mandolin. I dabble in a few other instruments. Whenever I go over to Afghanistan, I try to work on a little bit of gheyjak with the professor at the school who teaches the instrument. The version of the instrument I play has a pot and looks a lot like a banjo with a big wooden neck. It has two strings, actually one long metal piece which is wrapped around the bottom of the instrument and then comes up on the other side. It's tuned in a fourth. You sing and play it usually."

"Are you good on all the traditional instruments as you are, for example, on the violin?"

"No (laughs). I would say violin and voice are definitely my strongest instruments, and viola is getting up there too. Piano was my first instrument and was the one I was the most serious about until I was in high school. At that point I was being pulled in different directions. My violin teacher was saying, 'You need to practice four hours a day,' and my piano teacher was saying, 'You need to practice four hours a day.' I was really a pretty normal kid who liked to read, run around outside, and goof off (laughs). So I kind of focused on the violin at that point. But I've always loved the piano, and I still play. Now, I find that in some ways the piano is easier for me to play than it was when I was a teenager because I have worked out a lot of technical tension problems on the violin. So I can play the piano with much more fluidity now. So that's nice."

"What is your favorite instrument?"

"Oh, wow. I don't know. I love them all (laughs). Just depends on the day."

"Well, the piano has a greater range than the others."

"Piano has a great range. And I love the voice because you can take it wherever you go. Anybody and everybody has a voice. That's beautiful!"

"You know Eden, you are amazing! I've said so before. I'm surprised that you are not famous. I don't see a lot of musicians with your versatility and your ability to do them all so well. Here in Boston we will have to call you the musical Mookie Betts. Have you played classical violin with a symphony orchestra? I mean like Mozart, or the Mendelssohn violin concerto, or the Tchaikovsky concerto?"

"Oh yes, I've performed many times with orchestras. The Mendelssohn concerto was my competition piece when I was in high school, and I performed it with many different orchestras. I love that piece. And I've had some professional solo opportunities with orchestras as well."

"Is there a difference between playing the violin and fiddling?"

"Well, the words have different linguistic roots. One is Germanic and one is Latin, I believe. The differences really lay in the style of playing. Sometimes, in fiddle styles, people do different things to the instrument, they tune it differently sometimes, or they'll change the angle of the bridge, or whatever. But it's really the same instrument."

"How might you describe your performing technique?"

"It's hard to define what I do. I don't know. You could say I sing and I play and I dance, but I think what I do is creating a contemporary music that draws on all of these different influences on my life."

"How did the foot stamping come into it?"

"I started dancing when I was a teenager in Houston. I was hanging out with a folk community, and there were some musicians there that did a type of Appalachian percussive dancing called flat-footing. So I started picking that up from them a little bit, and over the years I've worked that and different kinds of body percussion more into my work as a soloist. It's another sound too, another concept to play with."

"I guess the fact that you do them all together comes into what we were discussing before about technical prowess, and what you do becoming part of your being. One might think that it's really difficult to do all those three things at one time?"

"The first time it's hard. Once you work on it and do it enough it becomes one thing. It's not three separate things, it's just one thing."

"Eden, it seems to me that not only do you have a nice voice, but great range. It sounds like you have a mezzo voice? Could you be an opera singer if you wanted?"

"If that had been my passion in life, I probably could have tried to do it."

"You could sing Cherubino in *The Marriage of Figaro?"*

"(Laughs) That would be fun. Maybe in my next lifetime that's what I'll do."

"Eden, please describe what you're doing in the composing field?"

"Just blending different genres and working with composing new classical music where I'm drawing on improvisation, folk styles, and different vocal skills. There's not a lot of people doing that kind of work."

"Who else does what you do?"

"Well, I don't know that anybody does exactly what I do. But there are a lot of really creative artists out there who are doing some very interesting things, each specific to their own interests – Iva Bittova and Carla Kihlstedt, for example, on the violin, or Fay Victor."

"Would you describe your first solo album, *My First Love Story,* as pop or classical?"

"That is difficult to say. The Vaughan Williams is classical, the Rumi songs are classical mostly, but there are some parts of the Rumi songs that definitely fit in more with folk music. There are pieces on that album that are very strongly based on Appalachian fiddling tradition. So it's been interesting with that CD to just see the way that people responded to it. People love it or are intrigued by it but don't really know what to do with it. They're like, 'Well, I would love to play this on my show, but I don't really know how to describe it.' It's really gratifying to me that *Boston Globe* critic Jon Garelick appreciates it as contemporary jazz because it is based on strongly based improvisation."

"Are you inventing a new style here?"

"Maybe (laughs). I might be. I'm part of a movement, a push that's been happening for a long time. Ran Blake was once at the forefront of that movement of artists taking the music that they love and creating a new genre and a new sound out of it. It's developing their own personal voice in a very special way."

"Is this movement attempting a fusion of different genres?"

"I wouldn't call it fusion so much. I'm not really trying to do anything. I'm just doing what I love. The way that I worked out the Rumi songs is that I read the poetry, loved it, and got really intrigued by it. Then I just started playing around with the rhythm of the words, and then I just started trying out some different ideas on the violin. But there was never a part of my mind that was like, 'OK, now I'm going to grab some Appalachian stuff, and now I'm gonna take some classical music.' It just sort of went in the direction that it went in. And I think that that's how Ran works too. He studies prolifically, just as I do. I'm very inspired by him. When he hears something he loves, he really gets into it. If Ran hears a Stevie Wonder song that he loves, he studies Stevie Wonder. He studies the whole album that that song goes with, and then he listens to every other Wonder album, and he really gets the sound into his own playing. He'll do the same thing with Gustav Mahler, and he'll do the same thing with Bach, he'll do the same thing with algebra!"

"And film noir."

"And film noir, right. And when he studies something that intensely it becomes a part of his musical vocabulary. As it does for me. So when I sit down to improvise, those new ideas and sounds start working their way out into my playing."

"So, how important in your musical life do you consider your own composition to be?"

"I think the work that I'm doing is essential to me, because it's one of the ways in which I'm shaping my own musical voice. But I wouldn't be me without drawing on all of the influences that have touched my life."

"How long have you been composing?"

"I wrote my first composition when I was about five."

"Have you published many of your compositions?"

"I self-publish my music. I have a work for mandolin orchestra that has been making the rounds internationally. So that's exciting! But I haven't published through a company."

"Have you written any other orchestral pieces?"

"Not for a traditional string orchestra or symphonic orchestra. I've composed and arranged many pieces for a chamber ensemble that I teach at NEC. The instrumentation for that varies every semester, so that has resulted in many different types of works. I've also written for solo instrument, mostly for myself. Also pieces for violin and viola."

"Eden, I'd like to ask you a few questions about some cuts on your album, *My First Love Story.* It received a terrific review in the *Boston Globe,* from Jon Garelick, who said it had 'epic musical and emotional range.' There is something about the way you sing and everything else you do that communicates feeling. Is that the first album you've put out?"

"Thank you. This is the first solo album I've put out. I've recorded several albums with my folk band, *Notorious Folk.* And I've played on a lot of other recording projects. But this is the first one that's mine, completely mine."

"Does its title relate to an actual love affair or when you first sat at the piano at four years of age?"

"Actually it was at two (laughs) when I started piano."

"That's younger than Mozart."

"(Laughs) After my mom read the liner note she said 'You have to change it. You were two when you started the piano.' But I couldn't change it at that point."

"Eden, let's take for example the first cut on the album, *Fourteen Miles,* the last lyric of which was 'wash away this pain.' Maybe I shouldn't ask you a personal question whether that had to do with a particular person?"

"No, not that song, I don't know where that song came from. Usually I know where my ideas come from, but that song I just wrote."

"Did you do it all on that song, the lyrics, the music, everything?"

"Yes. That's all me."

"Have you performed it quite a number of times?"

"Yes. I used to perform it mostly with the *Sail Away Ladies,* a quartet that I played with Sarah Jarosz and Ari and Mia Friedman, made up of two fiddles, cello, and mandolin. And we all sang. The night before I went into the studio to finish up this project, I was thinking about doing this piece solo. Then Hankus called, and said, 'You should do *Fourteen Miles.*' So then I really spent a lot of time working it out that night, and went in and did it."

"But it has no reference to a living person?"

"The only thing I can think of it could refer to is a relationship that I had been in where I left somebody, and I was hurting so much for him because I knew he was hurting. So it could have been from that. But it's years later, so I really don't know. I really don't know where it came from (laughs). I just wrote it."

"Have you written other songs totally by yourself? Ten, twenty, fifty?"

"Yes, I have, many of them. I've written a lot of tunes without lyrics, and I've written a bunch of songs. One of the other songs that I still play a lot is a song that I wrote about ten years ago after a bad coal mining accident in West Virginia. Thirteen miners were trapped underground, and after the week only one of them came out alive. It just really moved me a lot. So I set out to write it like a politically charged song about the coal mining industry. But then I ended up writing a much more introspective song from one miner's perspective that survived. I recorded it with my band and performed it a lot as a soloist."

"Eden, another cut I want to talk about is *Along the Field.* Of course, that references Vaughan Williams and A. E. Housman. Actually, it's seven or eight cuts. Tell us about that?"

"I played that piece first about fifteen years ago in Houston. I was working with a great singer, Tracy Rhodus, who wanted to perform it in a concert. She asked me to play the violin part. This was a piece that Vaughan Williams wrote for voice and violin for two separate performers. I loved doing it with Tracy, who is a classical singer with a beautiful, beautiful voice. But there was a part of me that was missing the folky side of the song, because there is so much English folk song in the composition. So I started thinking about what it would sound like with a folk singer. For years I kept thinking, 'I have to find the right singer to do this with.' And then as I was getting more into traditional fiddling and singing while I played, which is a strong part of Appalachian and other fiddle traditions, I started thinking, '*Well, maybe I could be the singer, maybe I could sing one part and play the other part.*' There are a couple of movements that are easier than others to do that with, that are more tonal and more in sync. So I began with those, and then over time I worked up to doing the whole piece. Some of them are very challenging in that respect, with the two instruments in different time signatures, different keys, different modes. It was really the first classical piece that I took on as a project as both a singer and a violinist at the same time. And that was a really exciting project!"

"Sounds like a turning point in your style?"

"Vaughan Williams had written these little interludes that were clearly for the purpose of giving the vocalist her pitches. So I started playing around with them and stretching them out and improvising more for the violin because I felt like the violin didn't get enough solo time. The singer got so much time to be in the limelight. But the violin, the fiddle, needed some more voice in there. So I started improvising interludes. Then I worked in some traditional English folk dance tunes that would've fit right in with the time period and the genre."

"What's the total mood that you think that all of them convey together?"

"I think it's full of longing. Housman, in his poetry, was always yearning for something that he couldn't have. He was homosexual, and in that time that wasn't something that could be acknowledged publicly, or at least he felt it couldn't be acknowledged publicly. It was the time when Britain was sort of recovering from the first war. There was a whole generation sort of feeling lost, that a country's innocence had been lost. A lot of the poetry comes out of Houseman's book, *A Shropshire Lad.* He'd never been to Shropshire. It was a part of the country that he was imagining, this idyllic place full of love and pastures and meadows. So the whole poetic work was full of his longing for an imagined world."

"There is one more cut in which I'm interested in called *Say Darling Say,* about your mother singing lullabies to you as a child?"

"We're a very musical family. There was always music in our house going on, and I have memories of my mother singing, 'Hush little baby, don't say a word, mama will buy you a mockingbird.' She would make up her own lyrics. There is an Appalachian, an Anglo-American, version of that song with a different melody, that I love. So I blended them together."

"I do have a few more questions as to whether you hear music in your head, inspired by my present reading of *Musicophilia* by Oliver Sacks. Do you hear music in your head, and, if so, do you hear the actual sound or only imagine what the music sounds like?"

"There is often music playing in my head, but I can usually control it. I think that I hear the actual sound, but it is difficult to say if I'm imagining the sound. It definitely sounds good! I don't think I've ever listened to music that sounds 'bad' in my head, though I've definitely had pieces stuck in my head. But they always sound good."

"Whose music do you hear, can you choose the music you hear, can you turn it on and off at will, does it come unbidden, does it ever interfere with normal life, is it classical music or some other genre, is the phenomenon a pleasure or a pain?"

"Anything and everything, ranging from favorite works by others to past recording sessions to current projects to pieces I'm in the process of creating. It can definitely come unbidden and be difficult to get rid of, but generally if I focus my mind on something else I can turn it off or change the channel."

"Have your greatest aural experiences in music occurred inside or outside your head?"

"Outside, I think. There is nothing like playing music, the sensation of being transported to another place emotionally and even physically. And there's nothing like playing good music with others or listening to a great live show."

"How do you compose? Is the notation being merely an afterthought, or do you sit at the piano and compose from note to note, idea to idea?"

"I usually write music in my head, so to speak, and often work it out completely before actually notating it. But I also sometimes work pieces out on an instrument. I very rarely sit down and work things out on paper without hearing them in my head first, but I enjoy sitting down to write counterpoint or other small pieces without starting them in my mind."

"Have your most beautiful or most profound hearings of your or any composer's music occurred inside your head?"

"I don't think so, although I enjoy hearing music inside my head. But there is something about being there with the music in a physical space that I really enjoy. I like to feel the instrument in my hands, or sense the vibrations through the floor, or share music with a good group of folks. I might be on my way home from a gig with my band, *Notorious Folk,* with whom I've toured since 2004, and often it was an amazing and satisfying weekend. There's nothing better than playing with some of your favorite people, family really! My face will hurt from smiling so much! We've had a great weekend together, and I feel energized and rejuvenated in spite of the lack of sleep that goes with the gigging and touring territory."

"That is wonderful! Turning to a topic somewhat more academic, what do you think the reason is that we have mostly male composers and very few female composers? Do you think there's a difference in the ability of one sex or another to compose music? Or do you think it's a social factor?"

"I think our awareness of male over female composers is a social gender factor. Our society as a whole is still suffering under the weight of gender stereotypes. I think that it will still take a while to get past that, but it is definitely changing. There are so many more young female composers and improvisers coming up these days. And that's really exciting to see. But the expectations for women in general, and the fact that women carry, and give birth, and nurse children affects that too. When you do those things you're expected to make changes in your life. And you want to make changes in your life to do it. But it is hard to do all of that and be a performer too. It's a challenging thing."

"Why haven't you become famous, Eden? Do you think that your musical life has been fragmented by the fact that you're so talented across such a broad range?"

"That could be it, partly. My path has always been very different from that of other people. I tend to follow the things that I love, so I don't necessarily home in on one area that might pop me into the public eye more than another. I also think my wanting to go back to school, wanting to study, wanting to teach, are important parts of my life on which I don't want to miss out. Fame isn't a goal that interests me, frankly. It has never been my goal, and I haven't devoted myself to that end. I think that if the right manager or promoter came along who really saw what I was doing and got excited about it, that person could really take it and fly with it. But for me to take on that role for myself would take so much time away from what I'm doing musically that it might not be worth it to me."

"Is there anything else you want to talk about?"

"You mentioned you spoke to Maestro Ben Zander yesterday. He's wonderful!"

"Do you know Ben?"

"I do. I actually met him when I was fifteen in Texas. He came down to conduct the All-State Orchestra. It was one of the most inspiring orchestral experiences that I have ever had. We played the first movement of Mahler's Second Symphony. I was sitting second chair violin, so I was right up front. I really got to work with him a lot. He's such an amazing teacher. He really inspired all of the orchestra to give our best. He gave such an inspiring speech at the concert, which they didn't record, although the concert was recorded. He really spoke passionately about how important music was to the world and to us growing up, how much it was an important and essential part of our lives. I remember people were crying. We were so moved on stage as young artists. We really worked hard for him. It was great!"

"Eden, I have asked you about all those things you do as a musician. You really can't tell me one that I was lying about, could you? They were all true."

"No, they were all true. All true."

The dictionary says "true" means genuine, sincere, loyal, and faithful, along with a host of other synonyms, all of which apply in equal measure to Eden MacAdam-Somer, whether in regard to her persona or her manifold musical talents. If there is anyone out there who would take issue with that extravagant statement, let he or she come forth to state the case. Halloo. Halloo. No one? I thought not. By unanimous vote we declare Eden MacAdam-Somer tried and true, first among many, musician extraordinaire and person extraordinaire. So sayeth I. So sayeth all!

CHAPTER
20

Monica Rizzio: Washashore Cowgirl, Singer, Songwriter, and Lady

Every so often something or somebody of great value washes up on shore. On Cape Cod they call that a "washashore." One day not so long ago, a washashore cowgirl by the name of Monica Rizzio, from a place called Quitman, deep in the heart of Texas, washed up there to our good fortune. She brought with her a golden voice, an eloquent guitar, a way with words and lyrics, a giving nature, and a deep love of music of whatever description. Equally at home on the stage of Symphony Hall in Boston performing the music of America with Tom Rush or seated in an audience there with her husband listening to the strains of Beethoven and Bernstein, Monica Rizzio is a pop artist who proves to us every day that music is music, and necessary to our happiness and civility. Her own life path demonstrates how the magic of music has propelled her from a favored albeit somewhat insular childhood and adolescence to a sophisticated view of the world and an appreciation of her own talents. Nearing midlife Monica Rizzio is already a great lady and an artist of distinction poised to rise to the highest level.

"We are very lucky to be here today with Monica Rizzio who is a folk singer, soul singer, jazz singer, every man's singer. A great singer and she's lots more. How are you today, Monica?"

"I'm doing good, Larry. It's a beautiful day."

"Oh, it is a beautiful day. Cloudless sky. And here we are, Monica, on Cape Cod on August 29th, 2018. Monica, you grew up in the Bible-heavy plains of Quitman, Texas, where Sissy Spacek came from. Quitman is way up there in the northeast corner of Texas. You've said you never saw the ocean until you left Quitman. Aroostook County in Maine, where they grow potatoes, is to us Bostonians like Quitman must be to people living in Dallas. I've never been to Aroostook. So what was it like growing up in Quitman?"

Americana singer and songwriter Monica Rizzio. Photo courtesy of Monica Rizzio.

"It was absolutely incredible. I grew up on a thirty-acre ranch. I grew up barrel racing, riding horses, and just had that really free childhood life which was pretty incredible."

"Is it Bible heavy?"

"Extremely. I think at the time when I was growing up there may have been 1,200 people in the town. There were something like twenty-five churches. Basically very Southern Baptist driven. But there were churches of all kinds."

"Were you religious when you were a kid? And how about now?"

"As a kid, yes. I still am, but it is a little bit different. I think I've really been able to expand my thinking living on the East Coast where you meet so many people who think so differently. In that little town everyone was kind of leaning to one side."

"How did they vote in the last election?"

"I would say that a lot of them were Republican voters."

"So you are up here living for the last decade on Cape Cod in Massachusetts, which is about the bluest state in the Union. Has your political thinking undergone a change over time?"

"Yeah, I think I've definitely expanded. Actually, I have a bit more of a liberal-minded view on everything."

"You grew up on Pleasant Valley Ranch, and you describe yourself as a tomboy, an outdoors girl, riding horses, riding in rodeos. Did you do all that stuff?"

"Yeah, I did. It was incredible. It was crazy to think that I barrel raced at like eleven years old. I had friends who used to do roping. I just kind of thought it was a normal thing that kids did. When I moved to New York my senior year of high school, I very quickly found out that I was in a big minority with regard to my interests at that point. In Texas I was on a horse at the age of probably seven and rode almost every single day."

"Do you still ride?"

"I haven't ridden since I moved to the East Coast. I do more Western Style, and there are not many Western riders in these parts. Here they get all dressed up in their equestrian wear. I think of a Western rider as more of the cowgirl style. In Texas we would either ride bareback just holding onto the mane of the horse or ride with a regular saddle. I would say Western Style is a little bit more relaxed, so to speak."

"Pleasant Valley Ranch sounds like a great place to grow up! I read you had a special musical bond with your father there? Does he still live down there?"

"My whole family now has relocated up to the East Coast. My dad was originally from right outside of New York City, my brother and sister now live in Connecticut, my mom and dad live in Westchester, New York. I'm the furthest one away. We are all pretty close to one another."

"So your dad introduced you to bluegrass and country music, and you would stay up with him all night listening to records when you were a little girl. That must have been fantastic."

"It was just like very normal. I think my parents kind of raised me very non-traditionally in that sense. Education was always encouraged, but instead of my dad saying, 'Did you read this book?' he said, 'Did you learn this song? Do you know how to do this Willie Nelson song or have you learned this Dean Martin song?' It was something that we were both so connected to. I think there is this huge bond with my father because we both love music. We can listen to it together for hours and hours."

"Is he a musician?"

"He used to play the accordion, and now he is a ukulele maker. So you'll get to hear my ukulele, which he built for me, at the show this evening."

"You said how different your life might have been if you didn't have to wait until after you went to music school in Nashville to learn the fiddle, ukulele, and guitar. Now at West Bend Music, the school you founded here on the Cape, you teach fiddle, banjo, mandolin, guitar, piano, and ukulele, so you plainly have a healthy respect for all those instruments."

"I do. I'm telling you if my parents had the means to put me through piano lessons or fiddle lessons, I would have been incredible. I remember picking up the flute when I was seven or eight. I would play for my parents who would have to say to put your flute down, you've got to come eat dinner. I was so enthralled and lost in the music because on the ranch there wasn't a lot to do besides go to church and to the football games. If someone were to have said, 'Hey, here's a fiddle, let's jam on the porch tonight,' I would have been all for it. There was a lot of that going on around me, but I didn't know that. I wish I had because as a child I was so competitive. I still play the flute."

"I read that by the time you were ten you knew you wanted to sing for the rest of your life. Is that true?"

"It's true, yeah. It's kind of crazy, right? At ten years old."

"No, not at all crazy. I mean you are doing what you love every day?"

"I do love it. I feel like some of us are fortunate to find out our passion sooner than others. I feel fortunate that at such a young age I was encouraged by everybody around me. That is so helpful."

"What do you think it was about singing and music that made you feel that way?"

"As a young child, and even later in middle school and high school, I had a hard time fitting in. To some degree I had some bullying going on in early middle school. I feel like music was my outlet. Later these kids who did bully me apologized at a high school reunion, saying we were just so jealous of you because you were doing all this cool stuff."

"Why jealous?"

"I would audition for the school play and get the lead part because there was a vocalist part. Or I would audition for a solo part and always I got the lead part. I was very athletic, so I did really well in sports. I was one of those kids that other kids either really liked or didn't like at all. Of course, I was friends with everyone. I would say in my freshman year most of my friends were seniors. I was very outgoing, I was in all the clubs, all the sports teams, but there was always that group of kids who were not very nice."

"Monica, you're the one who came out on the good side, I think. You then went off to the very fine Belmont University School of Music in Nashville, a great town for music. I read that you went out many nights to hear the great artists who perform there. You must have learned a lot in Nashville?"

"When I moved to Nashville in 2000, I had previously been going to Adelphi University where I had a full scholarship for music. That scholarship gave me the financial help I needed to attend college in the first place. When I moved to Nashville, I'll never forget just going out to those clubs and hearing my fellow peers play guitar and sing songs they wrote. At that point I had not yet learned to play the guitar. I was pretty much self-taught up to then. I was introduced to some of the best songwriters and players ever who were playing for big country stars or writing number one country songs. I had that incredible experience of meeting and becoming friends with a lot of great songwriters and artists."

"That's a wonderful experience! While you were there you met Demetrius Becrelis who is from Cape Cod, and you began writing folk and country songs together even after he went back to Cape Cod. Tell us about Demetrius?"

"Demetrius and I met in Nashville back in 2000 and starting writing music together. That is how I came to live on the Cape. We toured in a band called Tripping Lily for ten years and eventually started a business in 2008 called West Bend Music with his brother and a good friend."

"Monica, tell me about *Tripping Lily*? I know you sang with them for like ten years, but then you probably surprised them all when you said I'm out of here."

"Tripping Lily was an extraordinary quartet. I feel really fortunate. The four of us together had a very magical sound and we created a lot of harmonies. Our song writing was very eclectic. We all came from different genres. So I had more of that country jazz thing going on. Demetrius was very, very pop. His brother was kind of a mix of everything. We toured and played together for ten years. We were very close knit. I dated Demetrius, I was best friends with his brother, and we all lived and hung out together. Everything was together basically. Then in 2011 I ended the romantic relationship with Demetrius and left the band a year later."

"Was that because you ended the romantic relationship or did you have other motivations in leaving?"

"I think at that point I really wanted to play country music."

"Weren't you playing that with them?"

"We were playing acoustic folk pop music and we were performing around one microphone the way a bluegrass band would perform. I wanted to be the front lady. I wanted to sing and to have an electric guitar player. I just felt that at that point musically I was starting to explore other things. I wanted my own space. Demetrius and I have collaborated quite a bit since I left the group. He's played in some of my holiday shows and sat in on others. But I've definitely enjoyed having my own thing."

"Tripping Lily was known for soft and soulful pop which appealed to a big audience. Do you like that kind of music or do you like upbeat?"

"I don't think anything gets me more excited than like an old Loretta Lynn song, or Patsy Cline or Willie Nelson song. That makes me tick like nothing else."

"How would you describe those songs?"

"A little bit of twangy heartbreak upbeat, a little bit of soulful attitude in there. I just can relate to it so much. Growing up on a ranch in Texas, and growing up around a bunch of cowboys, just getting back to who I was as a kid. I think that I lost that part of me for so long. Or maybe I didn't. I didn't really think about the inner child, so to speak, for all those years in my twenties. When I turned thirty and I left the band and started doing my own thing, and I was writing for my first record, I had to almost musically find myself again. That was because I didn't know who I was without my two partners writing by my side. We were writing together all the time, we were together all the time. Breaking away caused me to have to really grow and stand on my own two feet."

"I hear one of the songs on your debut album, *Washashore Cowgirl,* had a relationship to your marriage?"

"Luckier Than You is the song on the album that I wrote in five minutes a couple of weeks before my wedding. I wanted to give my husband something different. Men tend to buy these beautiful rings for their ladies, and he had done that."

"Let the record show that Monica is wearing a very beautiful ring with lots of diamonds all around, and a nice big diamond in the middle. It is a very pretty ring, I noticed it before."

"Everybody who was coming to my wedding was very disappointed that I wasn't going to perform at the wedding. My mom and dad are like you're not going to sing, and I'm like no I kind of just want a night off, I want to get married and not have to worry about it. But little did they know that I had written *Luckier Than You* which no one had ever heard. It was a love song that I wrote for my husband."

"You described your marriage as a happy marriage."

"Life with Peter is wonderful!"

"What does Peter do?"

"He books all the bands for us. He's mainly a real estate agent owning his own real estate company."

"Do you have children?"

"I have a big fourteen-year-old boy. I became a full-time mom when I married my husband who was a single dad. I have the best of both worlds. I get to have a baby without actually having a baby (laughing)."

"Obviously, Monica, you have a very satisfactory life. If you were three times as famous and touring from city to city most of the year you might be a lot less happy."

"I feel like I've got a good thing going. I've got a great husband and a great support system. A fantastic nonprofit, Vinegrass, which gives back, and a really successful business in the school."

"How are your mom and dad doing these days?"

"My mom suffered a massive heart attack in January and 'died' three times but came back. That was a pretty incredible moment in my life. I would say it shook me up. I think spending the summers with my grandmother when I was a kid was a huge event even though she only lived across the pasture. She was a huge influence on me. She was the first person to get me to sing in church. She's not around anymore, but she was my go-to."

"What is your background, Monica?"

"I'm like 58% Sicilian, 20% Irish, and then the rest is German and English."

"What are your immediate plans with your new band?"

"We are planning a Texas and New Mexico tour to promote my upcoming record which we're going to record down in Nashville in January. The title is unannounced right now but it's going to be my sophomore record. I'm working with a producer down there. I'm really excited about it. I've been writing the past few years for the new record and I'm ready to get started on it."

"Do you think you would ever move back down to Texas?"

"I don't think so. My family is here, but it's not only that. I really love the East Coast. I love the charm, I love the food, I love the culture. But I could definitely see myself having some sort of little house in Texas where I could go and song write. It's kind of away from the pull of everyday life."

"Monica, let's talk about your debut album, *Washashore Cowgirl.* We should explain to the people reading this that that is an old expression here on Cape Cod meaning somebody who washes ashore on the Cape from someplace else. The cowgirl part is because Monica, as said, is a true cowgirl. *Washashore Cowgirl* was described as like a 'stiff cocktail,' autobiographical, with a hint of fiction, including a song about one of your idols, Willie Nelson. So the floor is yours to tell us why it was described like that? Stiff cocktail, start with that."

"OK, stiff cocktail. I always have to have a little something to get the creative juices flowing, if that makes any sense. I don't know as a writer if you have to do something to get to that spot. If I'm wanting to write a song that is very sad, I've got to get back to that place of how I felt then. Or trying to get to a state in which I can at least write about it or pretend that I ever went through it."

"It's similar with me because when I write a story it has to have a point of view. I always try to find the frame in which to write about this particular interviewee's life and why it is significant."

"Right, and don't you think that artists in general all have different ways of describing themselves? You're wearing so many different hats; you've got to internalize so many different aspects of your life. Where do you want your work to go? How do you want it to be perceived by other people? Does that make sense?"

"Everything you say makes sense, Monica."

"I just think Willie Nelson is a top-notch guy. I got to meet him a few years ago after I wrote that song, *Willie Nelson.* I went backstage and hung out with him a little before a show. I admire him because it was said he would never make it. He just persevered and persevered. And he made it. He made it so big! And he is so much his own person. He is not there to blow sunshine up your ass. He is just like Willie Nelson; he is who he is. He's not going to pretend to be somebody else. Great artist!"

"Washashore Cowgirl, 'autobiographical and with a hint of fiction.' What does all that mean? I think you do write songs that are autobiographical."

"Yeah, absolutely. At least in that album there are at least two or three autobiographical songs. But I think *Washashore Cowgirl* was from the perspective that I wanted my audience to see where I grew up because if you've never been there, you may not even be able to imagine how different it is than Cape Cod, Massachusetts, or Boston, or Brookline, or wherever it is. It's an extremely different world."

"Unlike many people, artists tend to let it all hang out. Let people know, 'I don't care.'"

"Why are you keeping that secret? It makes no sense. Yeah."

"I'm not ashamed of myself; let it all hang out. Are you that way?"

"Yeah, I think I got to be that way when I was writing for *Washashore Cowgirl.* I think there's a little bit of a pressure from the outside world, or even the industry, to be a certain way. For instance, I wrote a song called *A Little Time* which was just a song about me dealing with being really depressed and not knowing why I was feeling that way. I didn't want to put that song in the album. My husband encouraged me to put it in. He said, 'What are you hiding from? Why are you leading on your audience that you've got this perfect life when, in fact, you're not doing very well right now? Why don't you share that with them?' I said, 'Because I don't want to. I don't want people to know that I'm feeling shitty.' And that song has been more inspirational to me than anything. I've gotten so many emails, and so many people you wouldn't expect coming up after the show. Like young men come up and there are tears in their eyes, saying 'Thanks for writing that. I'm feeling that way and I didn't know anyone else felt that way.' So that was kind of a hard thing for me to do, but I just got to the point where I

American musician Willie Nelson, muse of Monica Rizzio.

Credit: joshbg2k, CC BY 2.0
<https://creativecommons.org/licenses/by/2.0>, via Wikimedia Commons

said to myself, 'You know what? I'm going to be a little bit more real, and not just say something to make someone say they are pleased. Instead I'll say how I'm really doing, actually pretty bad. I don't know why I'm feeling this way but I hope not to feel this way very much longer.' Writing that song was like a healing experience. I didn't feel bad anymore. It was a huge load that was just released. It was incredible!"

"It is said that you share intimate parts of your life with certain songs on that album like *Luckier Than You*, *Buttercups*, and *You and Me*, which was a song about getting cheated on. That happens to people in their lives. As you told, *Luckier Than You* was written for your husband. Would you call those others revelatory songs about negative experiences in your life?"

"I guess you could say *You and Me* is about the way that I dealt with moving on from a past love. But it was also very influenced by a few of my girlfriends who were also going through extremely difficult times with their husbands or boyfriends. So that song was probably one of the more fun songs that I've ever written because it was about the breakup, and getting cheated on, but I think at that point I kind of accepted it and moved on, very relieved that the relationship had ended."

"How many songs do you think you've written?"

"Maybe like fifty to seventy-five songs. I still consider myself a very young songwriter. I've always considered myself more of a vocalist than a songwriter, but that is slowly starting to change."

"It looks like you have chops as a vocalist, songwriter, lyricist, and teacher. Plus you have nonprofit charitable interests. You've got lots of stuff going on. I don't know whether this comes from becoming a more liberal northeasterner, but I think you are all over the map, which bespeaks a high level of commitment, decency, intelligence, whatever, those kinds of things?"

"I think I'm just inspired to grow. I can't stand the thought of mediocrity within myself. It just grinds at me when I feel like I'm being mediocre in my performing, or my teaching, or being a wife, or whatever it is. It's just disturbing. I feel like I'm just kind of being a slacker and that's not what I want to be, I want to be — this sounds so ridiculous — but you know I just want to be the best I can be and be able to give back. For me, that's how I feel. This whole nonprofit thing that I started, Vinegrass, is my way of giving back. There is nothing better than being able to give an instrument to a student or write a check and give that to someone who is going to college who needs money. I know how it feels growing up without enough. I can't say we were poor, because we weren't poor. We had a lot. We had the biggest house in town, we had a ranch, we had horses, but we definitely had no money growing up."

"Monica, your voice is great. What do you think is the quality in it that attracts people so much?"

"I think for a female I have a very different voice. A lot of people tell me that because I'm so petite they're surprised that a big voice comes out of a such a small body."

"How is your voice different?"

"My dad always used to say that all the good singers had a sound, and that's what you want. You've got to have that sound. When you listen to Barbra Streisand, you know it's her. I think I have a different sound for a female. I don't have that very ethereal high female like voice. I have a very low alto velvety type of country twang that I don't hear very often in female singers. I also believe my personality and feelings come out in my voice."

"In your various pursuits what is most important for you to accomplish? Let's take singing first."

"I think just pushing myself, pushing the envelope, singing genres I normally wouldn't sing. I ended a set recently with an Aretha Franklin song which I have never done. It was really out of my comfort zone, but I felt like I needed to do it. She was a legend and she had passed away. As an artist you have to pay tribute to those who came before you"

"Your new band is called, Monica Rizzio and Old Kings Highway. Do you sing your own songs with that group?"

"Primarily it's all original, I've got a Bob Dylan cover, a Loretta Lynn cover, a Willie Nelson cover in there, but for the most part, it's a lot of songs that I've written."

"There is an old expression that goes something like 'You can take the girl out of Quitman, but you can't take Quitman out of the girl.' Is that true of you, Monica?"

"I don't think you ever can take that childhood out of you. It's always going to be there."

"You've shared the stage with a lot of terrific people, Chris Botti, Diana Krall, the Cape Cod Symphony Orchestra. Tom Rush said he invited you to sing with him at Symphony Hall, and you took the stage away from him. I think he said it in good humor."

"I don't know what made him say that. I felt pretty alive on stage in Symphony Hall. You often wonder, 'How many chances am I going to get to play a stage like this?' It was a magical evening. I was his fiddle player and backup singer, and then he invited me to do my own songs. I was so high on performing that night that it took a while for me to come down from that show. It was absolutely incredible to be able to play with someone like that."

"What kind of stuff do you do with the Cape Cod Symphony which is a pretty well reputed community orchestra?"

"I think I've covered with them maybe five or six times. This last concert I did was last December at their holiday show. They hired me as a special guest singer. I did a few solo numbers, then I did some numbers with the symphony, and then some trio numbers with two other female artists, all pop, some sacred, some traditional holiday music. I've even done klezmer music with them. So I've done it all with the Cape Cod Symphony."

"Did you have any training in classical music?"

"I do. I had training for about a year in Nashville in classical piano and sang lots of arias and duets. I had to learn to sing in German and Italian. For example '*La ci darem la mano*' from Mozart's *Don Giovanni.*"

"Do you like classical music?"

"Oh, I love it. I love it. I listen to it and go to concerts. My husband and I went to Tanglewood to see some shows. We've attended concerts in the parks in New York City where they have some really cool classical concerts. I admire the discipline, and the music is so absolutely beautiful!"

"Could you imagine crossing over in any way?"

"I don't think so. I feel that at this point in my life that ship has sailed."

"Tell us about your teaching, Monica?"

"I love teaching. I love passing on that love of music. Nothing excites me more than getting a student to feel that way where they just can't wait to meet with me and learn from me every week. That's so inspiring. At this point in my life my biggest passion is touring and getting out on the road, but I love spending a lot of my time teaching at the school and focusing on my nonprofit."

"Seems to me you're absolutely a natural musician. Was opening the school your idea?"

"It was kind of all of ours. We kind of chatted about it, Alex, Demitrius, and our other co-owner, Clayton. *Tripping Lily* was touring a lot so we needed something that could provide an income and allow flexibility. That was teaching."

"Monica I'm very interested in your composing. Do you write the lyrics as well? And do you notate?"

"I normally just write up chord charts. I'll write up the lyrics with the chord charts over it. Then I'll get together with my band and we'll play through it. Possibly other arrangements may form at that point, but I don't notate it at that point, although I could."

"Do you have to work hard at the lyrics, or do they come to you pretty easily?"

"No, they are the hardest. My biggest struggle is the lyrics. They are very important to me."

"How do you access them?"

"You know what's so crazy, Larry? I feel that when I get my guitar out and I'm playing a melody the music speaks to me and basically tells me what to write. It is so far out, it's so weird, but it happens all the time. Some of my best songs are songs that were formed in that creative process."

"Do you hear music in your head?"

"Yes. I had a dream two nights ago. I wrote the best song. I was so mad when I woke up and couldn't remember it. But I remember that feeling of being, like wow, this is such a great song. So it's definitely happening while I'm sleeping."

"When you hear music in your head, is it just imagining what the music sounds like or do you actually hear the instruments?"

"It's weird, I can hear it but I can't tangibly put my finger on it."

"Is it always your music you hear?"

"It's always my music I hear, yeah."

"Does it ever become troublesome, or is it always a pleasant experience?"

"Oh, any time I hear it, yeah, it's always a pleasant experience. It's just frustrating that often I can't tangibly play it on my guitar or ever remember any part of the music. I just remember the feeling of being extremely satisfied with the end product."

"Did you ever write a song based on this kind of experience?"

"I wrote a song that Tripping Lily recorded and that we played with the Cape Cod Symphony called *Hello*. That was a song that woke me up in the middle of the night. Within like two seconds I grabbed my ukulele and I just wrote this song. It was right there, so I grabbed it before it got away from me."

"Does that experience happen to you during your waking hours?"

"It does, for sure. *Luckier Than You*, *Willie Nelson*, and *Buttercups* came that way."

"How would you describe your compositional process? Is it from the outside in or from the inside out? From dreams, color, impressions, experiences, light?"

"From experiences, dreams, surroundings, visions of the future, things that could be. Love inspires me a lot. Feelings inspire me. I'm trying to get away from that on my new record. It's easy for me to write about that stuff. It's harder to write about a person as opposed to writing about the emotional feelings within that person's story."

"Do you feel akin to any other pop composers?"

"I feel akin to some of those Texas songwriters like Blaze Foley, who died young, and Guy Clark. I loved Whitney Houston growing up. I feel like I could really connect with her. Judy Garland was another one. She was absolutely incredible! I feel like I know where Willie Nelson is coming from. Frank Sinatra was amazing, but Dean Martin had such a buttery voice. Dean Martin was the one who did it for me as a kid. Go figure, right?"

"Monica, can your music be distinguished from other composers?"

"I think so. There is a Texas twang and just a hint of vocal style. I feel my voice is very different, and that my songs tend to be like very emotional folk. They have somewhat of a catchy hook so that you find yourself singing them."

"How about Vinegrass*?* Was that your idea?"

"Yes, I would say it was a dual idea between my husband and me. I had always talked about wanting to start a nonprofit and give back to those in need. We talked about it and just said, let's do it. It's a great idea because before Vinegrass I used to produce shows in Yarmouth and I would book bands to come in, usually friends from Nashville who were touring. There was no venue on the Cape for a lot of people here who really appreciate this roots Americana music, so I said I'm going to bring it to them. We are going to charge for tickets and see what happens. It was so successful. One night too many people came and the café got shut down. There were like ninety people in a fifteen-occupant space."

"Monica, are you satisfied where you are now in your singing career?"

"I kind of wish that I did a little bit more of the grind touring in my early twenties because at that point, you are not that tied down to anything, no family, no children, nothing."

"Are you still ambitious enough to want to hit the top of the charts?"

"I would love to. I think at this point in my career I would love to play all the big festivals. I think I would say I've made it when I can sell out a five-hundred-seat theater."

"What is it that you want to convey most to your audience?"

"I want the audience to have a good time when they come to my show. I want them to forget any troubles. I want them to attend the show and leave saying, 'Wow, I kind of forgot about my life for an hour and a half, and the show made me feel really good.' Don't folks always go to a performance or an art event to forget about everyday life? Don't you pay that money to see a pop or classical show wanting to be artistically moved? You don't want to be thinking about all the things they have to do or need to do. I feel maybe I can fill a void for them."

"What do you think the appeal of rock, rap, country and other pop genres is?"

"I think it's fantastic. I think people can relate to all of it. I think a lot of the young people really look up to the artists who are doing it and are successful at it."

"How do the pop artists relate to their fans on and off the stage differently than classical artists and could this work for classical artists? Or are classical artists a little bit off-putting as opposed to pop artists?"

"Pop artists are a little bit more diva like. I don't know if you often hear about Hilary Hahn's relationships, but you will hear about a Katy Perry breakup. Classical is thought of in a whole different category. I often ask my husband, 'Why don't any of our friends go to the symphony? Why are we the youngest people there, and you are forty and I'm thirty-eight?' That is a constant conversation I've had with Jung-Ho Pak, the conductor of the Cape Cod Symphony. I have no idea why they don't come, but if you were to have a pop artist there, they would come. I go because I love the music. I go because I love the culture of it, I love where it comes from. I feel like all music is based on classical music to some degree, and I feel that some of the best musicians have been influenced by that music."

"One hundred years from now what's going to be more popular, pop or classical?"

"Probably pop. Sad but true. I think pop's popularity will continue indefinitely. I don't know if that is true of classical. I hope so. I really do. That's why we have to keep these music programs alive. We've got to have these kids learning classical music so that they can play it on a fiddle. I feel like it's an absolute must. I think that music and language should be incorporated in kindergarten all the way through high school. It does something for your mind. Something happens to someone when they hear their favorite song. The neurons in their brain go off like fireworks. They say that people in their older years who listen to music have sharper minds and delay any onset of dementia. It's sad that music education is overlooked."

"Could we live without music?"

"I don't think so. No way."

"What is music?"

"I think music is the universal language between people. I think it's the most emotional tangible item that you can feel and experience. At least, for me it is."

"Which has a deeper effect on people, pop or classical?"

"I think it depends on the person, could be 50/50. I think they're both great."

"How about women's lib? How do you feel about that? You have described a situation in which you took over your own life in a much bigger way."

"Yeah, I definitely am like an all-pro woman who thinks I can do anything that a man can do. (Singing) 'Anything you can do, I can do better. I can do anything better than you.'"

"You know all those old shows?"

"I know all those old shows. But you know honestly, Larry, I'm so absolutely relaxed that I'm a feminist to a point, but not to the point where I am uptight about it. I'm OK with opening the door for myself, but if a guy opens a door for me it's pretty awesome, thank you. But I don't expect that. I can open it myself. Some women are like I can do it all myself. I always joke with my husband that it's OK with me if you're the breadwinner of the household, that's fine, or even if I am. I'm fine either way. I still cherish the way that it was in the thirties and the forties between a man and a woman."

"I think that is a healthy attitude, Monica, because some of the rights that women have won are long past due, but I think mixing that with the natural relationship between a man and a woman is not a good thing."

"It's very equal with me and my husband. There is no expectation that you're the woman and you have to do this. It is just very laid back, it's great!"

"Please freely associate on any subject interesting to you whether musical, literary, political, national, or world?"

"So I can't tell you I am a huge basketball fan?"

"You can't (laughing). Are you?"

"I am, yeah, it's my favorite sport."

"Don't go by the categories because we're not going to have time to talk about them all. Just let it fly."

"Larry Ruttman, you really stumped me on this one. That's a really good one."

"I like to hear that. I like to hear when people say to me, 'I never heard that question before.' Maybe you want to tell us about how tough the music business is?"

"Oh yeah, I think that the music business is extremely annoying. I feel like all of these agents won't sign you until you can fill rooms, but then at that point you're thinking, 'Well then, why do I need to sign with you and give you a percentage of my split if I'm already doing all the work?' Labels won't look at you if you haven't had some success, radio won't play you if you haven't been at the top of the charts, but then how do you get there without their help? It's something I try not to get too discouraged about. I feel that I just have to keep pressing forward. I've had good radio press, and I have a good booking agent now. I just try to make it all evolve from the music and try not to think about what the business end wants me to do. If I do, then I have failed as an artist."

"You're not going to fail. You are going to do fine."

Having read Monica Rizzio's story and felt her presence, you probably feel as I do, that she can't fail because she has already succeeded in whatever she has touched with her beloved music, her relationships with family and friends, her teaching and giving, and in her powerful persona which steadily guides her to do what she believes is the right thing to do. One doesn't have to be a famous musician to be a great musician. I've heard her, and I know she is great. Her talent and sincerity go to the heart. There is a lot of luck in who becomes famous. Often there is a lot of denying of one's better instincts to attain that goal. More often than not, it seems to this writer, that that ultimately leads to a loss of self and bad results. For every talented artist who attains fame without losing their identity, there are several others who decline and fall in the tough world of entertainment. My guess is that it will never happen to Monica Rizzio, that her life will continue indefinitely to reward her hearers and all who know her far into the future whether she does or does not become a marquee attraction. Monica's deep understanding of music and what it does for her, and what she can do with it for others, guarantee that outcome.

American arts administrator, Peter Gelb, longtime General Manager of the Metropolitan Opera, who has achieved a superlative record in those challenging undertakings.

Credit: Peabody Awards, CC BY 2.0 <https://creativecommons.org/licenses/by/2.0>, via Wikimedia Commons

Part Five

MUSIC MANAGEMENT

Mark Volpe in the musical score library at Symphony Hall, accompanied by his composers here and gone.

Credit: Photo by Michael J. Lutch. Originally published in Boston Magazine. *Used by permission.*

CHAPTER
21

Mark Volpe: President of the Boston Symphony Orchestra, 1997–2021

The stars must have been aligned presciently in the night sky on the day Mark Volpe entered the world. One might have foreseen at that moment that Mark would have a future in classical music, given that his father was the second chair trumpet player of the Minnesota Orchestra (formerly known as the Minneapolis Symphony Orchestra). But no one would have predicted then that Mark's future would include assuming a leadership position for four major American symphony orchestras, the last of which in Boston is called "the aristocrat" of them all.

Not that Mark Volpe didn't aspire to play as a clarinetist in a major ensemble, but a summary and deflating decision by his auditors at an audition for one of the major West Coast orchestras sent him off on a beeline to law school where he used his musical knowledge to open a wedge into arts management. That vaulted him early on to preeminence in the field, ultimately resulting recently in his election to membership in the iconic American Society of Arts and Sciences. It might be argued that Mark is neither an artist or a scientist, but plainly his electors thought his skills in feelingly managing the fortunes of his orchestras and their players were worthy of such an esteemed recognition. Mark's accomplishments have been further recognized by five major universities that awarded Mark honorary doctorates.

So what were the family and life experiences which brought Mark Volpe to the humanistic values and business acumen sufficient to achieve his high place in the arts, and the sound judgment to steer clear of a crucial change of course in midstream into the likely far more lucrative wild world of wealth?

"Where did you grow up?"

"I grew up in Minneapolis, Minnesota. My father was the second trumpet player of the Minneapolis Symphony (now Minnesota Orchestra) for forty-three years before he retired. So I had a wonderful family consisting of my parents as well as a brother and two sisters. I grew up backstage on the University of Minnesota campus at Northrop Auditorium. The orchestra left the University facility and moved to its own hall in downtown Minneapolis in 1973. Upon my graduation from high school, I spent the next years playing clarinet professionally while attending music school, graduate school, and law school."

"Was your mother a musician?"

"No. My mother taught kids with learning disabilities. She primarily worked with kids who had pretty severe emotional behavioral issues. In the 1960s, autism was not well understood so only the students with the most severe issues warranted interventions."

"Were they both native Americans?"

"Yes. My father was born right after my grandmother arrived on the boat from Italy. And my mother was the third child of Greek born parents and the first one to marry someone non-Greek. Her two older sisters both had married gentlemen from Greece. So, I was confirmed twice and baptized twice, because at that point, the Greek Orthodox and Catholic churches did not recognize or observe each other's sacraments."

"Well only lately they've had a meeting."

"Yeah, exactly. The Pope finally met the Russian patriarch. My parents were married twice. I think they got married first in a Greek church, and then in the Catholic Church to appease my Italian grandmother."

"When did you first become interested in music? I guess it was part of the family. What was your first instrument?"

"Although all the Volpe children began our musical studies on the piano, we played trumpet shortly thereafter. That only worked for me for a brief period as my orthodontist recommended that I play clarinet. Back then, some dentists and orthodontists thought you could adjust bites by the instrument you played. They thought the clarinet would push my front teeth forward. Obviously, that thinking has been mostly discarded. Anyway, the net result is that I began clarinet in fifth grade, and it stuck. I played all through high school and began playing professional jobs at the age of fifteen. Then I went off to the Eastman School of Music for undergraduate school and Indiana University for graduate school. Big music school, in Bloomington, Indiana. Had a pretty good basketball team too, as I recall."

"So you were heading for a musical career?"

"Yes, I was. However, I just got tired of losing auditions. If you look at any position in the Boston Symphony or other major orchestras, you typically have a couple hundred people apply for each vacancy. The selection process involves submitting tapes from which forty or fifty players get invited to a live audition in the hall. After several rounds, the field is reduced to ultimately, one. I was auditioning for one of the big West Coast orchestras in 1978 or 1979. My net worth was about $620. I think I spent $610. of that getting out to the West Coast paying for a flight and hotel. And the way auditions work, you play short excerpts of specific pieces. So, if you're a clarinet player, you're always playing the Mozart Clarinet concerto and excerpts from Beethoven, Brahms, *Daphnis and Chloe*, Bartók's *Miraculous Mandarin*, etc. For that particular audition, I played a Brahms excerpt, and I played for maybe fifteen seconds, or eighteen seconds, and they said 'next.' And I turned the page and started playing the Beethoven excerpt, and they said no, 'next.' So it was at that very moment I decided to go to law school (laughs)."

"I guess that went OK?"

"I went to law school, and it was a great, great deal for me. I got my law degree in three years while continuing to play clarinet professionally. You graduated a few years before I did, Larry. But look at what kids are paying now for a law degree. I got my law degree in 1983 paying in-state yearly tuition in Minnesota which was less than $2,000 a year. Consequently, I got my law degree for under $6,000. It was fantastic because I graduated from law school with a condo and a car because I was making money. Unlike these kids who now graduate from law school and are $80,000 or more in debt. In the early 1980s, the state schools had these very sizable subsidies from state legislatures, whether you're talking Virginia, Michigan, Berkeley, Minnesota, or Wisconsin, if you were a state resident, it was just cheap. Now legislatures have cut the appropriations so while instate tuition remains cheaper than out-of-state tuition, it is still expensive."

"How did it go after law school?"

"I got a terrific legal education while at the same time I got to play a lot of clarinet. Although I considered working for a few law firms, was even recruited by a few, I just missed being around musicians. I had written several articles for legal periodicals when I was in law school on collective bargaining in the orchestral context. I also wrote on FCC broadcast issues as well as articles on intellectual property issues. And I sent some of these articles around to the fifteen largest orchestras and the three or four largest opera companies, I had three offers. Joe Meyerhoff, one of the great philanthropists who built the Baltimore Symphony Orchestra, hired me.

"Meyerhoff built and endowed the hall, and it's named after him. Then the gentleman who was serving as the Orchestra's Executive Director had massive brain surgery at Johns Hopkins and missed the first nine months of my tenure. Consequently, I, as the assistant executive director, basically was elevated to a senior role at the Baltimore Symphony. Six weeks out of law school, and I was in a major role at a major orchestra. So, it's sink or swim. I had very good friends in Baltimore, quite a few Eastman people and quite a few Indiana graduates as well, so a good third of the orchestra had my academic allegiances and were incredibly supportive, and I didn't sink. I was swimming fast at different times just trying to stay above water. But not to use mixed metaphors, somehow I got through."

"Well Mark, I want to come back to some other things. You were really the director at three places before you came here?"

"Well, in Baltimore, they quickly hired somebody over me ten months later when they recognized that I was too young. I then became the general manager in Baltimore. Then I got a call from a famous Minneapolis family — the Dayton family — which is the founding family of Target, and at that point they owned Hudsons, Marshall Fields, and Daytons department stores. They said, 'Do you want to be your father's boss?' I became the vice president and general manager of the Minnesota Orchestra."

"(Laughs) How old were you then?"

"Twenty something. I don't know, twenty-eight or twenty-nine. And I did that for two years. Then I got called from Steve Miller, who was the vice chair of Chrysler then under Lee Iacocca, who talked to me along with Edsel Ford, Henry Ford's great grandson, about my coming to Detroit. I was the Executive Director of the Detroit Symphony Orchestra for over six years. The Jewish community in Detroit is quite active and Max Fisher, another great philanthropist and political power broker, was the patriarch of the orchestra for a while. Peter Cummings, Max's son-in-law, as well. But that aside, then I got a call to come to Boston.

"The first guy who called me was Yo-Yo Ma. You know, that was what, twenty-five years ago. I was thirty-nine years old. And I was doing this substantial development in Detroit. I was partnering with Max and Peter Cummings, and a few other people, in a quarter of a billion-dollar development surrounding the concert hall. In Detroit I wasn't an orchestra manager. I was more of a developer. Given this, I initially told Yo-Yo, 'No, I have work to do.' I mean we had built an office building, a thousand-car parking garage, and we were in the process of going to every Detroit School Board meeting advocating that a performing arts high school be built on property we had acquired next to Orchestra Hall. Eventually a $100 million dollar bond issue was approved, and the high school was built."

"Sounds like you had good reasons to stay in Detroit."

"I kept on passing on Boston until Isaac Stern, one of my favorite people in the world, called me after I told Yo-Yo that I still had work to do in Detroit, and Isaac said, 'Are you crazy? It's the Boston Symphony. You're going. (laughs).' You know it's Isaac Stern."

"Well, he was right."

"Then he says, 'The school at Tanglewood is screwed and the school (Tanglewood Music Center) is one of the reasons that the Boston Symphony is the most important orchestra in America. I may be partial to the New York Philharmonic, but Boston is training the next generation of musicians and that makes Boston unique. You got to come do this job, Mark. Don't wait for the

New York Philharmonic. They'll call you too, but you got to come to Boston. And I'm a New Yorker.' I said, 'No, you were born in San Francisco. Who are you kidding, Isaac?' He laughed, you know."

"Tell me something, Mark, how long did you continue to play clarinet gigs while administrating orchestras?"

"I played a couple of summers in the Baltimore Symphony. The only assistant conductor we had was one of the clarinet players, so there are times where he had to conduct, and I played in the section. I also played some chamber music with members of the Baltimore Symphony as well full orchestra concerts, all in the late 1980s. I would like play second or third clarinet. So, I was on both sides of the negotiation. I was the highest paid second clarinet in the history of second clarinets. No, I'm joking. Every nickel I made playing in the Baltimore Symphony I contributed back to the orchestra. I didn't contribute my core salary back, I'm not that generous. But when I was playing, I would just turn it around as the union insisted that I be paid for playing in the orchestra. I had to protect both sides."

"Maybe that's why you can settle with the players union, why you can successfully negotiate contracts with the players. You have experience on the other side."

"My father was on the players committee in Minneapolis when I was a young kid, so I've been observing the dynamics of collective bargaining for close to sixty years. I remember committee meetings when I was six or seven years old. I don't know how many collective bargaining agreements I've observed or done. In my thirty-eight years with orchestras, the number is certainly fifteen or higher."

"When I was doing my book on baseball, two of the most interesting guys that I met were the union guys, Marvin Miller and Donald Fehr."

"Oh, Marvin Miller changed baseball. That's part of baseball history."

"And the other is Donald Fehr, terrific guy, very honorable, who succeeded Marvin. Their attitude toward the union was that they were not paternalistic. It was more like a community between each of them and the player reps and players. Did you play much baseball, Mark?"

"I played with the Harmon Killebrew kids and the Bob Allison kids growing up in a Minneapolis suburb where we lived. They all tried to outdo their dads, who played in the 1965 World Series against the Dodgers, batting third and cleanup against Koufax. Their kids killed themselves on the Little League field trying to be like their dads."

"When I was a kid, they had music in the grammar schools. I don't know about when you were a kid. But now they don't. I think they should."

"Absolutely. I think the Greeks and the Romans, going back to my heritage 2,500 years ago truly believed that to be educated there were seven disciplines and music was one of those seven disciplines. Of course, you had to have arithmetic. Of course, you had to have a sense of history. Of course, you had to have language skills. Of course, you had to have some understanding of the physical world, but music was one of the seven disciplines. The Chinese political leadership understands this and has structured many of the schools to include music. I mean there are about sixty million kids playing violin and piano and in the big urban environments: Beijing, Shanghai, Guangzhou, and Hong Kong. Obviously, as a music professional, I am totally biased interest as the best indicator for future attendance at concerts is having some experience in active music-making, playing instruments in a band or orchestra. Furthermore, I think it has been very bad public policy, at every level (local, state, and federal) to allow music programs to be gutted when the budget gets tight. Think about music education. I mean rhythm is math, acoustics is physics, not to mention the deductive reasoning and analytical reasoning required to play an instrument. Moreover, playing in an ensemble is the equivalent of playing on a team with all the resulting benefits of being part of something larger than yourself. Finally, when you are looking at a passage of music, it's an abstract language. To decipher the language, you have to problem solve, you must figure out something. Do you take it slower, do you subdivide, what articulation, etc. So music is integral to anybody's education. I think part of the real challenge in America is that the political types don't fully appreciate that they have diminished America by deemphasizing not just music education but art education in general."

"That's like when I was a kid, I took Latin too. Great base for the language skills."

"Any of the romance languages, French, Italian, Portuguese, whatever, Spanish."

"Yes. Do you think the liberal arts has been so diminished in our educational system that the life lessons, the life attitude, and the humanism that liberal arts teach are disappearing from our society?"

"I do not think they are entirely disappearing. That being said, the liberal arts certainly are being deemphasized. Both of my kids went to liberal arts colleges, so I certainly appreciate the value of a liberal arts education. My concern is that technology as a tool is fine, we disseminate musical content through technology, but technology as an ideology is a huge problem, and I think you're seeing a lot of that. I mean people don't have attention spans anymore. It's frightening."

"Only enough to look at a cell phone."

"It's an ever more competitive and cluttered global marketplace. I think we are really missing not only an opportunity, but also putting America at a disadvantage. My dad was born in Cleveland right after the family came over from Italy. And they had nothing. My grandfather had a second- or third-grade education. My grandmother had a third-grade education although she may have been the smartest person I ever knew. Dad got put into a public school on the east side of Cleveland, My grandparents had very limited English. Italian was the first language; Latin was the second language. Dad learned English right away in first grade. He had no choice. And then they handed him a trumpet. And there he is with his Italian friends, his Jewish friends like his friend Bernie Adelstein, who, later was the principal trumpet in the Cleveland orchestra for several decades. I know I'm talking to a lawyer. I will say this with all modesty intended. Law school is relatively easy compared to music school. To play an instrument at the highest level, to secure one of the sixty clarinet positions in the country so you can make a living, is an extraordinary accomplishment. And, unlike athletes who blow out their knees and are done in three years, clarinet players last thirty or thirty-five years, so there are one or two jobs a year that become available and there are thousands of people graduating with clarinet degrees in all the universities, all the music schools, all the conservatories. Today's market for law school graduates also has changed. When I was in law school, if you graduated in the top 75%, you had a job. That all being said, my legal education at the University of Minnesota was great. It helps me every day whether it's an issue regarding union negotiations, employment, real estate, intellectual property matter, etc. I had a great three years in law school. But, in terms of just knowing how to look at something, sort out what's relevant and what's not relevant, music was the best education I had."

"So, your powers of critical thinking are much more developed from your musical education?"

"Yes, from music. You can sit there and look at these complex abstract symbols on a page and sort it out. I'm not just talking contemporary music; I'm talking about as a kid looking at a Mozart concerto and having to decipher all the rhythmic harmonic and melodic relationships. Obviously, as a child your brain is developing, and music is certainly one way to further brain maturation."

"Do you think instruction in music and in some of the other arts is part of an answer to the divisiveness in our society?"

"Sure. I have visited well over twenty schools in the Boston public schools. In many of the schools, there are students from numerous countries speaking various languages. One of the things that brings these students from such diverse backgrounds together is music. Whether it's percussion instruments, or recorders for the young kids, or donated band instruments, I always marvel how talented music teachers inspire collective behavior. In a world where there are so many disparate parts politically and otherwise — it's fragmenting as we speak — you see how music can bring people together, and that's somehow lost among politicians."

"Well, given all that, I think that this election that we're experiencing now is a watershed election. To me it seems that if the election goes one way it could mean that the country changes from what we recognize to something else. What do you see as the future for classical music? Do you think that they are doing a lot better in some other countries?"

"Think about it. China has indigenous music, but classical music is very popular there, as it has been in Japan for a while, Seiji Ozawa is obviously a force there. Europe is obviously the home of much classical music, so I think there is always going to be a place there for classical music. It is not going away even in a world of niches. What do I see as the future of the Boston Symphony? Because of the genius of Henry Lee Higginson (Higginson, a Boston financier and Civil War hero, founded the Boston Symphony Orchestra in 1881 with his own funds for some years) in creating the Pops, which provides a wholly different orchestra experience for the audience, and because of Tanglewood, of course, not just the festival, but the school as well, we are probably as well positioned as any orchestra because of the multiplicity of offerings, along with Symphony Hall being a community resource. The annual budget is over $100 million. By GE standards that's a small number, but the BSO has the largest scale of operations of any orchestra in the world. Of course, many challenges remain, but I don't see a survival issue."

"Are other countries in the world doing a better job of nurturing or making sure that there is good ground for classical music?"

"Sure. In Europe you have governments that provide significant subsidy, whether you are talking opera companies, ballet companies, orchestras, venues. But America going forward is going to be very interesting. Basically, I've had my run, but I do not see the American approach to funding arts institutions radically changing in the near and mid-term.

"Classical music and many other artistic endeavors have always required subsidy. Initially it was the church providing support, or it could be the synagogue. Religious music has always been part of European tradition for centuries. Beyond the church, various dynasties provided support for the visual and performing arts. Haydn, Mozart, Beethoven, and many others worked for kings and princes. You read Mozart and Haydn and Beethoven letters, and you see they were always dealing with various titled people. Then, with the industrial revolution creating a mercantile class, the emerging bourgeois embraces various artist and artisans. Shortly thereafter, modern political states in Italy, France, Germany, etc. provide billions of dollars to subsidize culture."

"How about in America?"

"In America, basically, there was no subsidy of consequence for cultural institutions until the late nineteenth century. That's when the BSO was founded. Henry Lee Higginson founded and funded the Orchestra from his own resources. He would occasionally seek support from arts patron Isabella Stewart Gardner and a few others, but it was basically his 'show.' Then the income tax was introduced, and thereafter, as you know, when they started creating a complicated tax system, it was decided that it would be good public policy for certain activities to warrant preferential tax treatment such as education, religion, social services, and culture. So, when you contribute to the Boston Symphony, the Orchestra provides you a receipt allowing you to take a charitable deduction on your federal taxes. That's how America has chosen to support the arts. It's still a subsidy though indirect. We are dependent on philanthropy and ticket sales about equally. So ultimately what concerns me going forward in terms of talking about public policy is that

Symphony Hall 2021 as the Boston Symphony Orchestra and its Conductor, Andris Nelsons, accept the applause of the audience. Famed Symphony Hall also serves as the muse of Mark Volpe where he presented to the world a multitude of composers, conductors, and instrumentalists in his long tenure as President of the BSO.

Credit: Photo by Aram Boghosian for the Boston Symphony Orchestra.

there are occasional proposals to eliminate the tax deductibility of charitable giving for cultural institutions."

"What would you say your greatest ambition as the director of the Boston Symphony Orchestra is now looking forward?"

"Retiring. (Laughs) That's a bad joke. They want me to stay. But I've done it a long time. As I begin my next phase of teaching and writing, I feel assured that the BSO's financial situation is as secure, if not more secure, than any other American orchestra and that the orchestra is performing at the very highest level. I also leave knowing that the Orchestra's media strategy is well conceived and has been well executed and that touring plans are in place. Although we did not develop the area surrounding Orchestra Hall, the physical plants in Boston and Tanglewood remain the envy of every orchestra."

"How do you look upon the association of the BSO with the Leipzig Gewandhaus Orchestra with Maestro Nelsons sharing the podiums of both orchestras?"

"What people don't realize is how committed each orchestra is. Andris is with us twelve weeks plus touring, so fifteen, sixteen weeks, then four weeks or so at Tanglewood. His Gewandhaus commitment is twelve-sixteen weeks. If he had rejected Leipzig's offer, he would have filled in the time with numerous guest appearances requiring him to constantly travel. Consequently, it made so much sense to consolidate his conducting in primarily two places, Of course, he will occasionally guest conduct the Berlin Philharmonic and Vienna Philharmonic as well. Furthermore, there are many historical figures connecting the two orchestras. Charles Munch was the concertmaster of the Gewandhaus, Arthur Nikisch was music director of both places. Beyond that, Symphony Hall is patterned after the second Gewandhaus, which the Allies bombed to the ground in 1944. In Leipzig, they built a new hall when the orchestra was under Kurt Masur in the eighties."

"What single person in your life affected the course of your life the most, professionally and personally?"

"My father."

"What are the prime three personal qualities you possess which allow you to successfully handle the job?"

"Empathy and resilience. At this point, experience. I would also say intelligence."

"What personal quality do you wish you had in greater measure?"

"Patience. Also, I wish I didn't have to drive. I'm calm, but I wish it was easier to relax. It is a twenty-four-hour job where the phone rings nineteen of those hours. Ah, that's what my assistant Julie is doing out there, answering the phone."

"What is your greatest ambition musically for the rest of your life?"

"I didn't quite realize it. I wanted to play in a great orchestra. But now it's like any other discipline. I tell you; I was playing softball with the students like two years ago. I was a pretty good player. I was playing center field and the ball was hit over my head and I thought no problem, I figured out the geometry right away. Although my calculations were good, my legs could not deliver as the ball landed like fifteen feet beyond me. It's just remarkable. Now I'm only sixty-four, but I could fly when I was young. I could really run, and those days are gone. And likewise with the clarinet. Actually, the ambition I have is to have more time to practice the clarinet so I can play at a slightly better level than I'm playing now. I'll never play like I played in my prime. That ship has passed."

"What advice do you have for the next director of the BSO?"

"We are in a relationship business. People ask, what's your core competency. The BSO's core competency is presenting concerts. But in my position, you have to have relationships with all the various constituencies, the musicians, the staff, the trustees, the overseers, press, political leadership, business leadership, civic folks. It's about managing expectations. In other words, transparency. I talk to the players; I don't wait to negotiate contracts. I think of labor dynamics as something you do every day, not every three years when a new contract comes up. It's all about relationships. If you have a relationship, you can solve a problem."

"What has been the single most inspiring experience, musical or otherwise, you have had during your tenure at the BSO?"

"Oh, watching my kids grow up."

"What is the single greatest BSO performance you have ever heard?"

"Certainly, the grandest was when we played under Seiji Ozawa in Paris during the millennium in France in 2000. It was one of the greatest performances in terms of spectacle at the base of the Eiffel Tower with 350,000 or more people attending!"

"Are there any conductors or musicians whom you have met who have induced awe in you? I realize this would be hard to do because you are so experienced and have met many people of great name."

"Awe, never. I'm impressed, I'm moved, I'm inspired, but awe, like you're with a deity, I don't get that."

"We are all just human beings. That's the best attitude to have. Meet everybody on level terms. If you had it all to do over again, what would you do differently?"

"Only one thing. I don't mean to be disrespectful of Eastman School of Music, but I went to a school where there were eighty or ninety kids in my class. Rather than go to a music school, as good as Eastman is, I would go to a big university that has a great music program. Whether it's Yale or Michigan or one of the others. Now it's probably different at Eastman. In fact, I know it is different as they have embraced the school's relationship with the University of Rochester's River Campus. Furthermore, they have one of the first and best music leadership classes which I have visited on several occasions. However, that was not the case in the 1970s. I took a lot of classes elsewhere. I loved taking history at the University of Rochester. Also, I would try to go down to Cornell in Ithaca, which is long drive, so it made it so difficult to do. If I could do it over again, I would go to a liberal arts school or large University that has great music program. My brother, who was a trumpet player, went to Northwestern. It was a phenomenal experience. Had great classes in everything. I must be careful here. If you're a damn genius, maybe you should go to Julliard, but if you are not, you should get a broader education."

"You ended up in the right place, it's great for you. I just have the feeling that you are perfectly positioned to do what you really can do. So what do you picture yourself doing twenty-five years from now?"

"I really picture myself not doing this (laughs). But teaching, possibly writing."

"You'd be about my age then."

"Yeah, and frankly I'm inspired by your great health and energy. I think just being actively engaged in something, and keeping the mind going, keeping the body going as much as possible, that's great!"

"Can humans function without the arts and without music?"

"I don't think so. Babies before they say Dada or Mama begin verbalizing by humming stuff. Most kids make sounds."

"Unsuk Chin gave me a great answer to that. She said music is in a wave in the air, a wave that we hear."

"She's right, I'll give you another one. It starts inside here (Mark points to his heart). Everything comes from the heartbeat. It's the heartbeat! If something feels fast it's because it's faster than your heart, if something feels slow it's because it's slower than your heart. That's one of the definitions of slow and fast. Now it's all relative, but if (Mark banging) that's slow, (more banging) that's fast. This is faster than my heart (more banging), this is slower than my heart. You have this internal pulse. Without it, you don't live. You have all these rhythmic things going on, you know."

"Look how many tens of millions of times your heart beats in a lifetime! A question that occurs to me is do you think your ethnic background has a lot to do with your philosophy of life, as you have expressed it today?"

"It certainly is relevant; it certainly has some impact. I did grow up in a fairly ethnic environment, and my parents and friends were primarily musicians, academics, and teachers."

"Italians and Greeks are thought of as people with a lot of passion."

"Yeah, yeah, yeah. I'm the quiet one in the family by far. Occasionally I get a word in edgewise. I think it's true. There are other external factors, but I grew up mostly around Italians, some Greeks, and Jews. One of my sisters married a Jewish guy and I have a couple of uncles who are of Jewish heritage."

"I was just reading last night the whole Wilhelm Furtwangler story. How fascinating that he stood up to Hitler in favor of Jewish musicians. So the last question for you Mark is, what is music?"

"Music is life. It's life. Without music, you have family, but there is more to life. I'm a secular guy despite being around a lot of different ethnic types (knocking on the door). OK, I'm coming, I'm coming. Music is one of the few things that does unify. I'm a unifier, not a divider (knocking again)."

"Mark, great answer, great conclusion for this interview. Thanks so much."

To paraphrase the old expression, give a busy person something to do if you want it done right. So it is with Mark Volpe, whether it's answering the questions of an interviewer thoughtfully, but with dispatch in the vernacular of everyday people, negotiating a labor contract with heart and head, managing his orchestra with an eye on the bottom line and an ear to the quality of its sound, and always viewing his job with attention to the current milieu as well as to historical precedent. In short, a special man seeing his job as both art and science, and executing it to suit, an exemplar of humanistic values in a world existentially challenging those values.

Logo by Holly Sullo, Illustrator

Afterword

Thank you, dear readers, for reading this book. If you have come this far, you must have enjoyed it and love music. I took pains to have a very complete Index done for it so that if you wish to double back to find someone or something, you will find that easy to do.

All authors love to know what their readers think, whether about the book or anything. So if you want to write, I will love to receive. My email address is larry.ruttman@gmail.com. All up and/or down comments and questions invited.

The logo you see is by Holly Sullo, recognized Boston based artist and illustrator. I thought I would include it because a photo is often what the subject wants you to see rather than what another, especially an artist, sees, which is likely to be closer to the truth. Holly sure showed the few strands of hair I still have left. She seems to think I have three personalities: one, face-on, disarmingly smiling broadly, another serious and lawyerlike, and another devilish and Machiavellian with a curl of the lip.

Who am I to dismiss the perceptions of a gifted artist?

On a more serious note, I wish to share with you my own deep feelings about music in an essay entitled, *Why I Love Music So Passionately*, which I wrote for my soon-to-be-published memoir, *Larry Ruttman: A Life Lived Backwards — An Existential Triad of Friendship, Maturation, and Inquisitiveness.*

Why I Love Music So Passionately

Why do I love music so passionately? In trying to answer, I could never hope to emulate diva Susan Graham's amazing spontaneous and short reply to my question, "What is music?", which you have read in this book. Thinking I had completed this memoir some days before, I settled down to listen to and view the Metropolitan Opera's free stream of Mozart's *The Magic Flute*. I was disappointed to find that Sunday, not Saturday, was the night it was to be given. So I brought up *The Marriage of Figaro*, another Mozart favorite, on YouTube. That started me on a four-hour odyssey which had a transforming effect on me, as music always does. As one can do on YouTube, I allowed it to take me from Figaro to wherever and to whom it chose in clips of ten minutes or so highlighting great operatic stars and operas, some I hardly knew. As the evening unfolded, I could feel the smile on my face, the feeling of satisfaction in the pit of my stomach, the heightened awakeness, the sense of adventure and discovery, the feeling of loss that Mozart had died so young.

For me, to hear music is also to time travel to the time and place of the composers I'm hearing. All my life I've religiously read about the milieu from which these now-mythical figures have come. I've visited some of the places where they walked and talked, such as Beethoven's apartment in Vienna, where I purchased a small stamp of a lyre from the master's time which I stamp on some of my correspondence. I've been to Mozart's birthplace in Salzburg, the apartment in Vienna in the lee of St. Stephen's Cathedral where he composed *Figaro*, the opera house in Prague where I stood on the very spot he stood conducting that opera and *Don Giovanni*, at its world premiere a year later, and Saint Marx Cemetery outside Vienna where he is buried, but no one knows quite where, a story in itself. The result of this inquisitiveness, if you will, is that while listening I'm "beamed" to a long-ago time in a distant place, a dreamy, surreal, and sort of out-of-body experience, which impelled me to write this piece until 2 A.M. while the intensity of feeling persisted.

As great as I knew sopranos Renée Fleming and Joyce DiDonato are, I discovered on this night that each in their own way is bigger than life, that each has a talent, spirit, and understanding of life which inspires good thoughts in a fraught time or anytime. This experience in a greater or lesser intensity has happened to me every time I listen to music, especially since age thirty when my musical horizon broadened to include Mozart, Beethoven, and their many brethren composers. Music is music, and I get the same thrill and meaning whether I'm listening to Frank Sinatra, Doris Day, The Boss, or Robert Schumann, Sergei Rachmaninoff, or George Gershwin.

There is no other way than these words to try to convey to you why I believe, as many musicians and other people do, that music is life, and that we could not live without music in one form or another! Don't all people experience music? Wasn't music here when man arose? Won't music exist when man ceases to exist? Wasn't music here when the earth cooled and life began? Won't music be there when the earth disintegrates?

Index

Note: Page numbers in ***bold italic*** typeface refer to pages that contain captioned illustrations. Main headings that are the names of the interviewed musicians are in **bold** typeface.

B

D

E

F

G

I

J

K

L

R

S

Z